D1523413

REGIS COLLEGE LIBRARY
100 Wellesley Street West
Toronto, Ontario
Canada M5S 2Z5

Studies of the New Testament and Its World

Edited by
JOHN BARCLAY
JOEL MARCUS
and
JOHN RICHES

REGIS COLLEGE LIBRARY
100 Wellesley Street West
Toronto, Ontario
Canada M5S 2Z5

Constructing the World

Constructing the World

A Study in Paul's Cosmological Language

EDWARD ADAMS

T&T CLARK
EDINBURGH

BS
2650.2
A35
2000

T&T CLARK LTD
59 GEORGE STREET
EDINBURGH EH2 2LQ
SCOTLAND

Copyright © T&T Clark Ltd, 2000

All rights reserved. No part of this publication may be reproduced,
stored in a retrieval system, or transmitted, in any form or by any means,
electronic, mechanical, photocopying, recording or otherwise,
without the prior permission of T&T Clark Ltd.

First published 2000

ISBN 0 567 08689 5

British Library Cataloguing-in-Publication Data
A catalogue record for this book is available from the British Library

Typeset by Waverley Typesetters, Galashiels
Printed and bound in Great Britain by Bookcraft Ltd, Avon

REGIS COLLEGE LIBRARY
100 Wellesley Street West
Toronto, Ontario
Canada M5S 2Z5

Contents

Preface

This study originated in doctoral research undertaken at Glasgow University in the early 1990s. I wish to record my thanks to those who contributed to this project at that early stage. The work was supervised by Dr John Barclay. I am deeply indebted to him for his comments, criticisms, searching questions and continual encouragement. Better guidance I could not have received. I consider myself privileged to have studied under him. I am also grateful to Prof. John Riches who gave generously of his time and expertise throughout the research process. Thanks also go to Dr David Graham and Dr Todd Still for their support and friendship during this period, and to other members of staff and fellow researchers in the Department of Biblical Studies at Glasgow University, especially Prof. Robert Carroll, Dr Marion Carson, Prof. Ernest Best, Dr Joel Marcus, Dr Tom McGill and Dr Leslie Milton. I had the opportunity to present a paper on my research at the Paul Seminar of the 1993 British New Testament Conference, and I am grateful to those who raised questions and made comments then. I also wish to extend my gratitude to Tyndale House for use of the library and other facilities during a number of visits to Cambridge. During these visits, I benefited greatly from conversations with residents and researchers at Tyndale House, and from discussions with Dr Bruce Winter, Warden of the House. Others who deserve mention are Dr Todd Klutz, who drew my attention to critical linguistics, and Prof. Peter Stuhlmacher, with whom I discussed my work during a visit to Tübingen in 1993.

I should also like to thank those who assisted the process of revision. The Department of Theology and Religious Studies in King's College, London, has been an enormously stimulating environment for developing my ideas. I thank Dr Richard Burridge, Dr Douglas Campbell, Dr Crispin Fletcher-Louis and Dr Francis Watson for their willingness to discuss my work. I am particularly grateful to Prof.

Graham Stanton for his encouragement and advice. Thanks are also due to the New Testament teaching staff at London Bible college, especially Prof. Max Turner, for their interest and support.

The task of revising was considerably helped by the recommendations of my external examiner, Prof. James Dunn, and by the further comments and criticisms of Dr John Barclay and Prof. John Riches, in their capacity as editors of the series in which this book appears. John Riches read through several versions of the work strengthening both its methodology and argument. Shortcomings which remain are of course my own responsibility.

My thanks go to Alistair May, who proofread the manuscript, and to Katrin Gülden, who helped to check bibliographical details. I am also grateful for the assistance I have received from the staff at T&T Clark.

Justin Meggitt's book, *Paul, Poverty and Survival* (SNTW; T&T Clark: Edinburgh, 1998), appeared too late to be taken into account in this study. Meggitt challenges the "New Consensus" view that the Pauline churches contained some highly affluent groups and individuals, arguing instead that the communities were located among the poor. I do not think my study is in conflict with Meggitt's argument. In my analysis of the Corinthian Christian community, I focus on the church's boundaries. Unlike the studies which Meggitt criticizes, I do not build my reconstruction of Corinthian church life upon socio-economic divisions within the congregation. I do take it that 1 Cor 1:26 indicates the presence of some in the church who were of higher status than the others (as does Meggitt, pp. 105–6), who had at least a basic level of education and therefore some access to Hellenistic intellectual culture, and who probably constituted the leadership of the church. However, I decline to speculate on the size of the social gap between these individuals and the rest of the church. I do suggest that a few of the higher status members were patrons of the church, but I do not draw the inference that they therefore belonged to the upper classes. Meggitt points out that patrons could be found at the lower levels of Graeco-Roman society as well as the highest strata (p. 147).

Another important book which was published too late to be considered in this study is Philip Esler's *Galatians*, in the New Testament Readings series (Routledge: London and New York, 1998). In this book, Esler applies the work of Henri Tajfel on intergroup comparison and differentiation to the Galatian situation much as I do in chapter 8 of this study. I was first alerted to the work of Tajfel at a main paper given by Prof. Esler at the 1994 British New Testament Conference. In this paper, he employed Tajfel's theories to elucidate the Matthean Beatitudes. Reading Tajfel for myself, I saw the relevance of his ideas to the situation in Galatia and employed them in my own work. Esler's application of Tajfel's work to Galatians goes considerably beyond what I have done. But I see his analysis as a confirmation of my own.

The final word of thanks goes to my parents, Edward and Prudence Adams, for their practical and financial support throughout my years of research, and for all their love and encouragement. This book is lovingly dedicated to them.

EDWARD ADAMS
August 1999

Abbreviations

Abbreviations of biblical books, Pseudepigraphical and early Christian works, Dead Sea Scrolls, Mishnaic and other Rabbinic works, and reference works are as in *JBL* 107 (1988), 583–94. In addition to these, the following abbreviations are used in the main text and footnotes.

1. Primary Sources

Aeschines	*Falsa*	*De falsa legatione*
Alexander	*Fat.*	*On Fate*
	In. Ar. An. pr.	*On Aristotle's Prior Analytics*
	Mixt.	*On Mixture*
Apoc. Abr.		*Apocalypse of Abraham*
Apoc. Elijah		*Apocalypse of Elijah*
Aristotle	*Cael.*	*De Caelo*
	Cat.	*Categoriae*
	Eth. Eud.	*Ethica Eudemia*
	Metaph.	*Metaphysica*
	Meteor.	*Meteorologicum*
	Phys.	*Physica*
	Poet.	*Poetica*
	Pol.	*Politica*
	Probl.	*Problemata*
	Rhet.	*Rhetorica*
	Top.	*Topica*
Cicero	*De nat.*	*De natura deorum*
	Fin.	*De finibus bonorum et malorum*
	Off.	*De officiis*
	Rep.	*De Republica*
Dio Cassius	*Hist.*	*Roman History*

Dio Chrysostom	*Disc.*	*Discourses*
Dion. Halic.	*Ant.*	*Dionysius Halicarnassus, Antiquitates Romanae*
Epictetus	*Disc.*	*Discourses*
Epicurus	*Ep. Her.*	*Letter to Herodotus*
	Ep. Pyth.	*Letter to Pythocles*
Eusebius	*Ev. Prep.*	*Praeparatio Evangelica*
Ezek. Trag.		*Ezekiel the Tragedian*
Hesiod	*Theog.*	*Theogony*
Galen	*Intr.*	*Medical Introduction*
	Plen.	*On Bodily Mass*
Hippolytus	*Haer.*	*Refutation of all heresies*
Homer	*Il.*	*Iliad*
	Od.	*Odyssey*
Isocrates	*Panath.*	*Panathenaicus*
	Pan.	*Panegyricus.*
Jos. As.		*Joseph and Aseneth*
Josephus	*Ant.*	*Jewish Antiquities*
	Ap.	*Contra Apionem*
	Life	*Life of Flavius Josephus*
	War	*The Jewish War*
Justin	*Apol.*	*Apology*
Lanctantius	*D.I.*	*Divine Institutes*
Lucretius	*De rerum*	*De rerum natura*
Minucius Felix	*Oct.*	*Octavius*
Philo	*Abr.*	*De Abrahamo*
	Aet.	*De Aeternitate Mundi*
	Cher.	*De Cherubim*
	Conf.	*De Confusione Linguarum*
	Cong.	*De Congressu Eruditionis gratia*
	Decal.	*De Decalogo*
	Deus	*Quod Deus sit Immutabilis*
	Ebr.	*De Ebrietate*
	Flacc.	*In Flaccum*
	Her.	*Quis rerum divinarum Heres sit*
	Jos.	*De Josepho*
	Leg. All.	*Legum Allegoriae*

	Migr.	*De Migratione Abrahami*
	Mos.	*De Vita Mosis*
	Mut.	*De Mutatione Nominum*
	Opif.	*De Opificio Mundi*
	Plant.	*De Plantatione*
	Praem.	*De Praemiis et Poenis*
	Prov.	*De Providentia*
	Somn.	*De Somniis*
	Spec.	*De Specialibus Legibus*
Philostratus	*Vit. Ap.*	*Vita Apollonii*
Pindar	*Ol.*	*Olympian Odes*
Plato	*Criti.*	*Critias*
	Ep.	*Epistulae*
	Gorg.	*Gorgias*
	Leg.	*Leges (Laws)*
	Men.	*Menexenus*
	Phaed.	*Phaedo*
	Phaedr.	*Phaedrus*
	Phileb.	*Philebus*
	Polit.	*Politicus*
	Prot.	*Protagoras*
	Rep.	*Respublica (The Republic)*
	Symp.	*Symposium*
	Tim.	*Timaeus*
Pliny the Elder	*Nat. His.*	*Naturalis Historia*
Plotinus	*Enn.*	*Enneads*
Plutarch	*De An.*	*De Anima Procreatione in Timaeo*
	De E	*De E Apud Delphi*
	Par.	*Parallela Minora (Greek and Roman Parallel Stories)*
	Rom.	*Romulas*
	Comp. Lyc. Num.	*Comparison of Lycurgus and Numa*
	Pub.	*Publicola*
	St. rep.	*On Stoic self-contradictions*
Ps-Arist.	*Mund.*	Pseudo-Aristotle, *De Mundo*
Ps-Plato	*Epin.*	Pseduo-Plato, *Epinomis*
Quintillian	*Inst. Or.*	*Institutiones Oratoricae*

Seneca	*Ben.*	*De beneficiis*
	De consol. ad Marc.	**De consolatione ad Marciam**
	De prov.	*De providentia*
	Nat. quaes.	*Naturales quaestiones*
Sextus Empiricus	*Ag. Phys.*	*Against Physical Philosophers*
Strabo	*Geog.*	*Geography*
Suetonius	*Claud.*	*Claudius*
	Jul.	*Julius Caesar*
	Ner.	*Nero*
	Aug.	*Augustus*
Tacitus	*Ann.*	*Annals*
	Hist.	*Histories*
Tertullian	*Apol.*	*Apology*
Virgil	*Aen.*	*Aeneid*
	Ecl.	*Ecloge*
Xenophon	*Mem.*	*Memorabilia*

2. Other Abbreviations

fr.   fragment

D–K   H. Diels and W. Kranz (eds), *Die Fragmente der Vorsokratiker*, cited by volume and page number.

K–R   G. S. Kirk and J. E. Raven (eds), *The Presocratic Philosophers: A critical history with a selection of texts*, cited by page number.

L–S   A. A. Long and D. N. Sedley (eds), *The Hellenistic Philosophers*, 2 vols; *Volume 1, Translations of the principal sources with philosophical commentary; Volume 2, Greek and Latin texts with notes and bibliography*, cited by volume and page number.

NA 27   E. Nestle and K. Aland (eds), *Novum Testamentum Graece*.

NRSV   New Revised Standard Version. Unless otherwise indicated, quotations of the biblical text in English of four words or more are from the NRSV.

TLG   *Thesaurae Linguae Graecae.*

Full bibliographical details are provided in the bibliography.

Part I

Aims and methodology

1

The context of this study

1.1. Introduction

This study investigates Paul's usage of the words κόσμος and κτίσις, the main terms in his cosmological vocabulary (words belonging to the semantic area, "world"/"universe"/"creation"). It explores Paul's epistolary uses of these terms in relation to the social–historical situations within which they were employed, and seeks to assess what social functions these uses were designed to have in their original contexts of utterance. It attempts to relate Paul's socio–rhetorical usage to the sociological process of "world-construction" in Pauline Christianity and to the question of the type of "response to the world" we encounter in the Pauline letters.

This opening chapter locates the study within the scholarly discussions to which it relates, beginning with the current interest among New Testament scholars in "world-construction" and "world-maintenance" in earliest Christianity and then looking at the recent concern to analyze New Testament "responses to the world" in terms of church–sect typology. We then turn to the scholarly discussion of the words κόσμος and κτίσις in Paul's letters and show how the work which follows attempts to make a contribution to this area.

1.2. World-construction

Among the various sociological perspectives which have been applied to the New Testament in recent years, Peter Berger's theory of the construction and maintenance of social worlds has been especially prominent. Berger's paradigm has been seen to offer a ready framework for investigating the social formation of the early Christian communities and the world-views which helped to sustain them.

Berger developed his perspective with Thomas Luckmann in their co-authored work, *The Social Construction of Reality*, and subsequently applied it to the area of religion in *The Social Reality of Religion* (written by Berger alone). A brief account of Berger's perspective is in order.[1]

Berger first describes "world-construction".[2] He begins with the claim that every human society is an enterprise in world-building. Society is a dialectical phenomenon: human beings produce society, yet human beings are products of society. Berger highlights three stages in the dialectic: externalization, objectivation and internalization. Externalization, firstly, is the continuous outpouring of human beings into the world in which they find themselves. They enter an open world, a world which must be fashioned by their own activity. They must make a world in which they can locate themselves and realize their lives. The world that human beings construct, which Berger equates with culture, provides stability and firm structures for human life. Objectivation, secondly, refers to the phenomenon that the humanly-produced world becomes something "out there"; that is to say, it attains the status of objective reality.[3] It confronts its producers as a fact outside of themselves. As an objective reality, society offers human beings a world to inhabit, a world in which to develop as human beings: "This world encompasses the biography of the individual, which unfolds as a series of events *within* that world."[4] Internalization, the third stage in the process, relates to the internal appropriation of the constructed world by men and women.[5] Through internalization the structures of this world become absorbed within the human consciousness. The objective world becomes a subjective reality, shaping the identities and roles of individuals, as well as their attitudes and motives. The socially-constructed world is, according to Berger, above all, "an ordering of experience".[6] It constitutes a "nomos", both objectively and subjectively, for those who inhabit it: it shapes behaviour and gives coherence and meaning to life.

---

[1] See Berger 1969, 3–52. Berger stands in the phenomenological tradition. His thinking is particularly shaped by the phenomenology of Alfred Shutz: see Wuthnow, Hunter, Bergesen and Kurzweil 1984, 21–76, esp. 29–34.

[2] Berger 1969, 3–28.

[3] Berger 1969, 9.

[4] Berger 1969, 13.

[5] Berger 1969, 15.

[6] Berger 1969, 19.

For Berger, religion is part of this process. Religion is the particular form of the world-building enterprise by which a "sacred cosmos" is established. The cosmos posited by religion both transcends and embraces humanity. It confronts human beings as an immensely powerful reality beyond themselves and places them in an ultimately meaningful order.[7]

Having explained "world-construction", Berger turns his attention to "world-maintenance", the processes whereby the social world is sustained and "legitimated", that is, explained and justified.[8] Legitimations are answers to questions about the "why" of social institutions. Legitimation is important if the nomos of a society is to be transmitted from one generation to another so that the new generation comes to inhabit the social world. For Berger the highest level of legitimation is the "symbolic universe".[9] The symbolic universe is the "all-embracing frame of reference" within which all human experience can be conceived as taking place.[10] Symbolic universes serve as "sheltering canopies over the institutional order as well as over individual biographies" and "set the limits of what is relevant in terms of social interaction".[11] Berger and Luckmann's concept of symbolic universes corresponds to Clifford Geertz's notion of "world-views". According to Geertz, the world-view of a people is "their picture of the way things in sheer actuality are, their concept of nature, of self, of society. It contains their most comprehensive ideas of order."[12]

Berger's scheme has been seen to offer great potential for New Testament interpretation. Esler highlights the general applicability.[13] The early Christian congregations, for which the New Testament documents were written, may be regarded as social worlds in Berger's terms. The theologies expressed in the New Testament writings may be viewed as symbolic universes, legitimating and maintaining these fragile

---

[7] Berger 1969, 26. Berger (1969, 180) points out that on its own terms sociological theory will always view religion as a human projection. He stresses, though, that his argument does not preclude the possibility that projected religious meanings may be the reflection of an ultimate reality that includes both world and humanity (181).
[8] Berger 1969, 29–52.
[9] Berger and Luckmann 1966, 110–46.
[10] Berger and Luckmann 1966, 114.
[11] Berger and Luckmann 1966, 120.
[12] Geertz 1975, 127.
[13] Cf. Esler 1994, 11.

congregations, providing protective canopies for them in the face of external opposition and internal dissension.

A number of New Testament scholars have taken up Berger's paradigm.[14] Gager[15] and Kee[16] apply it to the early Christian movement as a whole. Meeks, in the first attempt by a New Testament critic to employ the theory, brings it to bear on the Johannine community.[17] In his later book, *The First Urban Christians*, he applies it to the Pauline churches.[18] A more extensive application to the Pauline communities is offered by Margaret MacDonald.[19] Wilde utilizes it with reference to Mark's Gospel.[20] The framework forms the basis for Esler's analysis of the Lucan community.[21] Overman takes up Berger's perspective in his study of the Matthean community.[22] Berger's notion of the symbolic universe is now firmly established as a standard heuristic tool in New Testament studies, being widely employed by interpreters.[23]

The recent concern to understand the New Testament texts within Berger's framework of social worlds and symbolic universes provides one of the stimuli for the present study. Viewing Paul's letter-writing activity as a mode of world-building, this project seeks to investigate how he uses the terms κόσμος and κτίσις within his epistles to try to construct the social and symbolic worlds of his readers. In doing so, it attempts to illuminate the larger phenomenon of world-creation in (what may be broadly termed) Pauline Christianity.

The crucial importance of language-use to the formation of social worlds is heavily stressed by Berger and Luckmann: "Language provides the fundamental superimposition of logic on the objectivated social world. The edifice of legitimation is built upon language and uses

---

[14] Many New Testament interpreters of course simply use the term "social world", in a general sense, to describe the social context of the early Christians, without any particular reference to Berger's theory, e.g. Pilch 1992; Stambaugh and Balch 1986; White and Yarborough 1995. On the rise of "social world studies" in New Testament studies, see O. G. Harris 1984.

[15] Gager 1975, 9–12.

[16] Kee 1980, 22–6, 30–53.

[17] Meeks 1972, 70–72.

[18] Meeks 1983a, esp. 8.

[19] M. Y. MacDonald 1988, esp. 10–11.

[20] Wilde 1978, esp. 47.

[21] Esler 1987, 16–23. See also Esler 1994, 6–12.

[22] Overman 1990, esp. 6, 90–1, 104, 130–1, 134.

[23] Barclay 1993, 518; Hays 1996; Kuck 1992, 36–7; Neyrey 1991; Räisänen 1990, 129–31; Syreeni 1994; Witherington 1994, 86–93.

language as its principal instrumentality."²⁴ Social worlds and symbolic universes are constructed largely by *linguistic* machinery. A study of Paul's language-use is therefore highly pertinent to the subject of world-construction in Pauline Christianity. The terms κόσμος and κτίσις are prominent among the words in Paul's linguistic repertoire which belong to the semantic domain, "world"/"universe"/"creation".²⁵ They are also, it is generally recognized, the most theologically significant words in this domain, figuring at key points in Paul's teaching and paraenesis. A study of *these* lexemes is thus especially relevant to a consideration of the making of social *worlds* and symbolic *universes*.²⁶

1.3. Response to the world

Another sociological framework which has found favour among New Testament scholars is the sociology of sects. Church–sect typology has been seen to offer a helpful schema for exploring and describing the early church's "response to the world".

The sociological distinction between "church" and "sect" was first made by Max Weber. It was expanded into a typology by Ernst Troeltsch, Weber's student, in Troeltsch's work on the sociological development of the Christian church. The two contrasting sociological types (which, according to Troeltsch, fully emerged as distinct social categories only in the medieval period) are described by Troeltsch as follows.²⁷ The church-type is conservative. It accepts the existing social order with its values and customs and supports the interests of the ruling classes. It is a mass organization, universal in outlook and seeking to embrace

²⁴ Berger and Luckmann 1967, 82. For a strong defence of the reality-constructing view of language, see Grace 1987.
²⁵ Other words and expressions belonging to this semantic domain which appear in the undisputed Pauline letters are αἰών, ὁ οὐρανός καὶ ἡ γῆ, οἰκουμένη and (τὰ) πάντα. αἰών with the sense "world"/"age" appears at Rom 12:2; 1 Cor 1:20; 2:6, 8; 3:18; 10:11; 2 Cor 4:4; Gal 1:4. γῆ ("earth") figures at Rom 9:17, 28; 10:18; 1 Cor 10:26; 15:47. All occurrences of γη except that at 1 Cor 15:47 are in quotations from the Old Testament. The expression εἴτε ἐν οὐρανῷ εἴτε ἐπὶ γῆς ("in heaven or on earth") occurs at 1 Cor 8:5. οἰκουμένη ("inhabited world") appears at Rom 10:18 in an Old Testament quotation. (τὰ) πάντα with the sense "universe" is found in Rom 9:5; 10:12 (possibly); 11:36; 1 Cor 3:21–22; 4:13; 8:6; 11:12; 15:27–28; Phil 3:21.
²⁶ The significance of κόσμος to an enquiry into world-construction is underlined by Kee 1980, 24–5.
²⁷ Summarized from Troeltsch 1931, 331–43.

everyone (offering redemption to all). It endorses the state and prevailing economic conditions. The church-type has an objective institutional character with hierarchy, traditions and rituals. Individuals are born into it. The ascetic ideal of the church-type (expressed in monasticism) consists in the repression of the senses, special religious achievements and the contemplative life. The goal of the church-type is world-dominion, an end which it can attain only through a process of adaptation and compromise. The sect-type, on the other hand, is radical in orientation. It is indifferent or hostile towards the state and society. It is connected with the lower classes and the marginalized in society. The sect is small – a select group of the elect. It is characteristically egalitarian, non-clerical and critical of religious officialdom. Individuals enter the sect by a conscious act of conversion. The ascetic ideal of the sect-type is expressed in terms of sharp opposition to the world and all its social institutions. Sects do not aspire to world domination but to inward personal perfection and love between its members. Sects usually arise as protest groups against the official church which they view as degenerate.

Troeltsch's classic definition of the sect-type has been refined and developed by subsequent sociologists of religion including Werner Stark[28] and especially Bryan Wilson. Wilson has produced a typology of sects based on sociological investigation not only of Christian groups but also of modern non-Christian religious movements in the Third World. Unlike Troeltsch, he does not define a sect over against a church-type organization as its opposite (a contrast which he points out derives from Christianity). For Wilson, sects may be defined as "deviant religious movements".[29] He classifies sects in terms of their "responses to the world", by which he means their "orientations to the wider society, its culture, values, and cultural goals, the experience of evil and the means of escaping it and attaining salvation".[30]

Wilson distinguishes seven different attitudes to the world.[31] For the *conversionist* sect, the world is evil because human beings are corrupt. To be saved human beings must be personally transformed, that is to

[28] Stark 1967.
[29] B. R. Wilson 1973, 26.
[30] B. R. Wilson 1973, 26.
[31] B. R. Wilson 1973, 22–6.

say, they must undergo a powerful experience of conversion. What is looked for is a change in the heart of individuals, not a change in the objective world (though it is often posited that at some future time objective reality will change to match the subjective sense of salvation). The *revolutionist* sect believes that the world, both the physical and the social order, must be totally destroyed if people are to be saved. The destruction and subsequent re-creation will come about only by divine action. The coming salvation in the shape of the transformed world is believed to be imminent. The *introversionist* response is to see the world as irredeemably evil and to find salvation in complete withdrawal from it. This response leads to the establishment of a separated and isolated community preoccupied with its own purity. The *manipulationist* sect, unlike the previous three, accepts the goals of the larger culture. What it rejects is the culture's means of attaining them. Salvation is neither other-worldly nor transcendental, but consists in health, wealth, happiness and success. It is achieved by learning universal principles concerning the relationship between human beings and the world. The new perception enables men and women to reinterpret and explain away the evil of the world. The *thaumaturgical* sect attempts to relieve present evils such as illness, grief and impending personal calamity, by supernatural means such as magic, miracles and oracles. Salvation is deliverance from specific woes and their particular incidence rather than from a universal principle of evil. The *reformist* sect largely accepts the world, but seeks to amend it in accordance with supernaturally given insights about the way society should be organized. The *utopian* response is to reconstruct the world (rather than just reform it) according to a divine plan, to establish by sheer human effort a radically new society in which evil is completely absent.

Church–sect typology has been applied by various scholars to the early Christian communities. Scroggs applies Stark's typifications of the sect to early Palestinian Christianity.[32] Tidball applies Wilson's typology to the New Testament in general.[33] Elliot uses Wilson's sub-type of the conversionist sect as an instrument with which to analyze the community behind 1 Peter.[34] Esler applies Wilson's sect-typology to

---

[32] Scroggs 1975.
[33] Tidball 1997, 106–12.
[34] Elliot 1981, 73–8.

the Lucan community.[35] Meeks[36] and Rensberger[37] engage in sectarian analysis of the Johannine community. Meeks,[38] Watson[39] and MacDonald bring the typology to bear on the Pauline social movement.

MacDonald's is the most thoroughgoing application of church–sect typology to Pauline Christianity. She charts the development of the Pauline communities through a three-stage process of "cumulative institutionalization",[40] in which a sect-type movement is transformed into a church-type one. The genuine Pauline letters represent the first stage of the process, the "community-building" phase. The deutero-Pauline letters, Colossians and Ephesians, represent the second stage, the "community-stabilizing" phase. The Pastoral epistles, which MacDonald dates in the early second century, represent the third period, the "community-protecting" stage. In each of the three phases, MacDonald investigates four areas: attitude to the world/ethics, ministry, ritual and belief.

Using Wilson's typology, MacDonald identifies Pauline Christianity in its first and second phases as a *conversionist* sect. Paul's genuine letters exhibit the characteristic conversionist tension between a desire to remain separate from the outside society and a desire to evangelize the world.[41] The typical conversionist "response to the world", MacDonald claims, is also evident in Colossians and Ephesians (though she sees in the household codes of Col 3:18 – 4:1 and Eph 5:21 – 6:9 an emerging concern for social respectability).[42] When we come to the Pastoral epistles, however, the orientation has shifted. 1 and 2 Timothy and Titus reveal a desire to gain the approval of outsiders, a strong universal outlook and a willingness to adopt the values of Graeco-Roman society. By this stage, then, Pauline Christianity is no longer a sect-type social group but a church-type body.[43]

Of all the sociological approaches to the New Testament, the application of church–sect typology has probably come under the heaviest fire. Criticism has focused on the historical and cultural

[35] Esler 1987, 46–70.
[36] Meeks 1972.
[37] Rensberger 1989.
[38] Meeks 1983a, 84–107.
[39] Watson 1986, 19–21, 38–48.
[40] MacDonald 1988, 16–18.
[41] MacDonald 1988, 32–42.
[42] MacDonald 1988, 97–102.
[43] MacDonald 1988, 163–6.

limitations of the typology,[44] its analytical imperfections,[45] and its "low degree of discriminatory power".[46] These criticisms are certainly valid, but they do not get to the heart of the problem. The difficulty with church–sect typology as employed by New Testament scholars, as David Horrell has recently shown, lies less in the typology itself as in its mode of application.[47] It has tended to be used in a "model"-based approach. A given type is imposed on the New Testament data as a sociological model and the data is then explained in the light of it. The typology is used to organize, explain and even shape the evidence on hand rather than to analyze and assess it. Such an approach is methodologically suspect since the conclusions of the examination are assumed at the outset. MacDonald exemplifies the error. She takes the conversionist sect-type as the starting-point for her analysis of earliest Pauline Christianity. She then proceeds to show that the evidence of the authentic letters fits the mould. In the process, important differences within the social data are either overlooked or obscured: differences between Paul's own beliefs and those of the communities he addresses, and variations in social outlook and ethos among the different communities themselves.[48] Her model-based application of sect-typology results in a simplistic and distorted view of the evidence.

Typologies, Horrell points out, are intended to offer "a classificatory scheme" facilitating the comparison of a wide range of examples.[49] Wilson insists that none of his seven types of response might ever appear in any high degree of purity in the real world, since the belief-systems of religious groups are often "volatile, inconsistent, many-sided, and internally contradictory".[50] The sect-typology, Wilson submits, is "useful as hypothetical points of orientation" for deviant religious movements.[51]

---

[44] The sociological notion of the sect, as noted above, was originally derived from the social history of Christianity. Thus Holmberg (1990, 110) points to the "circular reasoning involved in using Christian sects of later ages to analyze and explain that very movement that they all wanted to imitate to the best of their capacity". The application of Wilson's sect-typology, insofar as it draws from non-Christian religions, escapes this criticism. Even so, it is still open to the charge of historical and cultural unsuitability, given that Wilson's sect-types derive from study of *recent* religious groups in the *modern* world.

[45] Holmberg 1990, 110–12.

[46] Holmberg 1990, 113.

[47] Horrell 1996, 9–18.

[48] Cf. Barclay 1992.

[49] Horrell 1996, 11.

[50] B. R. Wilson 1973, 26.

[51] B. R. Wilson 1973, 27.

Used in this way, church–sect typology does have a positive contribution to make to New Testament interpretation. The typology offers a useful set of classifications for assessing (but not pigeonholing) New Testament attitudes to the world, though the interpreter must keep in mind the limited and provisional nature of the categories. The typology thus has some descriptive value. It does not, however, deliver explanations. In general, it assists in the distinction and schematization of various social responses to the world within and between religious groups, but provides little help in identifying the cause or purpose of any of these responses. The reasons for any particular response (or mix of responses) are largely to be found within the particular circumstances of the group's existence at a specific point in time.[52]

The renewed interest in New Testament attitudes to the world generated by the recent application of church–sect typology is another stimulus for the present study. In investigating Paul's uses of the terms κόσμος and κτίσις, there will be special consideration given to the question, To what extent is Paul employing these terms to inculcate in his audiences a certain "response to the world"? Again, the appropriateness of *these* terms to this area of sociological interest is self-evident.

In the course of exploring whether and how Paul employs the terms κόσμος and κτίσις to generate a particular orientation to the wider society, we shall interact with church–sect typology and, in the process, endeavour to advance our understanding of "response to the world" in Pauline Christianity beyond the generalized picture of the conversionist sect drawn by MacDonald.

1.4. κόσμος and κτίσις in Paul

We turn now to the scholarly discussion of Paul's usage of the terms κόσμος and κτίσις, beginning with κόσμος. A count of occurrences secures the place of κόσμος as Paul's main term for "world" or "universe": the word appears thirty-seven times in the undisputed letters, the highest number of instances in the New Testament outside the Johannine literature.[53] The term is not evenly distributed. There

[52] Cf. Horrell 1996, 24–5.
[53] In the Johannine writings, it appears 102 times. There are seventy-eight instances in the Gospel, twenty-three in 1 John and one occurrence in 2 John.

is a heavy concentration of occurrences in 1 Corinthians. It appears in this epistle twenty-one times, in comparison with nine times in Romans, three times each in 2 Corinthians and Galatians, and once in Philippians.

Treatments of κόσμος in Paul have tended to be brief and summary in form, confined mainly to dictionary articles and works of New Testament or Pauline theology. The most significant and influential accounts in the second half of the twentieth century have been those of Bultmann, in the first volume of his *Theology of the New Testament*,[54] and Sasse in his article on κόσμος in *TDNT*.[55] These are still regarded as the definitive treatments of the term.[56]

1.4.1. Bultmann on κόσμος in Paul

Bultmann treats κόσμος as a negative term for Paul. He sets it alongside "sin", "flesh", "death" and "the law", placing it under the heading of "Man Prior to the Revelation of Faith".[57] Bultmann stresses that κόσμος is an "*historical*" term with Paul rather than a "*cosmological*" one.[58] Apart from a few instances, κόσμος, he insists, is a term which has to do with humanity, denoting the human world and the sphere of human activity.[59]

For Bultmann, the most important feature of κόσμος in Paul's usage is that the term "often contains a definite theological judgment": κόσμος, implicitly or explicitly, serves as the "antithesis to the sphere of God or 'the Lord'".[60] This is the case, Bultmann points out, when κόσμος denotes human possibilities and conditions of life (appealing to 1 Cor 3:22; 7:31–34), human attitudes and estimations (1 Cor 1:20,

---

[54] Bultmann 1952, 254–9.
[55] Sasse 1965.
[56] For other discussions and reviews of κόσμος in Paul, see Bandstra 1964, 48–57; Baumgarten 1975, 160–2; Ladd 1975, 397–400; Painter 1993; Sampley 1991, 26–7; Sand 1967, 169–70; Stuhlmacher 1992, 269–73; Vos 1986, 12–14. On κόσμος in the New Testament generally, see Auer 1970; BAGD 446–8; Balz 1991; Bratcher 1980; Dinkler 1962; Guhrt 1975; G. Johnston 1963/64; Löwe 1935; Mussner 1961; North 1962; Zimmermann 1968. More generally, on Paul's/the New Testament view of the world, see Flender 1968, 2–7; Sampley 1991, 25–33; Schnackenburg 1968 (cf. also 1967); Schulz 1973; Völkl 1961.
[57] "Man under Faith" for Bultmann is marked by "*freedom from the world and its powers*" (1952, 351).
[58] Bultmann 1952, 254.
[59] Bultmann 1952, 254–5.
[60] Bultmann 1952, 255.

27–28) and human beings in their sinfulness (Rom 3:6, 19) and in their need of reconciliation to God (Rom 11:15; 2 Cor 5:19).[61] But it is particularly so, he stresses, when the expression ὁ κόσμος οὗτος is used (1 Cor 3:19; 5:10; 7:31b; cf. ὁ αἰών οὗτος in 1 Cor 2:6, 8; 3:18) or when κόσμος on its own carries the significance of ὁ κόσμος οὗτος (appealing to 1 Cor 1:20–21, 27–28; 2:12; 7:31a, 33–34; 2 Cor 7:10; Gal 6:14). Employed in this way, so Bultmann claims, κόσμος becomes a "time-concept" or more precisely "an eschatological concept", which

> denotes the world of men and the sphere of human activity as being, on the one hand, a temporary thing hastening toward its end..., and on the other hand, the sphere of anti-godly power under whose sway the individual who is surrounded by it has fallen.[62]

The power exerted by the κόσμος is interpreted by Bultmann in terms of suppression of individuality. The κόσμος (the macrosociety, as it were) gains the ascendancy over and masters the individual. It "comes to constitute an independent super-self over all individual selves".[63] This thought emerges from Paul's portrayal of the κόσμος in personal terms: when he speaks of the κόσμος as the bearer of wisdom (1 Cor 1:21; 3:19); when he attributes grief to it (2 Cor 7:10); when he speaks of the "spirit of the κόσμος" (1 Cor 2:12), which in modern terms, he argues, is "the atmosphere to whose compelling influence every man contributes but to which he is also always subject".[64] The believer has been rescued from the oppressive and anti-godly power of "the world" and is no longer determined by it (appealing to 1 Cor 2:12; 3:21–23; 6:2; 2 Cor 5:17; Gal 4:9; 6:14).

The "mythological" character of Paul's understanding of the κόσμος – that the κόσμος, though God's creation, is also "*the domain of demonic powers*"[65] (appealing to such texts as Rom 8:38; 1 Cor 2:6, 8; 2 Cor 4:4; Gal 4:3, 9) – is taken by Bultmann as expressive of a particular understanding of human existence. Through this notion a core insight is revealed: that individuals are not masters of their own lives, but are always confronted with the decision of choosing their lords. And, as

[61] Bultmann 1952, 255.
[62] Bultmann 1952, 256.
[63] Bultmann 1952, 257.
[64] Bultmann 1952, 257.
[65] Bultmann 1952, 257.

Bultmann puts it, "natural man has always already decided against God, his true Lord, and has let the threatening and tempting world become lord over him".[66]

1.4.2. Sasse on κόσμος in Paul

Like Bultmann, Sasse stresses the negative shading of κόσμος in Paul. For Sasse, the large majority of instances of κόσμος in Paul (as in the Johannine writings) fall into the category of "Humanity, Fallen Creation, the Theater of Salvation History".[67] He lays particular emphasis on the disjunction between God and the κόσμος in Paul's epistles.[68] He points out that the gulf between God and the κόσμος is traced back by Paul to the emergence of sin and death in the world as the consequence of Adam's sin (Rom 5:12). Now πᾶς ὁ κόσμος stands before God as guilty (Rom 3:19); the κόσμος falls under the judgement of God (Rom 3:6; 1 Cor 6:2) leading to condemnation (1 Cor 11:32). The true people of God are set apart from the κόσμος (appealing to 1 Cor 6:2; 11:32).[69] The full extent of the antithesis between God and the κόσμος can be appreciated only in the light of Christ, for only Christ can effect the reconciliation of the κόσμος (Rom 11:15; 2 Cor 5:19). In contrast to Bultmann, Sasse stresses that κόσμος can "transcend the framework of human history".[70] He points to the comprehensiveness of the term in 1 Cor 4:9, embracing even the supernatural powers. Appealing to Rom 8:22 (where κόσμος does not actually occur), he notes that the whole universe takes part in the history of salvation. Bringing these observations together, Sasse reaches the following definition of κόσμος in Paul:

> The κόσμος is the sum of the divine creation which has been shattered by the fall, which stands under the judgment of God, and in which Jesus Christ appears as the Redeemer.[71]

Sasse insists that Paul, like the other New Testament writers, refrains from using κόσμος when describing the redeemed world. He contends, "When the κόσμος is redeemed, it ceases to be κόσμος." The term "is

---

[66] Bultmann 1952, 259.
[67] Sasse 1965, 889.
[68] Sasse 1965, 892.
[69] Sasse 1965, 892.
[70] Sasse 1965, 893.
[71] Sasse 1965, 893.

reserved for the world which lies under sin and death". This, he claims "is very clear in Paul".[72]

1.4.3. Evaluation

Bultmann's exposition exhibits two characteristic emphases which mark his whole approach to Pauline theology. The first is his concern to reinterpret Paul in terms of existential philosophy. His existentializing is apparent in the emphasis on "decision" – one must decide either for God or for the κόσμος – and (especially) in the way he sets "the world" in antithesis to the *individual*. The opposition of the world, the collective humanity, to the individual is derived from Heidegger's existentialism. According to this analysis, the world subdues and smothers the fundamental individuality and distinctiveness of every human being. In order to achieve authentic existence, human beings must stand out from the world, act independently of it, exercise self-responsibility and take control of their own destinies.[73]

It is extremely doubtful, however, that a re-reading of Paul in existentialist terms does justice to his intentions. The central role which Bultmann credits to the individual, as Käsemann points out, owes more to the idealist tradition than to Paul.[74] Bultmann's analysis fails to take sufficient account of the corporate dimension in Paul's theology. It is highly questionable whether the threat posed by the κόσμος, when it is portrayed by Paul as a hostile force, can be adequately re-expressed as the threat of human collectivity to individuality. On close examination it will be seen that when κόσμος specifies a realm of opposition to God, it serves as the antithesis to the *community* of Christ, rather than to the individual believer (e.g. 1 Cor 1–3, especially 1:26–28; 6:1–2; 7:29–31). It may be objected that Paul's statement in Gal 6:14 – that the κόσμος was crucified to me (ἐμοί) – appears to have primary reference to the individual, but the context (vv. 12–13, 15–16) shows that Paul's words are oriented toward the community.[75]

---

[72] Sasse 1965, 893.

[73] For Bultmann, this is the key difference between New Testament anthropology and Greek and Hellenistic anthropology. Greek thought teaches human beings to find their security by incorporation into the κόσμος, while the New Testament directs men and women to find authentic life in the sphere of individual responsibility and decision (1955, 78, 83).

[74] Käsemann 1971a, 10–11.

[75] Barclay 1988, 102.

Secondly, Bultmann's approach betrays his typical stress on the anthropological orientation of Paul's theology. Bultmann's programme as a whole is marked by a concern to play down or reinterpret the cosmological and mythological elements in Paul's thought. It is now widely felt that Paul's theology cannot be so easily isolated from its apocalyptic and cosmic frame, at least not without seriously distorting its meaning.[76] One wonders, then, whether Bultmann's claim that κόσμος is a "historical" and not a "cosmological" term for Paul is more a reflection of his own theological prejudice than of Paul's actual usage. But this can only be determined as we explore the κόσμος texts.

Bultmann's and Sasse's accounts of κόσμος in Paul are based on a methodology which is now regarded as highly flawed. Bultmann and Sasse adopt a theological word-study approach to the analysis of κόσμος. In this style of lexical study, the word under investigation is treated like a technical term in a theological or philosophical treatise. The approach has been heavily and famously criticized by James Barr.[77] Barr points that it involves a basic confusion between "word-sense" and "concept". Terms are viewed as vehicles for theological ideas. The theological conception conveyed by a particular term is derived from a synthesis of the term's various occurrences. It is assumed that the final and general concept arrived at can then be read back into particular instances of the word as its technical meaning. Barr describes this linguistic fallacy as the "illegitimate totality transfer" error.[78] In the process of formulating the definitive theological meaning of a word, certain uses of the word are emphasized and occurrences which do not fit are either excluded or forced into the pattern.[79] Also, differences in epistolary usage are ignored. No thought is given to the possibility that the slant given to a word in one letter may be different to the perspective given to it in another.

Both Bultmann and Sasse conclude that κόσμος is a negative theological category for Paul. For Bultmann, "Man ... is indeed in the grip of the world and, so to speak, embedded in it – but for his ruin, not for his salvation."[80] For Sasse, the word κόσμος, not just for Paul but for the New Testament writers as a whole, is completely bound to a

---

[76] See Beker 1980; Käsemann 1969a; 1971a.
[77] Barr 1961, 206–62. See also Cotterell and Turner 1989, 106–28.
[78] Barr 1961, 218.
[79] Barr 1961, 219.
[80] Bultmann 1955, 78.

negative understanding of the world as estranged, fallen and condemned. One may wonder whether this conclusion is the result of the skewed methodology, Bultmann and Sasse downplaying or misreading part of the evidence in order to make it fit the scheme. Paul can use the word κόσμος with a positive sense: for example, Rom 1:8, 20; Phil 2:15. Such instances cannot be dismissed as uncharacteristic uses, unreflective of Paul's true theological thought. A proper account of Paul's employment of κόσμος must explore the full range of his usage and do full justice to his positive and neutral uses as well as his strongly negative ones.

Reviews of κόσμος in Paul since Bultmann and Sasse have been much less prone to the errors of theological word-study. However, these accounts are brief and cursory in nature and generally do not attempt to assess Paul's uses of κόσμος on a letter-by-letter basis.[81] None has supplanted Bultmann's and Sasse's accounts. These treatments continue to wield a wide influence.

There is thus a need for a detailed investigation of κόσμος in Paul which carefully examines the texts in which the word occurs, which is alert to differences in epistolary patterns of usage and which avoids, as far as possible, preconceived judgements about the meaning of the term in any particular occurrence of it. The present study attempts to address this need.

In the course of the investigation, interpretive issues raised by Bultmann's and Sasse's analyses will be kept in view. To what extent is κόσμος a "cosmological" term, and to what extent is it an "anthropological" term for Paul? To what extent and in what contexts is κόσμος used in a derogatory fashion by Paul? To what extent does Paul collocate the term with σάρξ, ἁμαρτία and θάνατος? Precisely how, in a given instance, is κόσμος linked with σάρξ, ἁμαρτία or θάνατος? Is κόσμος wholly consigned to the "plight" side of Paul's soteriology? Does Paul, to test Sasse's claim, ever use κόσμος with reference to the future redeemed world?

Paying attention to *epistolary* patterns of usage, the starting-point for the analysis will be the predominance of κόσμος in 1 Corinthians, with twenty-one of its thirty-seven occurrences in the undisputed Paulines concentrated in this letter.

---

[81] Painter (1993, 980–2) is one scholar who examines κόσμος epistle by epistle. His account, though, is extremely brief and is not specifically devoted to κόσμος.

1.4.4. κτίσις in Paul

The term κτίσις is employed by Paul much less often than κόσμος. It occurs only nine times in the commonly accepted epistles (Rom 1:20, 25; 8:19, 20, 21, 22, 39; 2 Cor 5:17; Gal 6:15).[82] Interestingly, in three of these it appears in close proximity to κόσμος (Rom 1:20; 2 Cor 5:17–19; Gal 6:14–15). The meaning of κτίσις in Rom 8:19–22 has been at the centre of a longstanding interpretive dispute. The main point at issue is whether the term refers to the human creation, the non-human creation, or both.[83] There is an emerging consensus that κτίσις denotes the wider creation apart from humanity. The meaning of the phrase καινὴ κτίσις in 2 Cor 5:17 and Gal 6:15 is also greatly debated. Again, the key issue is whether the denotation is anthropological, cosmological or both.[84] The state of this question is much less settled. Scholars are deeply divided over whether Paul has in view a new *cosmic* creation or a new *human* creation, and if the latter, whether the individual believer or the believing community.

κτίσις in Paul – or more specifically κτίσις in Rom 8:19–22, 2 Cor 5:17 and Gal 6:15 – thus suffers from no lack of detailed treatment in commentaries, articles and studies. In examining Paul's use of the term, therefore, this study is hardly plugging a gap in the research but rather adding to an already overwhelming body of literature!

Nevertheless, the concentration of occurrences of κτίσις in Romans is a fact which often goes overlooked in discussions of κτίσις in Paul. This important feature of Paul's usage calls for further attention. Every instance of κτίσις – as opposed to the expression καινὴ κτίσις – in the epistles commonly accepted as Pauline is found in Romans. κτίσις is a key term in the theological vocabulary of *this* epistle. This study, therefore, will treat Paul's use of κτίσις as an epistolary usage and will

---

[82] For κτίσις in Paul, see Baumgarten 1975, 162–79; Bultmann 1952, 227–32; Esser 1975; Foerster 1965; G. W. H. Lampe 1964; Petzke 1992; Stuhlmacher 1992, 269–73. On the general notion of creation in Paul, see Baumbach 1979; Becker 1989, 402–9; Schwantes 1962; Shields 1980 (on creation in Romans).

[83] Cranfield (1975, 411) lists eight suggestions: (1) the whole creation including human beings and angels; (2) all humankind; (3) unbelieving humanity; (4) believers; (5) the angelic world; (6) non-human creation together with angels; (7) non-human creation together with unbelieving humanity; (8) non-human creation. The fullest history of the interpretation of κτίσις in Rom 8:19–22 (though obviously dated now) is given in Gieraths 1950, 20–87.

[84] For the history of interpretation, see Aymer 1982, 17–37, and esp. Mell 1989, 9–32.

attempt to investigate it in relation to the particular theological themes, arguments and concerns of Romans.

Having reviewed Bultmann's discussion of κόσμος in Paul, it is appropriate to highlight his very brief reflections on Paul's use of κτίσις. As with his treatment of κόσμος, Bultmann's existentializing is apparent. He writes, "Paul's conception of the creation, as well as of the Creator, depends upon what it means for man's existence."[85] Human beings find themselves caught between God and creation and "must decide between the two".[86] Also evident is his desire to mitigate cosmic elements in Paul's theology. In Rom 8:19–22, Bultmann admits a non-human reference to κτίσις, taking the word to mean "the earth and its creatures subordinate to man".[87] However, he argues that the obscurity of Paul's words – the fact that the only thing that is clear from the text is that creation shares a history with humanity – "once again indicates how completely the cosmological point of view recedes for Paul behind that of his theology of history".[88]

An interesting feature of Bultmann's analysis is his emphasis on the ambiguity of κτίσις/creation for Paul. Observing that in Rom 8:38, κτίσις occurs in a list of cosmic powers "at enmity with God", he writes that for Paul,

> the creation has a peculiarly ambiguous character: On the one hand, it is the earth placed by God at man's disposal for his use and benefit . . . on the other, it is the field of activity for evil, demonic powers.[89]

Reflecting on the use of κτίσις in Rom 1:25, he argues that "'creation' becomes a destructive power whenever man decides in favor of it instead of for God".[90] Bultmann concludes that as to what "creation" actually means for human existence, Paul is "ambivalent".[91]

In studying Paul's use of κτίσις in Romans, the issues raised by Bultmann will be kept in mind. Is κτίσις – even if it can be shown to mean the non-human creation – as central to the main thought of Rom 8:19–22 as would appear? To what extent is κτίσις a destructive power

---

85 Bultmann 1952, 231.
86 Bultmann 1952, 229.
87 Bultmann 1952, 230.
88 Bultmann 1952, 230.
89 Bultmann 1952, 230.
90 Bultmann 1952, 230.
91 Bultmann 1952, 231.

for Paul? Does Paul, as Bultmann claims, have an ambivalent under-standing of κτίσις? Or, do Bultmann's comments betray his own concern to filter out those aspects of Paul's theology which have no direct meaning for human existence?

1.4.5. The particular contribution of this study

A major advance in Pauline word-study was made by Robert Jewett in his analysis of Paul's anthropological terminology.[92] Alert to the dangers of a theological word-analysis, on the one hand, and the limitations of a purely lexicographical treatment, on the other, he sought to account for the variations in Paul's uses of anthropological words in terms of the historical situation within which they were meant to operate. Alive to the situational nature of Paul's correspondence – that Paul's epistles (by and large) are occasional writings, responding to and interacting with specific situations in the communities addressed – Jewett, in his study, was concerned "to measure the impact of fresh historical circum-stances upon his [Paul's] anthropological usage".[93] He came to the conclusion that

> Each new connotation emerges in coherent relationship to a particular historical situation in the congregation Paul is addressing, is designed specifically to meet that situation, and tends to slip into disuse when the situation changes.[94]

The present study follows Jewett's lead, and attempts to explore the extent to which Paul's epistolary usages of κόσμος and κτίσις stand "in coherent relationship" to the situations being addressed.

Investigating this relationship involves asking two main questions: How does Paul's use of the terms *reflect* the social situation he is con-fronting? And, How is Paul's usage meant, in turn, to *affect* that situation? These are two sides of a dialectic. To the extent that they can be pursued separately, I am especially interested in the latter aspect: how far Paul intends his usage to exert an influence on his readers. In other words, I am concerned with the *social functions* or social impacts which Paul's usage of the terms may be designed to have within the community addressed.

---

[92] Jewett 1971.
[93] Jewett 1971, 7.
[94] Jewett 1971, 10.

It is by examining Paul's epistolary uses of the key terms in relation to the probable situational contexts and social objectives of the letters that I hope to make my primary contribution to the scholarly understanding of κόσμος and κτίσις in Paul.

1.5. Conclusion

To summarize, this project is a study of Paul's epistolary uses of the terms κόσμος and κτίσις. It attempts to investigate these uses within their original social settings, that is to say, in relation to the community situations which Paul is addressing. It will seek to identify, where possible, the intended social functions of Paul's uses.

Interpreting Paul's epistolary activity as an enterprise of world-building we aim to answer the question, How does Paul use the words κόσμος and κτίσις to try to construct the social and symbolic worlds of his readers? In other words, How does he use the terms to shape and influence the communities he addresses, their structures, norms and goals? Where relevant and appropriate, I also consider how Paul uses the terms to influence his communities' "response to the world", their orientation to their wider social environment.

Having now set out the context and aims of the project, the next chapter will endeavour to make clear the theoretical bases of the study and the methodology which will be implemented in the textual analyses to follow.

2

The method and approach
of this study

2.1. Introduction

This chapter constitutes the main theoretical and methodological part
of the study. It sets out the core theoretical assumptions on which
the investigation is based, and the interpretive method which will be
employed.

The chapter first identifies the limitations of Peter Berger's theoretical
perspective as an all-encompassing schema within which to conduct an
analysis of the terms κόσμος and κτίσις as instruments of world-
construction. We next discuss a more practically useful and theoretically
sound approach – the critical linguistics of Roger Fowler. After commenting further on theoretical issues, the interpretive method is set out.

2.2. The limitations of Berger's theory

The indebtedness of this project to Peter Berger's theory of world-
construction and world-maintenance was made clear in the previous
chapter. The project has, in some measure, been stimulated by the recent
application of Berger's theory to the New Testament. The present study
appropriates from Berger's work the basic heuristic concepts of the social
world and the symbolic universe, taking issue somewhat with his
understanding of the connection between them. According to Berger,
the symbolic universe operates to sustain and legitimate the social
world. To this should be added that the social world also serves to
support the symbolic world. In other words, social orders and symbolic
orders influence each other in a dialectical fashion. But we can agree
with Berger's basic point that the two are strongly correlated.

Taking up these concepts, then, this study assumes that the particular
communities to which Paul writes – or, to be more specific, the social
structures and norms embodied in these groups – may be viewed as
social worlds in the making. In other words, these communities

constitute emerging "worlds" for their members to inhabit, comprehensive social orders (potentially) shaping every aspect of their members' social experience: their social identity, social relations, attitudes and modes of behaviour. The developing world-views of these communities may be seen as symbolic universes, transcending and including the social worlds, giving symbolic meaning to them. And, Paul's letter-writing activity may be thought of as a world-constructing endeavour, an attempt to influence the social and ideological formation of the communities addressed.[1]

Berger's theory thus forms part of the broad framework of this investigation. However, it suffers from practical and theoretical limitations which make it unsuitable as a methodology for analyzing how Paul uses the terms κόσμος and κτίσις in his efforts to construct the social and symbolic worlds of his readers.

Firstly, Berger's theory gives a generalized account of large-scale social activities. It paints a picture of the origin and development of social movements in bold strokes. It is not a methodology for a penetrating analysis of the formation of specific social groups in specific social-historical contexts. Even less is it a framework for the detailed investigation of particular texts.

Secondly, despite his emphasis on the crucial role of language in the social construction of reality, Berger provides no precise analytical methods for the study of language as a reality-constructing medium. What Berger offers is a general perspective on language, not a linguistic theory, and certainly not an apparatus for linguistic analysis. Berger's "panoramic" framework is much less useful for the "close-up" study of language-use undertaken in the present work.

Thirdly, Berger describes the establishment and development of societies/social groups in terms of a two-stage process of creation and maintenance. Social worlds are built, then preserved. This schematization underestimates the extent to which social orders are continually made and remade by those who inhabit them, and does not adequately account for the fact that in this ongoing process structures may be both maintained and *changed*.[2]

Fourthly, Berger views the fashioning of social worlds and symbolic universes as the collective enterprise of human beings. Social orders,

---

[1] Cf. the building metaphor of 1 Cor 3:9–15 and Paul's use of the verb οἰκοδομέω (Rom 15:20; 1 Cor 8:1, 10; 10:23; 14:4 (×2), 17; Gal 2:18; 1 Thess 5:11).
[2] See Horrell 1996, 41–2.

according to Berger, are produced by collective entities. This obscures the role of "creative human actors".[3] Social worlds form and develop through a complex process of human interaction. Some individuals and sub-groupings have a greater capacity to influence the development than others.[4] The obscuration is clearly significant for the present study, since this is an investigation of the world-building efforts of one particular individual, that is, Paul.

A fifth limitation of Berger's scheme is his over-emphasis on *legitimation*. The theory fails to give a satisfactory account of language as an instrument of *critique*. For these and other reasons, Berger's theory is not an appropriate methodology for assessing how Paul uses language to structure and manipulate the social and symbolic reality of his addressees. A better line of approach is suggested by *critical linguistics*.

2.3. The "critical linguistics" of Roger Fowler

Critical linguistics is a branch of literary and cultural studies which explores the use of language in various modes of discourse to create, maintain and change social identity, roles and statuses, to confirm or manipulate social relations and structures and to effect or resist social control.[5] Its practitioners include R. Hodge, G. Kress, T. Trew, and especially Roger Fowler.[6] Fowler defines critical linguistics in these terms:

> its basic claims are that all linguistic usage encodes ideological patterns or discursive structures which *mediate* representations of the world in language; that different usages . . . encode different ideologies, resulting from their different situations and purposes; and that by these means language works as a social practice.[7]

---

[3] Giddens 1993, 718.

[4] Horrell 1996, 42.

[5] Fowler and Kress 1979, 190.

[6] Fowler's work, and that of the exponents of critical linguistics generally, is built on M. A. K. Halliday's functional theory of language. Halliday's basic premise is that "Language is as it is because of the functions it has evolved to serve people's lives" (1978, 4). He describes language as a "social semiotic" (1978, 2). He contends that by "the exchange of meanings" in a social context, "people act out the social structure, affirming their own statuses and roles, and establishing and transmitting the shared systems of value and knowledge" (1978, 2). Halliday views the relation of language to the social system as a "complex natural dialectic" in which language not only *reflects* the social system but also *influences* it (1978, 183).

[7] Fowler 1991, 89.

CONSTRUCTING THE WORLD

Fowler lays out his approach in chapters 2–4 of his book, *Linguistic Criticism*. He begins his account by discussing "Language and the Representation of Experience",[8] looking at the way in which language categorizes reality, orders experience and helps us make sense of the world. Language enables people to analyze the world and to impose structures upon it. It constructs cognitive categories: "it crystallizes and stabilizes ideas."[9] Yet, Fowler points out, linguistic codes do not interpret reality neutrally. They embody world-views and ideologies.[10] Through the social practice of language (mainly in conversation), and by convention, the categorizations of language and the ideologies which they encode, are accepted as common sense.

This leads to a consideration of "Official and Habitual Language".[11] The use of linguistic codes, Fowler notes, has a negative side: the twin problems of *legitimation* and *habitualization*.[12] Firstly, there is legitimation. The language which an individual acquires is the language of a society. It is an "official" language in that "it comprises the structures and the meanings authorized by the dominant interests of the culture".[13] Legitimated language dominates education, culture and the public arena. Its meanings are loaded in favour of controlling groups in society. Language encodes social categorizations and structures authorized by those in power and serves their interests. Since dominant groups control the means of legitimating the preferred systems of meaning – schools, libraries, media – language becomes a tool for preserving the prevailing order. Fowler writes, "It does this not only through propaganda, but also by inertia, the settlement towards stability and resistance to change which . . . is a characteristic of codes."[14] Secondly, there is habitualization. Conventional codes simplify knowledge and action. Consequently, they have the effect of making our perceptions automatic, unanalytical and uncritical. We recognize and accept rather than really "see" and examine. We uncritically accept legitimated meanings. Language-use, therefore, through legitimation and habitualization, has a propensity to

[8] Fowler 1996, 21–39.
[9] Fowler 1996, 29. Fowler at this juncture clearly stands in the Sapir-Whorf tradition, though, as will become clear, he rejects the linguistic determinism of that tradition. Cf. 1996, 46.
[10] Fowler 1996, 40.
[11] Fowler 1996, 40–53.
[12] Fowler 1996, 42–8.
[13] Fowler 1996, 43.
[14] Fowler 1996, 44.

reinforce its categories, to underpin the established socio-political order, to consolidate the inequities of society, and in fact to become an instrument of coercion and social control.

There are, however, linguistic practices which resist these tendencies: activities which promote "exploration, consciousness, change and creativity rather than stagnation and repression".[15] Fowler discusses these modes of linguistic usage under the heading "Linguistic Practice: Defamiliarization".[16]

The term "defamiliarization" (Russian, *ostraneniye*) is drawn by Fowler from Formalism. It was coined by Victor Schlovsky. He contended that, "The purpose of art is to impart the sensation of things as they are perceived and not as they are known. The technique of art is to make objects 'unfamiliar'".[17] The principle of defamiliarization is stated by Boris Tomashevsky: "The old and habitual must be spoken of as if it were new and unusual. One must speak of the ordinary as if it were unfamiliar."[18] This, as the Formalists demonstrated, can be achieved by an unlimited range of linguistic and literary devices (e.g. metaphor, use of unusual words, invention of new words, change of style, disruption of syntactical rules). The Formalists applied the theory of estrangement to poetic and "high" literary forms and saw no connection with social processes. Fowler understands defamiliarization as a general linguistic practice and one with important social implications. He defines it as "the use of some strategy to force us to look, to be critical".[19] In linguistic terms the process involves:

> *un*coding – disestablishing the received tie between a sign and a cultural unit – and optionally *re*coding – tying a newly invented concept to a sign and so establishing its validity. The ultimate process in linguistic creativity would be the formation of a whole new code, a system of new linguistic arrangements encoding a whole new area of knowledge.[20]

Defamiliarization, as defined by Fowler, is not only a literary effect; it is a linguistic activity which is capable of "reanalyzing people's theory of the way the world works".[21] It is a literary and linguistic practice which

---

[15] Fowler 1996, 55.
[16] Fowler 1996, 54–71.
[17] Schlovsky 1965, 12.
[18] Tomashevsky 1965, 85.
[19] Fowler 1996, 57.
[20] Fowler 1996, 55.
[21] Fowler 1996, 55.

questions existing conventions, challenges received perceptions of reality and promotes resistance and social change.

Fowler's perspective is a highly useful way of analyzing language as a means of world-construction and is appropriate to the nature and concerns of the present investigation. It is suitable for the study of particular uses of language in particular texts; it takes account of the social and cultural context of language-use; it is alert to the use of language to change existing social structures as well as to maintain them; it is alive to the ideological dimensions of the deployment of language; it is attentive not only to the role of language as an instrument of legitimation, but also to the use of language as a tool for social critique and resistance.

2.4. The uncoding and recoding of terms

Fowler's concept of defamiliarization, as a means of analyzing the "uncoding and recoding" of a particular *term*, needs to be filled out with a more precise account of linguistic and conceptual change. Fowler is interested in a variety of literary and linguistic techniques which produce a defamiliarizing effect of which the use of individual words or expressions in creative and unconventional ways is only one.

Also, as John Riches points out, his formulation of the linguistic process of defamiliarization is somewhat problematic. Fowler's talk of "*un* coding – disestablishing the received tie between a sign and a cultural unit" and "*re* coding – tying a newly invented concept to a sign", seems to presuppose a rather singular relationship between a linguistic sign and the aspect of experience to which it relates. According to Riches, the definition underplays the extent to which signs form part of a *network* of linguistic and experiential ties.[22] Since John Riches and Alan Millar have given considerable attention to the mechanisms of linguistic and conceptual change, it seems appropriate to use their insights to sharpen Fowler's notion of "uncoding and recoding".

Millar and Riches point out that the sense of a term is dependent on the sense of other terms with which it is linked. Thus, for example: "red" is linked with "coloured", "courage" with "bravery", "tiger" with "animal".[23] To understand the sense of a term one has to know the

[22] Riches 1995, 2.
[23] Millar and Riches 1981, 34.

senses of related terms. A term is linked with other terms in what Millar and Riches describe as "a more or less complex branching system". Terms are not only linked with other terms but also with aspects of sensory experience. Millar and Riches claim that "the term-to-term and term-to-experience links are constituted by regularities in linguistic use" and that "linguistic communication among the members of a community is only possible because the regularities which operate in that community are, for the most part, conventional".[24]

To say that the regularities of linguistic communication (especially the regularities governing the rejection and acceptance of utterances) are conventional is, according to Millar and Riches, to say that these conditions must hold of them: (1) Everyone conforms to them. (2) Everyone believes that everyone else conforms to them. (3) This belief generates a good reason for each person to conform. To the third condition, Millar and Riches add the qualification, "so long as one has an interest in the ends which the existence of the regularity promotes".[25] Since language is not only an instrument of communication, but also "a vehicle of truth", the attempt to promote a more adequate articulation of the truth will often lead to deviations from the regularities of language use, overriding the "good reason" of condition (3). To put this in Fowler's terms, since language is a means of expressing and reflecting on things in the world, and since conventional language-use leads to the problems of legitimation and habitualization, the attempt to reanalyze and question existing perceptions of the world will often involve deviating from the linguistic conventions, and resisting the ends which the conventions promote.

Riches argues that linguistic and conceptual change is to be understood as

> a process of modifying the network of associations which a term/sentence conventionally has in a particular natural language community at a particular time. In such a process, standard sentence to sentence links and sentence to experience links are modified (discarded and replaced with others) in order to generate new senses both continuous and discontinuous with former senses.[26]

The shift from talk of terms to talk of sentences in this definition is significant, since for Millar and Riches, meaning is not borne by terms

[24] Millar and Riches 1981, 34.
[25] Millar and Riches 1981, 37.
[26] Riches 1995, 1 n.1.

but by sentences. Thus, the sense of a term depends upon the sense of the sentence into which the term enters.[27]

Millar and Riches apply this approach to linguistic and conceptual change to the utterances of Jesus on the "kingdom of God", showing how Jesus rejected the conventional associations of the expression "kingdom of God", relating to punishment of enemies and sinners, and replaced them with others relating to forgiveness, healing and restoration.[28]

In the light of Millar and Riches' theory, the "uncoding and recoding" of a term may be more precisely explained as the modification of the term's network of associations, deleting some of the conventional links and adding others. It is by virtue of its established network of associations that a certain term may encode a world-view and ideology. It is by modifying the conventional linkages that that world-view and ideology may be subverted or repudiated and a new social meaning recoded.

2.5. Further theoretical issues

Before elaborating the interpretive method of this study, two further theoretical issues need to addressed. Word-study (of which this investigation is a type) is an area of inquiry which has suffered from a great deal of abuse in the past. Having already highlighted the errors committed by Bultmann and Sasse in their analyses of κόσμος we ourselves need to be especially careful to avoid such pitfalls. Like Bultmann and Sasse, we are interested not only in the sense of the individual *word* but also in the sense of the *sentence* into which the word enters. But, unlike Bultmann and Sasse, we need to make clear that we are not confusing the two things.

We shall distinguish, therefore, in the analyses that follow, between the sense with which Paul uses κόσμος and κτίσις in various contexts, and the way in which he deploys κόσμος and κτίσις alongside other linguistic expressions in those contexts in order to say what he has to say. Thus, for example, in Rom 3:6, the sense with which Paul uses κόσμος is "humanity", "human beings". This can be inferred from the way Paul links the verb κρίνω with the noun κόσμος as its object and the noun θεός as its subject: θεός and κρίνω are normally linked with

[27] Millar and Riches 1981, 38.
[28] Millar and Riches 1981, 41–2.

object expressions referring to human beings. The way that Paul deploys κόσμος along with other linguistic items is to express the belief that God will judge the human world. This working distinction will help us in discussing the sense of a sentence involving either κόσμος or κτίσις without creating the impression that that sense is being identified with the specific word itself.

The second theoretical point requiring clarification is what is meant by talk of the "social function" of Paul's uses of κόσμος and κτίσις. We need to make clear that using this phrase does not in any way imply a commitment to the sociological theory of functionalism.[29] The main methodological source of the notion of "social function" as employed in this project is again the work of Millar and Riches. The social function of an utterance – as understood in the present study – is "its *function for the speaker*, what the speaker aims to do in and through making it".[30] It relates to the speaker's intention "to persuade or otherwise affect those who might be addressed".[31] This is not to deny that an utterance may well have an outcome quite different from that intended by the speaker. But the actual social outcome of Paul's utterances is not a concern in this study, whose interest lies solely in the *intended effects* of his utterances upon the addressees.

In the chapters that follow, the term "social function" will vary with other expressions, such as "social impact", "social consequences" and "social implications". In each case, the qualification "as *intended* by Paul", if not explicitly stated, will be assumed.

To determine the social function of an utterance, we shall first explore the social impact of a statement involving κόσμος and κτίσις in relation to the meaning or content of that statement. Gager, at the outset of a study of Paul's apocalyptic language, expresses his intention to concentrate "on the *function* rather than the content or meaning of what have traditionally been called eschatological or apocalyptic motifs".[32] The present study eschews an approach of this kind. Millar and Riches point out that though it is permissible to draw a distinction between the *meaning* and *function* of utterances, the latter cannot be grasped without a grasp of the former.[33] Any inferences drawn about the social

[29] For a critique of this sociological perspective, see Horrell 1996, 33–8.
[30] Millar and Riches 1981, 30.
[31] Millar and Riches 1981, 30.
[32] Gager 1970, 327.
[33] Millar and Riches 1981, 32.

functions of Paul's uses of κόσμος and κτίσις in the course of this study will therefore be based on the meaning-content of Paul's statements. In some cases, the practical implications Paul derives or wishes his readers to derive from his statements on κόσμος and κτίσις will be obvious from their immediate contexts. In others, the social consequences will have to be teased out more carefully.

Secondly, we shall explore the social function of utterances involving κόσμος and κτίσις in a letter in relation to the social goals of that letter as a whole. Paul's letters strongly exhibit the qualities of cohesion, progression and thematization expected of well-formed and well-organized texts.[34] His epistles, by and large, present us with a progressive sequence of arguments and an interrelated (and to a large degree, integrated) set of ideas. Paul's epistles are also, for the most part, strongly *goal*-driven communicative texts. The various theological arguments presented in a letter contribute to the same practical ends. It seems reasonable to assume, therefore, that the social intention of particular utterances will be connected – on some textual level – to the social purposes of the whole texts.

2.6. The interpretive method

It is now appropriate to lay out the interpretive matrix within which this study will be conducted. We shall investigate Paul's epistolary uses of κόσμος and κτίσις (1) in their immediate literary and linguistic contexts within a letter, and (2) in relation to the epistles' larger communicative contexts. The latter will be discussed first, since this requires some filling out.

2.6.1. Contexts of utterance, culture and reference

The framework for exploring the contexts of the letters is drawn from the work of Roger Fowler. Fowler understands texts as units of communication "in contexts".[35] He highlights three contexts in which textual communication takes place.

Firstly, there is the *context of utterance*, "the situation within which discourse is conducted".[36] The context of utterance embraces the physical surroundings in which the communication takes places, the

---

[34] Fowler 1996, 82–3.
[35] Fowler 1996, 110.
[36] Fowler 1996, 112.

relation of the participants of the discourse to each other, and the channel of communication employed. In the case of a letter, the context of utterance is split; that is to say, the text is written and received at different times and in different places. Fowler points out that the settings of discourse are often perceived as institutions or routine settings (such as "church", "classroom", "television studio"). Thus the participants interact according to the roles assumed for or ascribed to them in those structures.[37]

Secondly, there is the *context of culture* which is "the whole network of social and economic conventions, all the institutions and familiar settings and relationships, constituting the culture at large, especially insofar as these bear on particular utterance contexts".[38]

Thirdly, there is the *context of reference*, which is "the topic or subject-matter of a text".[39] According to Fowler, defamiliarization occurs where the context of reference introduces elements which deviate in any way from the expected cultural context.[40] This threefold framework of contextual analysis is eminently applicable to Paul's epistles. His letters as whole units of communication lend themselves to this scheme of investigation.

Paul's epistolary discourse occurs within a split context of utterance. In exploring the utterance contexts of his letters, therefore, attention needs to be paid to the two sides of those contexts, the recipients in their social settings, on the one side, and the writer with his motives, aims and objectives in writing, on the other.

On the one hand, the social situation of the readers must be examined. As stressed in the previous chapter, Paul's (undisputed) epistles are situationally determined writings. They were written to and for specific communities – emerging social worlds – in specific locations, with specific needs. Until recently, it was common to view Romans as the exception to this rule. The contents of Romans were seen as purely theoretical, not directly related to the experience and needs of its readers. Now, however, a consensus has emerged that Romans too has a significant situational dimension (especially in chapters 14–16) even if the letter as a whole is not as clearly addressed to a specific congregational situation as 1 Corinthians or Galatians.

---

[37] Fowler 1996, 113.
[38] Fowler 1996, 114.
[39] Fowler 1996, 114.
[40] Fowler 1996, 115.

Reconstructing the community situations underlying Paul's letters is of course a precarious exercise. For the most part, all we have to go on is the evidence from Paul's letters themselves, and hearing only Paul's response, as Morna Hooker has famously stated, is very much like hearing one end of a telephone conversation.[41] Also, Paul's accounts are not disinterested reports, but partial, biased and selective presentations of events. But though "mirror-reading" is plagued with difficulties, it is not a hopeless exercise.[42] By a cautious and critical handling of the Pauline data, one can reach legitimate and plausible conclusions about the situations addressed.

In trying to establish the community situations this work will, by and large, depend and build on existing research. The communities concerned in this study are those in Corinth, Rome and Galatia. Much work has been done on the Corinthian Christian community in recent years and we shall draw on this material. Also, in recent scholarship, much has been done to advance our knowledge of the Roman Christian community (though here we can further the discussion). And, there is now a great deal of common ground among scholars as to the nature of the crisis at Galatia.

In reconstructing the audience situations, as well as using historical criticism, we shall draw upon the insights of sociology without, however, trying to superimpose any one sociological theory or concept on the data in a model-like fashion. Our procedure will be more eclectic and utilitarian, appropriating various sociological insights, using them as tools for illuminating the findings of historical research.

On the other side of the context of utterance, there is Paul in his place of writing, with his own motives and purposes in penning the letter. Paul's letters not only respond to community situations in a reactive way; they are clearly intended to affect and influence those situations. Paul writes with definite social aims in view, not only to consolidate, comfort and encourage the communities addressed, but to criticize, correct and to effect a significant change in their outlook and social behaviour. To achieve his goals for the communities addressed, Paul employs various rhetorical strategies, or modes of persuasion.[43]

[41] Hooker 1973, 315.
[42] See Barclay 1987.
[43] Recently, scholars have attempted to analyze the patterns and techniques of argumentation in Paul's letters in terms of Graeco-Roman rhetorical forms. This is no intention of mine here.

Precisely because Paul's various textual strategies are designed to secure social objectives, they may be appropriately described as *socio-rhetorical* strategies.[44]

Again, difficulty arises when trying to view Romans in this light, since the extent to which the theology of Romans is an argument used to achieve social aims in the community addressed is much debated. Any attempt to uncover a socio-rhetorical dimension to Paul's epistolary usage of κόσμος and κτίσις in Romans must therefore advance with caution. In view of the "special case" which Romans constitutes in this respect, we shall propose, at the appropriate point in this study, a special procedure to deal with it.

A review of the context of utterance of Paul's letters, using Fowler's approach, should also include some reference to the way in which the roles and statuses of letter-writer and letter-readers are being ascribed. Since this is not a main focus of the study, comments on this aspect of the utterance context in the chapters that follow will be kept brief.

Restraint must also be exercised in discussing the context of culture of Paul's letters. We shall consider only those aspects of the cultural context which are directly relevant to this present topic. The most crucial element of the cultural context for our purposes is the linguistic background of κόσμος and κτίσις, the conventional senses and associations of the terms. The next chapter will be given over to this area. Other facets of the context of culture will be drawn upon, where relevant, to shed light on the situation of the readers and on the social aims of Paul. In assessing the context of reference of a letter, we shall consider the broader theological perspectives and themes which pervade or dominate that letter and govern Paul's arguments therein.

2.6.2. The immediate linguistic contexts

In examining Paul's uses of κόσμος and κτίσις in their immediate literary and linguistic contexts within the given letter, we shall try to determine the sense of the term, whether κόσμος or κτίσις, and the meaning of the sentence of which it forms part. We shall scrutinize the descriptive expressions with which the term is linked, its verbal and its possessive relations, its associations with other nouns and noun-phrases

---

[44] The adjective "socio-rhetorical" is derived from Robbins 1984, though I am employing it differently here.

in the sentence and sentence-cluster, and so on. We shall explore, where relevant, the issues raised by Bultmann and Sasse in their theological analyses of the terms and seek to establish whether Paul is using the term in a standard or non-standard sense, and if the latter, what modifications of the conventional linkages he is making. Next we consider, from the immediate context, what practical implications Paul draws out or intends his readers to draw from his deployment of the term, and also give attention (again, where appropriate) to the ideological implications of Paul's usage, that is to say, probe the extent to which Paul is employing the term in its linguistic context either to legitimate or to challenge the dominant order and value system of Graeco-Roman society.[45] In working through the κόσμος/κτίσις texts within the epistle, we shall discern the extent to which Paul's uses evince a consistent, rhetorical pattern or strategy of employment.

Having conducted the analysis of the key passages, it will be useful to cast the net more widely – albeit very briefly – in an attempt to test whether any of the particular themes evident in Paul's utterances involving κόσμος and κτίσις may be seen to be part of a wider network of motifs and beliefs in the epistle.

Taking Paul's epistolary uses together, and relating them to the contexts of utterance, culture and reference, we shall consider the questions: What is the intended cumulative effect and overall social impact of these uses? What *kind* of social world does Paul's usage serve to construct? What type of "response to the world" does his usage function to generate?

2.7. *The focus on 1 Corinthians and Romans*

The study will concentrate on 1 Corinthians and Romans. It will do so for the obvious reason that in these epistles the key terms are over-whelmingly concentrated. But there are other good reasons for the focus on the linguistic usage in these two letters.

Firstly, in these letters, the terms are socio-rhetorically and theo-logically significant. κόσμος is socio-rhetorically and theologically significant in 1 Corinthians. More than half the total occurrences of the

---

[45] One might also enquire into how Paul uses the term to legitimate his own authority. But I am less interested in this aspect of ideology in the present study (though I shall touch on it in relation to 2 Cor 5:17).

word in Paul are located in this letter. κτίσις is significant in Romans. This letter contains every instance of κτίσις (as opposed to καινὴ κτίσις) in the undisputed Pauline letters. Also, κόσμος occurs nine times in Romans (the second highest number of occurrences next to 1 Corinthians), in most cases within an important theological statement.

Secondly, in both these epistles the social and ethical issue of relations with outsiders is prominent. With 1 Corinthians and Romans we are thus afforded the opportunity of exploring the links between Paul's uses of κόσμος and κτίσις and his teaching on community relations with the wider society.

Thirdly, these letters exhibit contrasting patterns of linguistic usage and betray contrasting theological emphases. They also emerge from distinctly different contexts of utterance. Highlighting and exploring the contrast between 1 Corinthians and Romans will be one of the main contributions of this study.

The use of κόσμος and κτίσις in Galatians and 2 Corinthians is much more limited, but still worthy of exploration. We shall consider the key texts (Gal 4:3; Gal 4:1–15; 2 Cor 1:12; 5:17–19; 7:10), applying the interpretive method outlined above, though discussing the contexts of utterance, culture and reference of Galatians and 2 Corinthians in much less detail. The single occurrence of κόσμος (with the sense "universe") in Philippians (2:15) will be dismissed from the field of the inquiry. It is neither theologically nor socio-rhetorically significant enough to the argument of the epistle to warrant attention by the level of analysis applied in this study.

2.8. Summary and procedure

This chapter has laid out the theoretical and methodological insights which inform this project and the method for analyzing the research data. The rest of this study will proceed as follows.

Chapter 3 will review the conventional senses and linkages of the key terms. This will help to reveal distinctives in Paul's usage and provide a basis from which to judge their socio-rhetorical impact on his audiences. Chapters 4–5 will look at the context of utterance of 1 Corinthians, focusing on the issue of weak group-boundaries in Corinth, and then examine the use of κόσμος in the epistle. Chapters 6–7 will examine the use of κόσμος and κτίσις in Romans, and then consider the context of utterance of the letter, focusing on the issue of social conflict with outsiders. Chapter 8 will briefly examine Galatians and 2 Corinthians. Chapter 9 will summarize the results of the investigation and present the main conclusions.

Part II

Linguistic background

3

The linguistic and historical background of
κόσμος and κτίσις

3.1. Introduction

The purpose of this chapter is to establish the standard senses and conventional associations of κόσμος and κτίσις in Greek (and Hellenistic–Jewish) language-use, and so to furnish the general linguistic background against which to interpret Paul's particular uses of the terms.

The chapter is mainly devoted to κόσμος. The concentration on this term is unavoidable since κόσμος is one of the most common and significant words in Greek literature. κτίσις is relatively infrequent by comparison and, in non-Jewish, pre-Christian Greek, exhibits a very narrow and stable line of usage. It can be treated briefly and incisively.

In carrying out a survey the main aim of which is to provide the linguistic backcloth to Paul's usage, a synchronic approach ordinarily would be given priority, since what we mainly need to know are the regular senses and conventional links of these words in contemporary usage.[1] However, a large part of the discussion of κόσμος in this chapter is conducted from a diachronic point of view. This approach can be justified on the basis of the historical and cultural significance of the term. κόσμος with the sense "world/universe" came to encode a world-view which, as Jaeger has shown, was one of the fundamental ideals which shaped Greek culture.[2] It will later be argued that Paul's usage of κόσμος in 1 Corinthians constitutes a deliberate challenge to and subversion of this world-view. It will be helpful, therefore, in view of the larger thesis, not only to set out the understanding of the world associated with κόσμος = world/universe but also to chart its origin, development and perpetuation.

---

[1] On the priority of synchrony in linguistic study, see Cotterell and Turner 1989, 25–6, 131–5.
[2] Jaeger 1965, 150–84.

It is not the intention here to offer a comprehensive review of κόσμος and κτίσις in Greek and Jewish usage. The profuseness of κόσμος in Greek writings renders such an investigation impossible, at least within these present confines. It is sufficient that the survey is representative and serves to establish my main points.

This chapter first lays out the conventional senses of κόσμος in Greek usage. We next focus on κόσμος with the sense "world/universe" – the sense most relevant to this study – concentrating on its use in Greek and Hellenistic philosophy and tracing the development of the world-view which κόσμος = world/universe came to evoke. The basic elements of this representation of the world are then set out. After exploring the social and ideological consequences of the designation of the world as κόσμος, we look briefly at Jewish uses of the word, and then turn attention to κτίσις in Greek and Jewish usage.

3.2. κόσμος in Greek usage[3]

The word κόσμος is attested from the time of Homer.[4] In early Greek usage, it has the basic sense of "order". As Puhvel states, the word conveys "a notion of ordering, arraying, arranging, and structuring discrete units or parts into a whole which is 'proper' in either practical, moral, or esthetic ways".[5] It is used for specific (interpersonal) orderings or arrangements, such as the seating order of rowers (Homer, *Od.* 13.73f), the order of troops (Homer, *Il.* 12.225), the Spartan system of government (Herodotus 1.65), and the order of cities (Plato, *Prot.* 322c). It is used to denote "order" in a general sense (Herodotus 2.52; 9:59),[6] as well as to express the notion of a social and moral order. Thus, we find the common adverbial construction κατὰ κόσμον meaning "in accordance with right and proper order", "as is fitting" (Homer, *Il.* 2.214; 10.472; *Od.* 8.179), and the use of κόσμος with the sense "orderly behaviour", "decorum", "discipline" (Thucydides 2.2.9).

---

[3] What follows is based primarily on LSJ 985. See also Balz 1991, 310; Cornford 1934, 1–2; Guhrt 1975, 521–2; Kahn 1960, 219–24; Sasse 1965, 868–80.
[4] The etymology of κόσμος is uncertain. See Haebler 1967; Puhvel 1976.
[5] Puhvel 1976, 154.
[6] In this sense, it is often used with or synonymously with τάξις (e.g. Herodotus 9:59). Cf. Sasse 1965, 869.

κόσμος is also used to mean "ornament", "decoration" and "adornment" (especially of women) (Homer, *Il.* 14.187; Herodotus 5.92). This line of usage is very frequent in classical Greek. Epithets (cf. Aristotle, *Rhet.* 1408a14; *Poet.* 1457b2) and songs (cf. Pindar, *Ol.* 11.13) can be referred to as "ornaments" of speech.

Other early attested senses of κόσμος are "form", "fashion", "structure" (Homer, *Od.* 8.492; Herodotus 3.22), and "honour" or "credit" (Herodotus 8.60; 8.142). A distinctively Cretan use is the application of the term to the chief magistrate (Aristotle, *Pol.* 1272a6; Strabo, *Geog.* 10.4.21–22).[7]

The meaning "world" emerges as a special sense of κόσμος among the philosophers. In Greek philosophy, the term κόσμος is first applied to the order by which the world is held together[8] and then to the world/universe itself as an ordered reality. κόσμος is also used with reference to distinct regions of the universe, especially the celestial realm (Isocrates, *Pan.* 179; Ps-Plato, *Epin.* 987b).[9] In later *koine* Greek, the sense "inhabited earth" arises. This meaning, however, is extremely rare in pre-Christian Greek, outside of the Septuagint.[10] It cannot be assumed, therefore, to be a conventional sense of the word at the time of Paul.

The earlier "non-cosmological" senses of κόσμος did not die out once the sense "world/universe" had become established, but continued in language-use alongside the later "cosmological" senses. This was certainly the case in the late first century BCE and first century CE.[11]

Jonas points out that κόσμος in Greek usage was generally a term of "praise and even admiration".[12] According to Kahn, when the word

---

[7] See Puhvel 1976, 154–5.
[8] The word διάκοσμος is also used with this sense, e.g. Parmenides fr. 8.60 (D–K 1:246).
[9] See also on Aristotle below, pp. 49–51.
[10] So LSJ 985; Sasse 1965, 880. The New Testament use of κόσμος for "inhabited world" and "humanity" derives from the LXX, see pp. 75–7.
[11] A few examples may be given to establish the point: "orderings" such as the order of government, Dion. Halic., *Ant.* 2.3.1; 2.7.2; "order" in general, Dio Chrysostom, *Disc.* 32.36, 37; 36:13; "decorum", Dio Chrysostom, *Disc.* 32.45, 46; Dion Halic., *Ant.* 7.15.4; 11.6.3; "ornament", "adornment", Dio Chrysostom, *Disc.* 13.34; 31.163; Diodorus Siculus, 5.27.3; 17.70.6; "form", "fashion", Dion. Halic., *Ant.* 1.21.1; 1.30.4; "honour", "credit", Dio Chrysostom, *Disc.* 31.146. For further examples, see pp. 58–64 (on Philo) and pp. 76–7 (on Josephus).
[12] Jonas 1963, 241.

κόσμος was used to designate the natural order of the universe, the "goodness" of that order was immediately implied.[13]

There is no need to explore each of the lexical senses of κόσμος. Our interest lies in κόσμος as it is applied to the world/universe. This meaning is most frequently found in Greek literature in the philosophical writings. κόσμος (world/universe) is in fact one of the most important terms in Greek philosophical vocabulary.

3.3. κόσμος in Greek and Hellenistic philosophy

While not an exhaustive or detailed account of the history of the use of κόσμος in Greek and Hellenistic philosophy, what follows is a broad outline, giving particular attention to the development of the conception of the world linked with the term.

3.3.1. The Presocratics[14]

As noted above, κόσμος was first used in Presocratic philosophy with reference to the order which inheres in the physical universe.[15] It is most likely that this usage goes back to the very beginnings of classical philosophy, in Miletus in the sixth century BCE. The Milesian philosophers, Thales, Anaximander and Anaximenes, laid the basis for the Greek world-view by adducing that the material universe is an organized structure characterized by regularities, stability and equilibrium.[16] It is the order that the world evinces which makes it conducive to rational explanation. Though there is no conclusive proof that the Milesians actually employed the word κόσμος to designate the world-order,[17] it is hard to imagine that they arrived at the idea of a world-order without themselves using the word, and that their successors picked up the term from elsewhere.[18]

---

[13] Kahn 1960, 222.

[14] For a review of the early philosophical uses of κόσμος, see Guthrie 1962, 208 n. 1; Kahn 1960, 219–30; Kerschensteiner 1962; Kirk 1954, 311–15; Kranz 1938; Vlastos 1955, 363–5. Occurrences of κόσμος in the sources for Presocratic philosophy are listed in D–K 3: 240–3. For wider reflections on the emergence of the Greek understanding of the physical universe as κόσμος, see Vlastos 1975, 3–22.

[15] E.g. Parmenides fr. 8.52 (D–K 1:239).

[16] Cf. Anaximander fr. 13; for text and translation, see K–R 134. On Anaximander's conception of a universe governed by law, see Kahn 1960, 166–96, esp. 188–93.

[17] We cannot be sure that the fragmentary doxographical evidence reflects the actual language used by the Milesians.

[18] So Kahn 1960, 219.

At some stage, philosophers began to employ the word to denote the world itself as an ordered structure. The exact origin of this usage is difficult to pinpoint. Plato (*Gorg.* 507e–8a) attributes it to the σοφοί. Similarly, Xenophon (*Mem.* 1.1.11) refers it to the σοφισταί. According to one doxographical tradition,[19] Pythagoras was the first to employ the term in this way. But it is impossible to gauge the accuracy of this tradition. The actual teaching of Pythagoras is notoriously difficult to reconstruct. None of his writings (if he wrote at all) has survived. There was also a tendency among later Pythagoreans to refer later philosophical advances back to the founder.

The earliest instance of κόσμος with the sense "ordered universe" may well be in Heraclitus fr. 30, though scholarly opinion is sharply divided on the meaning of the word in this passage. The relevant part of the text reads:

> This cosmos (κόσμος), the same for all, no god or man has made, but it was, is, and will be for ever: ever-living fire, kindling according to measure and being extinguished according to measure.[20]

Kirk argues for the meaning "things plus order" or "the natural world and the order in it", taking κόσμος as still having the primary sense of order.[21] Vlastos, however, takes κόσμος to mean "world". He points out that κόσμος stands in apposition to "ever-living fire" (πῦρ ἀείζωον), and since fire is the substance of the whole universe for Heraclitus, κόσμος must here denote the world itself (as an ordered entity).[22]

κόσμος appears in other Heraclitan fragments, notably in fr. 89,[23] where Heraclitus speaks of the κόσμος as "one and common". Again κόσμος, if not actually meaning "world/universe", comes within a hair's breadth of doing so.[24]

The first unambiguous attestation of κόσμος = world/universe is found in Empedocles fr. 134:5 (mid-fifth century BCE): the "holy,

---

[19] Diogenes Laertius 8.48.
[20] Vlastos' translation (1975, 4–5).
[21] Kirk 1954, 314–17; cf. K–R 199. "World-order" is the sense accepted by Guthrie 1962, 454–5, and Marcovich 1967, 268–73.
[22] Vlastos 1975, 4–7; cf. 1955, 346. This is also the conclusion of Burnet 1930, 134 n. 3, and Kahn 1960, 225.
[23] D–K 1: 171.
[24] The text, as Kirk (1954, 63–4) points out, shows signs of being reworded. Kahn (1960, 226–7), Marcovich (1967, 99) and Vlastos (1975, 8), however, accept it as genuine.

unspeakable mind" is described as "darting with swift thoughts over the whole world (κόσμος)".[25] The sense "world/universe" is also apparent in Diogenes of Apollonia fr. 2,[26] where "things that exist at present in the κόσμος" are identified as "earth and water and air and fire and all other things apparent in this κόσμος". In this text, according to Kahn, we have at last the "classic conception of the κόσμος".[27]

The sense of "world/universe" is frequently attested in the fragments relating to the Atomists, Leucippus and his more famous pupil, Democritus (c. 460–357 BCE).[28]

According to the Atomic hypothesis, minute and indivisible particles, "atoms", form the basis of all that exists. These atoms, which differ in size and shape, move randomly in infinite space. A κόσμος is formed when atoms collide, recoil and become entangled.[29] Since there is no limit to the number of atoms and since space itself is boundless, the number of κόσμοι is infinite.[30] There are innumerable κόσμοι both similar and dissimilar to our κόσμος.[31] Some are at their peak; some are in process of disintegration. A κόσμος is destroyed when it comes into collision with another κόσμος.[32]

According to Democritus fr. 34, Democritus described the human being as a μικρὸς κόσμος.[33] Though the citation is late (sixth century CE) and disputed, it is usually accepted that Democritus coined this

---

[25] Guthrie 1962, 208 n. 1; Kahn 1960, 227: K–R 159 n. 1. For text, see D–K 1: 366.

[26] Kirk (1954, 313) takes κόσμος here to mean "world-order". But see Vlastos's criticisms: 1955, 345. For the text, see D–K 2: 59–60.

[27] Kahn 1960, 228.

[28] D–K 3: 241–3.

[29] D–K 2: 70–1; K–R 409–10.

[30] D–K 2: 94. Whether a theory of a plurality of worlds/κόσμοι can be credited to philosophers earlier than the Atomists is one of the most controversial and debated issues in the study of Presocratic philosophy. The doctrine of ἄπειροι κόσμοι is ascribed to Anaximander by the later doxographers, Simplicius and Aëtius. Though accepted by Kerschensteiner (1962, 36–40), the ascription is almost certainly mistaken: see Cornford 1934; Guthrie 1962, 106ff; Kahn 1960, 46–51; K–R 121ff. The evidence for the theory prior to the Atomists is at best scanty and inconclusive. Leucippus and Democritus are the first to whom the concept can be unambiguously attributed: see Kahn 1960, 51–3; K–R 412 (cf. 123ff; 390).

[31] On the Atomists' theory of innumerable worlds and how these come into being, see the discussions in Guthrie 1965, 404–13; K–R 409ff.

[32] K–R 411.

[33] D–K 2: 153. The writings of the Atomists, Leucippus and Democritus, were entitled Μέγας διάκοσμος (Great World-system) and Μικρὸς διάκοσμος (Little World-system) respectively: D–K 2: 80, 90–1. The first recorded instance of the expression μικρὸς κόσμος is found in Aristotle, Phys. 252b26, where he applies it to animal life.

phrase.[34] The concept of the microcosmic relation of humanity to the physical universe, however, pre-dates Democritus.[35]

3.3.2. Plato

κόσμος with the sense "world/universe" was well established by the time of Plato, though it was apparently still a technical philosophical usage and not a part of everyday speech (*Phileb.* 29e; *Polit.* 269d). κόσμος with this meaning is frequent in Plato's writings (*Criti.* 121c; *Gorg.* 508a; *Leg.* 821a; 897c; *Phileb.* 28e; 29e; *Polit.* 269d–274d), though it does not entirely supplant other established terms for "world/universe" in his vocabulary: thus we also find τὸ ὅλον (*Gorg.* 508a; *Phileb.* 28d), τὸ πᾶν (*Polit.* 270b; 272de; *Tim.* 27a; 28c; 30b; 92c) and ὁ οὐρανος (*Polit.* 269d; *Tim.* 28b).[36] κόσμος, for Plato, designates the ordered unity in which heaven and earth, gods and human beings are bound together (*Gorg.* 507e–508).[37]

Plato's main cosmological treatise is the *Timaeus*. κόσμος (= world/universe) is found more frequently in this work than in any of his others.[38] The *Timaeus* is one of Plato's later writings and one on which his original philosophical thought is most emphatically stamped.

The cosmology expounded in *Timaeus*, like that of previous Greek cosmological thought, is dependent on the fundamental insight of Ionian natural philosophy that the physical world is an ordered system. Plato, however, departs from the Ionian tradition in a significant way: the order which the universe exhibits does not arise naturally;[39] rather it has been brought about by a divine intelligence.[40]

---

[34] Guthrie 1965, 471.

[35] Guthrie 1965, 471.

[36] We can still find a few examples in Plato of κόσμος with the older sense of "world-order" (*Tim.* 24c). Plato also uses κόσμος with reference to regions of the universe (*Phaedr.* 246c).

[37] Plato can also use κόσμος non-cosmologically. The following senses are found: specific "orders" or "orderings" such as the ordering of the market (*Leg.* 759a) and the civic order (*Leg.* 628ab); "order" in general (*Gorg.* 504a–c; *Phileb.* 64b; *Rep.* 430e); "adornment', "ornament" (*Criti.* 115c, *Gorg.* 523e; *Phaed.* 114e; *Symp.* 197e); "honour" (*Leg.* 717e); "credit" (*Ep.* 312cd).

[38] It appears at 24bc; 27a; 28b; 29a; 29e; 30b; 30cd; 31b; 32bc; 32c; 40a; 42e–43a; 47e–48a; 55cd; 62d; 92c.

[39] In *Leg.* 889b–c, Plato faults his predecessors for assuming that the universe and the order therein have come about by chance.

[40] Thus, what Heraclitus denied in his assertion that "this κόσμος . . . no man or god has made", forms the first principle of Plato's cosmology: so Vlastos 1975, 25.

The deity is set forth as a skilled craftsman (δημιουργός)[41] who moulds his raw materials into a copy of a model (παράδειγμα) before him. The model on which the finished work, the κόσμος, is based is the eternal forms.[42]

The κόσμος is fashioned as a living creature (*Tim*. 30cd), with soul and body.[43] Its body is spherical in shape (33b)[44] and consists of the four elements, earth, fire, water and air (32b).

Plato affirms the oneness of the κόσμος, rejecting the Atomists' claim that there is a plurality of κόσμοι (31ab; 55cd).[45] The uniqueness of the κόσμος reflects the uniqueness of the eternal forms (31b).

He also asserts the indestructibility of the κόσμος, again in opposition to the Atomists. The everlasting duration of the κόσμος is guaranteed for Plato in two ways. Firstly, it is ensured by the world's perfect construction: all available matter has been used up in the formation of the universe. There is thus nothing outside of the world which can act upon it to bring about its destruction (33a). And since the elements are linked together in perfect geometric harmony, the universe is also secure against dissolution by imbalance from within. The κόσμος, therefore, is not susceptible to destruction from any external or internal physical cause. Secondly, the indestructibility of the physical world is grounded and secured in the goodness and providential activity of the demiurge. Only the craftsman-deity has the power to undo his own handiwork (32c). But a good god who has fashioned such an excellent work would never wish to destroy what he has made. It is the will of the one who bound the elements together that that bond should remain forever (41ab). For both physical and theological reasons, therefore, the κόσμος must be considered indestructible, completely free from age and ailment (33ab).

[41] The deity is also given the titles, ξυνιστάς (29d), ποιητήν καὶ πατήρ (28c) and ὁ γεννήσας πατήρ (37c)

[42] Later in the discourse, we learn that there is another factor in Plato's scheme, the receptacle of all becoming (48e–49q) or Space (52a).

[43] The universe is also described as σῶμα in *Phileb*. 29e.

[44] On the Presocratic background of the sphericity of the earth, see Kahn 1960, 115–18.

[45] In *Tim*. 55cff, Plato makes the puzzling remark that it is questionable whether to speak of one κόσμος or five. Precisely what he means by this is unclear, confounding even ancient interpreters. Plutarch, *De E* 389–90, thinks Plato is referring to the four elements plus an additional fifth element, οὐρανός. For further discussion, see Cornford 1937, 220–1.

The κόσμος is described as good/beautiful (καλός) and as the best of all things that have come into existence (κάλλιστος τῶν γεγονότων, 29a).[46] There is a limit, though, as to how far the work can resemble the perfect model, given the materials at the craftsman's disposal. Consequently, an element of "bruteness" obtains in the construction, resistant to the imposition of order (47e–48a). This, however, does not detract from the noble quality of the object produced. This world is such a grand and praiseworthy work of art that it can be considered "a blessed god" (34b; cf. 55d, 68e, 92c).[47]

Plato gives a summary definition of κόσμος = world/universe in the closing words of *Timaeus*, drawing together the main themes of the cosmology expounded in the discourse. This κόσμος (ὅδε ὁ κόσμος)[48] is

> a visible Living Creature embracing the visible creatures, a perceptible God made in the image of the Intelligible, most great and good and fair and perfect in its generation … one Heaven sole of its kind. (92c)[49]

3.3.3. Aristotle

The use of the word κόσμος to designate the physical universe is commonplace in Aristotle.[50]

[46] The goodness of the divine maker provides the motive for the existence and goodness of the κόσμος (29e).

[47] Crombie (1963, 153) describes as absurd the "view which holds that Plato thought that the natural world is a deplorable place, and that the only proper way of treating it is to ignore it and study 'the ideal world' instead".

[48] The phrase ὅδε ὁ κόσμος (which also occurs in Heraclitus fr. 30; Diogenes of Apollonia fr. 2 (D–K 2: 49–60); Plato, *Tim.* 29a; 30cd; and frequently in Philo, *Cher.* 120; *Conf.* 97; *Decal.* 31; *Migr.* 220; *Opif.* 9) does not imply *this* κόσμος in contrast to *another* κόσμος or *many other* κόσμοι. The demonstrative functions as an emphatic form of the definite article.

[49] Discussion of the κόσμος (= world/universe), is also found in *Polit.* 269d–74, a cosmological account at variance with *Timaeus*. In *Polit.* 269d–74, Plato contradicts the principle of internal harmony outlined in *Timaeus*, when he portrays the κόσμος as having an endemic propensity to return to its original chaotic condition. The κόσμος is marked by alternating cycles: there is a time when the helmsman–deity steers the world along its course, and a time when the god lets go and the world revolves in the opposite direction, unwinding back into chaos. Plato insists, though, that the god always steps in to save the κόσμος from complete reduction to chaos. He thus still maintains the indestructibility of the κόσμος but on theological, not physical, grounds.

[50] *Cat.* 6a15; *Eth. Eud.* 1216a14; *Metaph.* 990a20ff; *Meteor.* 356b5ff; *Phys.* 196a25ff; 203b25ff; *Probl.* 892a25ff; *Top.* 104b5ff.

49

In Aristotle's cosmology,[51] the universe is conceived of as spherical in shape (*Cael.* 287b15ff) with a spherical earth at the centre, the sphere of the fixed stars at the circumference, and the revolving spheres of the planets in between. These heavenly spheres are viewed as successive layers enveloping the earth.[52] Aristotle can use κόσμος both with reference to the stars and their spheres, that is, to the celestial region (*Meteor.* 339b15ff), and to the region below the sphere of the moon, that is, the terrestrial region (*Meteor.* 339a15ff; 339b5ff; 340b10ff; 344a5ff; 344b10ff; 346b10ff).[53] This application of κόσμος to portions of the universe, as well as to the universe as a whole, corresponds to Aristotle's use of οὐρανός. In *Cael.* 278b10ff, Aristotle explains that οὐρανός, as he uses the word in this work, has three meanings: firstly, the outermost circumference of the universe; secondly, the region of the planetary spheres; thirdly, the universe as a whole. The interchangeability of κόσμος and οὐρανός for Aristotle, when referring to the whole universe, is apparent in *Cael.* 301a17–19 (συστῆσαι τὸν οὐρανόν . . . συνέστηκεν ὁ κόσμος).

It is in *De Caelo*, where Aristotle gives his most detailed discussion of cosmology, that κόσμος most frequently occurs. Most instances of κόσμος in this work occur in connection with the polemical themes of the singularity[54] and eternity[55] of the universe – key emphases of Aristotle's cosmology.

That there cannot be more than one κόσμος is the argument of *Cael.* 276a18–279b3. Aristotle asserts the unicity of the world in opposition to the Atomist notion of a plurality of worlds. Since there is no mass beyond the universe and since the world in its entirety (ὁ πᾶς κόσμος) is made up of all available matter, there can be no plurality of worlds: this universe is one, solitary and complete (279a8ff).

---

[51] For comprehensive discussions of Aristotle's cosmological system, see Elders 1965; Solmsen 1960.

[52] For Aristotle, it is not the planets and stars which rotate, but the spheres which hold them: see Elders 1965, 8.

[53] The terrestrial region is composed of the four elements, the celestial of a fifth element (*Meteor.* 339a).

[54] *Cael.* 274a28; 276a21; 276a31; 276b4; 276b14ff; 276b21; 277a6; 277b13; 278a27; 279a8. The question of innumerable κόσμοι is raised again in *Phys.* 250b15ff.

[55] *Cael.* 279b27; 280a23; 296a34; 300b17–20; 300b26. The use of κόσμος in connection with the eternity of the universe also crops up in *Meteor.* 356b4ff; *Top.* 104b5ff, 105b25ff.

Aristotle discusses whether the οὐρανός (universe) is ἀγένητος ἢ γενητὸς καὶ ἄφθαρτος ἢ φθαρτός in *Cael.* 279b4–283b24. Unlike Plato, he can find no place for a time πρὶν γενέσθαι τὸν κόσμον (*Cael.* 300b17). For Aristotle the κόσμος is without beginning or end.

He defends the thesis of the eternity of the κόσμος first of all, negatively, by attacking opposing viewpoints.[56] He builds his positive case mainly on a close analysis of the terms "ungenerated" (ἀγένητος), "generated" (γενητός), "destructible" (φθαρτός) and "indestructible" (ἄφθαρτος). He argues that the terms ἀγένητος and ἄφθαρτος logically imply each other.[57]

Aristotle also gave a defence of his doctrine of the eternity of the world in his treatise, *De Philosophia*, only a few fragments of which remain.[58]

3.3.4. Epicureanism

Epicurus (341–271 BCE) made a modified version of the atomic theory of Democritus, repudiated by Plato and Aristotle, the basis for his cosmology.[59] In line with the atomists, Epicurus envisaged a plurality of co-existent κόσμοι.[60] He defined a κόσμος as

> a certain envelopment of a heaven (οὐρανός). It envelops celestial bodies, an earth, and the whole range of phenomena. It is cut off from the infinite, and terminates in a limit which is either rare or dense, on whose dissolution all its contents will undergo a collapse.[61]

---

[56] He rejects Plato's view – that the κόσμος is created and indestructible – on the basis that it contradicts the empirical observation that anything which is generated is also perishable.

[57] For an explication of Aristotle's argument, see Williams 1966.

[58] It is generally agreed that at least three of the first four arguments which Philo presents in *De Aeternitate Mundi* in favour of the Aristotelian theorem of the eternity of the universe (*Aet.* 20–44), though probably not their original wording, are derived from this lost work. See Mansfield 1979, 141–4. Runia (1986, 191–3) posits that all four arguments in *Aet.* 20–44 come from Aristotle's *De Philosophia*. The two most celebrated of these arguments represent refinements and expansions of Platonic lines of reasoning. The argument of *Aet.* 20–24 amplifies Plato's physical argument for the indestructibility of the universe (*Tim.* 32c–33b). The argument of *Aet.* 39–43 develops Plato's theological axiom that a good god would not destroy the world he has made.

[59] Epicurus introduced the thought of the atoms as "weighted" (to account for their downward motion) and the notion of the spontaneous "swerve" (to explain how atoms collide and lock together).

[60] L–S 1: 57, 2: 54 (no. 13A = Epicurus, *Ep. Her.* 45).

[61] L–S 1: 57, 2: 54–5 (no. 13B = Epicurus, *Ep. Pyth.* 88).

The Epicureans explicitly criticized the Platonic thesis of a created and indestructible world,[62] arguing as Aristotle did, that there is no precedent in nature for something that has an origin but no end; similarly, there is no compound incapable of destruction.

Epicurus scorned any idea of the formation and preservation of the world by a deity. He did not deny the existence of the gods, only their activity in the physical realm. The existence of our world or indeed any world is due entirely to random and natural processes.[63]

3.3.5. Stoicism

The doctrines of Epicurus were faithfully preserved and defended by his school. Epicureanism, as a philosophical system, endured little change from its original formulation by Epicurus himself. In sharp contrast, Stoicism underwent considerable development from the views of its founder, a fact which must be borne in mind in any attempt to represent the "Stoic view". The Stoic system of philosophy was established by Zeno (333–262 BCE)[64] and maintained by a long line of successors. Of the early successors to Zeno, Chrysippus (280–206 BCE) stands out in importance. Chrysippus defended Stoicism at a critical time; through his reputation as a philosopher and dialectician, the system gained respectability and increased in influence.[65] Chrysippus also added key refinements to Zeno's doctrines. Important modifications and shifts in emphasis were also made by Panaetius (185–110 BCE) and Posidonius (135–55 BCE), and by the Roman Stoics, Seneca, Epictetus and Marcus Aurelius.

κόσμος, denoting the material universe, is a basic term for the Stoics. This is hardly surprising since, as Diogenes Laertius (one of our principal witnesses for Stoicism) tells us (7.132), the study of the κόσμος was one of the three main divisions of Stoic physics (along with the study of elements and the study of causes). The Stoics accepted the by now well-established tradition of the physical world as κόσμος. Indeed in Stoicism, the noble status of the κόσμος was raised to even greater heights.

---

[62] L–S 1: 60–1, 2: 59–60 (no. 13G = Cicero, De nat. 1.18–23).
[63] The Epicurean physical theory is set out in Lucretius, De rerum, esp. books 1–2, 5.
[64] Stoic dates are from Sandbach 1975, 7.
[65] On the life and reputation of Chrysippus, see Gould 1970, 7–17.

According to Diogenes Laertius (7.137),[66] the Stoics used the word κόσμος in three ways: firstly, for "god himself, the peculiarly qualified individual consisting of all substance, who is indestructible and ingenerable", and who "is the manufacturer of the world-order (διακόσμησις), at set periods of time consuming all substance into himself and reproducing it again from himself"; secondly, for the world-order (διακόσμησις); thirdly, for the combination of god and world-order.

This definition of κόσμος highlights the monism which obtained in Stoic thought. The god of Stoicism is not conceived of as independent from the world but rather as immanent in it.[67] According to Stoic cosmology, god, also called "nature", "reason", "soul", "mind", "creative fire", is both present in the substance of the world, and is the rational, controlling and ordering principle of the world. The κόσμος can be described as god since it is both pervaded and directed by a divine element.[68]

The existence and providence of god is open to rational perception by virtue of the microcosmic–macrocosmic link between the human mind and the cosmic mind.[69] In admitting a natural theology, the Stoics stood diametrically opposed to the Epicureans. A range of arguments, mainly teleological, can be found in Stoic texts aimed at proving the existence and providence of the deity.[70] In accordance with the monism of the Stoic system, arguing for the existence of god equates with demonstrating that the world is a living, rational creature.[71]

In the Stoic system, the κόσμος, even in the extended sense of "god himself . . . consisting of all substance", is not all there is. The Stoics also posited the existence of a void external to the κόσμος (into which the κόσμος expands prior to the conflagration).[72] In the light of this, a distinction is made between "the whole" (τὸ ὅλον) and "the all" (τὸ

---

[66] Text and translation are taken from L–S 1: 270, 2: 268 (no. 44F).

[67] On the monism and pantheism of the Stoic physical system, see Todd 1978.

[68] See L–S 1: 280–1, 2: 278–9 (no. 47C = Cicero, De nat. 2.23–5, 28–30); L–S 1: 323, 2: 321–2 (no. 54B = Cicero, De nat. 1.39); L–S 1: 326, 2: 325–6 (no. 54H = Cicero, De nat. 2.37–9).

[69] Gärtner 1955, 112.

[70] See texts and commentary in L–S 1: 323–33, 2: 321–32. For detailed discussion of the Stoic arguments, see Dragona-Monachou 1976.

[71] L–S 1: 323, 2: 321–2 (nos. 54A; 54B = Diogenes Laertius 7.147; Cicero, De nat. 1.39); L–S 1: 325, 2: 325 (no. 54G = Cicero, De nat. 2.22).

[72] On the Stoic conception of the void, see L–S 1: 294–7, 2: 291–5.

πᾶν): "the whole" is the κόσμος, but "the all" is the κόσμος and the void together; the whole, the κόσμος, is finite, but the all is infinite since the void is infinite.[73]

At the heart of Stoic cosmology, at least in the early period, lies the theory of cosmic conflagration (ἐκπύρωσις). According to this view, the history of the universe is cyclical. Each world-cycle begins and ends in a state of pure fire. A world-cycle begins when the primordial fire (to be distinguished from the element fire) cools to air then moisture, and eventually condenses into the four elements of which the world is constituted.[74] A world-cycle ends when the world recedes again into its fiery state (due to the gradual evaporation of water by fire causing air and earth to ignite).[75] The theory was probably an innovation on the part of Zeno, though it drew on earlier ideas, notably the ancient popular belief in periodically recurring natural disasters, mainly by fire and flood,[76] and the idea of the "Great Year", which first appears in Plato, *Tim.* 39d, though is generally thought to be much older.[77] Seneca (*Nat. quaes.* 3.27–30) expressly connects the conflagration theory with these traditions.[78]

In view of their belief in conflagration, the Stoics could speak of the κόσμος as having a definite beginning: γίνεσθαι δὲ τὸν κόσμον ὅταν ἐκ πυρὸς ἡ οὐσία τραπῇ δι᾽ ἀέρος εἰς ὑγρόν.[79] And more controversially (on Plato's and Aristotle's analysis), they could describe the κόσμος as perishable (φθαρτὸς ἄρα ὁ κόσμος).[80]

Affirmations of the destructibility of the κόσμος in Stoic writings, however, are somewhat offset by statements affirming or implying its immortality. Chrysippus insists that "the κόσμος must not be said to die" (οὐ ῥητέον ἀποθνήσκειν τὸν κόσμον).[81] In another recorded statement, he declares,

[73] L–S 1: 268, 2: 265 (no. 44A = Sextus Empiricus, *Ag. Phys.* 1.332).
[74] L–S 1: 275, 2: 272 (no. 46B = Diogenes Laertius 7.135–6).
[75] Cicero, *De nat.* 2.118.
[76] Plato, *Criti.* 111; *Leg.* 676–80; *Polit.* 269–74; *Tim.* 22a–23c; Aristotle, *Meteor.* 352a29ff; Ps-Arist., *Mund.* 400a23ff; Lucretius, *De rerum* 5.411–15; Dio Chrysostom, *Disc.* 36.39ff; Philo, *Aet.* 146ff; Josephus, *Ant.* 1.69–71.
[77] Plato does not associate the Great Year with periodic destructions. Aristotle, however, in *Meteor.* 352a29ff, does (if, as is probable, the "great period of time" mentioned here is a reference to the Great Year).
[78] Cf. L–S 1: 309, 2: 306–7 (nos. 52C, 52D = Nemesius 309.5–311.2; Eusebius, *Ev. Prep.* 15.19.1–2). See also Lapidge 1978, 181.
[79] L–S 1: 275, 2: 273 (no. 46C = Diogenes Laertius 7.142).
[80] L–S 1: 276, 2: 275 (no. 46J = Diogenes Laertius 7.141).
[81] L–S 1: 275, 2: 273 (no. 46E = Plutarch, *St. rep.* 1052c–d).

When the world (κόσμος) is fiery through and through, it is directly both its own soul and commanding-faculty. But when, having changed into moisture and the soul which remains therein, it has in a way changed into a body and soul so as to be compounded out of these....[82]

From this testimony, it emerges that what Chrysippus envisages as taking place at the conflagration is *change* rather than *destruction*.[83] In this connection, it is worth noting Eusebius' comment that "'destruction' is not used in an unqualified sense" by the Stoics, "They use the term destruction in place of natural change."[84]

The apparent conflict between affirmations of the mortality and the immortality of the κόσμος highlights the different senses accruing to κόσμος in Stoic usage, noted above. Insofar as κόσμος denotes a world-cycle, it can be described as destructible. But used in its broadest sense, encompassing the endless sequence of world-cycles and conflagrations, the κόσμος can be affirmed as everlasting.[85]

Another key aspect of Stoic cosmology is the cosmic πνεῦμα.[86] The cosmic "breath" is the sustaining principle of the universe.[87] πνεῦμα permeates everything that exists; it makes the world a unified and integrated whole.[88] It is the vivifying element in the universe, animating the various forms of life in it,[89] and the vehicle of divine intelligence.[90]

Cosmology has a direct bearing on ethics in Stoicism. The order which characterizes the world constitutes the basis of morality. The providentially arranged structure of the world is the guiding principle for human conduct. Doing "the good" lies in conforming to the rational law which imbues the world. Chrysippus states that

> There is no other or more appropriate way of approaching the theory of good and bad things or the virtues or happiness than from universal nature and from the administration of the world (κόσμος).[91]

---

[82] L–S 1: 275–6, 2: 274 (no. 46F = Plutarch, *St. rep.* 1053b).
[83] See further, Gould 1970, 123–5.
[84] L–S 1: 276, 2: 275 (no. 46K = Eusebius, *Ev. Prep.* 15.18.2).
[85] Cf. Philo, *Aet.* 4.
[86] L–S 1: 281–9, 2: 277–87.
[87] L–S 1: 282, 2: 280 (no. 47F = Galen, *Plen.* 7.525, 9–14).
[88] L–S 1: 283, 2: 283 (no. 47L = Alexander, *Mixt.* 223. 25–36).
[89] L–S 1: 284, 2: 284 (no. 47N = Galen. *Intr.* 14.726, 7–11).
[90] L–S 1: 284, 2: 284 (no. 47O = Diogenes Laertius, 7. 138–9).
[91] L–S 1: 368–9, 2: 364 (no. 60A = Plutarch, *St. rep.* 1035c–d). On the concept of natural law in Greek philosophy, see Köster 1973, 260–6.

The Stoics, as noted above, laid stress on the macrocosmic–microcosmic relation of human beings to the external world. Human beings are fundamentally connected to the universe as parts to the whole. There is a correspondence between the world's soul and the human soul, the latter being an offshoot of the former.[92] Thus, according to Chrysippus,

> our own natures are parts of the whole. Therefore, living in agreement with nature comes to be the end, which is in accordance with the nature of oneself and that of the whole, engaging in no activity wont to be forbidden by the universal law, which is the right reason pervading everything and identical to Zeus, who is this director of the administration of existing things.[93]

The determining ethical principle, therefore, is to live in conformity with nature.

The Stoics also developed the ethical implications of the long established image of the κόσμος as a city. Cicero writes,

> The Stoics hold that the world is governed by divine will: it is as it were a city and state shared by men and gods, and each one of us is a part of this world.[94]

The Stoic-influenced writer, Arias Didymus, comments,

> The world (κόσμος) is also called the habitation of gods and men, and the structure consisting of gods and men and the things created for their sake. For just as there are two meanings of city, one as habitation and two as the structure of its inhabitants along with its citizens, so the world is like a city consisting of gods and men, with the gods serving as rulers and men as their subjects. They are members of a community because of their participation in reason, which is natural law; and everything else is created for their sake.[95]

Each individual is constituted as a "citizen of the world"[96] and as such has a duty toward the κόσμος and the common good of society. According to Cicero, it is a "natural consequence" of each person's status as κοσμοπολίτης to prefer the common advantage to their own.[97]

---

[92] L–S 1: 319, 2: 321 (nos. 53X; 53Y = Diogenes Laertius 7.143; Cicero, *De nat.* 2.58).

[93] L–S 1: 395, 2: 390 (no. 63C = Diogenes Laertius 7.87–9).

[94] L–S 1: 348, 2: 346–7 (no. 57F = Cicero, *Fin.* 3.62–8). On the Stoic conception of the cosmic city, see Schofield 1991, 57–92.

[95] L–S 1: 431, 2: 426 (no. 67L = Eusebius, *Ev. Prep.* 15.15.3–5).

[96] L–S 1: 364, 2: 363–4 (no. 59Q = Epictetus, *Disc.* 2.10.1–12).

[97] L–S 1: 348, 2: 346–7 (no. 57F = Cicero, *Fin.* 3.62–8).

In the Stoic κόσμος, all events are causally linked. Reporting the views of the Stoics, Alexander of Aphrodisias writes,

> They ... say that since the world (κόσμος) is a unity which includes all existing things in itself and is governed by a living, rational, intelligent nature, the government of existing things which it possesses is an everlasting one proceeding in a sequence and ordering ... For nothing in the world (κόσμος) exists or happens causelessly, because none of the things in it is independent of, and insulated from, everything that has happened before. For the world (κόσμος) would be wrenched apart and divided and no longer remain a unity, for ever governed in accordance with a single ordering and management (οἰκονομία), if an uncaused process were introduced.[98]

The rational order of the κόσμος determines all events, past, present, and future. The ordered sequence of events, which includes every detail of the universal history, is, as it were, pre-programmed into the κόσμος at the beginning of every world-cycle. Thus the first-century CE Peripatetic philosopher Aristocles reports (as quoted by Eusebius),

> the primary fire is as it were a sperm which possesses the principles ... of all things and the causes of past, present, and future events. The nexus and succession of these is fate, knowledge, truth, and an inevitable and inescapable law of what exists. In this way everything in the world (κόσμος) is excellently organized as in a perfectly ordered society.[99]

The κόσμος of the Stoics is governed by a fate according to which all events are predetermined. Nothing happens which has not been determined by the universal plan.[100]

The determinism in the Stoic concept of the κόσμος is also apparent in the theory of endlessly recurring world-cycles. The universe generated out of the conflagration is conceived as identical or near-identical with the one which preceded it. This belief was expressed in a strong and in (marginally) less strong forms. The strong version was probably the original view and the one to which Chrysippus subscribed. According to this view, every detail of this world will be repeated in successive worlds. Thus,

> again there will be Socrates and Plato and each one of mankind with the same friends and fellow citizens; they will suffer the same things and they will

---

[98]   L–S 1: 337–8, 2: 338 (no. 55N = Alexander, *Fat.* 191. 30–192.28).
[99]   L–S 1: 276, 2: 274 (no. 46G = Eusebius, *Ev. Prep.* 15.14.2).
[100] Plutarch, *St. rep.* 1049f.

encounter the same things … and every city and village and piece of land return in the same way.[101]

On a less strong version, there are very slight differences from world to world; for example, a man who in one world has a mole on his face, in another world might not.[102]

The highly deterministic perspective in Stoic cosmology inevitably introduces a strongly passive and necessitarian element into the area of ethics. Every event in a person's life is fixed, and no one can stand in the way of providence.[103] Since people cannot resist their destinies, "virtue" lies in attuning one's mind to the cosmic mind and in willingly conforming to the course of life which destiny has mapped out.

This determinism appears to leave little place for free will and moral responsibility: Can human beings be held accountable for their decisions and actions, if these were destined to happen in the first place? The Stoics attempted to answer this problem in different ways.[104] One way was to emphasize the conjunction of fate and human conduct: the plans of providence are worked out by means of human decisions and actions. Another was to distinguish between causes. But the difficulty was never entirely and satisfactorily resolved.

3.3.6. Philo

To complete this review of κόσμος in Greek and Hellenistic philosophy, we turn now to a Jewish writer. In the work of Philo of Alexandria we find, to a degree that is unprecedented and unparalleled in the ancient world, a weaving together of Jewish tradition and Greek philosophy. The intermingling is such that it has been, and continues to be, a much debated subject whether we should think of Philo as a Hellenistic Jew or as a Jewish Hellenist.[105]

---

[101] L–S 1: 309, 2: 306–7 (no. 52C = Nemesius 309.5–311.2).

[102] L–S 1: 309–10, 2: 308 (no. 52F = Alexander, *In Ar. An pr.* 180.33–6; 181.25–31).

[103] This is well illustrated in the famous Stoic analogy of the dog tied to the cart: L–S 1: 386, 2: 382 (no. 62A = Hippolytus, *Haer.* 1.21).

[104] See texts and commentary in L–S 1: 386–94, 2: 382–9. On fate and the problem of fate and free will/moral responsibility in Stoicism, see Gould 1970, 148–53; Sandbach 1975, 101–8; Stough 1978.

[105] For the recent discussion, see Borgen 1984, 139–54. Borgen's conclusion (154) is that Philo fundamentally remained a Jew, though he "was on the point of ending up in a universalism where Jewish distinctiveness was in danger of being lost". See also Barclay 1996, 158–80.

κόσμος occurs far more frequently in Philo than in any other ancient writer.[106] Philo unreservedly accepts the Greek tradition of the world as κόσμος, which is an indication of how important and how widely disseminated that tradition had become by Philo's time. Philo also uses the term in some distinctive ways, but our main interest here lies in Philo's handling of the term κόσμος (= world/universe) insofar as it is representative of Greek and Hellenistic philosophy.[107]

In *Aet.* 4, Philo gives a definition of κόσμος (= world/universe), representing the classical view: κόσμος is "the whole system of heaven and the stars including the earth and the plants and animals thereon", "the world which consists of heaven and earth and life on them". Although this statement of meaning is intended to serve no more than for the discussion on hand, unquestionably it specifies what he most regularly means by the word.[108]

For his work as a whole, Philo draws heavily on Platonism, particularly the doctrines of the *Timaeus*,[109] and to a lesser extent, Stoicism. These influences, to the same degree, can be seen in his statements involving κόσμος (= world/universe).

The κόσμος, by definition, is characterized by order (*Aet.* 54; *Spec.* 4.237). The act of creation consisted in bringing order (τάξις) out of disorder (ἀταξία), (*Opif.* 21–23; 28; 33; *Spec.* 4.187). As an ordered structure, the created universe is also an object of beauty (*Opif.* 28).

Philo acclaims the goodness, beauty and perfection of the κόσμος with no less vigour and enthusiasm than Plato. He describes the κόσμος as the most perfect thing to have come into existence (*Opif.* 14; *Plant.* 131), the most beautiful and varied work of God (*Somn.* 1.207), the fairest, greatest and most perfect work of all (*Abr.* 74; cf. *Aet.* 26, 50, 73; *Her.* 199), a complete work, wholly worthy of its architect (*Cher.*

---

[106] Around 640 times, according to *TLG* (which contains most of the Philonic corpus).

[107] In the vast majority of instances in Philo, the word means world/universe. The following senses also appear: "order" in a general sense (*Somn.* 1.241; *Spec.* 4.210), "adornment" (*Abr.* 267; *Opif.* 53), "ornament" (*Cher.* 104; *Mos.* 2.243), "honour" (*Mos.* 2.145), the "host of heaven" (i.e. the celestial bodies, *Spec.* 1.15; a standard LXX use: see below, p. 75). Several times he refers to the heavenly realm as a κόσμος ἐν κόσμῳ (*Abr.* 159; *Flacc.* 169).

[108] Philo often uses the phrase ὁ σύμπας οὐρανός τε καὶ κόσμος (*Abr.* 57; *Mos.* 2.15; cf. Dio Chrysostom, *Disc.* 12.34). No distinction in meaning between οὐρανός and κόσμος is implied; the terms serve to reinforce each other.

[109] On Philo's utilization of Plato's *Timaeus*, see Runia 1986.

59

112).[110] The κόσμος may even be regarded as the younger son of God, νεώτερος υἱὸς θεοῦ (*Deus* 31; cf. *Aet.* 10, 20, where the κόσμος is described as a ὁρατὸς θεός). There are numerous passages in Philo's writings, where he waxes eloquent on the splendour and beauty of the various parts of the natural world, in both the terrestrial and celestial realms.[111] Philo's discursiveness on the majesty of the universe in fact contrasts with Plato's restraint.[112]

Philo, following Plato and the majority of Greek thinkers, emphasizes the unicity of the κόσμος,[113] though unlike Plato, Philo derives it from the oneness of God (*Opif.* 171–2).

Philo also maintains with Plato that the κόσμος is indestructible (ἄφθαρτος). Following Plato on both counts, Philo recognizes that what has been created is liable to destruction (*Decal.* 58),[114] but believes that the indestructibility of the κόσμος is assured on the basis of the preserving will (βούλησις)[115] and providential activity (πρόνοια)[116] of God. The Aristotelian viewpoint, that the κόσμος is ἀγένητος καὶ ἀίδιος, though favoured above Atomist, Epicurean and Stoic views of a generated and destructible κόσμος, is declaimed as "a worthless and baleful doctrine" (*Opif.* 11) which attributes a vast inactivity to God (*Opif.* 7), assigns anarchy to the κόσμος (*Opif.* 11) and credits God with no superiority over the κόσμος (*Opif.* 171).

Philo's firm rejection of Aristotle's dogma of the eternity of the κόσμος is, however, difficult to reconcile with his apparent support of it in the treatise, *De Aeternitate Mundi*. In this work, Philo discusses the philosophical question of the duration of the κόσμος. In the main section of it, he presents a series of twenty-four arguments in favour of the Aristotelian viewpoint. His endorsement of this view is all the more surprising since in the introductory section, *Aet.* 1–19, he has seemingly

[110] The exalted status of the κόσμος is also framed in biblical language: the κόσμος is the most true temple of God (*Spec.* 1.66, cf. *Somn.* 1.215); it is an offering dedicated to God (*Somn.* 1.243).
[111] *Opif.* 54, 78; *Praem.* 41–2; *Spec.* 1.210; 2.150–4; 3.187–8; 4.232–6.
[112] Runia 1986, 458.
[113] *Aet.* 8; *Migr.* 180; *Opif.* 172; *Spec.* 3.189. See Runia 1986, 174–6.
[114] In *Prov.* 1.6–23, Philo affirms that the κόσμος could indeed be destroyed, employing Stoic arguments and quoting from *Tim.* 38b to make the point. The emphasis which he lays here on the fundamental perishability of the κόσμος is unparalleled in his writings, see Runia (1986, 396–8).
[115] *Her.* 246; *Spec.* 2.5.
[116] *Decal.* 58; *Migr.* 181.

cleared the ground for a sound defence of the Platonic doctrine. A convincing explanation of this anomaly has been put forward by D. T. Runia.[117] Runia contends that the treatise belongs to the genre of θέσις. The genre is characterized by the use of the disputative method of arguing *pro* and *contra* a proposition.[118] The subject of the θέσις is εἰ ἄφθαρτος ὁ κόσμος, which we know from Aristotle and Quintilian was a typical theme for a θέσις.[119] But instead of having in the doxography (*Aet*. 8–19), two positions, the usual procedure in a θέσις, Philo sets out three opinions:

(1) that the κόσμος is created and destructible (γενητὸς καὶ φθαρτός),

(2) that the κόσμος is uncreated and indestructible (ἀγένητὸς καὶ ἄφθαρτος),

(3) that the κόσμος is created and indestructible (γενητὸς καὶ ἄφθαρτος).

These are clearly arranged in order of preference. The second, the Aristotelian position, is better than the first, the Atomist, Epicurean and Stoic view. But the third, Plato's view, is the best. Runia argues that the hierarchical sequence of the doxography was meant to foreshadow the intended structure of the tractate as a whole. He claims that Philo's aim in the main body of the treatise was to use the Aristotelian position to defeat Atomist, Epicurean and Stoic theories, and then having done so, to use the Platonist point of view to overthrow the Aristotelian dogma. The final section, however, in which Philo would have presented arguments favouring the view that the κόσμος is γενητὸς καὶ ἄφθαρτος is missing, and herein lies the cause of confusion to interpreters.

Aet. 1–19 makes abundantly clear where Philo's loyalties lie. Here he subscribes wholeheartedly to the Platonic doctrine, quoting *Tim*. 41ab. Making good use of the principle of *maior ex longinquo reverentia* (the older a belief the more truthful it is likely to be), Philo argues that this position was maintained by Hesiod, and before Hesiod, by Moses (*Aet*. 19; cf. *Opif.* 12).[120]

---

[117] Runia 1981.
[118] Runia 1981, 138.
[119] Aristotle, *Top*. 105b25; Quintilian, *Inst. Or.* 7.2.2.
[120] Philo locates the doctrine in Gen 8:22. The Genesis text does not actually affirm that the earth is everlasting but rather that, as long as the earth lasts (Πάσας τὰς ἡμέρας τῆς γῆς, LXX), the times and the seasons are guaranteed.

Occasionally, Philo can speak of the κόσμος as an intelligent living creature (*Aet*. 94, 95), though the κόσμος as a ζῷον is not a prominent theme in Philo's writings.[121]

An interesting departure from Plato is Philo's application of the word κόσμος to the eternal forms: he distinguishes between ὁ κόσμος νοητός[122] on the one hand, and ὁ κόσμος ὁρατός[123] on the other, referring to the world of ideas and the visible world respectively. The term κόσμος νοητός became a regular designation for the realm of ideas among the Middle Platonists. In Philo's writings we are afforded the earliest extant examples of its use. It would be presumptuous, however, to see this as an innovation on Philo's part, since this would overvalue his influence as a philosopher and accord to him a greater importance in the development of Platonism than he is probably due.[124] A unique emphasis of Philo is his presentation of the κόσμος νοητός as created (*Opif.* 16ff).

Philo takes up the philosophical metaphor of the κόσμος as a city. In *Opif.* 17–18, the creation of the κόσμος is likened to the founding of a city: the κόσμος νοητός is the plan, in accordance with which the divine architect/craftsman (both are combined in the one individual) constructs the city (cf. *Cher.* 127). In *Spec.* 1.13–14, the κόσμος is compared to a μεγαλόπολις, whose rulers (ἄρχοντες) are the stars and planets and whose subjects are all living beings which dwell on the earth.[125]

Utilizing Stoic natural theology, Philo argues that by observing the κόσμος, we can deduce its maker (*Leg. All.* 3.98–9). The image of the κόσμος as a city reinforces the argument. Human beings, coming into the κόσμος, encounter it as a μεγαλόπολις, well ordered, regulated by admirable laws, and exhibiting design and superintendence. This leads them to infer that God exists (*Spec.* 1.34–5) and that he cares for all that he has created (*Praem.* 41–2).

Like the Stoics, Philo lays stress on the microcosmic–macrocosmic relation of the human being to the κόσμος.[126] The human being is a

---

[121] Runia 1986, 157–8.
[122] *Opif.* 16, 19; cf. ὁ ἀσώματος κόσμος, *Opif.* 36, 55.
[123] *Abr.* 88; *Opif.* 16. cf. ὁ κόσμος αἰσθητός, *Congr.* 21; *Opif.* 25; ὁ φαινόμενος κόσμος, *Migr.* 105, 179; ὁ κόσμος οὗτος, *Her.* 75.
[124] So Runia 1986, 262.
[125] Cf. *Cher.* 120; *Prov.* 2–3.
[126] On the microcosm–macrocosm scheme in Philo, see Runia 1986, 465–6.

κοσμοπολίτης,[127] a βραχὺς οὐρανός (*Opif.* 82), and as such has a special place in the κόσμος (*Opif.* 143–4, 151).

Philo also adopts the Stoic concept of universal law, by which the κόσμος, the mega-city is regulated. Philo equates the universal law of nature with the Mosaic law.

> The world (κόσμος) is in harmony with the Law, and the Law with the world, and ... the man who observes the law is constituted thereby a loyal citizen of the world (κοσμοπολίτης), regulating his doings by the purpose and will of Nature, in accordance with which the entire world itself also is administered. (*Opif.* 3)[128]

Guidance for a moral life can be obtained by contemplation of the κόσμος:

> For anyone who contemplates the order in nature and the constitution enjoyed by the world-city whose excellence no word can describe, needs no speaker to teach him to practise a law-abiding and peaceful life and to aim at assimilating himself to its beauties. (*Abr.* 61)

The world-city, the μεγαλόπολις, has a single law commanding what should be done and forbidding what should not be done (*Jos.* 29; cf. *Praem.* 23).

The high regard for the κόσμος typical of the Greek and Hellenistic world-view evoked by the term κόσμος is thus well represented in Philo. But an important caveat must be entered: Philo's admiration for the κόσμος is tempered by his praise for the creator.[129] Philo insists that the κόσμος must not be assigned a disproportionate majesty (*Opif.* 7; cf. *Migr.* 194). The end for which the κόσμος was made was to display the goodness of its creator (*Cher.* 127). Though Philo can apply the word θεός to κόσμος (*Deus* 31; *Aet.* 10, 20) clearly it is not "God" in an unqualified sense. Philo constantly attacks the way in which the celestial bodies are identified as gods. In this connection, it is interesting to note that the teleological argument has a double function with Philo: not only does it serve to demonstrate God's existence and providence, it is also used to denounce astral worship.

The subordination of κόσμος to the creator, for Philo, is made clear in *Conf.* 98, where Philo discusses why Scripture speaks of the κόσμος

---

[127] Adam is κοσμοπολίτης in a special sense, in that he was the first man and the forefather of the race. *Opif.* 142.

[128] Cf. *Mos.* 2.49–51.

[129] Runia 1986, 458–61.

as God's footstool. He gives two reasons: firstly, that it may be shown that the efficient cause of the κόσμος is not to be found within creation; secondly, to emphasize that God is its sovereign ruler and regulator. It is this emphasis in his talk of κόσμος that most clearly indicates Philo's Jewishness and sets him apart from the mainstream of Greek philosophical thought.

3.4. The view of the world evoked by κόσμος

Despite the great variety of opinion in Greek and Hellenistic cosmological speculation, there were certain shared and fixed assumptions about the nature and character of the material universe upon which virtually all Greek cosmological discussion was built. These presuppositions formed a core understanding of the physical universe which the word κόσμος, when applied to it, tended to evoke.

The leading features of the Greek and Hellenistic view of the world connoted by κόσμος = world/universe can all be found in Plato's *Timaeus*. In terms of its influence on Greek and Hellenistic philosophy and its widespread cultural dissemination, particularly from the first century BCE onward,[130] Plato's *Timaeus* was the most important philosophical text of antiquity. It was widely read and studied, not only within philosophical circles but also by educated, cultured individuals in general. As Runia states,

> The very fact that it was regarded as the "Platonists' Bible" meant that its influence inevitably filtered down to men of letters and even those who had received only a smattering of learning. Indeed the *Timaeus* was the only Greek prose work that up to the third century A.D. every educated man could be assumed to have read.[131]

The beliefs associated with κόσμος (= world/universe) are as follows. Firstly, the κόσμος is *characterized by order*. The designation of the world as κόσμος suggests an *ordered* structure – a universe marked by regularity, harmony and purpose. The tenet that our world is an ordered world was the legacy of the Milesian philosophers and was the premise upon which all Greek and Hellenistic natural philosophy rested. As

---

[130] Reflecting the resurgence of Platonism as a major philosophical force: Dörrie 1973; Runia 1986, 46–57.
[131] Runia 1986, 57.

Jaeger states, it was the "spiritual discovery of the cosmos" that facilitated Greek philosophical speculation on the nature of the universe.[132]

When Plato comes to describe the generation of the world he depicts it as a fashioning of order out of a state of disorder (*Tim.* 29e–30a), a basic scheme which is repeated in Philo (*Opif.* 21–23) and Plutarch (*De An.* 1014bff).[133]

That the application of the word κόσμος to the physical universe entails the presupposition that this world is an ordered world is a fact frequently noted by philosophical writers.[134]

Secondly, the κόσμος is *marked by unity*. The word κόσμος connotes the idea of an ordering of distinctive parts into a *cohesive* unit. Insofar as the universe is a κόσμος, it is conceived of as a unity, with its varied and constituent elements, both animate and inanimate, heavenly and earthly, integrated into a perfect whole.[135] One of the main concerns of the Presocratic attempt to define reality was the relation between oneness and multiplicity: the appellation of κόσμος, first to the world-order, then to the world itself, conveniently functioned to highlight the essential unity of all that exists.

The unity and harmony of the κόσμος is stressed by Plato (*Tim.* 30d; 32b–c; 32d–33a). It is an emphasis of the Stoics[136] and is lauded in Pseudo-Aristotle's *De Mundo*.[137]

The thought of unity applies even where, with the Atomists and Epicureans, there is a plurality of κόσμοι, since each κόσμος, through the cohesion of atoms, is conceived of as a unity in its own right.

Thirdly, the κόσμος *is an object of beauty*. For the Greeks, order was a thing of beauty (cf. Philo, *Opif.* 28). In the earliest uses of κόσμος – for specific arrangements – as Vlastos writes, what is implied "is not just any sort of arranging, but one that strikes the eye or the mind as pleasingly fitting: as setting, or keeping, or putting back, things in their proper order".[138] When applied to the material world, therefore, κόσμος not only emphasized that the universe is an ordered structure

---

[132] Jaeger 1965, 160.
[133] The majority of Middle Platonists, however, rejected Plato's account as a literal cosmogony: Runia 1986, 54.
[134] Philo, *Aet.* 54; *Spec.* 4.237; Ps-Arist., *Mund.* 397a5ff.
[135] Cf. Plato, *Gorg.* 507e–508.
[136] Esp. Posidonius. See Sextus Empiricus, *Ag. Phys.* 1.79ff.
[137] *Mund.* 396b1ff: "out of plurality and diversity it achieves a homogenous unity capable of admitting every variation of nature and degree".
[138] Vlastos 1975, 3.

but also that the order inherent or displayed in it is of an aesthetically pleasing character; the connotation was indeed that of "a crafted, composed, beauty-enhancing order".[139]

The κόσμος is by very nature καλός. For Plato, the κόσμος is the quintessence, the perfect exemplar, of beauty (κάλλιστος, *Tim.* 29a; 92c). The beauty and perfection of the κόσμος are to be seen in its completeness (32c–33a), its freedom from age and sickness (33a), its sphericity (the sphere being the most perfect shape, 33b-c), its self-sufficiency (33d) and its circular motion (34a). Plato makes a deliberate play on κόσμος = adornment and κόσμος = world / universe at *Tim.* 40a.

The beauty of the κόσμος continues to be extolled in the first century CE (Pseudo-Arist., *Mund.* 397a5ff; Dio Chrysostom, *Disc.* 30.28; 36.60; 40.35–36; 48.14).

Fourthly, *human beings are related to the κόσμος as microcosm to macrocosm.* Since the κόσμος – the heavens and the earth and all life in them – is the sum of all its parts, human beings are related to the κόσμος as parts to the whole. The relationship of the human being to the κόσμος, however, is a special instance of the general part-whole rule. The human individual shares in the highest qualities of the κόσμος – life, intelligence, body, soul – and is indeed a microcosm of the κόσμος.

While Democritus may have been the first to articulate the notion of the human individual as the μικρὸς κόσμος, the idea is much earlier. The microcosmic–macrocosmic relation of the human being to the κόσμος runs through Plato's *Timaeus*, for example, at 30d; 44d–45b.

The implications of the human individual as the microcosm are most comprehensively worked out by the Stoics. From the Stoic point of view, men and women find their fulfilment in incorporating themselves into the unity of the κόσμος. Thus Cicero can say that human beings aré born to contemplate the world and to imitate it in their own conduct (*De nat.* 2.11–14).[140]

Human beings are microcosmically related to the κόσμος, not only individually but also collectively. There is a natural connection between the order of the κόσμος and the order of human *society*.[141] Hence, the

139 Vlastos 1975, 3.
140 Cf. Ps–Arist., *Mund.* 391a14.
141 On the Cynic dissent to this assumption, see p. 74.

comparison is frequently drawn between the πόλις and the κόσμος. The regulations and institutions of the city-state comport with the laws and structures of the κόσμος.[142] Again, the idea is elaborately developed in Stoicism.

Fifthly, the κόσμος *is an object of praise*. Classical Greek thought, without doubt, engendered an exceptionally high view of the world as κόσμος. Plato's *Timaeus* was pivotal in this respect: Plotinus can regard the dialogue as a hymn of praise to the κόσμος (*Enn.* 4.8.1.41).

One of the most powerful ways in which the high regard and reverence for the κόσμος was expressed was the ascription to it of immortality. That the κόσμος is everlasting was the mainstream view in Greek philosophical discussion, being upheld by both Plato[143] and Aristotle, the latter arguing for the *eternity* of the κόσμος.[144] Notwithstanding the Epicurean revival of the Atomist point of view, the Stoic theory of cosmic conflagration raised the most formidable challenge to the classic position. However, not all Stoics adhered to the doctrine of ἐκπύρωσις. The tenet of universal conflagration was abandoned by some notable Middle Stoics, including Zeno of Tarsus, Diogenes of Babylon, Boethus of Sidon, and Panaetius,[145] in favour of the doctrine of cosmic indestructibility. (The majority of the Roman Stoics in the first and second centuries CE, though, appear to have accepted ἐκπύρωσις.)[146] Also, as noted earlier, Stoic exponents of the doctrine from Chrysippus onward wanted to insist that in the process of conflagration the κόσμος does not die.[147] Rather it undergoes change. By using the word κόσμος with the broad sense of "god himself . . . consisting of all substance", the Stoics could indeed affirm the everlasting duration of the κόσμος, insofar as κόσμος, in this

[142] See further, pp. 69–70.

[143] Plato's view, that the κόσμος is created and indestructible, had already been expressed by Hesiod (*Theog.* 105–6; 116; 128), the father of Greek theology, in *c.* 700 BCE. It was probably also held by Pythagoras: so Guthrie 1962, 281–2.

[144] Though Aristotle considers himself the first to advance the theorem of the eternity of the κόσμος, his view may have been anticipated by Heraclitus (fr. 30): see Guthrie 1962, 454–9; Kahn 1960, 225–6; Kirk 1954, 317–24; 335–8; Luce 1992, 43–5. Also, in *Meteor.* 986b22, Aristotle credits Xenophanes with the doctrine.

[145] Philo, *Aet.* 76–7; Sandbach 1975, 79.

[146] Cf. Philo, *Aet.* 8. Reference to the cosmic conflagration is made by Seneca (*De consol. ad Marc.* 26.6; *Ben.* 6.22; *Nat. quaes.* 3.13.1–2; 27–30), Lucan (*Civil War*, 1:72–80; 2:7–10), and Epictetus (*Disc.* 3.13.4–5). Cf. also Dio Chrysostom (*Disc.* 36.56–7). On the cosmology of the Roman Stoics, see Lapidge 1989. On Lucan's distinctive utilization of the conflagration theme, see Adams 1997b, 336–42.

[147] See above, pp. 54–5.

extended sense, embraces the endless cycle of world-periods and conflagrations.

The Aristotelian thesis of the eternity of the κόσμος is strongly championed in two extant documents of the first century CE: *De Universi Natura*, attributed (wrongly) to Ocellus of Lucania,[148] and Pseudo-Aristotle's *De Mundo*.

The revered status of the κόσμος is clearly also evident in the attribution of divinity to the κόσμος. Plato described the κόσμος as a "blessed god" (*Tim.* 34b), a "self-sufficient and perfect god" (68e), a "perceptible god" (92c). The divinity of the κόσμος became increasingly stressed through the Hellenistic era. The Stoics, in their monist and pantheist cosmology, explicitly identified god and the κόσμος. Remarkably, even a Jewish writer like Philo, can apply the term θεός to the κόσμος (*Deus* 31; *Aet.* 10, 20).

With such a high view of the κόσμος obtaining in the Hellenistic period, the impulse was inevitably toward adoration and veneration of the κόσμος; hence Jonas speaks of "late-classical cosmos-piety".[149]

The world-view encoded by κόσμος (= world/universe), therefore, for the great part, is a positive and optimistic one. The world represented is basically a *good* (though not perfect) world. With regard to Greek cosmological speculation in general, Mansfield comments,

> the mainstream of Greek thought concerning the cosmos is optimistic; such less positive views as can be found, are, as a rule, against the current, or are only introduced for the sake of an argument.[150]

So, for example, Dio Chrysostom, the Stoic–Cynic popular philosopher, describes the view that

> This place which we call the universe (κόσμος) ... is a prison prepared by the gods, a grievous and ill-ventilated one, which never keeps the same temperature and condition of its air, but at one time is cold and frosty, and infected with wind, mud, snow and water, and at another time again is hot and stifling; for just a very little time of year it is endurable; it is visited by cyclones, typhoons occur, and sometimes the whole of it quakes to the very bottom. Now all these are terrible punishments. For men are invariably dismayed and terrified by them whenever they occur.[151]

[148] This work was known and read by Philo, *Aet.* 12.
[149] Jonas 1963, 247 n. 7.
[150] Mansfield 1981, 263.
[151] Dio Chrysostom, *Disc.* 30.11–12.

Dio, however, decisively rejects such an understanding of the κόσμος and affirms the consensus position that

> the universe (κόσμος) is a house very beautiful and divine, constructed by the gods; that just as we see houses built by men who are called prosperous and wealthy, with portals and columns, and the roof, walls and doors adorned with gold and with paintings, in the same way the universe has been made to give entertainment and good cheer to mankind, beauteous and bespangled with stars, sun, moon, land, sea, and plants, all these being, indeed, portions of the wealth of the gods and specimens of their handiwork. Into this universe comes mankind to hold high festival, having been invited by the King of the gods to a most splendid feast and banquet that they may enjoy all blessings.[152]

A highly negative and pessimistic assessment of the physical universe does, of course, emerge in the second and third centuries CE, with the rise of Gnosticism, Neo-Pythagoreanism and Neo-Platonism.[153] But, relatively few traces of such a disposition in Greek literature can be found before then.[154] Up to the end of the first century CE, κόσμος (= world/universe) in principle encoded a *positive* evaluation of the world.

3.5. The ideology of κόσμος

One of the elements of the world-view encoded by κόσμος (= world/ universe), outlined above, was the assumption that there is a natural relation between the social order and the cosmic order. The parallel may have been established at the very outset, when κόσμος was first used to designate the world-order. Up to then, κόσμος had been regularly used with reference to specific social orderings, including the order of the πόλις. It had also been used to express the idea of a general social and moral order. Kahn suggests that κόσμος was applied to the world-order "by conscious analogy with the good order of society".[155]

The conviction that the order of the universe is analogous to the civic order runs through Presocratic philosophy from Anaximander onward.[156] The parallel is drawn by Plato when he introduces the term κόσμος (= world/universe) in *Gorgias* (508a). He calls attention to the

---

152 Dio Chrysostom, *Disc.* 30.28–9.
153 Cf. Aune 1994, 296; Jonas 1963, 250–65.
154 The closest is probably the Epicurean cosmic system: so Mansfield 1981, 309–12.
155 Kahn 1960, 223. The continued co-existence of the earlier social senses of κόσμος alongside the later cosmological senses would have helped to keep the analogy alive.
156 Kahn 1960, 223. Cf. Jaeger 1965, 161.

bond of κοσμιότης καὶ σωφροσύνη καὶ δικαιότης ("orderliness, temperance, and justice") by which the constituents of the universe (earth, heaven, human beings and gods) are held together. He thus likens the κόσμος (= world/universe) to a well ordered city-state.[157]

As Ehrhardt states, the "order" of the universe, according to the world-view evoked by κόσμος (= world/universe), was understood to be "manifest in the unchanging courses of the stars in the sky, and upon earth in the stability of the city state".[158]

By encoding the assumption that the social system is a microcosm of the all-encompassing cosmic system, κόσμος (= world/universe), therefore, served to *legitimate* the prevailing social order.

According to Berger, the conviction that the social order is a reflection of the structure of the universe is one of the most effective forms of legitimation.[159] On this kind of scheme, the structures and stratifications of society are objectively grounded in the all-inclusive order of the universe. By participating in the socially established order, men and women participate in the divinely established order. Social norms and conventions, sanctions and punishments are all interpreted as concretizations of the cosmic structure; as Berger states, "humanly constructed nomoi are given a cosmic status".[160]

The scope of this type of legitimation is obviously wide. Berger writes,

This cosmization ... refers not only to the over-all nomic structures, but to specific institutions and roles within a given society. The cosmic status assigned to these is objectivated, that is, it becomes part of the objectively available reality of the institutions and roles in question.[161]

The microcosmic–macrocosmic scheme validates the whole institutional order of a society from the state to the institutions of kinship and family. It provides the ultimate sanction for the political and power structures of the day. The governing authority is conceived of as an agent of the gods; to obey the ruler is to be in "a right relationship with the world of the gods".[162] And it integrates the institutions of kinship into the life of the universe. Berger observes, "Every human family

---

[157] Kahn 1960, 223.
[158] Ehrhardt 1964, 206.
[159] Berger 1969, 34.
[160] Berger 1969, 36.
[161] Berger 1969, 36.
[162] Berger 1969, 34.

reflects the structure of the cosmos, not only in terms of representing but of embodying it."[163] Moreover, "cosmization" grounds the stratifications of a society in ultimate reality. Socio-economic divisions, social positions and the distribution of power are conceived as part of the rational ordering of the world, the very divine arrangement of things.

The effectiveness of this kind of legitimation, according to Berger, is seen, firstly, in the degree to which societal structures can be objectified. The institutions of a society are accorded "a semblance of inevitability, firmness and durability".[164] Social structures are raised above the level of historical contingency and are secured a place in the reality of the universe. Secondly, it is evident in the extent to which individuals can appropriate and identify with the roles ascribed to them. When the roles they are expected to play in society are accorded a cosmic significance, their identification with these roles is reinforced:

> He *is* whatever society has identified him as by virtue of a cosmic truth, as it were, and his social being becomes rooted in the sacred reality of the universe.[165]

But perhaps most of all, the strength of cosmic legitimation is apparent insofar as it bears a powerful built-in sanction against deviance. To challenge the social order and to resist one's prescribed role is to go against nature and the divine arrangement of things. Again Berger states that,

> When the socially defined reality has come to be identified with the ultimate reality of the universe, then its denial takes on the quality of evil as well as madness.[166]

By encoding the microcosmic–macrocosmic link between society and the cosmic order, therefore, κόσμος (= world/universe) served not only to justify and endorse the existing social and political order, but to do so in a comprehensive and powerful way.

The social and ideological consequences of κόσμος = world/universe were most fully drawn out by the Stoics. This is hardly surprising in view of the fact that the goal of Stoic ethics was incorporation into the social and cosmic order. It is also readily appreciable from the extreme

---

[163] Berger 1969, 34.
[164] Berger 1969, 36.
[165] Berger 1969, 37.
[166] Berger 1969, 39.

determinism of Stoic cosmology. In the Stoic system, all events are causally related and governed by πρόνοια. Thus both the social and institutional order and the position of every human being within that order are determined and fixed by fate.[167]

For the Stoics, the world-view evoked by κόσμος positively encouraged social integration, acceptance of one's social circumstances, political acquiescence and the preservation of the existing social order from the household to the state as a whole.[168]

In the Stoic-influenced work, *De universi natura* (43–51)[169] attributed to Ocellus Lucanus, the institution of the household is strongly upheld as part of the fabric of the κόσμος. The household is a microcosm of the city which is in turn a microcosm of the universe. As a member of both household and city-state (πόλις), and, most importantly, of the κόσμος, it is a man's duty to perpetuate these institutions. A man is thus obliged to marry, procreate and raise children and so replace those whom death takes from household and city. The make-up of the whole (τὸ ὅλον) and the all (τὸ πᾶν) is dependent on its parts. Each household and householder thus contributes to the cosmic system.[170]

Cicero, commenting on the fact that the world is a city and each person a part of it, writes,

> From this it is a natural consequence that we prefer the common advantage to our own ... This explains the fact that someone who dies for the state is praiseworthy, because our country should be dearer to us than ourselves.[171]

The whole, the state, has prominence over and gives meaning to its parts, the citizens. Citizens, therefore, are to find their fulfilment in the maintenance and preservation of the state. Within a perfectly ordered world-city, every person has a proper place. As the place which a person occupies at the theatre is rightly his or hers, Cicero continues, so too the place which one occupies in the city and the world. This extends to

---

[167] Long (1974, 198) states, "The external circumstances of his whole life are an episode in the life of universal Nature, and they are 'in his power' only to the extent that he can choose to accept them or not when they occur".

[168] On the political and social theory of the Stoics, see texts and commentary in L–S 1: 429–37, 2: 423–31. The mild radicalism of the earlier Stoics gave way to political and social conservation among the middle Stoics, a tendency which became more pronounced with the Roman Stoics.

[169] For translation of this section, see Deming 1995, 230–1.

[170] See further, Deming 1995, 70.

[171] L–S 1: 348–9, 2: 346–7 (no. 57F = Cicero. *Fin.* 3.62–8).

one's socio-economic position, since "no right is infringed by each man's possessing what belongs to him".[172]

It is particularly revealing in the light of Berger's observations that Cicero, following Panaetius and other Stoics, adopts the analogy of role-play in explaining the goal of human existence. In Cicero's view, each person is like an actor on a cosmic stage, with the responsibility of performing a role and playing that part well.[173]

Cicero equates civic law with universal law. In his judgement, whoever does not obey the true law "is fleeing from himself and treating his human nature with contempt".[174]

According to Dio Chrysostom, *Disc*. 30.28ff, one comes into the κόσμος as to a banquet held by a King. Each person is assigned a place. Some get better places and some are given inferior positions: "different persons have different things in greater abundance according to the tables at which they have severally reclined" (*Disc*. 30.30).

Epictetus exhorts his readers to contemplate and learn the administration of the κόσμος (ἡ τοῦ κόσμου διοίκησις, *Disc*. 1.9.4; 1.10.10). God directs and governs the κόσμος in such a way that the parts serve the whole (4.7.6). As a general stations a soldier to a post, so God has stationed each individual in some place and manner of life (1.9.24–26). One ought not to desert one's post (cf. 3.1.19–20).

Everyone must learn that they are citizens of the κόσμος (πολίτης τοῦ κόσμου, 2.10.3; cf. 1.9.6). It is the duty of the citizen, as a part of the whole, not to act like a detached unit and never to "exercise choice or desire in any other way but by reference to the whole" (2.10.4). Even if they were to know the future in advance, good citizens would continue to go down the path to which they had been assigned, even though that involved injury, disease or death. They would do so in the realization that their lot in the world comes from the orderly arrangement of the whole (2.10.5–6).

---

[172] L–S 1: 348–9, 2: 346–7 (no. 57F = Cicero, *Fin*. 3.62–8).

[173] L–S 1: 424, 2: 419–20 (no. 66E = Cicero, *Off*. 1.107–17). According to Cicero, each person is assigned four roles. The first relates to the common rationality possessed by all human beings which places them above the animals. The second relates to differences in intellect and temperament which mark out the individual. The third is imposed by "chance and circumstances", over which people have no say, e.g. noble birth, headship of state, public office, wealth and material conditions. The fourth, which admits a measure of human freedom, is the lifestyle and career which human beings choose for themselves.

[174] L–S 1: 432–3, 2: 428 (no. 67S = Cicero, *Rep*. 3.33).

One must not aspire to a higher place in the world than that which one has been given. In a well-ordered house, no one can assume the role of the lord of the mansion, except the one who bears this title. Anyone who attempts to do so will soon be brought down to their proper level. In this great city, the world, there is a lord of the mansion who assigns to each and every thing a fit place (3.22.5).

Even death is to be viewed from the perspective of the part and the whole and the viewpoint of the greater good of the κόσμος. Death is just a reconstitution of cosmic matter. Nothing that makes up the κόσμος is lost in the process; the elements are simply reorganized (4.7.15–16). What is born must die, so that the κόσμος advances on its planned course (4.7.27).

In deducing these social and practical inferences from cosmology, the Stoics were bringing to the fore an ideology already encoded in κόσμος (= world/universe). The determinist element in Stoic thought prompted them to express that ideology in an extreme form. But, essentially they were making explicit what was there implied.

κόσμος (= world/universe) formed part of what Fowler calls the "official language of legitimated meanings".[175] As noted at the beginning of this chapter, κόσμος (= world/universe) and the world-view it evoked belonged to the *paideia*, the ideals of Greek and Hellenistic education and culture. As part of official language, the social meaning of κόσμος (= world/universe) would have been transmitted in a routine and natural way. Through the process of habitualization, that meaning would have been tended to pass as common sense. As Fowler argues, legitimation and habitualization are the normal and inevitable tendencies of official language.[176]

This is not to claim that the social and ideological consequences of κόσμος (= world/universe) were never resisted. An extant example of such resistance (a rare example) is the early Cynics. They drew a sharp contrast between society and nature. For them the ideals of citizenship of the κόσμος and conformity to the cosmic order (which they enthusiastically accepted)[177] meant a rejection of the values and goals of contemporary society.[178]

---

[175] Fowler 1996, 43.
[176] Cf. Fowler 1996, 42–6.
[177] Diogenes Laertius 6:63, 72. On Cynic Cosmopolitanism, see Moles 1996.
[178] T. W. Martin 1996, 81–2.

The point is that the social meaning of κόσμος (= world/universe), transmitted by linguistic convention, was a powerful legitimating tool. Those exposed to official language (mainly through education, a smattering of which would have been sufficient) would have been susceptible to its influence. Whether individuals or groups resisted the ideological implications of κόσμος (= world/universe) depended on their critical capacities and their ability to combat "the dulling familiarity of conventional codes".[179]

3.6. Septuagintal and other Jewish uses of κόσμος

To round off this survey of the linguistic background to Paul's employ-ment of κόσμος, we briefly examine Hellenistic–Jewish usage of the term, especially in the Septuagint.

In the Septuagint,[180] κόσμος is used for צבא, "host" (of heaven), that is the celestial bodies as in Deut 4:19; Isa 24:21; 40:26. It is used with the sense of "ornament" or "adornment" as a rendering of various Hebrew words having this sense, for example, in Exod 33:5–6; 2 Sam 1:24; Prov 20:29; Jer 2:32. It has also this sense where there is no corresponding Hebrew word, as in Isa 49:18; Prov 18:17; Jdt 1:14.

The Septuagint normally speaks of οὐρανός and γῆ (translating תבל and ארץ) when referring to the universe.[181] κόσμος with the sense "world" (but with varying nuances) is found only in the later writings of the Septuagint, that is to say, in compositions whose original language is Greek. It occurs nineteen times in the *Wisdom of Solomon*, five times in 2 Maccabees and four times in 4 Maccabees.[182] The employment of κόσμος in the *Wisdom of Solomon* is the most interesting use of the term in a Jewish writing outside of the works of Philo.

In the *Wisdom of Solomon*, in addition to meaning "world/universe", κόσμος also bears the contextual senses, "the inhabited earth", "natural world" and "humanity".

The writer of this document makes a number of theologically significant statements involving κόσμος. With regard to the κόσμος, the physical universe, the author states the following. God gives

---

[179] Fowler 1996, 56.
[180] See Bytomski 1911; Guhrt 1975, 522; Sasse 1965, 880–2.
[181] See also κτίσις below, pp. 78–80.
[182] In 4 Macc 17:14, with the sense "world of spiritual beings".

knowledge of the structure of the κόσμος and the operation of the elements (εἰδέναι σύστασιν κόσμου καὶ ἐνέργειαν στοιχείων, Wis 7:17). God made the κόσμος (ἐποίεις τὸν κόσμον) by his word and formed humankind by his wisdom (9:9). God by his mighty hand created the world from pre-existent matter (κτίσασα τὸν κόσμον ἐξ ἀμόρφου ὕλης, 11:17, echoing the Greek concept of world-formation). God is sovereign over the universe: before him ὅλος ὁ κόσμος is "like a speck of dust that tips the scales, and like a drop of morning dew that falls on the ground" (11:22). People who were ignorant of God and foolish by nature supposed that the heavenly bodies were the gods that rule the κόσμος (13:2). The whole κόσμος (ὅλος ὁ κόσμος) was symbolically represented in the garment of Moses (18:24; cf. Philo, Mos. 133–5).

Concerning the κόσμος, the earth, the inhabited world, the author has the following to say. God created human beings to rule the κόσμος in holiness and righteousness (9:3). Idols did not exist from the beginning; they entered the κόσμος through human vanity (14:14). During the plague of darkness that fell on Egypt, that darkness remained on the land of the Egyptians alone. The rest of the κόσμος was illuminated with brilliant light and continued its work unhindered (17:20). The κόσμος (natural world) is said to be the defender of the righteous (ὑπέρμαχος γὰρ ὁ κόσμος ἐστὶ δικαίων, 16:17). In the final judgement, the κόσμος will join with God to fight against his foes (5:20).

Regarding κόσμος, the human world, the writer claims the following. Adam was the first-formed father of the human κόσμος (10:1). Death entered into the κόσμος through the devil's envy (2:24). In the days of the flood, the hope (i.e. the remnant) of the κόσμος, the seed of a new generation, took refuge in the ark (14:6). The multitude of the wise is the salvation (σωτηρία) of the κόσμος (6:23, 24).

The employment of κόσμος in this document serves as a useful parallel to some of Paul's uses of the term in Romans.

In Hellenistic–Jewish sources outside the Septuagint, the sense "ornament" or "adornment" predominates.[183] The sense "world/universe" is attested in the *Epistle of Aristeas*[184] and in *Aristobulus*.[185]

183 T. Jud. 12:1; Ezek. Trag. 16, 164.
184 Ep. Arist. 99, 210.
185 Aristobulus, Eusebius, Ev. Prep. 8.10.9; 13.13.3; 13.12.9; 13.13.5; 13.12.13.

κόσμος appears over one hundred times in Josephus. In the vast majority of instances, it has a non-cosmological application, denoting specific orderings such as the government (*Ant.* 3.84), the market-place (*Ant.* 3.289), the political constitution (*Ant.* 5.132), and having the senses, "order" in general (*Ant.* 1.81; 14.2), "ornament" (*Ant.* 1.249; 3.103), "adornment" (*Ant.* 3.167; 8.135) and "honour" (*Life* 274). The meaning "world/universe" is attested in a few passages (*Ant.* 1.21, 26, *Ap.* 2.284; *War* 5.459), as is the sense "earth", "inhabited world" (*Ant.* 9.242; 10.205; *Ap.* 2.138–9).

3.7. The linguistic background of κτίσις

Having now completed the review of κόσμος, in this section we come at last to κτίσις. This term, as indicated at the outset of the chapter, can be treated in a concise manner, in view of its limited range of usage.

κτίσις is a substantive derived from the verb κτίζω. It occurs in both Greek and Hellenistic-Jewish writings.

κτίσις is found early on in Greek usage, occurring in Pindar (*c.* 518–446 BCE), Thucydides (*c.* 500 BCE), Isocrates (436–338 BCE) and Aeschines (*c.* 390 BCE). In Pindar it has the sense "achievement", "accomplishment".[186] Pindar's use, however, is atypical. Elsewhere in Greek literature, it can mean "founding", "foundation", "settlement", and is applied to the establishment of cities.[187] Not surprisingly, it occurs most often in works of history. There is also a comparatively high frequency of instances in the writings of the geographer, Strabo. Plutarch comments that Trisimachus and Dercyllus both wrote series of books bearing the one-word title, Κτίσεων, *On the Founding of Cities,*[188] indicating that κτίσις was, at least by this stage, a technical term for the activity of city-establishing.

In the Septuagint, κτίζω and its derivatives are applied to the creative work of God.[189] This line of usage seems to be a linguistic innovation on the part of the translators of the Greek Old Testament. Interestingly, the

---

[186] Pindar, *Ol.* 13.83: κούφα κτίσις, "light achievement".
[187] Aeschines, *Falsa* 115.2; Dio Cassius, *Hist.* 46.21.4; Diodorus Siculus 1.15.2; 1.73.3; 2.3.1; Diogenes Laertius 9.20; Dion. Halic., *Ant.* 1.6.2; 1.66.1; 1.74.1; Isocrates, *Panath.* 190.1; Plutarch, *Rom.* 8.7; 12.1; *Comp. Lyc. Num.* 3.7; *Pub.* 6.4; Strabo, *Geog.* 1.3.15.3; 3.5.5.1; Thucydides 1.18.1; 6.5.3.
[188] Plutarch, *Par.* 307a; 313f.
[189] Nevertheless, κτίζω is not the main term for God's creative activity in the LXX: ποιέω, πλάσσω and θεμελιόω figure more often: Foerster 1965, 1023.

δημιουργέω word-group, which figures so prominently in the Greek cosmogonical tradition, is completely absent from the Septuagint. Foerster thinks that the translators preferred κτίζω and its cognates to the more obvious δημιουργέω for theological reasons. He comments,

> δημιουργεῖν suggests the craftsman and his work in the strict sense, whereas κτίζειν reminds us of the ruler at whose command a city arises out of nothing because the power of the ruler stands behind his word.[190]

Barr doubts that theological motivations played a part in the selection of κτίζω and its derivatives and rejection of the δημιουργέω word-group. He points out that κτίζω was already well established in the sense "make", "create". He thinks it more likely that the Septuagintal use of the κτι- word-group for God's creative activity simply followed from that lexical sense.[191] Whether or not the translators intended to make a theological point by choosing κτι- terminology over δημιουργέω and its cognates, the theological potential of this lexical choice is certainly exploited by Philo. He comments:

> God, when He gave birth to all things, not only brought them into sight, but also made things which before were not, not just handling material as an artificer (δημιουργός), but being Himself its creator (κτίστης). (Somn. 1.76)[192]

The word κτίσις is found sixteen times in the Septuagint.[193] In all but one of its occurrences (Ps 104[103]:24), there is no equivalent Hebrew term in the Massoretic text which it renders. It is noteworthy that instances of the word are concentrated in prayers extolling the sovereignty and power of God (Ps 74:[73]:18; Tob 8:5, 15: Jdt 9:12; 16:14; Wis 16:24; 19:6; 3 Macc 2:2, 7; 6:2).[194]

κτίσις carries the meaning "creature" or "created thing" in Tob 8:5, 15; Jdt 9:12; Sir 16:17; 43:26. It is used in the wider sense "creation / the created world" in Jdt 16:14;[195] Ps 74[73]:18; 104[103]:24; Sir 49:16; 3 Macc 2:2, 7; 6:2.

---

[190] Foerster 1965, 1026.
[191] Barr 1961, 225.
[192] Cf. Opif. 17. κτίζω, however, is less important for Philo than δημιουργέω.
[193] In Ps 105[104]: 21, Prov 1:13, and 10:15, on textual grounds, κτῆσις should be read instead of κτίσις: Foerster 1965, 1028.
[194] Esser 1975, 381.
[195] πᾶσα ἡ κτίσις here, though, may mean "every creature".

In the *Wisdom of Solomon*, the word κτίσις, which occurs four times (2:6; 5:17; 16:24; 19:6), refers to the natural world as distinct from human beings, that is with the sense "*non-human* creation". In Wis 2:6, the ungodly (cf. 1:16) reason together, "Come, therefore, let us enjoy the good things that exist, and make use of the creation (χρησώμεθα τῇ κτίσει) to the full". The "good things", with which κτίσις is linked, consist of wine, perfumes, flowers, rosebuds (vv. 7–8). In 5:17, the writer states that in the final judgement, God "will arm all creation to repel his enemies" (καὶ ὁπλοποιήσει τὴν κτίσιν εἰς ἄμυναν ἐχθρῶν). The arming of creation, as vv. 18–23 indicate, consists in God's harnessing of the forces of nature (lightning, hailstones, waters of the sea, rivers and a mighty tempest) to effect his judgement. κτίσις here is equivalent to κόσμος (= natural order) in 5:20. In 16:24, the writer states, that "creation . . . exerts itself to punish the righteous and in kindness relaxes on behalf of those who trust [God]". κτίσις in this verse is linked with the rain, hail, fire, snow, ice and hail referred to in 16:17–23 and interchanges with κόσμος (= natural order) in 16:17. In 16:24, κτίσις is firmly distinguished from righteous and unrighteous humanity. In 19:6, the writer declares that during the miracle of the Sea of Reeds, "the whole creation in its nature was fashioned anew (γὰρ ἡ κτίσις ἐν ἰδίῳ γένει πάλιν ἄνωθεν διετυποῦτο), complying with [God's] commands, so that [his] children might be kept unharmed".[196]

In Jewish writings outside the Septuagint, κτίσις is attested with the senses, "creature" (*T. Naph.*[197] 2:3); "creation" (*Ep. Arist.* 136; 139); "act of creation" (*T. Reub.* 2:3, 9, with reference to the creation of humanity; *Pss Sol* 8:7, ἀπο κτίσεως οὐρανοῦ καὶ γῆς). The meaning "nature/non-human creation" seems likely in *T. Levi* 4:1, where a description is given of the coming judgement, "when stones are split, when the sun is extinguished, the waters are dried up, fire is cowed down" and "all creation is distraught" (καὶ πάσης κτίσεως κλονουμένης).

κτίσις is not a favourite term with either Philo or Josephus. Philo only uses it in *Mos.* 2.51, with respect to the foundation of the great city, the world. Here it has the regular non-biblical sense of "founding", "foundation". Josephus also uses the term with the standard Greek

---

[196] On the theory of miracles in the *Wisdom of Solomon*, see Sweet 1965.
[197] πᾶσα κτίσις here meaning "every creature": cf. Hollander and De Jonge 1985, 303.

sense.[198] In *War* 4.533, however, we find the expression ἀπὸ τῆς κτίσεως, "from the act of creation".

3.8. *Summary and conclusions*

To summarize the main findings of the above survey, the word κόσμος had a variety of lexical senses in Greek usage – social, moral, aesthetic and cosmological. The majority of these meanings were current in the first century CE. κόσμος = "world/universe" began as a technical philosophical usage. It occurs most frequently in philosophical or philosophically informed works. Hence our concentration on this area of discourse.

The conventional associations of κόσμος (= "world/universe") in Greek usage relate to order, orderliness, regularity, stability, cohesion, continuity, harmony, fitness, beauty and integration. Such properties and values were judged positively in Graeco-Roman culture.[199]

κόσμος with the sense "world/universe" encoded a particular view of the world, that is to say, it was tied to a set of beliefs about the world: the world as an ordered reality; the world as a unified structure; the world as an object of beauty; the world as an entity to which human beings – both individually and collectively – are microcosmically related; the world as an object of praise and admiration.

κόσμος (= "world/universe"), encoding this world-view, was imbued (so to speak) with ideology. It functioned to legitimate, in the most comprehensive way, the dominant society with its structures, institutions, power-relations, norms and values. The designation of the world as κόσμος, because of the ideology it encoded, reinforced and endorsed the prevailing social order as the mirror-image of the cosmic order.

κτίσις in non-biblical Greek usage had the standard sense "founding", "foundation", "settlement". In Greek literature, it is employed in contexts relating to the establishment of cities. In Jewish usage, it was linked with God's creative/created work. It appears in the Septuagint and other Jewish writings with the senses "creature/created thing", "the

---

[198] *War* 6.269 (of the temple), 408, 437, 441; *Ant.* 18.373.
[199] To this extent, κόσμος (= "world/universe") may be described as a word of "emotive meaning". On emotive meaning, see Jackson 1988, 59–60. One may compare "freedom", "democracy", "justice", "rights", etc. in twentieth-century English-speaking societies.

created universe", "the act of creation". In the *Wisdom of Solomon,* κτίσις, as is clear from the linguistic contexts in which it is set, means "*non-human* creation".

The foregoing survey has provided us with a general linguistic background against which to compare and contrast Paul's specific uses of the terms κόσμος and κτίσις (and so to determine – as far as possible – whether Paul is using the words on particular occasions in standard or non-standard ways) and from which to judge the effects of those uses on the communities he addresses. This necessary investigation complete, therefore, the detailed analysis of the Pauline texts can now begin.

Part III

Textual analysis

4

Weak group boundaries at Corinth

4.1. Introduction

This is the first of two chapters devoted to a socio-rhetorical analysis of the usage of κόσμος in 1 Corinthians, and aims to explore the context of utterance of 1 Corinthians, the social and rhetorical setting within which Paul's uses of κόσμος are to be interpreted. The task mainly involves looking at the community situation which Paul is addressing and his social goals in writing. A short chapter like this can only sketch an outline of the utterance context of 1 Corinthians. We focus attention on the social and ideological boundaries of the Corinthian Christian community. This is the main point of contention between Paul and the Corinthians in the letter, the central issue around which most of the matters addressed by Paul revolve. Certainly (as will emerge during the course of this and the following chapter), it is the social issue most significant and relevant to Paul's usage of κόσμος in 1 Corinthians.

The present chapter begins with some general comments on the historical context within which Paul's discourse is conducted, then moves on to a discussion of the Corinthian "aberrations". The majority of the problems in the church, it will be argued, reflect the Corinthian church's weak boundaries. Further evidence of weak group boundaries is adduced from the areas of social intercourse with outsiders and social relations inside the group. After discussing what sociological category best fits the Corinthian church, we consider how the Corinthian Christians would have evaluated κόσμος (= world/universe).

4.2. Context of utterance: general comments

Paul was the founder of the Christian community in Corinth (1 Cor 3:6, 10; 4:14–15; 2 Cor 10:13–14). According to Acts 18:1–17, he established the church during an eighteen-month ministry in the city (his arrival in Corinth is usually dated 49/50 CE). When he moved on, it would seem that he left behind a flourishing congregation. Between the founding of the church and the writing of 1 Corinthians, other Christian teachers had visited Corinth, notably Apollos (1 Cor 1:12; 3:4–6) and possibly Peter (1:12; 3:22; 9:5). Also, Paul had written his converts a letter in which he instructed them "not to associate with sexually immoral persons" (5:9). As to the rest of the contents of that letter, we know nothing, though it has been suggested that a fragment of it is preserved in 2 Cor 6:14 – 7:1.

1 Corinthians was written by Paul in Ephesus (1 Cor 16:8, 19).[1] It was occasioned by oral reports Paul had received about the church, especially reports from a certain group he calls "Chloe's people" (1:11), and by a letter which the Corinthians sent to him asking for his "advice" (their motives were probably not quite *that* innocent) on various matters. Paul responds to the oral reports in the first part of the letter, from 1:10 to 6:20. Then at 7:1, he turns his attention to the matters raised in the Corinthians' written communication to him.[2]

It is clear that a number of "aberrant" (from Paul's point of view) developments had emerged or had come to fruition in the church by this time.[3] Paul writes to correct these false developments and to get the wayward church, as he sees it, back on the right rails.

According to 1 Cor 1:26, there were a few members of the church who were of some social status (οὐ πολλοὶ σοφοὶ … οὐ πολλοὶ δυνατοί οὐ πολλοὶ εὐγενεῖς).[4] Theissen has argued that this minority

---

[1] This study proceeds on the assumption that the letter is a unity; the argument in support of the integrity of 1 Corinthians is overwhelming. See the discussions in Conzelmann 1975, 3–4; Hurd 1965, 43–7; Kümmel 1982, 275–8; Schrage 1991, 63–71.

[2] Paul uses the prepositional phrase περὶ δέ when answering questions raised in their letter: 7:1, 25; 8:1; 12:1; 16:1. Cf. 1 Thess 4:9; 5:1. For an alternative, but less convincing, account of the arrangement of topics in 1 Corinthians and the discourse function of περὶ δέ, see Mitchell 1991, 191–2, and for criticisms of Mitchell, see Horrell 1996, 90.

[3] These aberrations were not the result of the propagating efforts of opponents who had infiltrated the church from outside but arose from within the church itself (4:18; 15:12). This epistle gives no hint of the presence of intruding agitators, though it is quite likely that the ministry of Apollos provided the catalyst for the Corinthian emphasis on wisdom.

[4] Moule (1962, 157) writes, "In the first place, the passage in 1 Cor I would probably never have been written had there not been educated Christians in that congregation who were contemptuous about the crudities of others. To some extent, then, it bears witness to the very reverse of the conditions it is often used to illustrate." On the σοφός, δυνατός, εὐγενής triad, see Wüllner 1973; 1982.

would have been a dominant minority in the congregation.[5] Effectively, these individuals would have constituted the leadership of the church.[6]

Paul portrays his relationship to his readers (his converts) as that of a father to his children (4:14–15). As their "father" he possesses a special right to direct and guide their lives. For the most part in this letter, Paul attempts to influence his converts through argument, persuasion and appeal, but on occasion he resorts to the language of threat and command (4:21; 5:3–5). Paul also describes himself as the "skilled master builder" who laid the foundations of the Corinthian community (3:10). The master builder determines how the structure should be fashioned. He thus writes to the Corinthians as the one who has the decisive say on how their new social world is to be constructed.

It is plain, however, that the authority which Paul claims for himself does not go unchallenged in Corinth. Though there is not as yet the outright opposition to Paul that will emerge in the situation underlying 2 Corinthians, a measure of resistance to him is clearly evident.[7] In the face of Corinthian criticisms, he is constrained to defend his manner of preaching (2:1–5), his style of apostleship (4:1–21), his refusal to accept their financial support (9:3–18) and (possibly) seeming inconsistencies in his conduct (9:19–23). To a certain extent, therefore, Paul has to justify his position of power to his readers.

The dominant issue of the letter is that of group boundaries.[8] The Corinthians were defining the lines of demarcation between the church and the surrounding society far too loosely for Paul's liking. Our 1 Corinthians may be interpreted as a sustained attempt by Paul to strengthen the social and ideological boundaries of the church.

4.3. The Corinthian "aberrations"

The Corinthian "aberrations" are largely failures in boundary maintenance. The Corinthians were insufficiently distinguishing

---

[5] Theissen 1982, 73–96.

[6] Erastus, the οἰκονόμος τῆς πόλεως, mentioned in Rom 16:23, would have belonged to this social grouping, as well as some of the other named individuals in the letter. On the evidence for identifying the Erastus of Rom 16:23 with the Erastus the aedile known from an inscription, see Theissen 1982, 75–83; and more recently, Clarke 1993, 46–56; Gill 1989.

[7] On the division between Paul and the Corinthians, see N. A. Dahl 1977; Fee 1987, 7–10.

[8] See Lindemann 1996 for a similar emphasis on group boundaries.

themselves from the surrounding society in their social practices and attitudes. Virtually every Corinthian "irregularity" stems from the social and cultural environment of the church. The majority of the problems in the congregation fall into one of two categories: conformity to the normal social practices and activities of the wider community; or, commitment to the ideals and beliefs of the dominant culture.[9]

4.3.1. Conformity to societal practices

Several of the Corinthian aberrations very plainly fit into this category: one brother taking another to court (6:1–11); going to prostitutes (6:15–16); participating in cultic meals (10:14–22). In resorting to litigation to settle their dispute, the offending believers were clearly following established norms of conflict resolution in Graeco-Roman society.[10] In consorting with prostitutes, the male members of the congregation involved were engaging in a commonplace activity in the Graeco-Roman world. Such conduct was not considered shameful or immoral (at least for the men involved) in pagan society. In attending idolatrous feasts, the Corinthian "strong" were obviously participating in normal cultural practices. The pressure to conform would have been high since such feasts were social occasions as much as religious rituals. Theissen has argued that the Corinthian "strong" are to be identified with the higher status members of the congregation.[11] They are the ones who would have been most integrated into Corinthian society and who would have found it most difficult to disengage from its religious aspects. Probably the "strong" at least included the "not many" of 1:26 but may have comprehended others in the congregation as well.

Conformity to the behavioural patterns of the larger society is probably also evident in the problem of grouping around names in

---

[9] The distinction between adopting the practices of outsiders and embracing the values and beliefs of outsiders reflects Barclay's (1996, 92–8) distinction between assimilation and acculturation in his study of Jews in the Mediterranean Diaspora.

[10] According to Clarke (1993, 59–71), one, and probably both, of the brothers going to court belonged to the socially prominent section of the church. He argues that the dispute between them may have been tied to a jockeying for position in the congregation.

[11] Theissen 1982, 130–1. Theissen's thesis that the "strong" and the "weak" of 1 Cor 8–10 can be divided on socio-economic lines has recently been contested by Gooch (1993). Gooch argues that the cornerstone of Theissen's argument, the vast difference in social use of food between rich and poor, is not borne out by the archaeological evidence (148–50). Horrell (1996, 108) agrees but argues that there are still other good reasons for identifying the Corinthian strong with the higher status members of the church.

1:10–17 and 3:3–5 and the problem of abuses at the Lord's Supper in
11:17–22. 1:10–11 indicates that there were divisions (σχίσματα)
and rivalries (ἔριδες) in the congregation. The Corinthians were
aligning themselves with Paul, Apollos and Cephas (and apparently
also Christ), and were boasting (3:21) about their affiliations with these
individuals.[12] The most plausible background to such quarrelling over
and grouping around names is, as Clarke and others have shown, the
Graeco-Roman practice of aligning oneself with someone of established
status and reputation in order to advance one's own status,[13] a practice
well established in the surrounding society in the areas of patronage,
politics[14] and sophistry.[15] The Corinthians were simply bringing this
normal societal practice into the life of the church. The problem of
abuses at the Lord's Supper is for Paul one of the most serious of the
Corinthian irregularities (11:17–18). It seems likely that the dis-
orderliness, drunkenness and inequality which characterized proceedings
at the celebration of the Lord's Supper at Corinth were being caused by
the Corinthian believers treating the occasion like a Graeco-Roman
dinner party.[16] At such an event, an evening meal (δεῖπνον) was
followed by a drinking party (συμπόσιον). Disorder and drunkenness
were typical of these occasions.[17] Also, it was the custom at these affairs
to assign place of prominence and quality and quantity of food according
to social rank, thus emphasizing the socio-economic differences among
those present. In their fellowship meals, the Corinthians appear to have
been following these practices, betraying how much they were
conditioned by the social patterns of the Hellenistic world.

4.3.2. Commitment to cultural values

A number of the Corinthian problems fall or may partly fall into this
category: the Corinthians' veneration of wisdom (1:18 – 3:23); their

[12] There is no indication that the groups referred to in 1:11–12 and 3:3–5 are divided on
the basis of theological differences: Clarke 1993, 91–2; Munck 1959, 135–67. It is
likely that the main division is over Paul and Apollos, ἐγὼ δὲ Κηφᾶ and ἐγὼ δὲ
Χριστοῦ being instances of "rhetorical hyperbole": so Pogoloff 1992, 178–80.
[13] Clarke 1993, 93–4.
[14] Clarke 1993, 94–5; Welborn 1987.
[15] Clarke 1993, 102–4; Witherington 1995, 100–1. According to Pogoloff (1992,172),
the Corinthians perceived Paul and Apollos as "high status rhetors suitable for divisive
allegiances". Competitive divisions over the supporters of such rhetors, Pogoloff
demonstrates, were a regular part of Hellenistic culture (173–8).
[16] See Theissen 1982, 145–68. Cf. Pogoloff 1992, 237–71; Witherington 1995, 243–7.
[17] Pogoloff 1992, 239.

toleration of the sin of incest (5:1–13); the sexual asceticism of some in the church (7:1–40); the offence which the Corinthians continued to take at Paul's refusal to accept their support during his ministry at Corinth (9:1–23); their emphasis on glossolalia (14:1–33); the denial of resurrection on the part of some in the church (15:1–58).

The nature of the wisdom prized by the Corinthians has been much debated by scholars: Paul uses the words σοφία and σοφός in such a variety of ways in chapters 1–3 of 1 Corinthians that it is difficult to pinpoint a precise and consistent target to his critique.[18] We can be fairly sure, however, that it at least partly involved Graeco-Roman rhetoric. As several recent studies have demonstrated, it is against a high regard for rhetorical sophistication that Paul's attack is mostly directed (1:17, 20; 2:1–5, 13).[19] The veneration of rhetoric was a mark of Graeco-Roman culture in the first century.[20] The high value which the Corinthians were placing on rhetorical eloquence thus reflects their adherence to a Hellenistic cultural ideal.[21]

The problem confronted in 5:1–11 is not simply the immoral behaviour of one member of the church but the acceptance of that behaviour by the rest of the church. A Corinthian believer was having sexual relations with his stepmother. In Graeco-Roman society, such a relationship was considered incestuous. It was forbidden by both Jewish and Roman law.[22] Yet, the Corinthians were letting his conduct go uncriticized and unchecked. Indeed, they remained proud (πεφυσιωμένοι ἐστέ, 5:2) and boastful (5:6). How is the church's toleration to be explained? The most popular explanation among scholars is that the Corinthians viewed the man's action as a legitimate expression of their new-found freedom in such matters as food and sex. The difficulty with this solution is that Paul makes no reference at this point to the Corinthian slogan, πάντα μοι ἔξεστιν (cf. 6:12).[23]

---

[18] σοφία is used sixteen times in 1 Cor 1–3. For a helpful analysis of σοφία and σοφός in the chapters, see Barrett 1964, 277–85.
[19] See esp. Clarke 1993, 102–5; Litfin 1994, 188–92; Pogoloff 1992, 108–27. Pogoloff argues persuasively that σοφία λόγου in 1:17 means "sophisticated speech" and must be understood against the background of the Graeco-Roman rhetorical tradition.
[20] See Litfin 1994, 109–34.
[21] It is likely that Paul was being unfavourably compared to Apollos: Witherington 1995, 124.
[22] Clarke 1993, 77–80.
[23] It is generally agreed that Paul cites Corinthian slogans at 6:12; 7:1; 8:1, 4, 8; 10:23; 15:12.

In separate studies, Chow and Clarke have recently proposed that the Corinthian congregation's acceptance of the man's behaviour is rather to be understood against the background of patronage. Chow and Clarke contend that the incestuous man was probably a patron of the church.[24] This fact alone, according to Chow and Clarke, is enough to account for the Corinthians' toleration of the man's indiscretion.

> For who would want to dishonour a powerful patron who could provide protection and benefaction to the church? On the contrary, as faithful clients, members in the Christian church should perhaps support and honour such a patron.[25]

If Clarke and Chow are right in their analysis of 1 Cor 5, in overlooking the man's actions the Corinthians were simply capitulating to the conventions of patron–client relations, and allowing these conventions to override the new ethical values of the church.

Notwithstanding the sexually promiscuous attitude of the men who were going to the prostitutes, some in Corinth took the view that, "It is well for a man not to touch a woman" (7:1). On the basis of this belief, some were practising celibacy within marriage, some appear to have been considering divorcing their partners, and some were thinking about breaking off their engagements to be married. The rationale for this sexual asceticism is much debated. But probably one of the influences on Corinthian thinking was a widespread and well documented belief in the Graeco-Roman world at the time: that by "avoiding sexual contact with another human being, one prepared oneself for union or communion with the divine".[26]

That Paul, during his ministry in Corinth, chose to remain financially independent of the Corinthians and support himself by means of his own trade was, as Fee puts it, "a festering sore between them" (cf. 2 Cor 11:7–12; 12:13–15).[27] It is likely that the dispute was partly due to the Corinthians perceiving Paul's actions according to the expectations and values of their social and cultural environment. Itinerant teachers and philosophers normally charged for their services or attached themselves – in a mutually benefiting and status-enhancing arrangement – to

---

[24] Chow 1992, 130–41; Clarke 1993, 80–5. Both Chow (135–8) and Clarke (84) suggest a financial motivation for the man's course of behaviour.

[25] Chow 1992, 140.

[26] Gundry-Volf 1996, 532.

[27] Fee 1987, 9.

patrons. Paul's refusal to accept their financial aid broke with this convention. His action probably displeased potential patrons in the church because it robbed them of the distinction of having him as their household teacher or philosopher.[28] It may even have been interpreted as a breach of the convention of friendship.[29] The fact that he supported himself by working with his hands may have added to the offence. Engaging in manual labour was generally looked down upon by cultured Greek society and considered demeaning for a philosopher. That the Corinthians were still smarting over the issue indicates the persistence of this attitude, moulded by the dominant culture, in the church.

The high premium placed by the Corinthians on glossolalia may also reflect a commitment to dominant cultural values. According to Martin, esoteric speech was viewed as high status religious behaviour in Graeco-Roman society.[30] In such a cultural context, the attraction of tongues-speaking to the status conscious Corinthians (cf. 4:8) is plain to see.

It is not easy to determine from Paul's argument in chapter 15 the actual position of the Corinthians who denied the resurrection of the dead (15:12). That they baptized for the dead (15:29), whatever exactly this practice was, at least implies that they believed in an afterlife of sorts.[31] In the light of Paul's extensive discussion of the σῶμα in resurrection in 15:35–50, it is very likely that what they particularly objected to was not the idea of the survival of the individual beyond death but that of a post-mortem existence which involves the body. In other words, their thinking was probably shaped by the hierarchical anthropological division of body and soul – with the body being accorded the lower status position – widespread in Hellenistic culture. They probably believed that at death the immortal soul is released from the mortal body. The denial of a cardinal element of the Christian faith (for Paul, the item on which his gospel stands or falls, 15:17) on the part of some Corinthian Christians on the basis of a Hellenistic cultural ideal, therefore, reflects not only their commitment to the dominant culture but also the *extent* of their commitment.

---

[28] Witherington 1995, 209.
[29] P. Marshall 1987, 245–7.
[30] D. B. Martin 1995, 88–92.
[31] D. B. Martin 1995, 107.

4.3.3. Paul's appraisal of the problems in Corinth

The overarching problem in Corinth was thus a failure to maintain clear lines of distinction between the Christian group and the wider society: the Corinthians were not sufficiently differentiating themselves in terms of their practices, beliefs and attitudes and their social and religious participation outside the church.

This is clearly Paul's diagnosis of the Corinthian aberrations. He views their quarrelling over names as "fleshly" (σαϱκικός) and "human" (κατὰ ἄνθϱωπον) behaviour (3:3), that is, as characteristic of the wider world. Their excessive interest in wisdom is for Paul a reflection of the high value placed on wisdom in Hellenistic society (1:22). Their acceptance of the conduct of the incestuous believer, as Paul sees it, betrays the "old leaven" in their midst, the pre-conversion mode of thinking of which they ought to have repented (5:6–7). In using the Graeco-Roman system to settle their dispute, the brothers of 6:1–11 were taking outside the church a matter which ought to have been resolved within the church (6:1). Those who were consorting with prostitutes were failing to realize that their bodies were now "members of Christ" (6:15). Those who were continuing in religious participation outside the church were failing to appreciate the exclusive nature of participation in Christ (10:21). Those abusing the Lord's Supper were failing to discern the distinctive nature of the social body which is the church (11:29).[32] It is not like any other Graeco-Roman *collegium*. At 15:33, in the midst of his defence of resurrection, Paul cites the epigram of Menander, "Bad company ruins good morals". Its intrusion into the argument is abrupt. Commentators labour at explaining its relevance to the polemic as a whole. But we can hardly doubt that this is a very carefully chosen saying, in Paul's opinion entirely apposite to the issue at hand. It seems to indicate a strong suspicion on Paul's part that the Corinthian deniers of bodily resurrection were simply adopting the values of their pagan friends. For Paul, therefore, the underlying problem in Corinth is weak social and ideological boundaries (cf. 6:9–11, where he has to remind the Corinthians of the decisive break from their pagan environment entailed in their baptism).

[32] Fee 1987, 564.

Excursus: Other explanations of the Corinthian aberrations

Other suggestions have been made by scholars as to the chief source of the problems in Corinth.[33] Without offering a full evaluation of all the alternatives, a brief review and assessment of the main suggestions is in order.

A once popular theory, now rightly out of favour, is that the main cause of the Corinthian deviations was Gnosticism.[34] To label the Corinthians "Gnostics" would be anachronistic, given that our evidence for Gnosticism comes from the second century CE and later. Some scholars, though, argue for an incipient or "proto-"Gnosticism in Corinth,[35] pointing to linguistic and conceptual links between Corinthian theology and later Gnosticism, for example, their claim to be πνευματικοί and possessors of σοφία and γνῶσις; their anthropological dualism and consequent devaluation of the body. But such links are superficial and misleading. Unlike the later Gnostics, the Corinthians do not appear to have considered themselves a special class of spiritual élite possessing a higher, esoteric wisdom and knowledge, concealed from the mass of ordinary Christians. In fact they claimed that "all of us possess γνῶσις" (8:1). As Martin writes, "This does not sound like the rigid epistemological hierarchy of later Gnosticism."[36] And their view of the body was not that it is evil, as the later Gnostics believed, but that it is relatively inferior to the soul or spirit.[37] Even to speak of an undeveloped or nascent form of Gnosticism at Corinth, therefore, is highly problematic, begging more questions than it answers.

Several scholars contend that Hellenistic–Judaism provides the main background to the problems at Corinth.[38] But though there are interesting parallels between Hellenistic–Jewish tradition and Corinthian Christianity, as Fee states, "what is less certain is that the parallels reflect what is essential to Judaism in this tradition rather than its helleniza-tion".[39] Certain aspects of Corinthian belief and practice simply do

[33] See Schrage 1991, 47–63.
[34] Jewett 1971, 23–40; Schmithals 1971; Wilckens 1971.
[35] Wedderburn 1987, 34–5; R. McL. Wilson 1982. Wilson (112) concludes that "what we have in Corinth . . . is not yet Gnosticism, but a kind of *gnosis*."
[36] D. B. Martin 1995, 71.
[37] D. B. Martin 1995, 71.
[38] Davis 1984; Horsley 1976; 1977; 1980; Pearson 1973.
[39] Fee 1987, 13.

not fit with Hellenistic Judaism: the sexual immorality highlighted in 5:1–13 and 6:15–20; the eating of food sacrificed to idols (8:1–13; 10:23–30); the continuing attendance of some at idolatrous feasts (10:1–22). At best the theory may account for the emphasis on wisdom,[40] but even the attempt to place the sapiential elements in Corinthian Christianity against a Jewish background inevitably founders on the fact that Paul specifically links wisdom with Greeks and not Jews (1:22).[41]

A more widely held view is that the main source of the Corinthian irregularities was an "over-realized eschatology".[42] On this analysis, the Corinthians spiritualized the resurrection, viewing it to have already occurred in their own experience (15:12). They supposed that they had already entered the kingdom and had already begun to reign (4:8). They believed that they had already come into the resurrection age and were already living "like angels" (Mark 12:25 par.). This belief, so it is argued, lies behind the problem of sexual asceticism, the problem of women praying and prophesying unveiled, the unruly behaviour at the Lord's Supper (the Corinthians supposing that they were already enjoying the abundance of the messianic banquet) and the inflated estimation of glossolalia (the Corinthians convinced that they were already speaking the language of heaven, 13:1).

But there are difficulties with this reconstruction. Firstly, the slogan of 15:12 suggests that the Corinthians doubters *denied* the resurrection of the dead; they do not appear to have been affirming (like Hymenaeus and Philetus of 2 Tim 2:17–18) that the resurrection had already taken place. Secondly, though the Corinthians would seem to have been boasting that they were fully enriched with every spiritual blessing, that they had attained the goal of their existence and were spiritually complete (τέλειος, 2:6), there is no evidence that they were advancing these claims from an eschatological standpoint.[43] In his mimicry of their boasts in 4:8, Paul makes no reference to resurrection.[44] The language here is more Stoic than eschatological. Litfin is probably right in his assessment that: "The eschatological element in this verse is purely the importation

---

[40] See Goulder 1991 for a statement of this position.
[41] Munck 1959, 148–50.
[42] Esp. Thiselton 1977/78.
[43] On the difficulties of drawing connections between Corinthian theology and the saying of Mark 12:25 par., see Deming 1995, 25–8.
[44] Cf. D. B. Martin 1995, 105.

of the Apostle and it functions as a rebuke of their attempt to emulate
... a worldly élite."[45]

It is not so much that the Corinthians lacked a *future*-eschatological
perspective. The problem seems more to be that they did not possess a
Jewish/Christian eschatological outlook at all. As Fee argues, they
probably, "translated such a view into their framework of 'spirituality',
in which they regarded their present spiritual existence as an assumption
of that which is to be, minus the physical body".[46] Their failure to
appropriate the apocalyptic dimensions of Paul's gospel is a reflection
of the continued dominance of Hellenistic patterns of thought within
the congregation.

Hurd suggests that Paul's earlier preaching in Corinth was to blame
for the defects in the Corinthian Christian faith. According to Hurd,
Paul's gospel underwent a radical shift between his founding mission in
Corinth and the writing of 1 Corinthians. Paul writes to the Corinthians
to bring them into line with his new theological and ethical position.
Hurd's thesis, however, attracts little support, due to the highly
improbable chronology and historical reconstruction on which it is
based. Hurd is obviously right to insist that Corinthian Christianity
derives from Paul's preaching. The differences between Paul and the
Corinthians that are evident in 1 Corinthians, however, are much more
readily explained by a "culturally-related ... hermeneutic"[47] at work in
the Corinthians' appropriation of Paul's gospel than by massive changes
in Paul's theology itself.

In several recent studies Stoicism has been suggested as a major
influence in Corinth.[48] The Corinthians boasts of 4:8, "Already you
have all you want! Already you have become rich! Quite apart from us
you have become kings!" fit the Stoic description of the enlightened
wise man.[49] Further points of contact with Stoic thought include the
Corinthian slogan, πάντα μοι ἔξεστιν, Corinthian views on marriage,
the Corinthian knowledge of 8:4–6 and the Corinthian claim to possess
ἐξουσία (8:9). That Stoicism was a factor affecting Corinthian thought
and practice is very likely. To admit this, however, does not undermine
the contention that the Corinthians' social and cultural environment

[45] Litfin 1994, 168–9.
[46] Fee 1987, 12.
[47] Barclay 1992, 67 n. 32.
[48] See Deming 1995; Malherbe 1994; Paige 1992.
[49] See Paige 1992, 183–4.

was the main source of the problems in the church. On the contrary. Stoic ideas and principles enjoyed a very wide currency in the first century CE and were part of the shared discourse of educated society. That the Corinthians seem responsive to certain aspects of Stoicism is no more than an indication of their receptiveness to currents of thought in their cultural environment in general.

Of the various theories proposed by scholars as to the chief source the Corinthian vagaries, the most plausible explanation is still the Corinthians' continued adherence to social and cultural norms and values. This is not to deny that there were other factors at work in the church at Corinth. But the conditioning influence of their Hellenistic environment remains the dominant force behind the beliefs and actions criticized by Paul.

4.4. Harmony with outsiders, discord within

Two further aspects of Corinthian Christianity point to the weakness of the community's boundaries. The first is the state of social harmony between Christians and non-Christians at Corinth. As John Barclay writes, "One of the most significant, but least noticed, features of Corinthian church life is the absence of conflict in the relationship between Christians and 'outsiders'."[50] Barclay highlights the contrast between the friendly relations with non-Christians enjoyed by the Corinthian believers with the social conflict and alienation experienced by the Thessalonian church in their social environment.[51] The contrast is all the more striking since these churches were founded by Paul during the same period of his missionary activity.

It has to be said that Paul is not totally disapproving of the Corinthians' close contacts with outsiders. He emphatically rejects the idea that the church should be a ghetto, divorced from the rest of society (5:10). He affirms that association with non-Christians is necessary and is to be encouraged (10:27), not least for the purpose of evangelism (14:23). He counsels believers in mixed marriages not to separate from their unbelieving spouses for the reason that "the unbelieving husband is made holy through his wife, and the unbelieving wife is made holy through her husband" (7:14). He recognizes that a degree of social

---

[50] Barclay 1992, 57.
[51] Barclay 1992, 56–60.

identification with unbelievers is necessary in order to bring them to Christ, and he offers himself as a positive example of this (9:19–23). The good social relations with outsiders enjoyed by the Christians in Corinth, then, are not unwelcomed by Paul insofar as they set up favourable conditions for the wider penetration of the gospel in Corinth.

He does, though, place certain constraints on their dealings with outsiders: by limiting some of the settings of their social interaction (6:1–11, 15–16; 8:10; 10:1–22); by advising unmarried Christians only to marry "in the Lord" (7:40); by warning them about the corrupting effects of spending too much time in the company of outsiders (15:33). And he is concerned to make the Corinthian Christians aware of the sharp social and ideological distinction between group members and non-group members. Thus he contrasts Christians and non-Christians as "saved" and "perishing" (1:18), "those who are inside" and "those outside" (5:12–13), "saints" and "unrighteous" (6:1) and "believers" and "unbelievers" (14:22–25).

The other pointer to the fragility of the church's boundaries is the lack of unity in the church. Social anthropology indicates that strong group boundaries go hand in hand with strong group identity and group solidarity. Conversely, the lack of internal cohesion in the Corinthian church suggests porous boundaries. First Corinthians reveals a number of social divisions in the church. There are the schisms over leaders in 1:10–12 (cf. 3:3–5), the dispute between the litigants of 6:1–8, the disagreement between the "weak" and the "strong" over εἰδωλόθυτα in chapters 8–10 and the divisions at the Lord's Supper in 11:17–34. From Paul's characterization of Corinthian church life, it would not appear that this is a cohesive community with a strong corporate identity. We do not gain the impression that the church is at all a close-knit group with a keen sense of "belonging *together*" (as opposed to belonging to parties within the congregation). By continuing to dine at the pagan temples, the Corinthian "strong" evince a higher regard for the approval of their non-Christians friends and associates than for the sensitivities of their "weaker" fellow believers.

The internal cohesion of the church is of major concern to Paul in this epistle. Throughout he lays heavy emphasis on group solidarity (1:13; 3:16–17; 10:16–17; 11:29; 12:12–27) and "brotherhood" (1:10, 26; 5:11; 6:5–8; 8:11–13). He asserts the right of the community to govern the lives of its individual members (5:1–13; 6:1–11). And he exhorts his readers to place concern for one's fellow group-members above one's own interests (8:10–13; 10:24). Whatever the other social circles to which the Corinthians belong, it is the ἐκκλησία which is now to be their primary network of social ties. Paul's desire for group solidarity in the Corinthian church comports with his concern for group boundaries since the one is the concomitant of the other.[52]

4.5. Categorizing Corinthian Christianity

Using Mary Douglas' social-anthropological group/grid model, as modified by Malina,[53] the believing community in Corinth may be defined as a "weak group" with a "high grid".[54] In this scheme of analysis, the parameter "group" measures the extent to which individuals perceive themselves as embedded in a particular social body in society (in this case, the ἐκκλησία). "Grid" relates to the degree to which those individuals assent to the norms, values and perceptions of the surrounding society (in this case, Graeco-Roman culture). A weak group, according to Malina, is marked by "fuzzy lines of distinction between ingroup and outgroup and highly porous boundaries between interfacing and interacting groups".[55] It is characterized by individualism and shallow group identity.[56] A weak group with a high grid closely adheres to the symbolic and value system of the larger culture, adopting societal patterns of perception and evaluation. Such a grouping, according to Malina, is both "socially and intellectually open".[57]

To what extent may the Corinthian church be described as a "sect"? There can be little doubt, in the light of the foregoing analysis, that the category "sect" as classically defined by Troeltsch is quite inapplicable

---

[52] For Mitchell, church unity is the overriding burden of 1 Corinthians: Paul's aim in writing is to "urge reconciliation of divided factions" (1991, 303). While fully recognizing Paul's stress on community solidarity, it is on strong group boundaries that his main emphasis lies. The basic problem of weak group boundaries underlies the internal divisions of the congregation.

[53] Douglas 1973, 77–92; Malina 1986. Cf. Carter 1997.

[54] Malina 1986, 17–19, 45ff.

[55] Malina 1986, 18.

[56] Malina 1986, 18–19.

[57] Malina 1986, 52. There are other features of the Corinthian church as portrayed by Paul which correspond to the weak group/high grid type (Malina 1986, 47–54): the priority of the individual over the group rite (11:17–34); an instrumental and practical view of the physical body as the means to an end (cf. 6:13); the prizing of status and achievement (1:26–31; 4:8–13); tolerance of different beliefs and standards of behaviour; a stress on individual freedom (8:9).

to the Corinthian congregation. The church at Corinth exhibits none of the characteristic traits of Troeltsch's sect-type.[58] It is not radical in social disposition. It is not indifferent or hostile to the world. It is not egalitarian. It is not characterized by a strong sense of love between its members. What then of Wilson's sect sub-types?[59] Even though some similarities between the church at Corinth and one or two of Wilson's sect-types may be found, the Corinthian Christian community fails to meet the basic criterion for inclusion under one of Wilson's categorizations: it is not a "deviant religious movement". The Corinthian believers neither consider themselves as religious deviants in their socio-religious environment nor are they defined or treated as such by others. To be sure, the Corinthian Christians distinguish themselves from the rest of society, as πνευματικοί to ψυχικοί; but, as Barclay notes, that distinction engenders neither a sense of hostility nor a sense of exclusivity.[60] Their involvement in the church is not accompanied by any significant social or moral change.[61] They are able to practise their faith while remaining fully integrated into Corinthian society, taking part in the social, economic, civic, legal and even religious aspects of life in the city. The Corinthian Christian community, as Barclay puts it, is a club, in which the Corinthians "could gladly participate . . . as one segment of their lives. But the segment, however, important, is not the whole and not the centre."[62] In sum, on the accepted sociological definitions of a "sect", the Corinthian congregation must be judged thoroughly *un*sectarian.

4.6. The Corinthian evaluation of κόσμος

It can be taken for granted that the Corinthians would have used and understood the term κόσμος in accordance with standard Greek linguistic usage. For them, κόσμος would have had its usual positive connotations of order, unity, beauty, perfection and so on.

Those members of the congregation with any level of education (a very basic level would have been enough) would almost certainly have been acquainted with the world-view evoked by κόσμος (= world/

---

[58] See pp. 7–8.
[59] See pp. 8–9.
[60] Barclay 1992, 69–70.
[61] Barclay 1992, 70.
[62] Barclay 1992, 71.

universe). This understanding of the world, as the previous chapter shows, belonged to the common cultural discourse of educated society and was part of the Corinthians' cultural heritage.[63] Judging by their commitment to cultural values, they would probably have broadly accepted that world view and its ideological implications.

It is no accident that the most positive use of the word κόσμος in the whole epistle is located in a Corinthian slogan cited by Paul. The twin affirmations of 1 Cor 8:4, οὐδὲν εἴδωλον ἐν κόσμῳ and οὐδεὶς θεὸς εἰ μὴ εἷς, were being advanced by the Corinthian strong as the theological grounds for their freedom to eat meat sacrificed to idols and to dine in the temples. It can be judged from 1 Cor 8:4–6 – it is likely that these verses as a whole reflect their cosmological perspective – that the Corinthian strong (whose position seems to be the dominant ethos of the church) viewed the κόσμος (= world/universe) as a positively valued ordered unity, entirely free of malignant forces and devoid of corrupting influences, flowing from God, governed and directed by him.[64]

It is possible that another glimpse of the Corinthian evaluation of κόσμος may be found in 5:10b. Again κόσμος here has the standard sense "world/universe". In 5:9–13, Paul corrects a Corinthian misunderstanding of a charge he had given them in his previous letter, namely, that they should dissociate themselves from sexually immoral people. Paul insists that he was referring then to immoral Christians and not to sexually immoral people in general since that would involve completely withdrawing from the κόσμος. As Fee points out, it seems likely that the Corinthians themselves had exploited the ambiguity of Paul's words in his earlier letter, highlighting, in their letter to him, the absurd consequences of his advice if taken at face value. If this is the case, then Paul could well be repeating here a Corinthian rejoinder from their letter to him: "it is as you say, if I had meant that, you 'would then need to go out of the κόσμος (= world/universe)'".[65]

It may be conjectured, then, that the Corinthians combined a high view of the world as κόσμος, in line with Greek and Hellenistic tradition, with Jewish and Christian ideas. One may perhaps draw a

---

[63] See pp. 41, 64.
[64] See pp. 140–1.
[65] Cf. Fee 1987, 222–3. Thus, their original claim may not have been dissimilar to Philo's assertion (*Leg. All.* 3.5) that it is impossible to leave the κόσμος (= world/universe).

parallel with Philo. Very clearly, Philo develops a Greek philosophical view of the world as κόσμος, heavily indebted to Platonism and Stoicism. Yet he endeavours to harmonize this basic world-view with the tenets, traditions, and Scriptures of his Jewish faith. Within a Christian context, one can imagine a similar *modus operandi* in the church at Corinth.

The view persists that the Corinthians held to a radical physical / spiritual dualism (often referred to as "Hellenistic dualism") which eschews and disparages the material world.[66] But as emphasized in the previous chapter, such an extreme interpretation of Platonic dualism did not emerge in the ancient world until the second and third centuries CE. It is, therefore, both misleading and anachronistic to import this conception into a first-century situation.

The Corinthians' broad acceptance of the view of the world encoded by κόσμος, would have encouraged and legitimated their interaction with and participation in the larger society. The most acculturated members of the church would have seen the whole κόσμος (embracing the whole social order) as worthy of positive engagement (with even fewer barriers than Philo, judging from 1 Cor 8–10) and would have viewed integration into the κόσμος as a highly laudable endeavour. The ideology linked with κόσμος (= world / universe) would also have legitimated the church's imitation of the practices of the wider society and absorption of the values of the general culture. The Corinthians would have viewed their new religious club, or *collegium,* as a microcosm of the larger society and of the whole κόσμος.[67] They would have sought to mirror in their group norms and intra-group relations the norms and values of the dominant culture.

4.7. Conclusion

This chapter has sketched the context of utterance of 1 Corinthians. The main social issue at stake in the letter, we have suggested, is group boundaries. The Corinthians were drawing their social and ideological boundaries far too loosely for Paul's liking. Paul writes to sharpen the distinction between the church and the surrounding society. His social goal is to build up the boundaries of the Corinthian community and to

---

[66] E.g. Fee 1987, 11.
[67] Pogoloff 1992, 274.

engender in the congregation a clearer sense of its distinctive religious, moral and social identity.

The Corinthians would have understood and employed the term κόσμος in line with standard usage. They would probably have accepted, at least in broad terms, the world-view and ideology linked with κόσμος. That ideology would have encouraged and reinforced the Corinthians' integration into the larger society and their modelling of the church on dominant cultural norms and values.

This, then, is the social and rhetorical context within which Paul's uses of κόσμος and their social functions are to be interpreted. To the investigation of these uses, we now turn.

5

κόσμος in 1 Corinthians

5.1. Introduction

There are three broad features of Paul's usage of the term κόσμος in 1 Corinthians which the problem of weak group boundaries, highlighted in the previous chapter, immediately helps to explain. Firstly, there is the term's frequency of occurrence. More than half of the total uses of the term in the undisputed Pauline letters are found in this epistle. Secondly, there is the tone of Paul's usage. The term is almost consistently used in a negative way throughout the letter. Thirdly, there is the sociological edge to Paul's usage. There is a fairly constant stress in Paul's usage on the contrast between the κόσμος and the church. These general observations are sufficient to show that the pattern of usage of κόσμος in 1 Corinthians is highly context-specific. It *reflects* the situation which Paul is addressing – specifically the issue of group boundaries at Corinth – and it is intended to *affect* that situation.

Precisely how Paul's deployment of κόσμος is meant to operate within its original context of utterance is the central concern of the present chapter. What follows is thus a close examination of the κόσμος texts in 1 Corinthians, observing how Paul's specific uses of the term in their immediate linguistic and literary contexts work toward his larger social goal. Before launching into this task, however, it is necessary to highlight briefly the main theological context of reference for his usage.

5.2. The theological context of reference

Chapter 2, drawing on the insights of Roger Fowler, indicated that there are three larger contexts influencing the linguistic content of Paul's epistles: the context of culture, the context of utterance and the context of reference. Chapter 3 discussed the cultural and historical context of

Paul's usage of κόσμος (and κτίσις). Chapter 4 dealt with the utterance context of 1 Corinthians. Mention must now be made of the epistolary context of reference. By this is meant, modifying Fowler somewhat, the theological theme or themes dominating the epistle, or the theological point of view which determines most or much of what Paul has to say in the letter.

The dominant theological perspective of 1 Corinthians is an apocalyptic one. The term "apocalyptic" is widely used in biblical studies. However, there is no commonly accepted definition of the term. One could almost say that there are as many definitions of "apocalyptic" as there are scholars who employ the category. Nevertheless, there are certain characteristics of the apocalyptic outlook upon which there is a measure of scholarly agreement. These features are listed by Wayne Meeks:[1]

1. Secrets have been revealed to the author or prophet.

2. These secrets have to do with a cosmic transformation that will happen very soon. Time moves toward that climax, which separates "this age" from "the age to come."

3. Central among the events to happen "at the end of days" is *judgment*: The rectification of the world order, the separation of the good from the wicked, and assigning the appropriate reward or punishment.

4. Consequently the apocalyptic universe is characterized by three corresponding dualities: (a) the cosmic duality heaven/earth, (b) the temporal duality this age/the age to come, and (c) a social duality: the sons of light/the sons of darkness, the righteous/the unrighteous, the elect/the world.

These elements are all present in 1 Corinthians. The gospel is set forth by Paul as "secret and hidden" wisdom "which God decreed before the ages" (2:7) and which he has now revealed (ἀπεκάλυψεν ὁ θεός, 2:10) to believers. Paul speaks of "the present crisis" (7:26) and declares that the time "has grown short" (7:29). The climax to which all time is moving is cosmic in scope (15:27–28). History is divided into two ages, though Paul only speaks of "this age" (ὁ αἰὼν οὗτος, 1:20; 2:6–8; 3:18), not of the coming age. This is because, for Paul, the new age has already dawned as a result of the death and resurrection of Christ. Hence, believers are those "on whom the ends of the ages have come"

---

[1] Meeks 1983b, 689. For a review and critique of the use of the term "apocalyptic" in Pauline scholarship, see Matlock 1996.

(10:11). God will finally consummate the ages with the revelation (ἀποκάλυψις) of Jesus Christ (1:7; cf. 11:26; 15:23; 16:22). This is an event which believers eagerly anticipate (ἀπεκδεχομένους, 1:7). Paul equates this event with the eschatological "day of the Lord" (1:8; 5:5). On that "day" each person's work will be revealed with fire (3:10–15). Paul states that when the Lord comes he will "bring to light the things now hidden in darkness" (4:5). The judgement will affect angels (6:2–3) and the principalities and powers (15:24). As well as judgement (5:5; 6:2,3; 11:32; 15:24–26), Paul expects the return of Christ to be accompanied by the resurrection of the dead (6:13–14; 15:12–57). Jesus' resurrection was the first stage of the general resurrection (15:20–23). In the light of the apocalyptic event of Christ, reality is now characterized by the cosmic duality of heaven and earth (15:47–49), the temporal duality of this age and (implicitly) the age to come (or kingdom of God, 4:20; 6:10–11; 15:50), and the social and ethical dualities of "saved" and "perishing" (1:18–21), "believers" and "unbelievers" (14:22–25), "saints" and "unrighteous" (6:1–2).

First Corinthians is thus shot through with apocalyptic motifs and structures of thought. The major arguments and discussions of the letter take place within an apocalyptic frame of reference: the treatment of wisdom and Corinthian factionalism (1:18–31; 2:6–16; 3:10–15, 18–23; 4:5); Paul's responses to the issues of incest in the church (5:5, 9–13), going to the courts (6:1–11), going to prostitutes (6:14), marriage and celibacy (7:25ff), eating food offered to idols (10:11, 14–22), abuses at the Lord's Supper (11:27–32); Paul's reflections on love (13:8–12); the discussion of resurrection (15:1–58). The whole epistle opens and closes with a reference to the return of Christ (1:7; 16:22). The apocalyptic viewpoint pervades the letter. It is this theological perspective, as I will show, which largely governs Paul's usage of κόσμος in the letter.

5.3. Examination of texts

κόσμος appears in 1 Corinthians at 1:20, 21, 27(×2), 28; 2:12; 3:19, 22; 4:9, 13; 5:10(×2); 6:2(×2); 7:31(×2), 33, 34; 8:4; 11:32; 14:10. There is a noticeable concentration of occurrences in the first main section of epistle, 1:18 – 3:23, where Paul deals with the issue of wisdom. κόσμος is found in this section eight times. The word occurs ten times over the next four chapters, four of these instances in the space of a few verses (7:31–34). After the occurrence at 8:4, the rate of usage drops significantly. It appears only twice in the rest of the letter.[2]

5.3.1. The world's wisdom overturned by the cross (1:20–21)

In 1:18–25, Paul develops the theme of the gospel as the power and wisdom of God. To unbelievers it appears as folly, but in the cross God has overturned the world and its wisdom. Paul's aim in this section (and up to 2:16) is to combat the overvaluation of culturally defined wisdom among his readers. The gospel is true σοφία and this is the complete opposite of the world's wisdom.

In v. 18, Paul sets out a soteriological and social contrast using the present participles ἀπολλυμένοι and σῳζομένοι. The division of humankind into "those who are perishing" and those "who are being saved", it becomes evident in vv. 22–24, overrides the old division of humanity (from a Jewish perspective) into Ἰουδαῖοι καὶ Ἕλληνες. The distinction between the ἀπολλυμένοι and the σῳζομένοι is expressed in their reactions to the cross. To those who are perishing, the message of the cross appears as foolishness. To those on their way to salvation, that message is the power of God. The soteriological contrast of v. 18, however, is not the central antithesis of this section but rather paves the way for it. The fundamental contrast emerges in vv. 20–21: the contrariety between the wisdom of the world and the wisdom of God.

κόσμος in vv. 20–21 is linked with θεός as its contextual opposite and ὁ αἰὼν οὗτος as its contextual synonym. The opposition of κόσμος and θεός is clear from the contrast between ἡ σοφία τοῦ κόσμου and ἡ σοφία τοῦ θεοῦ. The synonymous relation of κόσμος and ὁ αἰὼν οὗτος is evident from the interchange of the phrases τοῦ αἰῶνος τούτου and τοῦ κόσμου in the related clauses of v. 20 (cf. 3:18–19). These linkages indicate that κόσμος is being used with the sense "this world" in accordance with apocalyptic two world/age dualism.[3]

---

[2] We shall not be looking at the occurrence of κόσμος in 14:10 where the word bears the sense "inhabited world". In 14:10, Paul notes that there are many tongues in the κόσμος. This is a simple statement of fact on Paul's part. It is clear that the word κόσμος is not at all in the foreground and has no rhetorical significance in Paul's discussion of glossolalia in chapter 14.

[3] Paul, it is true, does not actually use the full phrase ὁ κόσμος οὗτος at this point (though, he will do so at 3:19, 5:10 and 7:31b). The parallel with ὁ αἰὼν οὗτος, however, clearly indicates that this is an instance of κόσμος on its own bearing the sense of ὁ κόσμος οὗτος. Cf. Bultmann 1952, 256.

In his definition of apocalyptic thought cited above, Meeks empha-sizes the temporal aspect of the two world / age dualism: "this age" and "the age to come". But the dualism also had a spatial aspect: "this world" and "the world to come".[4] That the dualism could be expressed in terms of two successive ages and two successive worlds reflects the fact that the future blessing was conceived of in Jewish apocalyptic thought both as a new era and as a new or renewed creation. It also reflects the fact that the underlying Hebrew term עדלם in post-biblical Hebrew under-went a development in meaning from "age" to "world".[5]

The doctrine of the two ages or worlds developed gradually in Jewish thought. It is rooted in Old Testament eschatology. It is implicit in Qumran talk of the "epoch of wickedness" (CD 6:10, 14; 15:7; 1QpHab. 5:7–8). There is no uncontested evidence for the explicit contrast between the two world / ages, however, in Jewish texts written before 70 CE.[6] The distinction is found in the *Similitudes of Enoch* ("this age of unrighteousness", *1 Enoch* 48:7; "the age that is to become", 71:15). But the dating of this work is vigorously debated by scholars, though many would affirm a pre-70 CE date. [7]

The dualism is explicitly expressed in the classic Jewish apocalyptic writings, *4 Ezra* and *2 Baruch. 4 Ezra* 7:50 states that "the Most High has made not one world but two". According to *4 Ezra,* the present world is full of sadness, infirmities and evil (4:27–28). Its entrances are "narrow and sorrowful and troublesome; they are few and evil, full of dangers and involved in great hardships" (7:12). The present world is marked by corruption and sinful indulgences (7:112–14). The future world, on the other hand, is full of glory (7:112). Its entrances "are broad and safe, and really yield the fruit of immortality" (7:13). It is marked by righteousness and truth (7:113–14). The author states that

---

[4] *4 Ezra* 7:50, 111–13; *2 Apoc. Bar.* 15:8; 51:14–16.

[5] See esp. Jenni 1952; 1953; also Guhrt 1978, 827–9; Holtz 1990, 45–6; Stone 1989,149–80; summarized in 1990, 218–19.

[6] Tob 14:5 mentions the "time of that age", when the Jews return to Jerusalem, but there is no contrast in this passage with the present age. The later Syrian text of Sir 18:10 distinguishes between "this age" and "the age of the pious", but the earlier Greek text simply reads ἐν ἡμέρᾳ αἰῶνος. *T. Iss.* 4:6 talks of "the world's error", but again there is no reference to a world to come. In *1 Enoch* 16:1, the phrase "great age", ὁ αἰὼν ὁ μέγας, appears, referring to the duration of the world's history. But this probably reflects the influence of the Platonic "Great Year" rather than the two world/age scheme: so Sasse 1964b, 203.

[7] See the discussion in Suter 1979, 23–32.

while this world was made for the sake of the many, the world to come was made for the sake of the few (8:1). The dividing point between the two worlds is the day of judgement (7:113).

According to *2 Baruch* this world is "a struggle and an effort with much trouble" (*2 Apoc. Bar.* 15:8). It is polluted by great wickedness (21:19) and present evils (44:9). It is a world characterized by affliction (51:14) and corruption (40:3) and is of limited duration (48:50). The coming world, on the other hand, is "a crown with great glory" (15:8). It is a "world that does not make those who come to it older" (51:16; cf. 44:12) and which itself has no end (48:50).[8]

Paul, at 1 Cor 1:20–21 and elsewhere in his writings, not only reflects apocalyptic two world / age dualism, he is one of the earliest witnesses for it. Depending on the dating of *Similitudes of Enoch,* he may be *the* earliest witness for the antithesis, though of course Paul (in the undisputed letters) talks only of the present world / age. The two-age scheme is attested in the traditions of the sayings of Jesus in the Synoptic Gospels,[9] but as written works the Synoptic Gospels post-date Paul, whatever earlier material they may contain. More significantly, Paul is the earliest witness for the use of the word κόσμος to designate "this world". If 1 Corinthians precedes Galatians, 1 Corinthians contains the earliest recorded examples of the apocalyptic employment of κόσμος in ancient literature.[10]

The apocalyptic sense of κόσμος constitutes a significant departure from standard Greek usage of κόσμος = world/universe. The referent is still the social and physical world of common experience. But there is a substantial change in the understanding of the referent. As indicated in the previous chapter, the Corinthians would have used and understood κόσμος in accordance with the linguistic conventions, and would probably have been influenced by the world-view established by these conventions. 1 Cor 8:4 certainly points in this direction. It is scarcely imaginable that Paul would have been unaware of the provocative nature

---

[8] Cf. also *Apoc. Abr.* 17:17; *Bib. Ant.* 3:10; 19:7; 34:3; *2 Enoch* 42:3; 43:3; 50:2; 61:2; 65:1, 3–4, 8; 66:6, 8. The two world/age scheme also occurs in rabbinic literature: *'Abot* 2:7; *Gen. Rab.* 44:22.

[9] Matt 12:32; Mark 10:30 = Luke 18:30; Luke 16:8; 20:34–35. Cf. the phrase ἡ συντέλεια αἰῶνος / τοῦ αἰῶνος in Matt 13:39, 40, 49; 24:3; 28:20.

[10] The deprecatory use of κόσμος, informed by apocalyptic two world/age dualism, is attested in different strands of New Testament thought (John 1:10; 8:23; 12:25, 31; 15:18–19, etc.; James 1:27; 2:5; 4:4; 2 Peter 1:4; 2:20; 1 John 2:15–17; 3:13; 3:17, etc.). It is not, therefore, a distinctively *Pauline* contribution to Christian vocabulary.

of his new apocalyptic deployment of the term for a relatively cultured Gentile audience. He must have known that he was utilizing the term in a way that ran counter to his readers' linguistic expectations and cultural values, even if he had already introduced them to this usage in his ministry in Corinth or in his previous letter.[11] It seems highly likely that he both anticipated and aimed at the unsettling effect. It is generally agreed that in 1:18 – 3:23, Paul is engaged in a terminological battle with his readers, taking up and redefining Corinthian watchwords: σοφία, σοφός, πνευματικός, ψυχικός, τέλειος, νήπιος. We know from 8:4 (and possibly 5:10b) that κόσμος *is* an item of *their* vocabulary. It seems to reasonable to suppose that κόσμος is one of the Corinthian catchwords which Paul in 1:18 – 3:23 is – quite deliberately – polemically re-using. The relatively high number of instances of the word in this section supports this conclusion.

κόσμος in 1:20–21 embraces humanity, both Gentile and Jewish humanity (vv. 22–24). It comprehends "culture",[12] again both Graeco-Roman and Jewish culture,[13] but it is also more than human culture. It is a "cosmological" reality as well as an "historical" one,[14] in line with apocalyptic thought in which the present world/age is a spatio-temporal entity. As the sphere of opposition to God, it probably includes spiritual opposition to God as well as human, since Paul states in 2:6–8 that the present age is dominated by ἄρχοντες τοῦ αἰῶνος τούτου, spiritual powers operating behind human leaders, who are doomed to perish.[15] There is, however, particular emphasis in these verses on the human aspect of "this world" (cf. τῶν ἀνθρώπων, 1:25).

Having announced in 1:19, the apocalyptic fulfilment of God's promise to "destroy the wisdom of the wise" and thwart "the discernment of the discerning" (Isa 29:14), and having taunted the wise man, the

---

[11] 1 Cor 5:10 and 8:4 seem to indicate that if he had done so, the apocalyptic usage had not caught on with his readers.

[12] Meeks 1993, 62.

[13] γραμματεύς in v. 20 is a Jewish technical term for a rabbi or teacher of the law; see Pogoloff 1992, 160. The triad σοφός, γραμματεύς, συζητητής in v. 20 is thus probably meant to cover the wise and learned of both Greek and Jewish cultures.

[14] *Contra* Bultmann 1952, 254.

[15] Interpreters are divided over whether the ἄρχοντες τοῦ αἰῶνος τούτου of 2:6–8 are human rulers (esp. those responsible for the crucifixion of Jesus) or evil supernatural powers, with an increasing number suggesting that both are in view. ἄρχοντες probably refers jointly to human and spiritual rulers. The dual reference is in line with the apocalyptic world-view which sees a struggle between God and evil spiritual forces behind events in human history (e.g. Dan 10:20–21). It is also in accord with a theme in the

scribe and the debater of "this age" in the light of this, Paul asks in v. 20b, οὐχὶ ἐμώρανεν ὁ θεὸς τὴν σοφίαν τοῦ κόσμου; "Has not God made foolish the wisdom of the world?" The genitive τοῦ κόσμου indicates belonging: God has nullifed the wisdom which is *possessed* by the world. As Conzelmann states, κόσμος "appears here as . . . the bearer of 'its' wisdom".[16] With ἐμώρανεν Paul indicates that God has actively *made* the wisdom of the world to appear as foolishness. God has turned the world's wisdom into its very antithesis, foolishness. As Godet states, "He has, as it were, *befooled* wisdom."[17] God's mockery of the world and its wisdom corresponds to the destruction (ἀπολῶ) of the wisdom of the wise, as predicted by Isaiah. The thought is thoroughly apocalyptic. In the event of the cross, God has initiated the change of the ages. The old world/age, the κόσμος, has been judged and condemned. Its wisdom has been destroyed, cast aside and ridiculed.

In v. 21 Paul states, ἐν τῇ σοφίᾳ τοῦ θεοῦ οὐκ ἔγνω ὁ κόσμος διὰ τῆς σοφίας τὸν θεόν, "in the wisdom of God, the world did not know God through wisdom". The verb γινώσκω is used here with the Hebraic sense of acknowledging and obeying.[18] The knowledge of God which Paul has in view here is thus what might be called a "saving" knowledge of God. Paul insists that the world has not come to know God in a saving way. The κόσμος is outside the scope of salvation.

The linkage of κόσμος with the verb γινώσκω has the effect of presenting the κόσμος as a sentient subject. The semi-personification of κόσμος in this verse, and perhaps also in the previous verse, might suggest that the κόσμος is being cast here in the role of an apocalyptic anti-godly power, incognizant of and inimical to God's purposes.[19]

It will not do, therefore, in the light of vv. 20–21, merely to say that the wisdom of the world has been superseded or transcended by a fuller

---

Gospel tradition: that spiritual forces were at work in the events leading up to the crucifixion of Jesus (e.g. Luke 22:3, 53). For a defence of this interpretation, see esp. Kovacs 1989. Cf. Bockmuehl 1990, 163 (arguing for a dual reference with particular emphasis on the human side); D. B. Martin 1995, 62–3; Reid 1993, 748; Theissen 1987, 374–8; Wink 1984, 44–5.

16 Conzelmann 1975, 43.
17 Godet 1886, 94.
18 Schmitz 1976, 395–7.
19 Cf. Bultmann 1952, 257.

revelation.[20] The world's wisdom and the word of the cross are here set in complete antithesis. There is no continuity between them. There are on entirely opposite sides of the apocalyptic divide.

1 Cor 1:20–21, then, presents us with a very different assessment of the world as κόσμος to that of the Greek and Hellenistic world-view. The κόσμος is linked with the old outgoing age (ὁ αἰὼν οὗτος). Its wisdom has been made foolish (ἐμώρανεν) by God. It has not known (οὐκ ἔγνω) God. These are hardly the standard linguistic or conceptual linkages of κόσμος for educated (or moderately educated) Greek readers.

Paul's deployment of κόσμος in vv. 20–21 can be understood in terms of linguistic defamiliarization, or uncoding and recoding, as discussed in chapter 2.[21] Paul takes up a familiar term, a word of high emotive meaning (since the ideal it stood for belonged to the Greek *paideia*), uncodes some of its standard associations and recodes new links. In the process he challenges the world-view and ideology borne by the conventional linkages and encodes a different and new social meaning.

Chapter 3 argued that κόσμος (= world / universe), as official and legitimated language, tended to endorse and reinforce the norms, values, structures and goals of the existing social order. By habitualization (uncritical acceptance), the encoded social meaning tended to be seen as natural. Paul skilfully turns the conventional ideological associations of κόσμος to his advantage. By linking κόσμος with ὁ αἰὼν οὗτος, the old age deposed in the apocalyptic judgement of the cross, Paul sets the dominant social and value system conventionally associated with, and legitimized by, κόσμος in *antithesis* to God's new order. He cleverly stands the ideology of κόσμος on its head. As suggested in the previous chapter, the Corinthians would probably have accepted, to some extent, the ideology of κόσμος and may well have appealed to it to justify their social and ideological integration into the larger society and dominant culture. By discrediting the κόσμος Paul thus undermines what may well have been one of the main theoretical bases for their society-conforming style of faith.

---

[20] According to Héring (1962, 11), the wisdom of the world is human philosophy insofar as it is equipped for recognizing the revelation of God in nature. For Davis (1984, 73), it is the prior revelation of God in the Torah. Neither suggestion can be sustained from the text.

[21] See pp. 27–30.

In 1:18–25, then, Paul builds an apocalyptic contrast with the σῳζόμενοι/πιστεύοντες/κλητοί on the one side, and the ἀπολλυμένοι and the κόσμος on the other. Paul counts his readers among the σῳζόμενοι, and thus on the right side of the apocalyptic fence. They stand in antithetical relation to the κόσμος and at complete variance with its values (though Paul will later accuse his readers of acting as though they still belonged to the old world/age, 3:1–4). Paul, therefore, utilizes κόσμος negatively in this context to press the *distinction* between the church and the wider society and to construct for his readers an *alternative* social world and symbolic universe.

5.3.2. The world's values overturned in the church (1:26–28)

In 1:26–31, Paul argues that God's overturning of the world's value-system is evident in the social make-up of the Corinthian church itself. Paul contends that God's elect is not society's élite. God does not work with the canons of honour and value operative in the dominant culture. Indeed, he has shattered these conventional canons in the cross. The social composition of the Corinthian community thus bears witness to God's reversal of the world's estimations of wisdom, power and social worth.

He invites his readers to consider their social circumstances at the time of their "calling" (κλῆσις). "Not many" (οὐ πολλοί) of their number, he reminds them, could be counted among the σοφοί, δυνατοί and εὐγενεῖς of Graeco-Roman society. To this triad, Paul attaches the term, κατὰ σάρκα. The word σάρξ here carries apocalyptic associations and signifies the sphere of opposition of God.[22] κατὰ σάρκα is the point of view which is characteristic of this sphere. The prized social distinctions of the Hellenistic world are thus consigned by Paul to the old world/age. They have no relevance to God and no place in the church.

God's way of working, Paul argues in vv. 27–28, stands in the sharpest possible contrast to the value-system of the κόσμος, the present world. God has chosen τὰ μωρὰ τοῦ κόσμου, τὰ ἀσθενῆ τοῦ κόσμου and τὰ ἀγενῆ τοῦ κόσμου καὶ τὰ ἐξουθενημένα. The genitive τοῦ κόσμου does not indicate "belonging to", as in v. 21, but has the

---

[22] The phrase κατὰ σάρκα carries apocalyptic connotations at Rom 8:4, 5, 12, 13; 2 Cor 5:16; 10:2, 3; 11:18; Gal 4:23, 29. On σάρξ as an apocalyptic term, see Barclay 1988, 205–15.

sense of "in the estimation of" or "from the perspective of".[23] Paul's point is that God chose what is regarded as foolish, weak, low and despised from the point of view of the κόσμος. The expression τοῦ κόσμου thus correlates with κατὰ σάρκα in the previous verse. God's purpose in operating in this way, Paul indicates by the three ἵνα clauses, is to shame the wise and powerful and to destroy the existing order of things. The third ἵνα clause, ἵνα τὰ ὄντα καταργήσῃ, points to God's ultimate aim.[24] The terminology here is significant. τὰ ὄντα is an expression used in Greek cosmological discussion for the things of which the physical universe is comprised.[25] The verb καταργέω is employed by Paul with reference to final eschatological destruction.[26] Paul, therefore, seems to be claiming here that it is God's ultimate intention to demolish the established cosmic order. God's overturning of the values of the κόσμος is part and parcel of an apocalyptic judgement on the κόσμος which will culminate in its total destruction.[27] Correspondingly, God's call of the Corinthians is part of his purpose, which he is now working out, to establish a brand new creation.

Paul, here, thus continues his defamiliarizing use of κόσμος. He links κόσμος with σάρξ, a realm separated from and in rebellion against God. With the contrasts τὰ μωρὰ/τοὺς σοφούς, τὰ ἀσθενῆ/τὰ ἰσχυρά, and τὰ μὴ ὄντα/τὰ ὄντα, Paul sharpens the opposition between θεός and κόσμος, established in vv. 20–22: God has chosen (ἐξελέξατο ὁ θεός) the very things and people written off by the κόσμος. However, the linkage with τὰ ὄντα indicates that

[23] To take the genitive as meaning "the foolish element in the world" would imply, as Barrett (1968, 58) states, "a world that is partly foolish and partly wise, and it is doubtful whether Paul intended to be as complimentary as this".
[24] Conzelmann 1975, 50.
[25] Kahn 1973, 445–6.
[26] The verb occurs in this letter at 1:28; 2:6; 6:13; 13:8(×2), 10, 11; 15:24, 26. Each time it refers to final eschatological destruction
[27] The cosmological sense of ἵνα τὰ ὄντα καταργήσῃ is resisted by most commentators. Fee (1987, 83) rejects a cosmological reading of this phrase on the basis that Paul's language is rhetorical and eschatological. But the rhetorical style of vv. 27–28 hardly rules out the inference that Paul is making a theological/cosmological statement. And the eschatological nature of Paul's language hardly precludes its also being cosmological since apocalyptic eschatology is cosmic eschatology. The cosmological interpretation is supported by the Jewish apocalyptic background: the notion that God will bring the existing spatio-temporal world to a cataclysmic end is a standard apocalyptic motif. It is also supported by Paul's affirmation in 7:31b: παράγει γὰρ τὸ σχῆμα τοῦ κόσμου τούτου. See further below, pp. 130–6.

Paul is retaining the cosmological overtones of the term in conventional Greek usage of κόσμος (= world/universe). The term continues to bear the core sense "world", established in the standard usage and continues to be linked with the social and physical world of his readers' actual experience. He casts that world, though, in a quite different light.

In vv. 27–28, Paul sets the church, and here it is quite specifically the Corinthian church, in antithesis to the κόσμος. The Corinthian church, Paul claims, was founded on the basis of criteria entirely at odds with the values of the κόσμος. The church is the reverse-image of the dominant cultural value-system. The Corinthians' continued adherence to the practices and ideals of the general society was the main cause of the problems in the community. The Corinthians may have wanted their community to be a microcosm of the larger society and of the κόσμος, reflecting in its norms, values and structures those of the wider world. Paul strikes at the heart of such thinking. The Christian congregation is not to be a *micro-*κόσμος but an *anti-*κόσμος.

5.3.3. The spirit of the world (2:12)

Having claimed in 2:6–8 that God's secret wisdom is hidden from "this age" and from "the rulers of this age", Paul declares in 2:10b that God's purposes have been "revealed to us through the Spirit". In v. 12, Paul insists that the Spirit whom he and his readers have received is not τὸ πνεῦμα τοῦ κόσμου but τὸ πνεῦμα τὸ ἐκ τοῦ θεοῦ, "so that (ἵνα) we may understand the gifts bestowed on us by God".

κόσμος here is again "this world", as viewed from the apocalyptic standpoint (cf. ὁ αἰὼν οὗτος in 2:6–8). As in the previous two texts we have considered, κόσμος is clearly set in opposition to God (τοῦ κόσμου ... ἀλλὰ ... τοῦ θεοῦ).

It is a matter of debate whether Paul is talking here about a "spirit" of the κόσμος analogous to the Spirit of God, a demonic counterpart to the Holy Spirit,[28] or whether τὸ πνεῦμα τοῦ κόσμου is no more than a rhetorical equivalent to τὸ πνεῦμα τὸ ἐκ τοῦ θεοῦ.[29] Probably the latter is in view. Rather than speaking of two different spirits, Paul has in mind the one Spirit – the Spirit which believers have received.

[28] So Ellis 1978, 29–30. Cf. "the ruler of the power of the air, the spirit that is now at work among those who are disobedient", Eph. 2:2.
[29] So Fee 1987, 113; Theissen 1987, 368 n. 1.

His point is that this Spirit is not τοῦ κόσμου but ἐκ τοῦ θεοῦ. One may compare Rom 8:15. In this text, Paul states, οὐ γὰρ ἐλάβετε πνεῦμα δουλείας … ἀλλὰ … πνεῦμα υἱοθεσίας. The meaning here is that the (one) Spirit which believers have received is not one which leads them into slavery but one which brings about adoption. As Dunn observes, the contrast is epochal: it is not between one spirit and another but between the old epoch and the new.[30] If the similar rhetorical structure of Rom 8:15 may be used to shed light on 1 Cor 2:12, Paul's claim in the latter is that the Spirit possessed by Christians does not belong to the κόσμος (τοῦ κόσμου, possessive genitive), the old world / age. The Spirit is rather from (ἐκ τοῦ θεοῦ, genitive of origin) God and is the power of God's new world / age.

Perhaps the Corinthians, adopting Greek, and principally Stoic, ideas about the cosmic role of πνεῦμα, regarded their possession of the Spirit as incorporating them more fully into the unity of the κόσμος. The Stoics commonly viewed the πνεῦμα as the life-principle sustaining and permeating the κόσμος (= world / universe).[31] The πνεῦμα, from the Stoic point of view, was seen as mediating between the macrocosmos and the microcosmos. The Corinthians, had they been accustomed to such notions, may have viewed their experience of the Spirit as helping them to achieve the goal of integration into the social order of the κόσμος.

Whether or not Paul is concerned to counter such thinking, the effect of his remark in 2:12 is to reinforce the disjunction between the Corinthians and the κόσμος. He is making the point, once again, that his readers do not belong to the world and the present age. Their reception of God's Spirit sets them apart from the κόσμος. The use of the first person plural in this verse serves to sharpen the social distinction (ἡμεῖς, ἐλάβομεν, εἰδῶμεν, ἡμῖν). Paul sets himself and his readers over against the κόσμος.

Even though τὸ πνεῦμα τοῦ κόσμου is probably only a rhetorical phrase, Bultmann rightly notes that it nevertheless conveys the impression that the κόσμος is a "compelling influence", a force to which those who belong to the κόσμος are always subject.[32] The κόσμος is conceived of as a power structure, a sphere of belonging. A further

[30] Dunn 1988, 452.
[31] See p. 55.
[32] Bultmann 1952, 257.

implication of Paul's remark in 2:12, therefore, might be that since his readers have God's Spirit, and as the Spirit is diametrically opposed to the κόσμος, they ought, through the power of the Spirit, to resist the world's pull on their lives. Put in sociological terms, they should resist the conditioning influence of the larger society and assert their social and ideological distinctiveness.

5.3.4. The wisdom of the world is foolishness with God (3:18–23)

The section 1 Cor 3:18–23 forms a summary conclusion to the argument so far,[33] drawing together the twin issues of the Corinthians' pre-occupation with wisdom and their grouping around the names of the apostles.

Having largely dealt with the problem of factionalism in 3:1–17, Paul returns in v. 18 to the theme of the Corinthians' interest in wisdom and drives home the point of his foregoing discussion. Those who think of themselves as wise ἐν τῷ αἰῶνι τούτῳ are to become fools so that they may become truly wise. ἐν τῷ αἰῶνι τούτῳ here means "according to the standards of this age" and is a variation on κατὰ σάρκα in 1:26 and τοῦ κόσμου in 1:27–28. The Corinthians had indeed considered themselves to be wise (the formula used by Paul here, εἴ τις is generally taken as pointing to claims which were actually being made by the Corinthians; cf. 8:2; 11:16; 14:37). But, says Paul, they are deceiving themselves because they are judging wisdom by the wrong criteria. The wisdom to which they have latched on belongs to the old, out-going age (ὁ αἰὼν οὗτος, 1:20, 27–29; 2:6–8). Paul urges his readers to adopt a stance which is a complete reversal of worldly standards, a perspective consonant with God's new age. He accentuates the personal cost which this will involve: they should become fools in the estimation of the wider world.

In 3:19a Paul gives the reason (γὰρ) for this injunction. It is that ἡ σοφία τοῦ κόσμου τούτου μωρία παρὰ τῷ θεῷ ἐστιν. The statement effectively summarizes what Paul has argued in 1:18–25. As in 1:20–21, κόσμος stands in substitutional sense relation with ὁ αἰὼν οὗτος and is placed in contrast to θεός. Here, though, Paul attaches the demonstrative pronoun to the noun κόσμος, making clearer the parallel with ὁ αἰὼν οὗτος and sharpening the antithesis with the (implied) world / age to come.

---

[33] Schrage (1991, 311) describes the section as *peroratio*.

In 1:20, Paul stated that God "made foolish" the wisdom of the world. Here he expresses the foolishness of the world in God's sight as a settled fact (μωρία παρὰ τῷ θεῷ ἐστιν).

In 3:19b–20, Paul cites two Old Testament scriptures, beginning with Job 5:13, "He [God] catches the wise in their craftiness". The image is that of the hunter and his prey. God, the hunter, uses the cunning of the wise as the means of their entrapment. Paul then cites Ps 94:11, "The Lord knows the thoughts of the wise, that they are futile." Harking back to 1:10–12 and 3:1–9 and picking up his remarks on "boasting" in 1:29–31, Paul draws the practical conclusion (ὥστε) in v. 21a, "So let no one boast about human leaders."

In 3:21b–23 Paul gives a further reason for the injunction of 3:21a. There is to be no more boasting about human beings because, claims Paul, "all things are yours". There then follows a list of these "all things". The list begins with Παῦλος, Ἀπολλῶς and Κηφᾶς. These are the names which were at the centre of the Corinthians' internal wrangling (3:3). The catalogue then suddenly enlarges. The πάντα possessed by believers includes κόσμος, ζωή, θάνατος, ἐνεστῶτα and μέλλοντα.

In this context, κόσμος could have the neutral sense of "inhabited world", "earth", or even the positive sense of the "universe" as God's good creation and everlasting possession.[34] It seems more likely, however, that the word continues to bear the negative sense "this world" in accordance with Paul's apocalyptic line of usage so far. The four terms with which κόσμος is linked in this cluster, ζωή, θάνατος, ἐνεστῶτα and μέλλοντα probably all have pejorative senses. θάνατος certainly does. In 1 Corinthians θάνατος is "the last enemy" (1 Cor 15:26); it is destined to be destroyed (15:26) and to be "swallowed up" in victory (15:54). ζωή, ἐνεστῶτα and μέλλοντα appear together in Rom 8:38–39, in a list strikingly similar to this one, where they form part of a series of entities which threaten believers and attempt, unsuccessfully, to thwart God's good purposes. κόσμος as "this world" would hardly be out of place among these bedfellows. It may be objected, though, that the apocalyptic sense of κόσμος is difficult to square with Paul's claim that πάντα γὰρ ὑμῶν ἐστιν. How could Paul be saying that "this world", which is the enemy of God and which is doomed to pass

---

[34] The majority of interpreters see a neutral or positive sense here: Barrett 1968, 95–6; Bruce 1971, 46; Fee 1987, 154; Morris 1958, 73; Robertson and Plummer 1914, 73.

away (7:31), "belongs" to the believer? But the inclusion of θάνατος in the list entails this kind of problem anyway.

The genitive of possession in these verses, πάντα γὰρ ὑμῶν ἐστιν ... πάντα ὑμῶν, is clearly intended to pick up the genitives of 1:12 (ἐγὼ μέν εἰμι Παύλου, ἐγὼ δὲ Ἀπολλῶ, ἐγὼ δὲ Κηφᾶ, ἐγὼ δὲ Χριστοῦ) and 3:4. Paul is deliberately inverting the Corinthian slogans "I belong to Paul", and so on, into "they belong to you". The rest of the items on the list are also things which may dominate or possess the Corinthians: the world with it shaping influence, life with its concerns, death, present circumstances and future uncertainties. Paul's point is that their standing in Christ places them above all dominations. The leaders in whom they boast, and all the things which currently determine their lives belong to the Corinthians, not the Corinthians to them. The rhetorical effect of including κόσμος in this list is to say "With all its menacing and tempting possibilities", the κόσμος "lies ... beneath their feet; they have mastered it".[35] The practical implication which Paul expects his readers to draw from this, I think, is clear. Having mastered the κόσμος through Christ, the Corinthians must not live as if the κόσμος has mastered them. Now that they have gained the ascendancy over the κόσμος, they must not let themselves be possessed by it all over again.

5.3.5. The apostles' relation to the world: a paradigm for the Corinthians (4:9, 13)

In 4:7–13,[36] Paul draws an ironic contrast between the Corinthians and the high spiritual status they claim for themselves and the apostles, their leaders, whose social position is the lowest imaginable. His aim in this section is to deflate the exalted opinions which some of his readers evidently had of themselves (cf. 4:18). For the purpose of his argument, he adopts the perspective τοῦ κόσμου attacked in 1:27–28. He describes how things look from the old world/age point of view. As 4:14–16 make clear, Paul's depiction of the apostles' miserable lot has a paradigmatic intent: in describing the social experience of the apostles, he is setting out the parameters of Christian existence in general.[37]

---

[35] Bultmann 1952, 257.
[36] On the structure of 4:7–13, see Fitzgerald 1988, 129–32.
[37] Paul presents himself here as a "counter-example": so Fitzgerald 1988, 122.

Fiore points out that in 1 Cor 1–4, Paul makes use of the rhetorical model, covert allusion.[38] This is especially evident in 4:6–13, where Paul employs hyperbole, contrast, irony and metaphor to arrest his readers' attention and to challenge their assumptions. Fowler equates such devices with the techniques of defamiliarization.[39]

Paul describes the Corinthians in v. 8, in terms of their own perception of their new spiritual status. He exclaims, "Already you have all you want! Already you have become rich! Quite apart from us you have become kings!" These notions of theirs, however, are illusory and fundamentally misguided. Paul retorts, "I wish that you had become kings, so that we might be kings with you." But far from being kings, Paul explains in v. 9, the apostles have been apportioned the lowest place in the cosmic hierarchy. He asserts that "God has exhibited us apostles as last of all, as though sentenced to death, because we have become a spectacle to the world."

The words τῷ κόσμῳ καὶ ἀγγέλοις καὶ ἀνθρώποις can be coordinated in three different ways: (1) "to the world, and to angels and to human beings", in which case κόσμος, ἀγγέλοι and ἀνθρώποι constitute three separate entities; (2) "to the world, both angels and human beings", in which case the phrase καὶ ἀγγέλοις καὶ ἀνθρώποις specifies the denotation of κόσμος: κόσμος is the "intelligent universe", the sum of angels and human beings; (3) "the world, including angels and human beings", in which case κόσμος has the standard sense "world/universe", and ἀγγέλοι and ἀνθρώποι specify the inhabitants of the κόσμος. Of these three options, the first is the least likely. If Paul had intended κόσμος, ἀγγέλοι and ἀνθρώποι as three separate entities, one might have expected him to use the article before each of the nouns instead of just κόσμος. In the linguistic context, there is nothing which would favour the second option over the third or *vice versa*. What tips the balance in favour of the third approach is that κόσμος with the sense of "the aggregate of angels and human beings", appears to have no exact precedent in prior Jewish and Greek usage.[40] With Barrett[41] and Fee[42] I thus take κόσμος to mean "world/universe" in line with standard Greek usage, and the phrase καὶ ἀγγέλοις καὶ

---

[38] Fiore 1985, 89.
[39] Fowler 1996, 56.
[40] In 4 Macc 17:14, κόσμος has the sense "totality of spiritual beings".
[41] Barrett 1968, 110.
[42] Fee 1987, 175.

ἀνθρώποις to refer to the universe's inhabitants. But whatever the precise sense of κόσμος, it is plain that the κόσμος is not a "bad" thing. κόσμος in this verse does not have the pejorative associations of the word in chapters 1–3. Nothing is said or implied about the moral character of the κόσμος or its inhabitants.

Paul likens the apostles to those condemned to die in the arena, either by fighting gladiators in mortal combat or by being thrown to the wild beasts.[43] The spectacle is played out before the whole universe, with all its citizens, both angelic and human, beholding the events. The apostles plainly do not stand in a positive relation to the κόσμος. The word θέατρον has a pejorative meaning, as is clear from the preceding ἐπιθανατίους. They are not a spectacle to the κόσμος as brave men, of fortitude and strength,[44] but rather as criminals sentenced to death, a spectacle of utter humiliation. Thus, although κόσμος in this verse cannot be said to bear a "bad" sense, the usage may be still be classed as negative, since the apostles are linked to the κόσμος in a negative way. To the κόσμος the apostles have been made objects of shame. They are on display in the universal arena as exhibits of disgrace and dishonour. This is plainly not how the Corinthians would have conceived of *their* standing in the κόσμος. As Fee states, Paul's words "must have aimed at their discomfort".[45]

The difference between the apostles' life-experience and that of the Corinthians is further laid out in the antitheses of 4:10. The Corinthians, on the one hand, are wise, strong and held in honour (φρόνιμοι ... ἰσχυροί ... ἔνδοξοι). Paul and the rest of the apostles are fools, weak and held in disrepute (μωροί ... ἀσθενεῖς ... ἄτιμοι).[46] He then goes on in vv. 11–13 to present a catalogue of hardships and privations elucidating the abasement which characterizes the apostolic ministry. That such dishonour surrounds the apostles "to the present hour" and "to this very day" is emphasized at the beginning and end of the list, in

[43] Fee's (1987, 174–5) opinion that Paul is thinking in terms of the Roman triumph procession rather than the events of the arena is based on 2 Cor 2:14.
[44] As in the Stoic use of the metaphor, e.g. Seneca, *De prov.* 2.9.
[45] Fee 1987, 175.
[46] Paul in 4:10 is not referring to the socio-economic status of the Corinthians. His remarks are directed at the whole congregation, and he has already indicated in 1:26–28 that there is only a minority in the church with relatively high status. What 4:10 does seem to indicate, though, as Barclay (1992, 57) observes, is "a consciousness among the Corinthians that, whatever their social origins, their status had been enhanced by their adoption of Christianity".

sharp contrast to the "already" which marks the Corinthians' outlook (v. 8). Paul lists nine hardships: hunger, thirst, lack of clothing, ill-treatment, homelessness, and having to work with one's own hands, abuse, persecution, slander. Manual labour, though not a hardship as such was, as indicated in the last chapter, something which the Corinthians found particularly objectionable in Paul's missionary practice. The last three hardships are set in the form of antitheses, contrasting the ill-treatment which the apostles receive with their non-retaliatory reactions. Paul, in summary, rounds off the catalogue with the claim that, "We have become like the rubbish of the world, the dregs of all things", ὡς περικαθάρματα τοῦ κόσμου ἐγενήθημεν, πάντων περίψημα.[47]

The similarity between the clause θέατρον ἐγενήθημεν τῷ κόσμῳ in v. 9 and the words περικαθάρματα τοῦ κόσμου ἐγενήθημεν in v. 13 strongly suggests that κόσμος carries the same sense, "world/universe", in both verses. The cosmic dimension of the apostles' humiliation in v. 9, it seems, is being picked up again in v. 13. The cosmic note probably continues into the following clause with πάντων meaning "all things", that is, the universe, rather than "all people", "humanity".[48]

The nouns περικαθάρματα and περίψημα are virtually synonymous. Both refer to the dirt removed in the process of cleansing, either sweepings from the floor (περικαθάρματα) or dirt from the body (περίψημα).[49] Both words by extension became terms of contempt.[50] Both words, in certain contexts, could also be used with a sacrificial sense.[51] This has prompted some interpreters to see an expiatory reference here: the apostles are acting as scapegoats for the world.[52] But this idea is quite remote from the context.[53] The stress is on the ignominy of the apostolic lot.

---

[47] Although different Greek words are used in the LXX, there is a very close correspondence between the metaphor here and the words of Lam 3:45 ("You have made us filth and rubbish among the peoples").

[48] πάντων could either be masculine plural genitive or neuter plural genitive.

[49] Fee 1987, 180.

[50] For περικάθαρμα in this connection, see examples in Hauck 1965, 430 n. 3. For περίψημα in this connection, see examples in Stählin 1968, 89–90.

[51] Hauck 1965, Stählin 1968, 85–8.

[52] Barrett 1968, 112–13.

[53] Fee 1987, 180.

As in v. 9, κόσμος does not bear a negative meaning. The word has its standard sense, "world / universe". It is the (paradigmatic) relation of the apostles to the κόσμος which is presented in negative terms. They are linked to the κόσμος in a disdainful way as περικαθάρματα and περίψημα. It is for this reason that we would classify the use of κόσμος in v. 13 as a negative one.

The portrait of the apostles' relation to the κόσμος in v. 13 is even more scandalous than in v. 9. The apostles are not only a shameful and dishonourable spectacle to the κόσμος, they are the scum of the κόσμος. Writing from a "this-worldly" perspective, Paul is working within the parameters of the Graeco-Roman understanding of the κόσμος (= world / universe) and its social ordering. Within that frame of reference, Paul portrays the apostles as occupying the place of social and cosmic outcasts.

In clear contrast to the social harmony experienced by the Corinthians in their social context, Paul in 4:9 and 13 sets up a model of Christian existence exemplified by the apostles, in terms of social alienation and dislocation. The social acceptability of Corinthian Christianity within the wider Corinthian society (4:10) is completely at odds with the marginalized position of the apostles. Paul deploys κόσμος alongside θέατρον, περικαθάρματα and περίψημα in these verses to challenge the social and cultural integration enjoyed by the Corinthians and to construct an ideal of social disjunction.

5.3.6. Taking leave of the world (5:10)

In 5:1–13, Paul responds to the problem of incest in the congregation, demanding that the offender be expelled from the church (v. 5, 13). He rounds on his readers, excoriating them for having allowed the man's conduct to go on unhindered (vv. 6–8). They ought to have known that "a little yeast leavens the whole batch of dough"(v. 6). Paul's main worry about the situation, it is clear, is that the community will become corrupted by the presence of sin within its boundaries. The "old yeast" must be thrown out, therefore, so that the new batch can flourish (v. 7).

In vv. 9–13, Paul turns to settle the Corinthians' misunderstanding of an instruction in his previous letter. Since his intent in this earlier letter had been to forbid precisely what was now taking place, Paul judges this an appropriate point in the present letter to resolve the issue. Chapter 4 argued that the Corinthians' misunderstanding of Paul's earlier advice was probably intentional: they deliberately accentuated the vagueness of Paul's words (his meaning may have been quite clear in its original context) in order to brush it aside altogether. This makes better sense than either of the two main alternatives: that the Corinthians were making a polite request for clarification, or simply that an unintentional misunderstanding arose.[54]

Paul insists that when he instructed them not to associate with "sexually immoral persons", he meant those who call themselves "brothers" and yet are sexually immoral or greedy or idolaters, revilers, drunkards or robbers. He did not mean the immoral, the greedy and robbers or idolaters τοῦ κόσμου τούτου. To cut off social relations with all such people, Paul concedes, "you would then need to go out of the world", ὠφείλετε ἄρα ἐκ τοῦ κόσμου ἐξελθεῖν.

ὁ κόσμος οὗτος in 5:10a obviously bears the negative apocalyptic sense of "this world". The genitive indicates belonging: Paul is speaking of the sexually immoral, greedy, and so on, *who belong to* this world. κόσμος in 5:10b has the basic sense "world/universe". It was suggested earlier that this sense was dictated by Corinthian usage, Paul here repeating the Corinthians' words from their letter to him. But whatever links κόσμος may have had in its original context in the Corinthian letter, Paul in this linguistic setting casts κόσμος negatively. The κόσμος is a world which is populated by immoral and corrupt people, so numerous that believers cannot avoid contact with them. In the immediate linguistic context, there is no substantial difference in meaning between τοῦ κόσμου τούτου in the first clause and τοῦ κόσμου in the second. Paul, in 5:10b, is not switching from a negative deployment of κόσμος to a neutral or positive one. Rather, he is continuing his strategy of defamiliarizing κόσμος (= world/universe), suppressing the usual positive linkages of the term and collocating it with the negative terms πόρνος, πλεονέκτης, ἅρπαξ and εἰδωλολάτρης.

In agreeing that one cannot leave the κόσμος, Paul is not in any way softening his stress on the social and ideological boundaries of the church. He is merely indicating that his concern for the boundaries of the Corinthian church does not extend to a desire for the congregation's complete separation from the rest of society. He is not giving his readers

---

[54] As Fee (1987, 223 n. 15) states, "Neither of these can account for the vigorous rhetorical style of Paul's response."

complete freedom to interact with outsiders in all circumstances. Acknowledgement here of the basic fact that contact with non-Christians is an inescapable part of Christian life will not preclude Paul from later disallowing (6:1–11, 14–15; 7:40; 10:1–22) or warning against (15:33) certain sorts of associations with the world. Far from moderating his earlier insistence on the social and ideological boundaries of the Corinthian church, these verses function to confirm them. On the one hand, Paul strongly presses the *social distinction* between the church and the larger society. He differentiates between the sexually immoral τοῦ κόσμου τούτου and an ἀδελφός (even if only a "so-called" brother) who is sexually immoral. In 5:12–13, Paul distinguishes "those outside" from "those who are inside". The implication of v. 5 is that the realm "outside" the church is the sphere of Satan. There is no compromise, therefore, on the fundamental social duality of 1:18–25. On the other hand, Paul stresses the *ethical distinctiveness* of the Christian community (5:6–8). His primary concern is for the purity of the community. That purity must not be spoilt by "the disguised presence within the church of a representative from the outside, from the cosmos that should be 'out there'".[55] Paul's social intention here, then, is very clearly to reinforce the boundaries of the community, and not at all to encourage openness to the world. The qualification which 5:10b introduces to his earlier talk of κόσμος is that the social duality of church and world is not to be expressed in ghetto-like withdrawal from the wider society. Though Christians cannot do otherwise than live side by side with unbelievers, the social and ideological distinction remains. Believers may not be able "to go out of the world", ἐκ τοῦ κόσμου ἐξελθεῖν, but they are not to be "of this world", τοῦ κόσμου τούτου.[56] They cannot avoid the evils of the present world, but in their values and practices they are to demonstrate that they belong to a new world.

5.3.7. The saints will judge the world (6:1–2)

In 6:1–11, Paul confronts the problem of brother taking brother to court. He begins by venting his sense of scandal at the state of affairs (τολμᾷ, v. 1) . What is being allowed to happen is, as he sees it, an affront and a shame to the congregation (πρὸς ἐντροπὴν ὑμῖν λέγω,

[55] D. B. Martin 1995, 170.
[56] The formulation, then, is Paul's variation on John 17:15–16.

v. 5). With stinging sarcasm, probably expecting the Corinthians still to be reeling from his earlier offensive against their claims to possess wisdom, he asks (v. 5), "Can it be that there is no one among you wise enough to decide between one believer and another?" He argues that, whatever the eventual outcome of the litigation, whoever wins the case, to have lawsuits at all is already a defeat for the church (v. 7). He asks his readers (v. 7), "Why not rather be wronged? Why not rather be defrauded?" But in fact it is *they* (ὑμεῖς, Paul's remarks are aimed at the whole community, not just the offending brothers) who do wrong and defraud (v. 8).

The outrage, for Paul, lies in the fact that a dispute between believers is being taken "before the unrighteous" instead of "before the saints" (ἐπὶ τῶν ἀδίκων καὶ οὐχὶ ἐπὶ τῶν ἁγίων, v. 1).[57] A disagreement between two brothers (ἀδελφὸς μετα ἀδελφοῦ) is being brought "before unbelievers" (ἐπὶ ἀπίστων, v. 6). This is scandalous not because it constitutes a "bad witness to the world".[58] Paul is not concerned here about the church's mission to the world. It is outrageous because it is an inversion of the eschatological relationship of the church and the world. This is made clear in the rhetorical questions of v. 2: "Do you not know that the saints will judge the world? And if the world is to be judged by you, are you incompetent to try trivial cases?"

κόσμος is used in both questions: οὐκ οἴδατε ὅτι οἱ ἅγιοι τὸν κόσμον κρινοῦσιν; καὶ εἰ ἐν ὑμῖν κρίνεται ὁ κόσμος, ἀνάξιοί ἐστε κριτηρίων ἐλαχίστων; In the first, κόσμος is the object of the active verb κρίνω. The subject is οἱ ἅγιοι. In the second, which restates the premise of the first and draws a consequence from it, κρίνω is in the passive voice and κόσμος is its subject. ὑμεις substitutes for οἱ ἅγιοι as the agent of the action. The verb κρίνω, with the sense "to pass or execute judgement",[59] is normally linked with object nouns or

[57] Paul's objection is not based on the corruption inherent in Graeco-Roman civil legal system: *contra* Winter 1991. The word ἄδικοι is not being used with reference to the moral character of the judges or the juries who pronounced verdicts in civil cases. As Robertson and Plummer (1914, 110) remark, "The term reflects, not on Roman tribunals, but on the pagan world to which they belonged." Pagan judges and juries are unsuitable arbitrators not because they are corrupt, but because they belong to the ranks of the ungodly.
[58] *Contra* Witherington 1995, 164.
[59] Some commentators (e.g. Robertson and Plummer 1914, 111) argue that κρίνω in v. 2 bears the sense "to rule over". Paul's contention would thus be that the saints will reign over the world (the earth). But this is unlikely. The sense, "to pronounce or carry out

noun phrases referring to human beings (notwithstanding ἀγγέλους κρινοῦμεν in v. 3). οἱ ἅγιοι (and ὑμεῖς) are obviously set apart from κόσμος. The distinction between οἱ ἅγιοι and κόσμος in v. 2 mirrors the distinction between οἱ ἅγιοι and οἱ ἄδικοι in the previous verse. It can thus be inferred that ὁ κόσμος is contextually synonymous with οἱ ἄδικοι. Since οἱ ἄδικοι refers to unrighteous humanity (in contrast with the righteous), the sense "unrighteous / ungodly humanity" can be deduced for κόσμος.

With his claim that the saints will judge the unrighteous world, Paul refers to an established theme of Jewish eschatology, that God's elect will be involved in his judgement of the wicked.[60] In the light of this reality, their current disputes are trivial (ἐλαχίστων). Paul's argument in v. 2 is an *a fortiori* one. In using the pagan court system to resolve their disagreements, the Corinthians are allowing the respective roles of ungodly world and sanctified church on the greater occasion of the final judgement to be completely reversed in the present (comparatively) insignificant situation.[61] The depth of feeling which Paul evinces here indicates for him the absurdity of the whole affair – the κόσμος, the world which consists of unrighteous human beings, in the shape of its judges and arbitrators, is being permitted to settle the petty disputes of those who will be its assessors at the last day.

In v. 3, a second eschatological premise is utilized to consolidate and intensify the first. Paul asks, "Do you not know that we are to judge angels – to say nothing of ordinary matters?" Here he alludes to the motif of the judgement of the fallen angels, found in intertestamental Judaism and also picked up by other New Testament writers.[62] As Fee writes, "So inclusive will be ... participation in God's eschatological judgment that not only the world but even the angels will be judged by the newly formed eschatological people of God."[63]

---

judgement", is the sense with which the verb κρίνω is used in 5:3, 12, 13; 6:1, 6. The thought of the saints judging the unrighteous also forms a more obvious contrast with the fact that the saints are presently *being judged by* the unrighteous (6:1).

[60] Dan 7:22 (LXX). Cf. *Jub.* 24:29; *1 Enoch* 1:9; 38:5; 48:9; 95:3; 98:12; 1QpHab. 5:4: Rev 20:4.

[61] The word κριτηρίων in v. 2 can either mean "law courts" or "legal cases". Hence, the apodosis of v. 2 can read either, "are you unworthy to sit in the lowest courts?" (so Barrett 1968, 136) or "are you not competent to judge trivial cases?" (so Fee 1987, 233).

[62] *1 Enoch* 67–69; 91:15; 2 Pet 2:4; Jude 6.

[63] Fee 1987, 234.

In 6:1–11, Paul uses κόσμος among other terms to construct a strong theological, moral and social contrast, setting his readers apart from those outside the Christian community. That contrast may be set out as follows.

οἱ ἅγιοι	οἱ ἄδικοι ὁ κόσμος οἱ ἄγγελοι (vv. 1–3)	
ἡ ἐκκλησία	οἱ ἐξουθενημένοι (v. 4)[64]	
ἀδελφοί	ἄπιστοι (vv. 5–8)	
βασιλεία θεοῦ	οἱ ἄδικοι	πόρνοι εἰδωλολάτραι μοιχοί μαλακοί ἀρσενοκοῖται κλέπται πλεονέκται μέθυσοι λοίδοροι ἅρπαγες (vv. 9–11)

The Corinthians once belonged on the wrong side of the divide. But having been washed, sanctified and justified (v. 11), they are now on the positive side. Hence Paul, in v. 2, specifically equates οἱ ἅγιοι with ὑμεῖς, the Christian community in Corinth.

Again, in these verses, Paul can be seen to be defamiliarizing κόσμος, uncoding the term's standard positive links and recoding negative ones. The κόσμος is the totality of non-Christian humanity, consisting of the sexually immoral, idolaters, adulterers, and so on. He utilizes the term, along with other pejorative expressions to press the distinction between the Christian community and the rest of society, in accordance with his larger purposes of establishing strong group boundaries in Corinth.

---

[64] That οἱ ἐξουθενημένοι refers to unbelievers, "those who have no standing in the church", is strongly argued by Fee 1987, 235–6.

5.3.8. The form of this world is passing away (7:29–31)

In 7:29–31, Paul attempts to define for his readers what their attitude to life in the world ought to be.[65] As Wimbush states, these verses

> not only describe the *model* of Christian existence in the world Paul deems appropriate, but also the *rationale* behind this model. In no other passage does Paul *directly* address these matters.[66]

It is hardly accidental that such a passage should be found in 1 Corinthians given the Corinthians' lack (on Paul's analysis) of strong group boundaries and an adequate "response to the world". This short unit is especially significant because here Paul recommends an approach to life in the world based on an apocalyptic perception of the future demise of the world.

These verses occur in the context of Paul's treatment of issues relating to sex and marriage. Paul deals with these matters in response to questions raised by the Corinthians in their letter to him (7:1). In 7:25ff, he addresses the question of whether virgins should marry. The advice he gives is that they should remain single in view of "the present distress" (διὰ τὴν ἐνεστῶσαν ἀνάγκην, v. 26). If his preference for singleness is rejected and they do in fact get married, he assures them that they will not have sinned, but they will have "tribulation" (θλῖψις, v. 28) in this life, and Paul's wish is that they should be spared this.

Paul's mention of "the present distress" in v. 26 is usually understood as a reference to the sufferings and stresses which, according to various strands of Jewish tradition, immediately precede the end of the world.[67] ἐνεστῶσαν can either mean "impending" or "present". The meaning "present" is to be preferred because this is the sense with which the word is used elsewhere in Paul's writings (1 Cor 3:22; Rom 8:38; Gal 1:4). It also accords with Paul's conviction that Christians have already been experiencing the suffering and distresses which herald the end since Christ's death and resurrection.[68]

---

[65] Several studies of Paul's attitude to the world concentrate on this passage: Hierzenberger 1967; Schrage 1964; Wimbush 1987.

[66] Wimbush 1987, 83.

[67] For the word ἀνάγκη in this regard, see Luke 21:23. On this theme of Jewish eschatology and its New Testament interpretation, see esp. Allison 1987. The end-time period of tribulation was conceived of as being esp. harrowing for the married: *2 Apoc. Bar* 10:13–14; Mark 13:17; Luke 23:29.

[68] Cf. 1 Thess 3:4. See Allison 1987, 62–9; Witherington 1992, 158–9.

In 7:29–31, verses which constitute one sentence in Greek, Paul makes explicit the apocalyptic viewpoint hinted at in v. 26. He outlines a general approach to life in the world embracing marriage, the joys and sorrows of life, the acquisition of money and possessions, and the "use" of the world. In these verses Paul is not just addressing the virgins with their particular dilemma in view (the introductory words of v. 29a, τοῦτο δέ φημι, ἀδελφοί, signal the importance of what is to follow for *every member* of the congregation). He moves, for the moment, beyond the issue on hand and speaks to the Corinthian community at large, urging the whole church to adopt a more avowedly apocalyptic outlook on life in the world.

He argues that the time has been shortened (ὁ καιρὸς συνεσταλμένος ἐστίν, v. 29a). It has been shortened (we must presume) as a result of the apocalyptic event of the death and resurrection of Christ. As Fee states, "the event of Christ has now compressed the time in such a way that the future has been brought forward so as to be clearly visible".[69] Therefore, from this point onward (that is, from now until the parousia), believers should adopt a dispassionate attitude toward worldly affairs, guided by the ὡς μή principle articulated in the five clauses of vv. 29b–31a (my translation):

those who have wives	are to be	as though	they had none
those who mourn		as though	they were not mourning
those who rejoice		as though	they were not rejoicing
those who buying		as though	they were not possessing
those who use the world		as though	they were not overusing it

οἱ ἔχοντες γυναῖκας	ὦσιν	ὡς μὴ	ἔχοντες
οἱ κλαίοντες		ὡς μὴ	κλαίοντες
οἱ χαίροντες		ὡς μὴ	χαίροντες
οἱ ἀγοράζοντες		ὡς μὴ	κατέχοντες
οἱ χρώμενοι τὸν κόσμον		ὡς μὴ	καταχρώμενοι

The word κόσμος in the final ὡς μή clause, in view of the linkage with the verbs χράομαι ("use") and καταχράομαι ("use to the full", "consume"), appears to mean the (neutrally valued) "inhabited world". The expression οἱ χρώμενοι τὸν κόσμον calls to mind Wis 2:6.[70] In that text, the ungodly resolve, "let us make use of the creation", χρησώμεθα τῇ κτίσει. "Making use of the creation", it emerges from

---

[69] Fee 1987, 339 n. 14. Cf. Doughty 1975, 69.
[70] Discussed in chapter 3, p. 79.

the immediate context in Wis 2, consists in making, we suggest, full and unhindered use of creation's resources. κόσμος in 1 Cor 7:31a refers to the physical environment which people inhabit – not only the natural environment but also (and especially) the built environment, that is, material constructions produced by human beings to serve their needs – houses, buildings, roads, streets. Paul's phrase χρώμενοι τὸν κόσμον is intended to cover the whole range of his readers' interactions with their natural and created environment, and their various utilizations of the world's resources (cf. ἀγοράζοντες ... κατέχοντες in the previous clause), both natural resources and humanly produced commodities.

What Paul is calling for in the five ὡς μή clauses of 7:29–31a is certainly not complete disengagement from the world (cf. 5:10). He is plainly not saying that husbands and wives should now separate and live celibate lives. The goal he seems to have in mind for his readers is akin to the Stoic ideal of inner detachment from or aloofness to the world.[71] They are to be involved in the world, but not to be absorbed by it. As Conzelmann puts it, they are to "maintain freedom in the midst of involvement".[72] But such inner detachment also requires a measure of outward restraint. They are to make "use" of the κόσμος but not "full use" of it.

The assertion of v. 31b, παράγει γὰρ τὸ σχῆμα τοῦ κόσμου τούτου,[73] supplies the reason why they are to assume this disposition. This statement has provoked a great deal of scholarly discussion. The point of contention is whether Paul is advancing a "cosmological" claim and, more specifically, whether he is talking about the end of the spatio-temporal world. The debate revolves not only around the meaning of ὁ κόσμος οὗτος but also the force of the tense of παράγει and the significance of σχῆμα. The majority of scholars reject the idea that Paul is making a cosmological statement.

The conceptual background to v. 31b, most would agree, is the apocalyptic expectation of coming cosmic change. The expectation in

[71] The ὡς μή statements of vv. 29b–31a appear to betray Stoic influence. There are significant parallels with Epictetus (*Disc.* 2.21.6; 3.17.24; 3.22.67–76; 3.24.60; 4.7.5). See further, Braun 1962, 159–67; Chadwick 1954/55, 267; Deming 1995, 190–1.

[72] Conzelmann 1975, 133.

[73] The closest parallel to Paul's phrase τὸ σχῆμα τοῦ κόσμου τούτου in non-biblical Greek literature is Philostratus, *Vit. Ap.* 8.7: καὶ τί τὸ σχῆμα τοῦ κόσμου τοῦδε; but it can shed little light on the meaning of 1 Cor 7:31b.

Jewish apocalyptic writings is thoroughly "cosmological" in that what is looked for is a transformation of the physical, as well as the socio-political, world. In Jewish apocalyptic texts, the expected change is depicted either in terms of the renewal of the present creation,[74] or, more radically, as the dissolution of the present world and the establishment of a completely new creation.[75] Paul (like the author of 2 Pet 3:10–13) seems to be reflecting the more radical version of the apocalyptic belief. The question is, however, Is he handling the apocalyptic conception in such a way as to reduce or eradicate its cosmological meaning? In other words, Is he historicizing and demythologizing it? To answer this question, we need to look carefully at the linguistic components of v. 31b.

Firstly, what does Paul mean by κόσμος? Defenders of the non-cosmological interpretation of 7:31b refer to Bultmann's definition of κόσμος as a "historical" term for Paul and not a "cosmological" one.[76] But, as stressed at the outset of this study, whether κόσμος has a narrow anthropological sense or a wider cosmological sense must not be prejudged but determined on a case by case basis. In this instance, Paul uses the apocalyptic expression ὁ κόσμος οὗτος. "This world" in Jewish apocalyptic discourse is the whole created order, both human and non-human, which stands or has been caught up in evil and opposition to God and which is destined to pass away. There are no linguistic indicators among the surrounding words and expressions to suggest that ὁ κόσμος οὗτος is being employed with exclusive reference to or particular emphasis on (as in 1 Cor 1:20–21) human beings. It seems, therefore, that the apocalyptic/cosmological meaning ought, in principle, to stand. Specifically against an anthropological/historical meaning is the use of κόσμος with reference to the physical world in the immediately preceding clause. The γάρ indicates a strong link between v. 31a and v. 31b. This is not to contend that the word κόσμος has exactly the same meaning in both clauses, but there must surely be a significant overlap in referent if Paul's argument is going to work.

Secondly, what is the force of the present tense of παράγει? The verb παράγω (used intransitively) means "pass by", "depart", "pass

---

[74] *1 Enoch* 45:2–5; *Jub.* 1:29; 4:26; *4 Ezra* 7:29–31; *2 Apoc. Bar.* 29:1–8; 32:6; 57:2; *Bib. Ant.* 32:17.
[75] *1 Enoch* 72:1; 91:16; *2 Enoch* 65:5–11; *4 Ezra* 7:39–43; *2 Apoc. Bar.* 40:3; *Bib. Ant.* 3:10; *Apoc. Elijah* 5:38. See further Volz 1966, 338–40.
[76] Deming 1995, 185; Doughty 1975, 69; Hierzenberger 1967, 58–60.

away", "disappear". It is not a typically Pauline word. It occurs only in this passage in the whole Pauline corpus.[77] As Schmidt points out,[78] it is synonymous with the verb παρέρχομαι in affirmations of the future "passing away" of heaven and earth (Matt 5:18; 24:34–35; Mark 13:31; Luke 16:17; 21:33; 2 Pet 3:10; Rev 21:1). Wimbush argues that the choice of the present tense of the verb over the future is significant. He claims that by using the present tense, Paul is substantially altering the apocalyptic notion he is reflecting. According to Wimbush, he employs the present tense to de-eschatologize the motif of the dissolution of the cosmos and to emphasize instead "the *perennial* state of affairs in the present order".[79] However, the present tense of παράγω is best understood as reflecting the present or inaugurationist aspect to the eschatology of 1 Cor 7:25–31 (the *present* distress, 7:26; the time *has been* shortened, 7:29). It functions not to de-eschatologize the apocalyptic belief in a coming cosmic change, but to indicate that the eschatological process which culminates in the dissolution of the present world has now been set in motion:[80] this world is already on its course toward final destruction.

Thirdly, what is the significance of the word σχῆμα? It is often argued that Paul excludes any thought that the spatio-temporal world is *en route* to destruction by emphasizing that it is the σχῆμα of this world which is passing away. On the assumption that σχῆμα denotes the external appearance of a person or thing in contrast to the inner essence, it is claimed that what Paul envisages as passing away is not the κόσμος itself but rather its outward form or pattern.[81] Though a widespread interpretation of 1 Cor 7:31b, this suggestion faces several difficulties. Firstly, had Paul wanted to make the distinction between a temporary σχῆμα and an enduring κόσμος, he is more likely to have said τὸ σχῆμα τοῦ κόσμου or τοῦτο τὸ σχῆμα τοῦ κόσμου. Secondly,

---

[77] The verb is used in the parallel Johannine text, 1 John 2:17.
[78] Schmidt 1964, 130.
[79] Wimbush 1987, 34, cf. 47.
[80] Schmidt 1964, 130.
[81] Thus what is passing away not the world but "its outward pattern, in social and mercantile institutions" (Barrett 1968, 178); "the world's social and economic 'infrastructure'" (Deming 1995, 185); its "institutions, morals and ideals" (Wimbush 1987, 34). Cf. Harrisville 1980, 125–6; Kuck 1992, 247; Morris 1958, 118; Robertson and Plummer 1914, 156; Ruef 1971, 64. For a summary of the various ways in which scholars have interpreted σχῆμα, see Hierzenberger 1967, 62. On σχῆμα see BAGD 797; Schneider 1971, 954–8.

Paul is talking here about ὁ κόσμος οὗτος. In apocalyptic thought, "this world" is conceived of as dominated by evil, suffering, corruption, and so on. It hardly seems likely, therefore, that he would wish to imply that it is only the external appearance or outer husk of such a world which passes away, while its intrinsic and essential reality lives on. As Héring point, out, "When 'this world' is mentioned, what is always is meant is our present world as something which must perish, over against . . . 'the world to come'."[82] Thirdly, the linguistic basis for the assumption that Paul is implicitly differentiating between "outward form" and "essence" must be questioned. While the word σχῆμα focuses on the physical and visible appearance, shape or structure of a thing, it need not denote these qualities in contradistinction to the quality of essence or inner reality. Such a distinction might stand if σχῆμα were being used in contrast to μορφή but no such or equivalent contrast appears in 1 Cor 7:31b. In the only other New Testament occurrence of σχῆμα, Phil 2:7 (in the context of the Christ-hymn), where the term is used in connection with Christ's humanity, it is clear that it embraces both "outward form" and "essential reality".[83] In 1 Cor 7:31b σχῆμα is most likely both a "*Formbegriff*" and a "*Wesensbegriff*":[84] it denotes not only the form of ὁ κόσμος οὗτος, but also its essence.[85] The σχῆμα of "this world" is its whole state of existence. The rhetorical function of the insertion of σχῆμα, thus, is not to emphasize how discriminating the "passing away" will be but how extensive.

There is no compelling reason, therefore, to reject the inference that Paul is using κόσμος in 7:31b to make a thoroughly "cosmological" claim. There is no contextual warrant for assuming that the cosmological overtones of the traditional apocalyptic motif which Paul is taking over here are either being eliminated or played down. Indeed, the only difference between Paul and Jewish apocalypticists is that Paul believes that the cosmic change has in some sense been activated. The apocalyptic event of the cross and resurrection has, in principle, set in motion the process that will lead to final cosmic destruction.

---

[82] Héring 1962, 59. Cf. Hierzenberger 1967, 58.

[83] Schneider 1971, 956.

[84] The terminology is Hierzenberger's (1967, 65).

[85] So Conzelmann 1975, 134; Orr and Walther 1976, 219; Schrage 1995, 176, though Schrage believes that what is in view in 1 Cor 7:31b is not "*Weltuntergang*" but "*Weltende im Sinne der Weltwende*".

In 7:29–31, then, Paul deploys κόσμος together with other terms to generate a wide-ranging "response to the world", embracing family ties, joys and sorrows, wealth and possessions, engagement with the physical environment and use of material resources. His readers' lives are not to be absorbed by such things because these things are part of a world which is destined for dissolution.

What Paul says in v. 31b, therefore, continues his critique of the Greek cultural ideal of the world as κόσμος. As noted in chapter 3, according to the world-view associated with κόσμος = world / universe, the κόσμος was to be held in the highest regard. One of the ways in which this reverence for the κόσμος was expressed was the ascription to it of immortality.[86] Paul takes a radically different stance on the future of the κόσμος to that of Plato and Aristotle. The present κόσμος is not indestructible or eternal. It is not an ever-enduring reality. It is of limited duration, and its time has grown short.

Though Paul does not specifically relate his talk of κόσμος in 7:29–31 to the problem of weak group boundaries in Corinth, it nevertheless serves his larger epistolary goal of strengthening the church's social and ideological barriers. It calls into question the Corinthians' high degree of participation in and commitment to the larger culture. For the Corinthians to concentrate all their energies on social and cultural integration into the existing social order, on the logic of 7:29–31, is to invest in a dying world and is tantamount to setting out deck-chairs on the *Titanic*. The effect of Paul's usage of κόσμος here is to discourage over-involvement and enmeshment in the wider world.[87]

5.3.9. The things of the world and the things of God (7:32–35)

At 7:32, Paul returns to the issue of whether virgins should marry, reiterating his advice that they should stay as they are. What Paul says in vv. 32–35 is directed more toward this group than, as vv. 29–31, to the community in total. Nevertheless, he has the whole congregation in view in v. 32a, when expressing the wish that they should be free from anxieties (θέλω δὲ ὑμᾶς ἀμερίμνους εἶναι).[88]

Verses 32b–34 form a well crafted rhetorical unit. The structure and symmetry of vv. 32b–34 becomes clear when the text is set out:

[86] See pp. 67–8.
[87] Kuck (1992, 248) completely misses the point of 1 Cor 7:29–31 when he states that Paul is drawing on apocalyptic eschatology to counsel openness to the outside world.
[88] In the New Testament ἀμέριμνος appears elsewhere only at Matt 28:14.

a. ὁ ἄγαμος μεριμνᾷ τὰ τοῦ κυρίου, πῶς ἀρέσῃ τῷ κυρίῳ·

b. ὁ δὲ γαμήσας μεριμνᾷ τὰ τοῦ κόσμου, πῶς ἀρέσῃ τῇ γυναικί, καὶ μεμέρισται. καὶ

c. ἡ γυνὴ ἡ ἄγαμος καὶ ἡ παρθένος μεριμνᾷ τὰ τοῦ κυρίου, ἵνα ᾖ ἁγία καὶ τῷ σώματι καὶ τῷ πνεύματι·

d. ἡ δὲ γαμήσασα μεριμνᾷ τὰ τοῦ κόσμου, πῶς ἀρέσῃ τῷ ἀνδρί.

Despite the careful rhetorical crafting, the precise meaning of Paul's words in these verses has proved less than straightforward to discern. Two exegetical issues in particular have to be resolved: (1) What is the meaning of the verb μεριμνάω in each of its four occurrences? (2) What is the force of δε in clauses *b* and *d*?

As to the first issue, three main views have been proposed, none of which is without its difficulties. According to the traditional interpretation, Paul uses μεριμνάω in both a positive and a negative way. Thus, as Robertson and Plummer state, "there is a right kind of μέριμνα as well as a wrong".[89] The problem with this view is that it gives the same verb two different senses in parallel clauses. A second approach, favoured by Barrett, takes the verb as having a uniformly negative meaning.[90] On this view, Paul is desirous that married and unmarried should be free from anxiety, both anxiety about the things of the world and about the things of the Lord. The difficulty with this view is that Paul in v. 32b equates anxiety about the things of the Lord with the desire to please the Lord, and elsewhere in Paul "pleasing the Lord" is a thoroughly laudable endeavour (Rom 8:8; 2 Cor 5:9; 1 Thess 2:15; 4:1). A third approach, taken by Fee, understands the verb as having a uniformly positive sense.[91] Thus, caring for the things of the world and caring for the things of the Lord are both legitimate activities. However, a consistently positive use of μεριμνάω would seem to fly in the face of Paul's wish expressed in v. 32a, that all should be ἀμερίμνους. Regarding the function of δέ, the question is whether the connective is to be understood as having its full adversative force, setting up a strong antithesis between concern for τὰ τοῦ κυρίου and concern for τὰ τοῦ κόσμου, or as indicating a simple contrast between two different but equally improper (as Barrett argues), or equally proper (as Fee

---

[89] Robertson and Plummer 1914, 157.
[90] Barrett 1968, 179–80. So also Balch 1983, 434–5.
[91] Fee 1987, 344–5.

argues), areas of interest. Both issues can best be resolved by focusing on the phrases τὰ τοῦ κμρίου and τὰ τοῦ κόσμου themselves.

Too often interpreters have homed in on the verb μεριμνάω alone, forgetting that its meaning cannot be determined in isolation from other parts of the sentence. The sense with which the verb is used, as Wimbush rightly insists,[92] is dependent on its object: in lines *a* and *c* the object is τὰ τοῦ κυρίου, and in *b* and *d* the object is τὰ τοῦ κοσμου. τὰ τοῦ κυρίου, the Lord's business, is incontestably something positive. It ought to follow then that μέριμνα about τὰ τοῦ κυρίου is understood by Paul as a valid and commendable activity. What then of τὰ τοῦ κοσμου? The term κόσμος in these verses has to be understood in the light of vv. 29–31 and especially v. 31b. In 7:31b, Paul uses κόσμος with the sense of "this world". Given the close proximity of vv. 32–33 to v. 31b, we probably ought to infer (in the absence of linguistic indicators to suggest otherwise) that the negative sense "this world" established in v. 31b is meant to carry over into vv. 32–33. That τὰ τοῦ κυρίου is the contextual antonym of τὰ τοῦ κόσμος also points in this direction. The contrast between κυρίος and κόσμος corresponds to the antithesis between θεός and κόσμος in 1:20–21; 2:12; 3:19. Moreover, in 7:29–31, Paul lists having wives as one of the things that should be treated "as though not", in view of the fact that the present world is in decline.[93] Having just made the connection between marriage and ὁ κόσμος οὗτος, it is quite likely that he is now building on it.

If the apocalyptic sense of κόσμος is accepted, μέριμνα about τὰ τοῦ κοσμου can hardly be viewed as a legitimate activity.[94] Thus, the traditional view on the verb μεριμνάω remains the most plausible: the verb has a positive meaning when used in connection with the affairs of the Lord and a negative meaning when used with reference to the affairs of the world. The contrariety of τὰ τοῦ κυρίου and τὰ τοῦ κόσμου also means that the δέ in lines *b* and *d* functions to signal a strong contrast between the two types of concern.

The point that Paul is making in vv. 32b–34, then, is that the married state for both the believing husband and the believing wife entails a

[92] Wimbush 1987, 51–2, 64.
[93] According to the saying of Jesus in Luke 20:34–35, marriage belongs to "this age", not to "that age".
[94] Cf. Matt 13:22, ἡ μέριμνα τοῦ αἰῶνος.

greater exposure to and engagement in the affairs of the world, and this is bad (or at least not desirable), whereas being single means having more opportunity for attending to the affairs of the Lord, and this is good. Thus singleness is preferable to marriage. It is not that marriage in itself is bad. What is disagreeable to Paul is the concern for worldly things which inevitably accompanies it. Also, Paul is not saying that the married believer's *sole* concern is the world's affairs, but that a spouse faces a conflict of interests (καὶ μεμέρισται), presumably a conflict between serving the Lord and attending to worldly matters. That such a division of interests is Paul's real reservation about marriage in this passage is made clear in v. 35, where Paul states the purpose of what he has been saying: that they all might live before the Lord in an unhindered (ἀπερισπάστως) way.

In 7:32–35, then, Paul again brings the distinction between "this world" and the sphere of God and church into his practical teaching. He justifies his preference for singleness on the grounds that the married state has a tendency to embroil believers in the sphere of this world/ age, lessening their effectiveness for God.

As noted in chapter 3, the ideology of κόσμος served to legitimate the institution of marriage.[95] Marriage and procreation, it was argued, were necessary for the perpetuation of the established order. To be married and have children was a duty incumbent on responsible citizens. The maintenance of the family was a means of ensuring the stability and continuity of the socio-political order. Paul here completely overturns this line of thinking. It is precisely because marriage involves a certain level of commitment to the present worldly order, an order judged in the cross and destined to pass away, that remaining single is the better option for those who belong to the new world. Again, Paul uses κόσμος in a defamiliarizing fashion to uncode the encoded ideology.

As in 7:29–31, Paul does not explicitly relate his negative talk of κόσμος to the social problem of weak group boundaries. However, his continuing appeal to the distinction between the κόσμος and the realm of God in his ethical argumentation and his constant undermining of the ideology of κόσμος – an ideology which justified extensive participation in and conformity to the larger society – clearly serves his overall social aim of erecting solid boundaries.

---

[95] See p. 72.

5.3.10. God, idols and the world (8:4–6)

In 8:1–6, Paul begins to deal with the issue of food sacrificed to idols. The twin claims of v. 4 (along with the assertion, πάντες γνῶσιν ἔχομεν, in v. 1), it is generally accepted, are slogans of the Corinthian strong – claims made by them in justification of eating εἰδωλόθυτα. It is also likely that, with the exception of the parenthetical remark in v. 5b, vv. 5–6 is largely material quoted from the Corinthian letter (though in v. 6, the Corinthians are probably citing a creedal statement).[96] At the very least, Paul expects the Corinthian "strong" to recognize in vv. 5–6 an accurate reproduction or continuation of their own line of thought. 8:4–6 as a whole, then, may be taken to represent the γνῶσις to which the Corinthian "strong" appealed to justify their actions.

The first assertion of v. 4, οὐδὲν εἴδωλον ἐν κόσμῳ, is slightly ambiguous: οὐδὲν can either be understood as an attribute ("no idol exists in the world") or as a predicate ("an idol is nothing in the world"). Most scholars favour the first approach in view of the parallelism with the clause which follows. The Corinthian claim is that an εἴδωλον has no genuine reality. An idol has no real existence in the world. The second assertion, οὐδεὶς θεὸς εἰ μὴ εἷς, "there is no God but one", gives the reason for the first. Monotheism rules out the existence of other gods. Verses 5–6 comprise a single sentence in Greek. The γάρ of v. 5 signals a link with the preceding assertions. The gods of Graeco-Roman religion are only "so-called" (λεγόμενοι) gods. "For us", there is one God, the Father, and one Lord, Jesus Christ. God is the source of the universe (ἐξ οὗ τὰ πάντα) and Jesus is the mediator of creation (δι' οὗ τὰ πάντα).[97]

It is clear from the immediate context of 8:4–6 that κόσμος in 8:4 has the conventional sense "world/universe". ἐν κόσμῳ in v. 4 correlates with ἐν οὐρανῷ ... ἐπὶ γῆς in v. 5. κόσμος is also contextually equivalent to the phrase τὰ πάντα in v. 6. The "all things" of v. 6 are defined as flowing from God and sustained by him. Taking vv. 4–6 as a unit and not just v. 4a, οὐδὲν εἴδωλον ἐν κόσμῳ, as an isolated remark, it seems likely that κόσμος here, in the context of an affirmation

---

[96] Willis 1985, 83–7. The view that Paul's quotation of the Corinthians letter continues into vv. 5–6 is also taken by Grosheide (1953, 192), Parry (1937, 127–8) and Winter (1990, 220–1).

[97] 1 Cor 8:6 has the appearance of a creedal formula. As Dunn observes (1980, 180), it is striking for the way it splits the *Shema* (Deut 6:4), the classic expression of Jewish monotheism, and the familiar Stoic formula ἐξ οὗ ... δι' οὗ, between God and Christ.

of the universe as God's *good*[98] creation, carries the favourable connotations it usually has in standard Greek usage: order, unity, beauty. As previously noted, this use of κόσμος – a Corinthian use – stands out as the most positive in the whole letter. These verses, taken as a whole, betoken a positive assessment of the world informed by Hellenistic beliefs as well as Jewish and Christian ones: the κόσμος is a good world, ordered and controlled by God and completely empty of baneful spiritual influences.

It is not difficult to infer how the Corinthian "strong" used their knowledge of God and the κόσμος to legitimize eating εἰδωλόθυτα. The κόσμος is free of spiritual beings in competition with the one God. Since the whole world is God's, there is no part of it which is off-limits to believers. This includes Graeco-Roman temples. Since the gods are utterly powerless to contaminate any food or make any place dangerous, one cannot be harmed by eating their "sacred food" or by entering their "sacred space". Engaging in meaningless religious ceremonies is a completely value-free activity.

What, then, does Paul make of the cosmological perspective of the Corinthian "strong"? At first glance, he does not appear to dispute it. Instead, so it seems, he calls on the "strong" to act lovingly toward the weaker members of the congregation. He argues that love has primacy over knowledge (8:1–3) and places limits on the exercise of authority, even if that authority has a legitimate basis (8:7–13). He appeals to his own conduct as an example of this (9:1–27). He urges the "strong" not to seek their own advantage but that of others (10:23–11:1). In 10:23–30, Paul endorses the basic approach of the Corinthian "strong" to εἰδωλόθυτα in the practical cases of buying meat from the market and attending meals hosted by unbelievers (10:23–30).[99] He justifies his advice in v. 26 by citing Ps 24:1, "the earth and its fullness are the Lord's" (cf. 1 Tim 4:4). Paul, like the Corinthian "strong", argues from theological and cosmological principles.

On closer inspection, however, it becomes clear that Paul does not give his full endorsement to the cosmological viewpoint of 8:4–6. As he had previously done at 6:12–14 and 7:1, in 8:4–6 he cites Corinthian claims precisely in order to qualify and correct them. He obviously accepts that "there is no God but one" and that God is source and

---

[98] Conzelmann 1975, 144.
[99] That the host here is an unbeliever is persuasively argued by Horrell 1996, 147.

sovereign of the whole creation (τὰ πάντα).[100] But he parts company with the Corinthian strong on their understanding of the non-reality of idols and "so-called gods". As noted above, at 8:5b he inserts a qualification (ὥσπερ εἰσὶν θεοὶ πολλοὶ καὶ κύριοι πολλοί) into the Corinthian remarks.[101] Paul assents to the Corinthian claim that the gods of Graeco-Roman religion are not true deities, but he disagrees with the contention that they have no existence. He indicates in v. 7 that the θεοὶ πολλοὶ καὶ κύριοι πολλοί have a subjective reality for those who are accustomed to them. He goes on to explain in 10:19–22 that they also have an objective reality. Standing behind the pagan gods are real supernatural powers. What pagans sacrifice, they sacrifice unwittingly to δαιμόνια (10:20).[102] To take part in a cultic meal, therefore, is to become partners with demons.[103]

It becomes clear in the larger discussion of 1 Cor 8–10 that Paul regards the cosmological perspective of the Corinthian "strong" as both partial and misleading. It affirms the world as the creation of the one true God but fails to reckon with cosmic evil. It denies the existence of other deities in the κόσμος, but fails to account for the presence of malevolent spiritual beings. It is a world-view which accommodates and encourages religious participation outside the church. Paul seeks in this letter to press upon his readers an apocalyptic view of the world, a perception of reality which (he hopes) will function to inhibit cultural and religious integration into pagan society.

The passage 1 Cor 8:4–6 indicates that the Corinthian "strong" (whose views probably constituted the dominant perspective in the church) had assimilated the Jewish and Christian belief in the world as God's good creation. This emphasis resonated with the high view of the world as κόσμος which obtained in educated Hellenistic culture. But they had failed to take on board the apocalyptic conviction that the

[100] It should be noted, though, that the emphasis here is on *believers* (ἡμεῖς), not the universe as a whole, as the object of God's and Christ's *redeeming* activity.
[101] Willis 1985, 86.
[102] The word δαιμόνιον in Greek and Hellenistic usage refers to divine intermediary beings with no necessary connotations of evil: Foerster 1964, 8–9. Paul, though, refers to hostile spiritual powers.
[103] Paul reiterates an established line of polemic against the gods in Judaism. The idea that idols represent evil spirits is already present in the Old Testament: Deut 32:17; Ps 106:37; Isa 65:3, 11; Bar. 4:7. For examples in Intertestamental Jewish literature, see *Jub.* 11:4–6; 22:16–22; *1 Enoch* 19; 99:6–10; *T.Naph.* 3:3–4.

present world – from which they were being rescued – is dominated by evil and oppression and is under the control of spiritual forces opposed to God. It is Paul's aim in this letter to reconstruct the symbolic worlds of his readers in these terms.

5.3.11. Condemned with the world (11:32)

The last occurrence of κόσμος in 1 Corinthians to be considered in this analysis is in 11:32, at the conclusion of Paul's reply to the problem of abuses at the Lord's Supper. Paul ends his response to this issue on a sombre note with the theme of judgement (11:29–32). He asserts that those who eat and drink without "discerning the body" bring God's judgement upon themselves. The community has in fact already fallen under God's judgement. It is for this reason that "many" of the community are ill and that some have died. But, Paul explains, the judgement they are experiencing is disciplinary in nature. Its aim is to ensure final salvation. It has been administered so that they might not be condemned with the κόσμος.

Since κόσμος here is the object of God's judgement, it can be inferred that the word has a human sense. Given that the readers are distinguished from κόσμος, the reference is to unbelieving human beings. The sense of κόσμος in this verse is then the same as in 6:2: "unrighteous human world".

This statement thus builds on what Paul has said about the κόσμος in 6:1–2. Clearly, Paul is not applying the contrast between the church and the κόσμος to the issue of group boundaries. But again, at a deep rhetorical level it functions to reinforce the distinction between the non-believing world and the church which he has been pressing throughout.

5.4. Related themes and emphases

To complete this analysis, we turn briefly to related motifs and emphases. Three correlative themes may be highlighted: the separation of human beings into the "saved" and the "perishing"; the cosmic eschatology of 15:27–28; the contrast between the σῶμα ψυχικόν and the σῶμα πνευματικόν in 15:42ff.

5.4.1. The saved and the perishing

The implicit contrast between this world/age and the new age in 1 Corinthians is accompanied by a radical soteriological division of humankind into the σῳζόμενοι and the ἀπολλύμενοι (1:18–25). The latter distinction stems from the former in that those who are being "saved" are those whom God rescues from the present age which is on its way out. Those who still belong to this world are in process of "perishing" along with it.[104]

In this letter, Paul operates with a strongly particularist understanding of salvation. There is little, if any, hint that salvation is universal in scope (that Christ's death was for the benefit of "all") let alone that all in the end may be saved. It has sometimes been claimed that the notion of universal salvation is present in 15:22[105] and 28.[106] But this cannot be sustained. The immediate context makes clear that ἐν τῷ Χριστῷ πάντες ζῳοποιηθήσονται in 15:22 refers to believers, not to all human beings.[107] The purpose clause of 15:28, specifying the goal of God's redeeming work, that God might be πάντα ἐν πᾶσιν, hardly implies the final salvation of all.[108] It simply indicates that God will reign supreme. God's redemptive goal does not preclude the final ruin of unbelievers (indeed, on the logic of vv. 24–26, it could be argued that it requires their destruction). The particularist understanding of salvation that is found in 1 Corinthians, with its clear stress on the distinction between the saved and the lost, serves to reinforce the boundaries of the Christian community.

5.4.2. Cosmic eschatology in 15:27–28

The cosmic eschatological perspective of 1:26–27 and 7:31b correlates with the affirmation of cosmic eschatology in 15:27–28. Paul expects "all things" (τὰ) πάντα, to be subjected to Christ under the overall rule of God. Plainly, he has in mind a "cosmic" event. The allusion to Adam in the citation of Ps 8:6b in v. 27 suggests that Paul is thinking in terms of a perfected creation. But whether the establishment of God's intended cosmic order comes about by the transformation of the existing creation or, as in 1:26–27 and 7:31b, by the destruction of the present creation and the creation of a new world is not specified. It is noteworthy, though, that the language of destruction is prominent in

104 Fee 1987, 69.
105 de Boer 1988, 112–13.
106 Boring 1986, 280.
107 So Barrett 1968, 352; Conzelmann 1975, 269.
108 *Contra* Boring 1986, 280.

144

vv. 24–26.[109] While, then, 15:27–28 chimes with the cosmic eschatology of 1:26–27 and 7:31b, it does not so obviously correlate with the *radical* cosmic perspective of these verses. But, at the same time, it is not in tension with that perspective.

5.4.3. The present body and the resurrection body (15:42–50)

The radical discontinuity between this world/age and God's new world, implied in Paul's talk of κόσμος (= "this world") comports with his emphasis on the discontinuity between the present body, the σῶμα ψυχικόν, and the resurrection body, the σῶμα πνευματικόν, in the discussion of 15:42–50.[110] The term σῶμα for Paul denotes a person's bodily participation in and with their environment. The σῶμα ψυχικόν is the mode of bodily existence in the present world/age. The σῶμα πνευματικόν is the form of bodily existence appropriate to the coming world/age. [111]

In 15:42–50, the σῶμα ψυχικόν and the σῶμα πνευματικόν are *quantitatively* distinct. This is clear from the construction of v. 44b, Εἰ ἔστιν ... ἔστιν καὶ.... Paul is not talking about the one body viewed from two different angles but about two different bodies. As Witherington writes, "We may perhaps urge that Paul saw a continuity in the form or shape of the two bodies, but we cannot argue that he held that the resurrection body is the *same* body."[112] Moreover, the two σῶματα are *qualitatively* distinct. The σῶμα ψυχικόν is characterized by φθορά, ἀτιμία and ἀσθένεια; the σῶμα πνευματικόν is marked by ἀφθαρσία, δόξα and δύναμις (vv. 42–43). The present body partakes of the attributes of this world: mortality, dishonour and weakness. The resurrection body shares the qualities of the new world: immortality, glory and power. It should be noted that the σῶμα ψυχικόν is for Paul the body given to Adam at creation (cf. the citation

---

[109] E. P. Sanders (1991, 31) suggests that cosmic dissolution is implied in the purpose clause of v. 28.

[110] The relation of the σῶμα ψυχικόν to the σῶμα πνευματικόν in 1 Cor 15:44ff is much debated. Those who stress continuity include M. E. Dahl 1962, 94–5; Ellis 1990; Fee 1987, 777; Gillman 1988; Sider 1975. Those who stress discontinuity include Conzelmann 1975, 281; Dunn 1977, 290; M. J. Harris 1983,126; Witherington 1992, 189ff.

[111] In Intertestamental Judaism there is a "correlation between mode of existence and location of existence": so Cooper 1989, 86. A similar correlation is thought to be present in Paul: so M. J. Harris 1983, 165–71.

[112] Witherington 1992, 197

of Gen 2:7 at v. 45). [113] The implication, therefore, is that φθορά – as a property of the present physical body as originally created by God – is an inherent and innate characteristic of the present created order. Furthermore, the two σώματα are *materially* distinct. This idea emerges at v. 50, where Paul indicates that "flesh and blood cannot inherit the kingdom of God". [114] The lack of material continuity between present existence and resurrection life is also apparent at 6:13b, where Paul adds to the Corinthian slogan, "Food is meant for the stomach and the stomach for food", the qualification, "and God will destroy both one and the other". [115]

The sharp distinction between the present body and the future body mirrors the discontinuity of the different worlds to which they belong. The present physical body cannot inherit God's kingdom, because it is part of the "form of this world" which must pass away. [116]

---

[113] Several scholars dispute the point, arguing that the σώμα ψυχικόν is for Paul the physical body, insofar as it bears the effects of Adam's sin; e.g. Clavier 1964, 351; Kim 1984, 264 n. 1; Sider 1975, 433–4. Kim argues that the idea of Adam's fall is implicit in these verses. He states, "The reason why Paul contrasts Christ and Adam nevertheless without making an explicit reference to the latter's fall in 1 Cor 15:44–49, is because for Paul Adam is always a sinner . . . What Adam was before his fall does not interest him." What Kim fails to recognize, however, is that even an implicit reference to the fall of Adam would undermine Paul's argument at this stage. As Lincoln (1981, 43) emphasizes, Paul is not arguing *a fortiori*: if there is a physical body subject to corruption how much more must there be a body of glory. Rather Paul is saying that from the beginning a different kind of body has been in view. Lincoln draws attention to the observations of Vos (1986, 169 n. 19) "the Apostle was intent in showing that in the plan of God from the outset provision was made for a higher kind of body . . . From the abnormal body of sin no inference could be drawn to that effect. The abnormal and the eschatological are not so logically correlated that one can be postulated from the other. But the world of creation and the world to come are thus correlated, the one pointing forward to the other." Cf. Ridderbos 1975, 542 n. 152.

[114] Jeremias (1955/56) argues implausibly that by "flesh and blood" Paul means "the living", in contrast to "the dead". For a critique of Jeremias, see Witherington 1992, 199–200.

[115] This relation of 6:13b to 6:13a is of course a debated issue. Is v. 13b agreeing with v. 13a (and if so, is v. 13a a statement made by the Corinthians or is it Paul's own comment?), qualifying it, or contradicting it? The question is discussed in detail by Fee (1987, 254–7) and Wedderburn (1987, 28–32). Fee understands v. 13b as the continuation of the Corinthian slogan in v. 13a, and Wedderburn sees it as Paul's own comment, but one to which the Corinthians would have assented. I take the view that v. 13b is Paul's own statement and that it is intended to support the Corinthians' slogan of v. 13a – but from Paul's own apocalyptic perspective, a viewpoint which the Corinthians did not share.

[116] Admittedly, a greater sense of the continuity between present and future modes of bodily existence emerges in 1 Cor 15:51–54, where Paul speaks of "change" and employs the metaphor of clothing, connoting transformation, rather than exchange and replacement: so M. J. Harris 1983, 127. This is partly due to the fact that, as Witherington

5.5. Summary and conclusion

Paul's usage of κόσμος in 1 Corinthians may be understood in terms of a linguistic and socio-rhetorical strategy of defamiliarization (as defined in chapter 2). He "makes strange" a term which would have been familiar to his readers, a term which evoked a world-view and which was impregnated (so to speak) with ideology. That ideology would have legitimated the Corinthians' social and cultural integration into the macrosociety. Paul uncodes some of the standard associations of κόσμος (= world/universe) in customary usage and recodes new ones. In the process, he radically subverts the world-view and ideology conventionally linked with the term. He recodes a quite different perspective on the world. He rejects the ideal of *integration* into the social order of the κόσμος and replaces it with that of *distinction* from the κόσμος.

Paul modifies the conventional network of associations of κόσμος (= world/universe). He generates a number of unexpected, negative linkages. κόσμος is placed in the collocational "bad" company of ὁ αἰὼν οὗτος, ἀπολλυμένοι, σάρξ, τὰ μωρά, τὰ ἀσθενῆ, θάνατος, περικαθάρματα, περίψημα, πόρνοι, πλεονέκται, ἅρπαγες, εἰδωλολάτραι, ἄδικοι, ἐξουθενημένοι, ἄπιστοι, μοιχοί, μαλακοί, ἀρσενοκοῖται, κλέπται, μέθυσοι and λοίδοροι. It is set in opposition to God, the church and the kingdom of God. Paul retains the standard associations of order and unity. Moreover, he maintains the conventional term-to-experience link. In the majority of cases, with κόσμος Paul refers to the human and natural world in which his readers participate. Yet, even the standard positive links are turned into adverse ones: κόσμος is the "ordered" and "unified" "world" of opposition to God. Paul's usage thus treads a line between maintaining a recognizable identity with conventional usage of the term, while at the same time working against and subverting the conventions.

Paul uses κόσμος in a predominantly negative way. For the most part, κόσμος bears the negative apocalyptic sense "this world". In 6:2 and 11:32, it has the negative meaning "unrighteous human beings".

(1992, 201) states, Paul in these verses is dealing with "the question of what happens to the living at the parousia *vis-à-vis* what happens to the dead". "Change" as the broader metaphor can be applied to both groups. "Resurrection" can be applied only to the dead (v. 52).

In some instances, the negative element in Paul's usage emerges not in the sense borne by the word but in its deployment in relation to other terms. Thus in 4:9 and 13, the apostles are linked negatively to the κόσμος (= world/universe) as θέατρον, περικαθάρματα and περίψημα. In 5:10 the κόσμος (= world/universe) is seen to be full of immoral and corrupt people. In 7:31a "using" the κόσμος (= inhabited world), though not a "bad" activity, is relativized in view of the fact that παράγει τό σχῆμα τοῦ κόσμου τούτου.

κόσμος is the main negative term of the epistle. Of the negative quartet, ἁμαρτία, θάνατος, σάρξ and κόσμος, the latter is far and away the most prominent. ἁμαρτία appears only four times in the letter (15:3, 17, 56(×2)). θάνατος occurs eight times, mainly in chapter 15 (3:22; 11:26; 15:21, 26, 54, 55(×2), 56). At 3:22, it is associated with κόσμος. σάρξ occurs eleven times (1:26, 29; 5:5; 6:16; 7:28; 10:18; 15:39(×4); 15:50). Only at 1:26, where it is linked with κόσμος, does it designate a realm of hostility to God.[117]

Paul challenges the world-view linked with κόσμος (= world/universe). The κόσμος is no longer the well-ordered, beautiful, praiseworthy and ever-enduring world, to which human beings are microcosmically linked. It is now the anti-godly, hostile world which is under God's judgement and doomed to destruction. Paul also subverts the ideology of κόσμος (= world/universe). The value-system and social ordering which κόσμος (= world/universe) had come to encode is seen to have been overthrown in the apocalyptic event of the cross. God's new creation community operates with completely different values and structures.

Paul utilizes κόσμος to promote a "response to the world" which, given the standard sociological definitions, may be described as sectarian. Of the seven sectarian responses outlined by Wilson, it seems that Paul's usage (and his theological perspective in the letter as a whole) corresponds most closely to the *revolutionist* response.[118] This world, according to Paul in his statements on κόσμος, is a corrupt and hostile place. The present world and those who belong to it are in the process of perishing. Salvation consists in being rescued from this world/age and being relocated in God's kingdom. 1 Cor 7:29–31 provides little incentive

---

[117] It may, though, bear this sense in 5:5 in the phrase "the destruction of the flesh".
[118] 5:10 rules out the *introversionist* response.

for reforming the world outside the church. The world is not to be reformed; it is to be destroyed.

Paul views the situation at Corinth as one of social and ideological compromise. The church is failing to maintain its distinctiveness within its wider social and cultural environment. He uses κόσμος to try to build strong group boundaries and to construct a social world *distinct* from the larger society, embracing alternative forms of sociality, patterns of living and community ideals.

6
κόσμος and κτίσις in Romans

6.1. Introduction

In comparison with his talk of κόσμος in 1 Corinthians, Paul's usage of κόσμος and κτίσις in Romans is much less accessible to socio-rhetorical analysis. The investigation of 1 Corinthians in the preceding chapters was facilitated by the comparatively large amount of information in that epistle about the situation of the readers and the clarity with which Paul's motives and goals in writing could be identified. When we come to Romans the path is not so smooth.

In recent years, there has been a lively debate over Paul's purpose in writing Romans: Ought the epistle to be viewed as arising out of Paul's own concerns or as a response to the particular needs of the Roman churches? A consensus has emerged that no one single purpose can account for Paul's writing to Rome and that due attention must be paid to both Paul's own interests and the socio-historical situation of the readers. Moreover, as a result of the rehabilitation of chapter 16,[1] it is now more readily recognized that Paul had a fair degree of knowledge about the character and structure of the Roman Christian community as he wrote.[2] Yet in spite of these advances, it remains an unsettled question how far the theological arguments of Rom 1:18 – 11:36 (where with one exception [1:8] occurrences of κόσμος and κτίσις are located) were shaped with the concrete needs and actual circumstances of the Roman readers in mind.[3]

---

[1] Following Gamble's (1977) exhaustive text-critical analysis, Rom 16, once commonly regarded as a later addition, is now viewed by the majority as an integral part of the original epistle.

[2] On the evidence which can be gleaned about Roman Christianity from Rom 16, see esp. P. Lampe 1987, 124–53; 1991.

[3] Watson's study (1986, 88–176) remains the most ambitious attempt to relate the theological discussion of Rom 1–11 to the actual situation of the Roman Christians.

In view of this uncertainty, in investigating Paul's usage of κόσμος and κτίσις in Romans, the approach adopted in the previous two chapters will more or less be reversed. This chapter will analyze in detail Paul's uses of κόσμος and κτίσις. The next chapter will consider how those uses might have been intended to function in the social and historical context of utterance.

The present chapter will first look at the theological context of reference for Paul's usage of κόσμος and κτίσις in Romans, then conduct a close examination of the key texts in their immediate literary and linguistic contexts, before looking briefly at related themes and emphases.

6.2. The theological context of reference

The sustained exposition of Rom 1:18 – 11:36 is the closest Paul comes to a systematic account of his theology. One of the most significant, but often neglected, features of the theological development is the prominence of creator/creation motifs.[4]

Heavy emphasis is laid on the understanding of God as creator (1:19, 20, 25; 4:17; 9:19–24; 11:23–24, 36). Concern is shown to correlate God's redeeming activity very closely with his role and activity as creator. In a highly revealing statement, Paul describes God as the one "who gives life to the dead and calls into existence the things that do not exist" (4:17b),[5] linking God's redeeming work (giving life to the dead) with his creative work. The discussion of the place of Israel in God's plans in Rom 9–11 closes with a doxology affirming God as the source (ἐξ αὐτοῦ), mediator (δι᾽ αὐτοῦ) and goal (εἰς αὐτόν) of the material creation (τὰ πάντα), thus showing that the sweep of God's purposes in the course of salvation history is encompassed within an all-embracing purpose for creation (11:36).

There is good reason for believing that the creational dimension of God's saving activity is implied in the key expression, the "righteousness of God", widely regarded as the dominant theme of the

---

[4] See Achtemeier 1985, 15–26; Byrne 1990; Garlington 1990; Kraftchick 1987; Shields 1980; Stuhlmacher 1987, 9–11.

[5] See the reflections of Käsemann (1971b, 90–3; 1980, 121–4) on this statement. Cf. Shields 1980, 51–4. The first part of the designation corresponds to the second of the Eighteen Benedictions (cf. Jos. As. 8:9–10; 20:7), on which see Moxnes 1980, 233–9. Hofius (1971/72) highlights the similarity between Rom 4:17b and 2 Macc 7:28.

epistle.[6] Käsemann circumvented the impasse in the traditional debate as to whether δικαιοσύνη θεοῦ signifies God's own righteousness (taking θεοῦ as a subjective genitive) or the righteousness which comes from God and which God imparts (taking θεοῦ as an objective genitive) by asserting that δικαιοσύνη θεοῦ has both a "power" and a "gift" character.[7] Interpreting Paul's view against the Old Testament and Jewish apocalyptic background, Käsemann argued that God's righteousness for Paul is a broad concept with cosmic significance. The phrase δικαιοσύνη θεοῦ, for Käsemann, speaks of God's faithfulness toward the whole of creation. He writes, "God's power reaches out for the world, and the world's salvation lies in its being recaptured for the sovereignty of God."[8] Although Käsemann's views are by no means uncontroversial, his emphasis on the comprehensiveness of the conception has won large support.[9] If Käsemann is right, the "righteousness of God" is a conception which for Paul (in Romans) underlines the unity of God's creative and redemptive activity.

Creation motifs figure at significant points in the argument of chapters 1–8. Rom 1:18–32 contains a number of echoes of Gen 1–2. The reference to the act of creation in Rom 1:20 points back to Gen 1:1. The list of animals in Rom 1:23 (καὶ πετεινῶν καὶ τετραπόδων καὶ ἑρπετῶν) reflects the influence of Gen 1:20–25.[10] The terms θῆλυς and ἄρσην in Rom 1:26–27 allude to the statement of Gen 1:27 that God created human beings male and female. The use of εἰκών in Rom 1:23 hints at Gen 1:27 and the statement that God created humankind in his own image.[11] The words οἱ τὰ τοιαῦτα πράσσοντες ἄξιοι θανάτου εἰσίν in Rom 1:32 may point to the prohibition and the threat of death in Gen 2:17.[12] These echoes serve to depict Gentile wickedness as a radical and paradoxical departure from God's creatorial intentions for men and women.[13] In Rom 2:7 Paul declares that those

---

[6] Stuhlmacher's 1991 essay is a recent restatement of this point of view.

[7] Käsemann writes (1969b, 174), "the gift which is being bestowed here is never at any time separable from its Giver. It partakes of the character of power, in so far as God himself enters the arena and remains in the arena with it."

[8] Käsemann 1969b, 182.

[9] See the review of the discussion in Brauch 1977; Onsetti and Brauch 1993.

[10] See Hyldahl 1955/56.

[11] Wedderburn 1980, 416.

[12] Dunn 1988, 69.

[13] Following Hooker (1959/60) and Jervell (1960, 312–31), a number of scholars believe that Paul is modelling the critique of Rom 1:18–32 on the story of Adam's fall in Gen 3: e.g. Bruce 1985, 80; Dunn 1988, 53; Milne 1980, 10–12; Ziesler 1989, 75. But while

who do good works in pursuit of δόξα, τιμή and ἀφθαρσία will be rewarded with eternal life on judgement day. According to Jewish theology, δόξα, τιμή and ἀφθαρσία were ends God had in view for his human creatures when he created them.[14] In 2:14–15 Paul argues that the Gentiles "by nature" (φύσει) – that is to say, as a result of God's creative act[15] – have a law within their hearts, an instinctual moral awareness, which functions in certain respects as an equivalent to the Jewish law. Paul's summary charge in 3:23, πάντες γὰρ ἥμαρτον καὶ ὑστεροῦνται τῆς δόξης τοῦ θεοῦ, implies that every human being has replicated the sin of Adam.[16] In 4:20, Paul comments that Abraham, the exemplar of faith, "gave glory to God" (δοὺς δόξαν τῷ θεῷ). Giving glory to God was specified in 1:21 as the required response to the revelation of God the creator, a response which the disobedient Gentiles failed to render (γνόντες τὸν θεὸν οὐχ ὡς θεὸν ἐδόξασαν).[17] Paul thus depicts Abraham's faith as proper creaturely submission to the creator. In 5:12–21, Paul develops the Adam / Christ parallelism. Christ, the new Adam, has reversed the calamitous effects of the disobedience of the old Adam. Much of the discussion that follows in chapters 6–8 operates within that Adam / Christ framework. Christians have been liberated from the regimes of sin and death introduced by Adam, and have been transferred into the realm of righteousness. The eternal life forfeited by Adam (Gen 2:9, 17; 3:22), the hallmark of the restored creation (Rom 5:21), is the present possession of believers (6:4, 11, 13, 22–23). Paul declares in 6:6 that "our old self" (ὁ παλαιὸς ἡμῶν ἄνθρωπος) has been crucified, signalling believers' disengagement from the old solidarity with Adam.[18]

---

there are good reasons for hearing echoes of Gen 1–2 in Rom 1, the evidence for the influence of Gen 3 is much less convincing: see Scroggs 1966, 75–6 n. 3; Wedderburn 1980, 413–19.

[14] Dunn 1988, 85–6, 168. Cf. Ps 8:5. For the restoration or the intensification of glory as a future hope, see 1 Enoch 50:1 (in conjunction with "honour"); 2 Apoc. Bar. 15:8; 51:1–3; 54:15, 21; CD 3:20; 1QS 4:23. That God created human beings for ἀφθαρσία is affirmed in Wis 2:23.

[15] See Shields 1980, 9–19.

[16] Dunn 1988, 168; Scroggs 1966, 73–4. In a strand of Jewish thinking, one of the consequences of Adam's transgression was the loss or distortion of glory: Apoc. Mos. 21:6; cf. Sir. 49:16; 2 Enoch 30:11–18. For rabbinic references, see Str-B 4.887.

[17] For other textual links between Rom 1 and 4, comparing and contrasting Abraham and the rebellious Gentiles, see Adams 1997a.

[18] Moo 1991, 390.

The Adamic background of 7:7–13, where Paul discusses the relation of law to sin, is widely recognized.[19] It is quite likely that the allusion to Adam carries over into 7:14–25,[20] where Paul describes the debilitating experience of living under the law without the aid of the Spirit.[21] An allusion to Adam's fall, it is generally accepted, is present in 8:18–23.[22] Adamic Christology and soteriology are in the foreground in 8:29–30: Christ is the founder of a new eschatological humanity (πρωτότοκον ἐν πολλοῖς ἀδελφοῖς); through Christ, God's original creative purposes for human beings – bearing God's εἰκών and reflecting his δόξα – are now being brought to fulfilment (συμμόρφους τῆς εἰκόνος ... ἐδόξασεν).[23]

The proliferation of creation motifs in 1:18–32 and 8:18–39, the opening section and the climax of the main discussion, indicates their key position in the structure of Paul's argument. The whole exposition of 1:18–11:36 begins and ends with a focus on God the creator (1:20–25; 11:36).

In the light of the above, it is difficult to disagree with Achtemeier's conclusion that the sweep of Paul's thought in Romans concerns "the course of the history of God's dealing with his creation, from its rebellion against him to its final redemption".[24] The strong emphasis in this letter on God as creator and providential ruler and on the world as his creation, which tempers the apocalyptic dualism of the present evil world/age and the future world/age, is the main perspective informing Paul's use of κόσμος and κτίσις.

6.3. Examination of texts

κόσμος occurs at 1:8, 20; 3:6, 19; 4:13; 5:12, 13; 11:12, 15. κτίσις is found at 1:20, 25; 8:19, 20, 21, 22, 39. It can be seen that occurrences

---

[19] Allusions to the story of Adam and Eve in this subsection are listed by Theissen 1987, 202–8, and Watson 1986, 152. See also Dunn 1988, 379–80; Wedderburn 1980, 420–2.

[20] Cf. Longenecker 1964, 114. Watson (1986, 155) writes, "7:14–25 ... is to be linked with v. 13 and thus with the passage as a whole. The present tense merely indicates that Paul is discussing the enduring effects of the primal event described in vv. 7–12."

[21] For a detailed defence of this view of Rom 7:14–25, see Kümmel 1974. For the point of view that Paul in this passage is describing Christian experience, see Dunn 1975, and more recently, Garlington 1990.

[22] See further below, pp. 174–5.

[23] Dunn 1988, 482–6.

[24] Achtemeier 1985, 13.

of κτίσις are concentrated in the passages 1:18–32 and 8:18–39, where, as noted above, creation motifs proliferate.

We begin the analysis with Rom 1:20–25, gliding over the instance of κόσμος in 1:8, where the word has the sense of "inhabited world".[25] Appearing in the epistolary thanksgiving, κόσμος here is of no direct significance for the argument of the main body of the epistle. Yet such an innocuous occurrence at the beginning of the letter could be taken as an early signal that the usage of κόσμος in Romans is not going to be as polemically or as negatively charged as it was in 1 Corinthians.

6.3.1. God has revealed himself through the created world (1:19–20)

Within Rom 1:18–3:20, which describes the human plight and culminates in a charge of universal sinfulness,[26] 1:18–32 serves as an indictment against pagan society.[27] It is true that Paul never actually specifies "Gentiles" or "Greeks and barbarians" (cf. v. 14) in this sub-section, but his appeal to God's revelation through creation as the standard of judgement (and not at all to the law) indicates that Gentiles and not Jews are in view.[28] The passage strongly echoes standard Jewish polemic against the Gentiles, especially the anti-Gentile polemic of *Wisdom of Solomon* (particularly Wis 13:1–19; 14:22–31). It is widely held that Paul made direct use of this document in the formulation of his argument. The parallels, both linguistic and conceptual, are striking,

---

[25] Paul's statement that the Roman believers' faith is being "proclaimed throughout the world" (ἡ πίστις ὑμῶν καταγγέλλεται ἐν ὅλῳ τῷ κόσμῳ) is clearly rhetorical exaggeration: cf. BAGD 447; Cranfield 1975, 75 n. 2.

[26] The mainline view that 1:18 – 3:20 aims or partly aims at demonstrating that every human being has sinned has been questioned recently by several scholars: Bassler 1982; 1984; G. N. Davies 1990; Ziesler 1989, 41–2. The weight of evidence for the traditional viewpoint, however, remains overwhelming. 3:9 indicates that Paul clearly regards the previous part of his argument as laying down the charge that all are under sin (προῃτιασάμεθα γὰρ Ἰουδαίους τε καὶ Ἕλληνας πάντας ὑφ' ἁμαρτίαν εἶναι); that there are no exceptions to this charge (οὐκ ἔστιν, οὐδὲ εἷς, ἕως ἑνός) is hammered home in the catena of 3:10–18. On the rhetorical coherence of Rom 1:18 – 3:20, see Aletti 1988.

[27] Bassler (1982, 128–33) challenges the traditional division of the text at 1:18 and 2:1, arguing for the unity 1:16 – 2:11. For criticisms of this approach, see Moo 1991, 117–18.

[28] Cranfield (1975, 105–6), Bassler (1982, 122), Jervell (1960, 316–19) and others argue that Jews are also included in the indictment, pointing to Paul's appropriation in v. 23 of the language of Ps 106:20 and Jer 2:11, texts which refer to Israel's fall into idolatry. But in picking up the wording of these texts, Paul is not thereby accusing Jews. Rather, as Fitzmyer (1993, 271) states, Paul "is simply extrapolating from such incidents in the history of the chosen people and applying the ideas to the pagan world".

and as Dunn states, are "too close to be accidental".[29] It is not until 2:1 that Paul begins to implicate the Jews, implicitly from 2:1 to 2:16, then explicitly from 2:17.

Rom 1:18–32 develops the initial declaration of v. 18, that God's wrath is being "revealed against all ungodliness and wickedness of those who by their wickedness suppress the truth". (Ἀποκαλύπτεται γὰρ ὀργὴ θεοῦ ἀπ᾽ οὐρανοῦ ἐπὶ πᾶσαν ἀσέβειαν καὶ ἀδικίαν ἀνθρώπων τῶν τὴν ἀλήθειαν ἐν ἀδικίᾳ κατεχόντων.)[30] Paul argues that as a consequence of their rejection of the revelation of God the creator (vv. 19–23), Gentiles have been abandoned by God (παρέδωκεν αὐτοὺς ὁ θεός, vv. 24, 26, 28) to the results of their own sinfulness.

κτίσις and κόσμος occur together in v. 20 in the expression, ἀπὸ κτίσεως κόσμου. κτίσις plainly has the sense "act of creation".[31] κόσμος clearly means "world / universe", in accordance with standard Greek usage. In view of the preceding κτίσεως and the following τοῖς ποιήμασιν, κόσμος has the particular nuance here of the "universe" *as created by God*.

κτίσις occurs again at v. 25. Paul states that the disobedient Gentiles ἐσεβάσθησαν καὶ ἐλάτρευσαν τῇ κτίσει παρὰ τὸν κτίσαντα. Here κτίσις means "created thing", "creature". Paul does not specify whether by κτίσις he has in mind the lifeless idols or the actual human and animal creatures which the idols are intended to represent (ἀνθρώπου καὶ πετεινῶν καὶ τετραπόδων καὶ ἑρπετῶν, v. 23). The reference is probably intentionally broad, since Paul is expressing here a general truth (as he sees it) about the nature of idolatry – that it consists in an essential confusion of creator and created things.[32]

---

[29] Dunn 1988, 56–7. Cf. Romanuik 1967/68; Sanday and Headlam 1902, 51–2; Wilckens 1978, 96–7.

[30] The suggestion that God's wrath, like his righteousness (v. 17), is revealed in the gospel, advanced by Bockmuehl (1990, 138–41), Cranfield (1975, 109–10), Leenhardt (1961, 60–1) and Wilckens (1978, 102), should be rejected. Paul goes on to describe God's wrath in vv. 24–32 in terms of sin and its consequences, which, in comparison with the gospel, he could hardly have thought of as something new. Cf. Travis 1986, 36. Nevertheless, the repetition of ᾽αποκαλύπτεται in v.18, which implies that the two revelations are eschatologically linked (so Bornkamm 1969, 62–3), indicates that the wrath of God, though always operational, has somehow been brought into sharper focus by the gospel events.

[31] Cf. *T.Reub.* 2:3, 9; *Pss. Sol.* 8:7; Josephus, *War* 4.533.

[32] This is a standard Jewish theme: e.g. Ep. Jer. 59ff; *Ep. Arist.* 132ff; *Jub.* 12:1ff; *T. Naph.* 3:1ff; Josephus, *Ap.* 2:190ff; Philo, *Abr.* 75, 88; *Ebr.* 108ff; *Decal.* 53ff, 66–7; *Spec.* 1:15ff; Wis 13:1–10.

As noted in chapter 1, Bultmann claims that Rom 1:25 casts a dark shadow over κτίσις – "'creation' becomes a destructive power whenever man decides in favor of it instead of for God".[33] Yet the context makes clear that the κτίσις is not inherently ambiguous. It is not the κτίσις which seduces and tempts human beings away from God. If human beings stand in an ambiguous relation to creation, it is due to *their* misperception and misappropriation of it, to *their* distortion of its true character. Paul is not casting aspersions on κτίσις but on those who misuse it.

In v. 20, κόσμος (= world / universe) is contextually equated with τὰ ποιήματα. It is by means of the "things he has made" that God has made himself known to the Gentiles (τοῖς ποιήμασιν νοούμενα καθορᾶται). Effectively, then, the κόσμος is understood as the instrument of God's universal revelation. As Dunn writes, what Paul has in view in this passage is "a revelation of God through the cosmos, to humankind as a whole, and operative since the creation of the cosmos".[34]

Paul's argument in this verse draws on Stoic natural theology.[35] As observed in chapter 3, the Stoics contended that the existence and providence of God can be deduced by rational reflection on the κόσμος. This is possible, they argued, because of the affinity between the rationality of the human mind (νοῦς) and the rationality manifest in the κόσμος. The term νοούμενα indicates Paul's acknowledgement of such an affinity.[36]

The revealed[37] knowledge of God (τὸ γνωστὸν τοῦ θεοῦ, v. 19) is not merely a potential knowledge but an actual knowledge. It is actually

---

[33] Bultmann 1952, 230.

[34] Dunn 1988, 57.

[35] Longenecker (1964, 54) states that Greek natural theology has "partially penetrated" Rom 1:19–20.

[36] Cf. Dunn 1988, 58. The words ἐν αὐτοῖς in v. 19 may also reflect the belief in the continuity between human rationality and the rationality evident in the whole universe: so Dunn 1988, 57. As we might expect, as well as similarities there are also marked differences between Rom 1:18–32 and Stoic thought; these are highlighted by Gärtner 1955, 133–44. Gärtner, however, in his concern to emphasize the Jewishness of Paul's thought, refuses to allow even a discriminating use of Stoic concepts on Paul's part.

[37] Although Paul indicates that the knowledge of God the creator is acquired through reason and sensory perception (νοούμενα καθορᾶται, v. 20; cf. Demarest 1991, 140–1), it is still better to describe what Paul has in view in Rom 1:19ff as "natural *revelation*" rather than "natural *theology*". According to the classic definition in Christian thought, "natural theology" is truth about God which can be discovered by the unaided faculty of human reason, in contrast to a knowledge of God which is "revealed". But here, the

possessed by the Gentiles. This is clear from v. 21, where Paul states that the Gentiles "knew God" (γνόντες τὸν θεόν, cf. τὸ δικαίωμα τοῦ θεοῦ ἐπιγνόντες, v. 32). Paul's charge is not that they have missed the truth of God (though they could have apprehended more, v. 21), but rather that they have deliberately suppressed it. As Gärtner writes, "The compassing of the natural revelation is not only a positive but unrealisable potentiality in man – he *has realised* it."[38] The questions are raised, What is the content, aim and capability of the knowledge of God made available through the κόσμος? Is the revelation of which the κόσμος is the vehicle a negative revelation or a positive one?

It is clear that the revelation through the κόσμος has a definite and positive content: Barth's reading of Rom 1:19–21 that what creation reveals is the fact that God cannot be known,[39] simply cannot be sustained. What God has made evident are his "invisible qualities", τὰ ἀόρατα αὐτοῦ, clarified as his "eternal power" and "divine nature", ἥ τε ἀΐδιος αὐτοῦ δύναμις καὶ θειότης.[40] Moreover, God has revealed himself as the world's *maker*. This is implied both by ἀπὸ κτίσεως κόσμου and τοῖς ποιήμασιν in v. 20, and in v. 25, Paul specifically refers to God as τὸν κτίσαντα. The accusation that Gentiles have confused creation with the creator could hardly have stood if Paul had not thought such a distinction were apparent from the revelation through the created world. What is revealed through the κόσμος is, therefore, the presence, power and nature of its creator.

The effect of the revelation through creation is to leave Gentiles "without excuse", ἀναπολογήτους (v. 20). Whether the construction, εἰς τὸ εἶναι, is to be taken as expressing purpose or result is debated by commentators.[41] The difference, however, is not as significant as has sometimes been assumed. If understood consecutively, the consequence or effect is plainly conceived of as having been intended by God. And if

knowledge of God made accessible through the κόσμος is the result of a definite self-revelation of God. This is made clear in the statement, ὁ θεὸς γὰρ αὐτοῖς ἐφανέρωσεν (v.19); cf. Hooker (1959/60, 299–300).
[38] Gärtner 1955, 79. Barth (1952, 46) comments, "When we rebel, we are in rebellion not against what is foreign to us but against that which is most intimately ours, not against what is removed from us but against that which lies at our hands."
[39] Barth 1952, 46–7.
[40] ἀΐδιος and θειότης are both Hellenistic philosophical terms. For ἀΐδιος, see Sasse 1964a; for θειότης, see Kleinknecht 1965.
[41] See the discussion in Moo 1991, 118.

taken purposively, it emerges from v. 21 that the purpose is to be seen as a secondary and conditional one. In either case, the essential thought is this: God has designed that if the Gentiles should fail to honour him, they should be denied the excuse of ignorance.

That the Gentiles are rendered guilty is the *outcome* of this revelation, but it is not the *aim* of it. God's primary intent in revealing himself, Paul makes clear in v. 21, was not to condemn but to lead people to obedient faith in him. This is apparent from Paul's description of what the Gentiles failed to do when confronted with God's revelation: "they did not honour him as God or give thanks to him", οὐχ ὡς θεὸν ἐδόξασαν ἢ ηὐχαρίστησαν. Barrett correctly perceives the significance of these words. He comments,

> As God's creature, man was bound to render glory and thanksgiving to his creator; this means not merely to acknowledge his existence, and to employ the words and rites of religion, but to recognize his lordship and live in grateful obedience – in fact (in the Pauline sense) to believe, to have faith.[42]

As noted above, in Rom 4:20 Abraham's faithful response to the creator is expressed as his giving δόξα to God. In 15:6 the verb δοξάζω is specifically used with reference to the obedient and worshipful response of Christians toward God (cf. 15:9).

If God's revelation through the κόσμος aims at bringing the Gentiles into a right relationship with him, it must (in Paul's view) have the capacity to achieve that end. That the revelation through creation, as Paul envisages it here, is capable of leading people into a proper standing with God is denied by many interpreters. Moo, for instance, writes, "This limited knowledge falls far short of what is necessary to establish a relationship with Him."[43] Such an approach, however, leaves Paul with a seemingly intractable logical problem: the Gentiles are condemned for rejecting a right relationship with God, but that relationship was never on offer in the first place. As Paul sees it, it is not that the revelation through the created order is limited – that it cannot lead to a true standing with God – it is rather that men and women deliberately distort the truth they have received and never reach the goal for which that truth was intended. The inadequacy of the revelation through the κόσμος for Paul lies not in the revelation itself but in its

42 Barrett 1957, 36.
43 Moo 1991, 102.

160

misappropriation due to sin.[44] Moo's objection is therefore quite misconceived. It lays the emphasis on a deficient revelation rather than on an inappropriate response. It is precisely the sufficiency and clarity of the revelation which make its rejection so incriminating.[45]

The revelation of which the κόσμος is the instrument, then, has to be judged as a positive one. It is sufficient in itself to lead human beings into a worshipful relationship with God. That it has a negative outcome, securing the condemnation of the disobedient Gentiles, is due to its subversion by human sinfulness. Even the incriminatory effect of the revelation, Paul leaves his readers in no doubt, is fully part of God's design (as much as the sin-exposing function of the law in Rom 7:7–13). The revelation through the κόσμος, in the thought of Romans, stands in a positive relation to the gospel. It exposes and defines a dilemma which finds its resolution in the gospel. And it prepares for and finds its fulfilment in God's climactic revelation in Christ.

In Rom 1:20, κόσμος carries its conventional associations of orderliness, stability, cohesion, splendour and so on. Paul, in vv. 19–21, appears to presuppose aspects of the view of the world conventionally linked with κόσμος (= world / universe): the world as an ordered structure, the world as a unity, the world as an object of beauty (cf. Wis 13:3–7), the world as an order to which human beings are intimately and intricately related.

The notion of a well-ordered world comes further to expression in vv. 22–32, where Paul sets Gentile disobedience within the context of a universal moral order. Paul appeals to the category "nature", φύσις, in vv. 26–27, where he denounces homosexual activity. He describes female homosexual practice as the exchange of the "natural intercourse for unnatural" (αἵ τε γὰρ θήλειαι αὐτῶν μετήλλαξαν τὴν φυσικὴν χρῆσιν εἰς τὴν παρὰ φύσιν) and male homosexual activity as "giving up natural intercourse with women" (ἀφέντες τὴν φυσικὴν χρῆσιν τῆς θηλείας). Paul argues on the basis that there is a rational, natural order, at least in the area of sexual relations, in accordance with which one is expected to live.[46] The notion of living in harmony with the

---

[44] According to Calvin (1894, 71), God's manifestation in creation is "sufficiently clear" in itself, but because of "our blindness" it is insufficient: we are prevented by our blindness, "so that we reach not to the end in view".

[45] What the revelation through creation is incapable of doing is overcoming the human sin which thwarts its purpose.

[46] The appeal to a natural order in connection with aberrant sexual behaviour is found in *T.Naph.* 3:2–5. cf. 2:8–9.

CONSTRUCTING THE WORLD

natural arrangement of things, as observed in chapter 3, is a Stoic (and Cynic) one. Paul freely draws upon this theme. The main difference between Paul and the Stoics is that for Paul the natural order is specifically the order intended by the creator. In vv. 28–30, Paul takes up another Stoic notion: "that which is fitting/proper", τὸ καθῆκον. The vices listed in vv. 29–30 are summarily introduced as τὰ μὴ καθήκοντα. In Stoic moral argumentation τὸ καθῆκον denotes "the demands and actions which arise out of the claims of environment and which critical reason sees to be in harmony with ... nature".[47] Verses 28–30 are thus predicated on the assumption that there is a good and proper moral order which the vices catalogued violate.

That idea of a universal moral order is further intimated in Paul's description of the manifestation of God's wrath in vv. 24ff. C. H. Dodd observed that the progress of evil in society is depicted in 1:18–32 as a natural process of cause and effect.[48] Dodd mistakenly dissociated the retributive process from the direct activity of God: the words παρέδωκεν αὐτοὺς ὁ θεός in vv. 24, 26, 28 clearly point to the *deliberate* act of God.[49] Even so, it is clear that God's action amounts to giving the Gentiles over to the inevitable consequences of their actions.[50] As Robinson states, God's wrath is

the process of inevitable retribution which comes into operation when God's laws are broken ... he leaves pagan society to stew in its own juice. The retribution which overtakes it, resulting in automatic moral degradation, is what "comes on" almost like a thermostat when, as it were, the moral temperature drops below a certain point. This is part of God's order and it works automatically ...[51]

[47] Schlier 1965, 438. On the Stoic concept of proper functions, see L–S 1:359–68; 2:355–64. The negative form in Rom 1:28 (which also occurs in 2 Macc 6:4; 3 Macc 4:16; Philo, *Cher.* 14) differs from the usual Stoic formulation τὸ παρὰ τὸ καθῆκον.
[48] Dodd 1932, 29. The belief that the world exhibits inherent laws of action and consequence is the presupposition of the Jewish wisdom tradition: see Von Rad 1972, 124–43.
[49] So Cranfield 1975, 120. It may be that the passives ἐματαιώθησαν, ἐσκοτίσθη and ἐμωράνθησαν in vv. 21–22 are also meant to be understood as references to God's action: so Michel 1966, 65.
[50] God's judgement is to let the Gentiles drift into further involvement in sin. This line of thought may be compared with the dictum of Wis 11:16, "one is punished by the very things by which one sins".
[51] J. A. T. Robinson 1979, 18; cf. Travis 1986, 38. Paul reflects a standard Jewish belief that there is an inevitable regression from idolatry to sinful conduct more generally: Deut 28:13–14; Hos 5:15–6:11; Ezek 36:25ff; Wis 14:22–29; *2 Apoc. Bar.* 54:17ff; *1 Enoch* 99:7–9; *2 Enoch* 10:1ff; *T. Naph* 3:1ff.

162

In his explication of the outworking of the divine wrath, Paul places emphasis on the "fitness" of God's response to Gentile sin (the notion of appropriate punishment is extensively developed in *Wisdom of Solomon*, 11:15–26; 16:1–19:17). In each subsection, vv. 22–24, vv. 25–27 and vv. 28–32, a deliberate suppression of the truth is matched with a corresponding and appropriate response by God.[52] The exchange of the glory (δόξα) of God for idols (v. 23) results in their being given over to the dishonour (ἀτιμάζεσθαι) of their bodies (v. 24).[53] The exchange (μετήλλαξαν) of the truth of God for a lie (v. 25) leads to an exchange (μετήλλαξαν) of natural sexual relations for unnatural ones (vv. 26–27). The failure to give due recognition to God (οὐκ ἐδοκίμασαν, v. 28) leads to an unfit mind (ἀδόκιμον νοῦν, v. 28).

In vv. 22–32 Paul draws a picture of a morally ordered universe maintained by a universal natural law and an in-built retributive process which comes into play when the moral order is contravened.

In Rom 1:18–32, then, Paul uses κόσμος and κτίσις, alongside many other terms and expressions, to construct a positive assessment of the world as God's created and providentially ordered world. The created κόσμος is set forth as the vehicle of a revelation which is sufficient in itself to lead the inhabitants of the world into a correct relationship with their creator. In building this symbolic universe for his readers, Paul takes up Greek and Hellenistic as well as Jewish ideas. He embraces, to a considerable degree, the view of the world customarily associated with κόσμος (= world/universe) and appropriates the Stoic notions of the world's inherent rationality and orderliness and of the natural order of the world as a basis for theological and moral knowledge.[54]

Certainly, Paul draws a bleak analysis of Gentile society in this passage, as dark as anything we find in 1 Corinthians. But unlike 1 Corinthians, he does not depict pagan society as part of an all-encompassing evil and God-opposed κόσμος. Rather, he places the rebellious Gentiles within a well-regulated, morally structured, God-revealing and God-controlled κόσμος. The problem with Gentile society, on this assessment, is that it is out of harmony with the cosmic and natural

[52] Klostermann 1953. Cf. Bussmann 1975, 119–20; Hooker 1966/67; Jeremias 1954; Popkes 1982.
[53] Paul uses ἀτιμία as the opposite of δόξα in 1 Cor 11:14–15; 15:43; 2 Cor 6:8.
[54] The picture of the world Paul paints is similar in many respects to the picture drawn by the author of *Wisdom of Solomon*, though Paul avoids the more fanciful elements of this author's view of reality. On the world-view of *Wisdom of Solomon*, see Sweet 1965.

order. The critique presupposes the ideal of human integration into the created κόσμος.[55]

The standard conceptual linkages of κόσμος (= world/universe) which for situational reasons Paul subverted in 1 Corinthians, he now feels free to exploit. Paul largely builds his argument in Rom 1:18–32 on the world-view conventionally associated with κόσμος = world/ universe (though by elucidating the *disjunction* between pagan society and the cosmic order he is able to resist, for the time being at least, the ideological consequences of that world-view). The extent to which Paul appropriates and commits himself to this view of the world is striking in view of his opposition to it in 1 Corinthians.

6.3.2. The world liable to judgement (3:6)

The diatribe style directs the flow of argument in 3:1–8.[56] In chapter 2 Paul attacked the privileged status of Israel. At 3:1, he raises the issue, What has happened to the covenantal advantage of the Jew? What is the point of being a Jew if God shows no partiality? Paul insists that the value of being a Jew is "much, in every way" (v. 2). He argues that even though some have been unfaithful, their unfaithfulness will not nullify God's faithfulness (v. 3). This claim elicits the rejoinder from the imaginary interlocutor, If human unrighteousness only serves to draw out God's righteousness, is not God unjust when he inflicts his wrath?[57] Paul simply and decisively rejects this suggestion (μὴ γένοιτο). If God were unjust, he states, how then could he judge the world? (ἐπεὶ πῶς κρινεῖ ὁ θεὸς τὸν κόσμον;) On the day of reckoning[58] God is going to judge every human being. He could not do so if he were unjust.[59] Paul's line of reasoning in refuting the objection is clear enough. His procedure is to dismiss the initial suggestion – that human sin intensifies God's faithfulness – by showing that it leads to an impossible conclusion.[60]

[55] At a very basic level, the contrast Paul draws between social behaviour and the order of nature is similar to that drawn by the Cynics.
[56] The precise structure and thrust of Paul's argument is notoriously difficult to uncover. For fuller discussion, see Campbell 1991; Hall 1983; Stowers 1984; Watson 1986, 124–8.
[57] ὀργή in v. 5 probably embraces the present (cf. 1:18–32) and the future (cf. 2:5) aspects of the divine wrath.
[58] Punctuating κρινεῖ as a future tense. Cf. Dunn 1988, 135.
[59] Cf. Gen 18:25; Deut 32:4; Job 8:3; 34:10–12; Ps 9:8; 97:2; Isa 30:18; 41:1; Jer 12:1; Ezek 7:27; Mal 2:17.
[60] The same objection is reformulated in v. 7 in terms of human untruthfulness and divine truthfulness.

In 3:6, κόσμος, as the object of the verb κρίνω with ὁ θεός as its subject, has a human sense. It refers to the world of human beings.[61] Unlike 1 Cor 6:2 and 11:32 where, as we have seen, κόσμος as the object of judgement refers to *unbelieving* human beings in contrast to believers, here κόσμος embraces *all* human beings. There is no distinction between believers/saints and unbelieving humanity in this passage. The term has no pejorative reverberations. It is reading too much into the word to claim, as Bultmann does, that κόσμος in this instance denotes human beings "in their sinfulness and enmity toward God".[62] The κόσμος (= humanity) is certainly placed over against God, but this does not in itself imply the existence of enmity between the two parties. Neither does the fact that the κόσμος will be judged necessarily insinuate the wickedness of the κόσμος, since God's final judgement brings deliverance as well as doom, vindication as well as accusation (Rom 2:5–11). Even believers will have to stand before the judgement seat of God (Rom 14:10). Paul's evaluation of κόσμος is left unstated since the emphasis in this verse is plainly on the character of the God who will exercise judgement and not of those who will be judged. Paul's employment of κόσμος in 3:6 may thus be classed as a neutral use of the term.

6.3.3. The world condemned (3:19)

Rom 3:9–20 forms the climax of the epistle's opening argument, focusing on the universality of human sinfulness. The fact of universal sin is driven home in a series of Old Testament quotations in vv. 10–18.[63]

In 3:19 Paul asserts that the law speaks above all to those who are under it – his point being that the scriptural indictments just cited, which were originally aimed at non-Jews, apply just as much to Jews as to Gentiles[64] – "so that (ἵνα) every mouth may be silenced, and the whole world may be held accountable to God", πᾶν στόμα φραγῇ καὶ ὑπόδικος γένηται πᾶς ὁ κόσμος τῷ θεῷ.

κόσμος in 3:19, as in 3:6, has a human sense. πᾶς ὁ κόσμος means "all humanity".[65] This is clear from the preceding πᾶν στόμα

---

[61] Cf. BAGD 447; Cranfield 1975, 185; Dunn 1988, 135; Fitzmyer 1993, 329; Wilckens 1978, 166.
[62] Bultmann 1952, 255.
[63] On this subsection, see Keck 1977.
[64] Dunn 1988, 150–1.
[65] BAGD 447; Cranfield 1975, 197; Dunn 1988, 152; Fitzmyer 1993, 337.

and the parallel phrase πᾶσα σὰρξ in the following verse. But unlike
3:6, unambiguously in this context, there is the thought of the
sinfulness of the κόσμος. Humanity is "held accountable" for its
sin and unrighteousness (3:9–18). Rom 3:19 in fact gives us Paul's
least favourable remark involving κόσμος in the whole epistle.
Even so, it is clear that there is a lesser degree of negativity attach-
ing to κόσμος here than to the pejorative uses of the term in
1 Corinthians. κόσμος is not the apocalyptic "this world" of 1 Cor
1:20–21, 27, 28 and so on. The sense of alienation between God
and the κόσμος in Rom 3:19 is much less sharply expressed than
in the negative remarks on κόσμος in 1 Corinthians. Moreover, there
is no hint here of the social and ethical dualism between believers
and the κόσμος that so dominates that epistle. It hardly needs to be
pointed out that Paul's negative estimation of κόσμος (= humanity)
in this verse is deeply rooted in his development of the human
predicament in these opening chapters, the argumentative foil for
his presentation of the solution in Christ which begins at 3:21.

It would be imprudent to overestimate the theological and rhetorical
contribution of the term κόσμος to Paul's exposé. πᾶς, not κόσμος,
is the key word in the phrase πᾶς ὁ κόσμος. ὁ κόσμος, it would
seem, is simply added to πᾶς in 3:19 for stylistic variation (cf. γὰρ
Ἰουδαίους τε καὶ Ἕλληνας πάντας, v. 9; πάντες v. 12; πᾶν
στόμα, v. 19; πᾶσα σάρξ, v. 20).

The phrase πᾶς ὁ κόσμος in 3:19 is probably not without a
polemical edge. If Dunn's reading of the opening argument of the epistle
is correct, Paul's critique has been substantially directed against Jewish
presumptions of privileged status on the basis of election and possession
of the law. The universal charge of 3:19, then, would have this target in
view. Dunn writes,

> That *every* mouth (πᾶν στόμα) and *all* the world (πᾶς ὁ κόσμος) are thus
> left defenseless (3:9) before the indictment of the *Jewish* scriptures, confirms
> that Paul pens his *universal* indictment with a view to denying *Jewish* claims
> to a special defense at the final judgment ... his object is ... to show that
> their own scriptures place his own people just as firmly "in the dock" along
> with everyone else.[66]

---

[66] Dunn 1988, 152.

6.3.4. The future world, the inheritance of believers (4:13)

Paul's purpose in the section 4:13–17a is twofold: negatively, to break the association, current in Jewish theology, of the law and the covenant promise to Abraham (vv. 14–15); positively, to show that just as membership of Abraham's family is defined by faith (vv. 11–12), so faith determines who are the heirs of Abraham's promised inheritance (vv. 13, 16–17a).

The promise to Abraham is encapsulated in the phrase in v. 13, τὸ κληρονόμον αὐτὸν εἶναι κόσμου, "that he would inherit the world". The meaning of κόσμος here has to be determined on the basis of the tradition which the expression τὸ κληρονόμον αὐτὸν εἶναι κόσμου reflects. In the Genesis accounts what is promised to Abraham is the land of Canaan (Gen 12:7; 13:14–15, 17; 15:7, 18–21; 17:8). In later Jewish thought the promise of land evolved to cosmic proportions. It is generally agreed by modern commentators that the formulation τὸ κληρονόμον αὐτὸν εἶναι κόσμου reveals the influence of this tradition.[67] The reinterpretation of the promise was already well under way by Paul's time:

> Therefore the Lord assured him with an oath,
> that the nations would be blessed through his offspring;
> that he would make him as numerous as the dust of the earth,
> and exalt his offspring like the stars,
> and give them an inheritance from sea to sea
> and from the Euphrates to the ends of the earth. (Sir 44:21)

> And he [Abraham] remembered the word which was told to him on the day that Lot separated from him. And he rejoiced because the LORD had given him seed upon the earth so that they might inherit the land. And he blessed the Creator of all with all his eloquence. (*Jub.* 17:3)

> May He strengthen you and bless you.
> And may you inherit all of the earth. (*Jub.* 22:14)

> And I shall give to your seed all of the land under heaven and they will rule in all nations as they have desired. And after this all of the earth will be gathered together and they will inherit it forever. (*Jub.* 32:19)

> But to the elect there shall be light, joy and peace and
> they shall inherit the earth. (*1 Enoch* 5:7)

---

[67] Cranfield 1975, 239; Dunn 1988, 213; Fitzmyer 1993, 384; Käsemann 1980, 119–20; Leenhardt 1961, 120; Nygren 1952, 176; Wilckens 1978, 269; Ziesler 1989, 129.

> And this, in accordance with the divine promise, is
> broadening out to the very bounds of the universe
> (κόσμος), and renders it inheritor of the four quarters
> of the world, reaching to them all. (Philo, *Somn.* 1.175)

> And so as he abjured the accumulation of lucre, and the
> wealth whose influence is mighty among men, God rewarded
> him by giving him instead the greatest and most perfect
> wealth. That is the wealth of the whole earth and sea
> and rivers, and of all the other elements and the
> combinations which they form ... He gave into his hands the
> whole world (κόσμος) as a portion well fitted for His
> heir. (Philo, *Mos.* 1.155)

The tradition of the extended promise is also found in the post-70 CE apocalyptic writings *4 Ezra* (cf. 6:59) and *2 Baruch*. In the latter, the inheritance of the righteous is the world to come. The eschatological, cosmic inheritance is a prominent theme in this document.[68]

> Therefore, they leave this world without fear and are confident of the world
> which you have promised to them with an expectation full of joy. (*2 Apoc.
> Bar.* 14:13)

> And as for the glory of those who proved to be righteous on account of my
> law ... their splendor will then be glorified by transformations, and the shape
> of their face will be changed into the light of their beauty so that they may
> acquire and receive the undying world which is promised to them. (*2 Apoc.
> Bar.* 51:3)

The wider promise is also attested in later rabbinic tradition. The saying of R. Nehemiah (*Mek. Exod.* 14:31) may be cited as an example:

> Thus wilt thou find of Abraham that he has taken possession of this and the
> future world as a reward of faith, as it is written, He believed in Yahweh and
> he reckoned it to him for righteousness.[69]

Almost certainly, then, the construction τὸ κληρονόμον αὐτὸν εἶναι κόσμου relates to the reinterpreted promise to Abraham in which the promised inheritance is no longer just the land of Palestine but the whole world.[70]

---

[68] Cf. *2 Apoc. Bar.* 14:17–19; 15:7; 21:24–25; 44:13.

[69] Quoted from Käsemann 1980, 120. For further rabbinic references, see Str-B 3.209.

[70] The tradition of the expanded promise is also reflected in Matt 5:5, "the meek ... will inherit the earth".

κόσμος in this verse is often simply taken to mean "world" in the sense of the "habitation" of humankind.[71] In the light of the tradition of the enlarged promise, κόσμος in 4:13b refers not just to the environment of human beings, but to the *eschatological* environment of the people of God, the "world" which is to be the eschatological inheritance of God's elect, that is to say, the new or restored creation.

This inference is also drawn by Moxnes.[72] But having made the deduction, he then goes on to reject it. κόσμος here cannot mean what it appears to mean – the future eschatological world – since, quoting Sasse, κόσμος "is reserved for the world which lies under sin and death", and "When the κόσμος is redeemed, it ceases to be κόσμος."[73] Moxnes argues that Paul's focus in the construction τὸ κληρονόμον αὐτὸν εἶναι κόσμου is on the word κληρονόμος not κόσμος. The content of the promise, the future hope, is not developed in any way in the following verses. He writes, "It is the structure and identity of the community of the 'heirs to the world' with which he is concerned."[74] The community emphasis, he points out, is clear in Paul's use of κληρονόμος and his application of the Abrahamic promise in Gal 3–4 and Rom 8:12–17.[75] Paul utilizes the extended promise in Rom 4:13, Moxnes argues, to stress the universality of the promise (i.e. to emphasize that Gentiles are also included), as vv. 11–12 and 16–18 show. He concludes that in Paul's reinterpretation, the formulation τὸ κληρονόμον αὐτὸν εἶναι κόσμου refers to "the charismatic community, viewed from an eschatological perspective".[76]

Moxnes is right to insist that Paul's main interest in the subsection lies in the question, Who are the heirs? not, What do the heirs inherit? This does not mean, however, that the substance of the promise is of no concern to Paul, nor that the formulation of 4:13 gives us no clue as to his understanding of it. It is difficult to imagine how Paul could take up the wider form of the promise without wishing to associate himself with it. The fact that Paul offers no elaboration or correction of it more obviously suggests that he accepts rather than discards, or is ambivalent toward, the view of the future inheritance which it entails. It is true, as

---

[71] E.g. BAGD 447.
[72] Moxnes 1980, 247.
[73] Sasse 1965, 893.
[74] Moxnes 1980, 249.
[75] Moxnes 1980, 248.
[76] Moxnes 1980, 249.

Moxnes insists, that vv. 11–12 and 16–18 focus on the universality of the promise, but Paul draws out this theme from the promise of fatherhood to many nations (citing Gen 17:5 in v. 17a), not from the motif of cosmic inheritance.

The choice of the embellished promise over its original Genesis form is a deliberate one. By opting for the enlarged version, Paul is able to avoid a narrow focus on the land of Palestine and a more nationalistic understanding of the Abrahamic promise which would have been counter-productive to his argumentative purposes in Romans. The very use of κόσμος is probably significant in this respect: κόσμος, as opposed to γῆ,[77] eliminates any suggestion of a reference to Palestine.[78]

It is also likely that Paul takes up the widened form of the promise because he sees in it "the promise of the ultimate restoration to Abraham and his spiritual seed of man's inheritance (cf. Gen 1.27f) which was lost through sin".[79] What God promises to Abraham and Abraham's spiritual heirs is, as Dunn states, "the restoration of God's created order, of man to his Adamic status as steward of the rest of God's creation".[80]

In his study of Paul's concept of inheritance, J. D. Hester argues that the geographical reality of the land does not cease to play a part in Paul's theology: "He simply makes the Land the eschatological world."[81] This is clear, he argues, from Rom 8:17–23, where Paul is concerned to show that creation will be a suitable inheritance for the people of God.[82] Hester concludes:

> when Paul speaks of "heirs of the world", he looks back to the Promise to Abraham and summarizes it as this, and looks forward to the fulfillment of Abraham's Promise in the Kingdom of God. The Inheritance is everything that God promised and gave to Abraham – justification, formation of the people of God, a Land in the form of the New Creation, and the future blessed existence that is part of living in the realm of the fulfilled Promise.[83]

---

[77] γῆ is used in Matt 5:5.
[78] Hester 1968, 80 n. 3.
[79] Cranfield 1975, 240.
[80] Dunn 1988, 213. Cf. Byrne 1990, 54; Wilckens 1978, 269.
[81] Hester 1968, 81.
[82] Hester 1968, 82.
[83] Hester 1968, 89. W. D. Davies in his extensive treatment of New Testament views of the land (1974) fails to take adequate account of Hester's observations, when the former argues that Paul interprets the promise in "a-territorial" terms. Davies (1974, 178) contends that in Romans "Paul ignores completely the territorial aspect of the promise." Tellingly, he does not discuss the phrase τὸ κληρονόμον αὐτὸν εἶναι κόσμου in Rom 4:13.

It is precisely the question which Paul passes over in 4:13–17a that is taken up in his development of the theme of believers as "heirs" in 8:17–23: namely, the content of the promised inheritance. Christians are declared to be heirs (κληρονόμοι) of God and joint-heirs (συγκληρονόμοι) with Christ (8:17). They are destined for "glory" – a glory that is to be shared with the liberated κτίσις (8:21). Without pre-empting the discussion of 8:19–22, the association of ideas in 8:17–23 strongly suggests that the inherited κόσμος of 4:13 is to be equated with the emancipated κτίσις of 8:21. If this interpretation is sufficiently accurate, 8:18–23 may, on one level, be understood as an explication of the construction τὸ κληρονόμον αὐτὸν εἶναι κόσμου.

The wider promise with its cosmic focus, therefore, is not at all inconsistent with Paul's polemical purposes or with his theological development in Romans. The indications are that Paul has taken over the tradition not unthinkingly, but approvingly, lending significant weight to it. This leads back to the initial observation: on the basis of the tradition of the enlarged promise and Paul's acceptance of it, κόσμος must in 4:13 denote the future eschatological world, the restored creation.

Rom 4:13 thus indicates how positively Paul can use κόσμος in this epistle, in marked contrast to 1 Corinthians. This brief discussion has also further highlighted the weakness of an analysis which aims at a final theological definition of κόσμος in Paul: almost inevitably it leads to the imposition of a framework which permits some senses and excludes others, causing Paul's uses to be read in a predetermined way, like forcing a foot into a badly fitting shoe. This verse is a clear instance of κόσμος having the contextual sense ruled out by Sasse – the future, redeemed world.[84] That this fact has gone almost wholly unnoticed by interpreters reflects how Sasse's definition of κόσμος has hindered, however much it has also helped, interpretation of Paul's usage of κόσμος.

6.3.5. The world occupied by the enemy forces of sin and death (5:12–13)

In Rom 5:12–21, Paul launches into a comparison and contrast of Adam and Christ, the purpose of which is to demonstrate that Christ's

---

[84] Cf. Murray 1959, 142.

redeeming work has undone the fateful effects of Adam's rebellious act and has provided a comprehensive solution to the universal plight.[85]

In the argument of 1 Cor 15:21–22, 45–49, Adam and Christ were largely representative figures, typifying two qualitatively different modes of existence. In this passage Adam and Christ are determinative figures – individuals whose actions have affected the destiny of all/many.[86] A basic similarity between the two individuals is assumed (v. 14); they are contrasted on the basis of the nature and consequence of their deeds: Adam's disobedience resulting in sin, death and condemnation for all; Christ's obedient act bringing life, grace and righteousness for all. There is clear emphasis on the superiority of Christ's deed over Adam's (indicated by the formula πολλῷ μᾶλλον in vv. 15, 17 and the words περισσεύω, περισσεία and ὑπερπερισσεύω in vv. 15, 17 and 20, respectively): Christ has "more than counterbalanced the sin of Adam".[87]

The lines of continuity Paul traces from Adam to Christ and the historical overview of vv. 13–14, suggest that to a limited degree a salvation–historical perspective is operative in this passage (i.e. the belief in a progressive unfolding of God's saving purposes in a chain of historical events).[88] But this outlook is qualified by an overriding apocalyptic frame of thought which builds on radical contrasts, antitheses and opposites and utilizes "power" language. The "cosmological–apocalyptic" character of Paul's exposition in 5:12–21 has been emphasized by de Boer. He points particularly to the personification of sin and death, on the one hand, and grace on the other; these entities, he argues, are presented as "cosmological rulers in conflict".[89]

κόσμος appears in vv. 12 and 13. In v. 12, Paul states that through Adam "sin came into the world ... and death came through sin", ἡ ἁμαρτία εἰς τὸν κόσμον εἰσῆλθεν καὶ διὰ τῆς ἁμαρτίας ὁ θάνατος. In v. 13, he comments, "sin was indeed in the world before

[85] On the structure of 5:12–21, see de Boer 1988, 158ff; Dunn 1988, 271; Gibbs 1971, 48–9. The ὥσπερ of v. 12 introduces a protasis which has no immediate apodosis, Paul interrupting the parallelism to develop parenthetical lines of thought (vv. 12c–14, 15–17); the comparison is not actually completed until vv. 18,19, or on de Boer's chiastic analysis, v. 21.
[86] *Contra* Ziesler 1989, 143ff; 1990, 52–7. Note Dunn 1988, 272–3.
[87] Barrett 1962, 93.
[88] See the definition of salvation history in Cullmann 1967, 74–8.
[89] de Boer 1988, 160.

the law", ἄχρι γὰρ νόμου ἁμαρτία ἦν ἐν κόσμῳ. Though Gibbs argues that κόσμος in these verses has the meaning, "the dwelling place of humanity",[90] and Shields, questioning the distinction between a human κόσμος and a general κόσμος, understands the word "as referring generally to the created world as the context of life – human and otherwise",[91] the sense "human world" is to be preferred here. This is how the majority of commentators understand the word. The construction εἰς τὸν κόσμον in v. 12b stands parallel to εἰς πάντας ἀνθρώπους in v. 12c. As the exposition proceeds, the determinative events, Adam's sin and Christ's act of obedience, are only ever conceived of as affecting human beings (cf. εἰς πάντας ἀνθρώπους again in v. 18). The reference to Adam and the Gen 3 background of the passage give κόσμος (= humanity) the particular contextual nuance, "humanity" *as God's creation.*

There are two key points to note about κόσμος in these verses. Firstly, the κόσμος is not inherently sinful or mortal. Sin "entered" (εἰσῆλθεν) the human κόσμος, and death entered it through sin. The wording ἡ ἁμαρτία εἰς τὸν κόσμον εἰσῆλθεν καὶ διὰ τῆς ἁμαρτίας ὁ θάνατος calls to mind Wis 2:24, where we read that "through the devil's envy death entered the world" (θάνατος εἰσῆλθεν εἰς τὸν κόσμον). As already indicated, it is quite likely that Paul was familiar with *Wisdom of Solomon,* and it may well be that he is picking up its language here, highlighting the role of Adam rather than that of the devil in the introduction of death into the κόσμος. Sin is plainly assumed to have existed prior to the transgression of Adam, standing in the wings as it were, awaiting a moment to steal centre stage. Yet, Paul leaves his readers in no doubt that neither sin nor death were part of God's original creatorial intention for the human κόσμος. Their existence in the κόσμος constitutes a distortion and contradiction of God's creative aims. κόσμος here is a morally neutral entity.

Secondly, despite the collocation of κόσμος with ἁμαρτία and θάνατος in 5:12–13, κόσμος does not rank alongside these "cosmological–apocalyptic" power-structures on the wrong side of the apocalyptic divide. The κόσμος is not here the alien and hostile power of 1 Cor 1:20, 21; 3:19, 22. Rather it is represented as having been

---

[90] Gibbs 1971, 51 n. 2
[91] Shields 1980, 63. So too Wilckens 1978, 315 n. 1037.

"overpowered" by hostile forces. To take up and extend de Boer's imagery of apocalyptic conflict, the κόσμος has been invaded and placed under enemy rule. The evil intruders, sin and death, secured the bridgehead through Adam. From there they swept through the entire κόσμος, subjugating it and establishing their dominion over it. The κόσμος is thus occupied territory. But, as Paul goes on to show (vv. 15–21), God through Christ has acted to deliver the human κόσμος from its enemy occupants. The process of liberation is already underway.

6.3.6. Creation groaning, awaiting liberation (8:19–22)

In 8:18–30 Paul takes up the theme of suffering in hope, expanding his earlier train of thought in 5:2–4. Paul ended his discussion in the previous paragraph (vv. 12–17) with the assertion in v. 17b that believers share in the sufferings of Christ so that they may also be glorified with him (εἴπερ συμπάσχομεν ἵνα καὶ συνδοξασθῶμεν). He now elucidates the inherent relation between present suffering and future glory.

The "thesis" which he sets out in v. 18 is that the afflictions which now must be endured are a necessary prelude to the coming glory. They intrinsically point forward to that glory and are completely outweighed by it (cf. 2 Cor 4:17; Phil 1:20). A threefold evidence for this thesis is provided in the next three subsections:[92] the expectation of creation, vv. 19–22; the groaning of believers, vv. 23–25; the present experience of the Spirit, vv. 26–27. The final subsection, vv. 28–30, is to be understood either as a further testimony, or, more likely, as a conclusion. The passage is shot through with an "already"/"not yet" tension – the frustration of having received a foretaste of the inheritance to come (v. 23), on the one hand, and having to wait to enter into the fullness of that inheritance, on the other (v. 24–25).

The thrust of Paul's argument in vv. 19–22 is that the present "groaning" of creation is a stage in a forward-moving divine process, the climax of which is liberation and glory. It is generally agreed that

---

[92] This analysis of the text goes back to Zahn (1865) and is accepted by many interpreters. Criticisms of Zahn's structuring have been made and alternative suggestions advanced, e.g. by Christoffersson (1990, 141–3), Luz (1968, 370, 377) and Paulsen (1974, 107–8). Zahn's structuring, though, remains the simplest and most convenient. The division ought to be made, however, not on the basis of the threefold groaning motif (as Zahn suggested), but according to the main subject of each subsection: creation, vv. 19–22, Christians, vv. 23–25, the Spirit, vv. 26–27.

Paul alludes in these verses to Gen 3:17–19,[93] where God curses the earth because of Adam's sin. In so doing, Paul stands in a developing line of reflection in Jewish – especially Jewish apocalyptic – theology which speculates on the effects of Adam's transgression on the world of nature,[94] and which finds in the Adamic fall an explanation for the miseries and afflictions of life.[95] In addition to Gen 3:17–19 and the traditions associated with it, he also alludes to the apocalyptic conception of the re-creation or renewal of heaven and earth.

Bindemann points out that while almost every motif in 8:19–22 can be found scattered individually throughout Jewish apocalyptic writings, there is no exact parallel to this passage in any of the apocalyptic works known to us.[96] Nor is there an equivalent in any other extant Jewish text. Thus, while Paul is here utilizing existing Jewish traditions, at the same time, as far as we can tell, he is creatively handling the traditional material and developing his own distinctive emphases.[97]

The meaning of the term κτίσις in this passage has been much debated. In the history of interpretation, a range of suggestions has been put forward.[98] In the modern period of New Testament study,

---

[93] Christoffersson (1990) disputes the scholarly consensus on the Gen 3 background to our passage. He argues that it is rather the "flood tradition", which grew out of Gen 6–8, which furnishes the backcloth to this text. But his contention is to be rejected for the following reasons. Firstly, while the story of the Watchers provided the earliest Jewish explanation of the origin of evil in the world (1 Enoch 1–36), by the end of the first century CE, it had been virtually supplanted by an account based on the story of Adam and Eve. From the perspective of the history of religious thought, therefore, it seems more reasonable to connect Rom 8:19–22 to an emerging tradition than to pitch it against the background of a declining one. Secondly, the flood story has otherwise no place in Paul's thinking. The Adam and Eve story, on the other hand, features significantly. Adam motifs, as we have seen, are especially important in Romans, particularly in chapters 5–8. Thirdly, the parallels which Christoffersson claims to have found are, on close scrutiny, not at all strong, and at points the attempt to explain Rom 8:18–30 in the light of the flood tradition leads to skewed exegesis of the text, e.g. his astonishing contention (120–4) that the υἱοὶ θεοῦ of v. 19 should be identified as angels, when Paul has already referred to Christians as υἱοὶ θεοῦ in vv. 12–17.

[94] Jub. 3:29; Apoc. Mos. 10–11; Gen. Rab. 11:2–4; 12:6. On the Adamic fall as affecting nature in Jewish writings, see Tennant 1903, 127, 150–1, 193, 197, 203, 21. For rabbinic references, see Str-B 3: 249–55.

[95] 4 Ezra 7:11–14; 2 Apoc. Bar. 56:6–10; Apoc. Mos. 7–8; 39; Adam and Eve 1–4; 6; 18–21; 32–34; 47; 49–50. These passages are discussed by Levison 1988. See also W. D. Davies 1962, 38–39; A. L. Thompson 1977, 7–14.

[96] Bindemann 1983, 29.

[97] Cf. Balz 1971, 38.

[98] For the history of research, see Gieraths 1950, and more recently Christoffersson 1990, 33–6.

however, only three options have merited serious scholarly attention: (1) κτίσις as the unbelieving human world;[99] (2) κτίσις as unbelievers and the non-human creation;[100] (3) κτίσις as the non-human creation.[101] In recent interpretation, a consensus has emerged favouring the last meaning.

In order to determine what Paul means by κτίσις in these verses it is necessary to consider the established senses of the term, on the one hand, and the various links between κτίσις and other terms and expressions in the immediate linguistic context, on the other. The established Jewish senses of the term are "act of creation", "creature", "created universe", "non-human creation".[102] Of these only "non-human creation" is possible in 8:19–22. The senses "act of creation" and "creature" are obviously inadmissible. The wide sense "created universe" (the whole creation embracing heaven, earth and every human being) is ruled out since believers are distinguished from the κτίσις in vv. 22–23 (πᾶσα ἡ κτίσις συστενάζει ... οὐ μόνον δὲ, ἀλλὰ καὶ αὐτοὶ ... ἡμεις καὶ αὐτοὶ ἐν ἑαυτοῖς στενάζομεν). This means that of the three main suggestions as to the meaning of κτίσις in these verses advanced by scholars, only "non-human creation" is an established sense prior to Paul's usage. If Paul is using the term to designate unbelieving humanity or unbelievers together with the natural world, he is employing it in a non-conventional sense. It seems therefore, that lexical priority has to be given to the natural sense "non-human creation". If this meaning is ruled out, it has to be excluded on the basis of clear linguistic signals in the text pointing to one of the other two suggested senses.

The case for a reference to unbelievers is advanced primarily on the grounds of Paul's application of personal language to the κτίσις. The κτίσις "waits with eager longing" and "has been groaning in labour pains until now". This more obviously suggests, so it is claimed, an anthropological denotation than a cosmological one. And since believers are distinguished from the κτίσις, the human referent must be non-

---

[99] Gager 1970, 327–30; Pallis 1920, 102; Schlatter 1935, 270; Walter 1989.

[100] Balz 1971, 47–9; Gerber 1966; Gibbs 1971, 40; Käsemann 1980, 233; Viard 1952.

[101] Bindemann 1983, 73; Byrne 1979, 105; Christoffersson 1990, 139; most modern commentators.

[102] See above pp. 78–80. The standard non-Jewish sense, "founding", "foundation", is inapplicable here.

believers. This line of argumentation involves an exceptionally rigid and unrealistic view of language-use which takes little or no account of metaphor. The application of personal language to the natural world is in fact one of the best attested metaphors in ancient literature. The imagery is extensive in the Old Testament, particularly in the psalms and prophets.[103] The use of anthropomorphic language, and especially feminine imagery, in depictions of the earth is also widespread in Greek and Roman writings.[104] The argument from personification, therefore, bears little weight. Another argument put forward in favour of κτίσις as denoting non-Christians is that since Christians are called καινὴ κτίσις in Gal 6:15 and 2 Cor 5:17, κτίσις in Rom 8:19–22 must by implication refer to unbelievers.[105] Again, this is an extremely tenuous line of reasoning. Neither in Gal 6:15 nor in 2 Cor 5:17 does Paul contrast καινὴ κτίσις with κτίσις, so nothing at all can be deduced from these texts as to the possible meaning of κτίσις in Rom 8:19–22.

A close look at what is predicated of κτίσις in these verses should make clear that the sense "unbelievers" is improbable. Paul states that the κτίσις "waits with eager longing for the revealing of the children of God". Whatever Paul 's view of the ultimate fate of non-Christians, this seems, from his perspective, a rather unlikely description of their present disposition. Also, given Paul's stress elsewhere on human culpability for sin, it is highly doubtful that Paul would say that unredeemed humanity was subjected to futility and enslaved to decay "not of its own will", that is, through no fault of its own (οὐχ ἑκοῦσα). For this reason, it is difficult to accommodate any reference to non-Christians within the embrace of κτίσις in these verses. The suggested meanings "unbelievers" and "unbelievers and the non-human creation" would seem equally implausible.

The linguistic evidence thus adds support to the consensus view that κτίσις in 8:19–22 denotes the "non-human creation". It is an established

---

[103] Deut 32:1; Job 7:1–9; Ps 19:1; 68:16; 96:12; 98:8; Isa 1:2; 14:8; 35:1; 45:12; 55:12; Jer 4:28; 12:4; Ezek 31:15; Hab 2:11. Note also the personification of creation in *4 Ezra* 10:9–17; *2 Apoc. Bar.* 11:6–7.

[104] "Earth is a mother" metaphors were very common in the ancient world, found in both poetry and philosophy. According to Plato, it is not earth which imitates woman but woman–earth (*Men.* 238). Philo takes up the image of the mother–earth in *Opif.* 129ff.

[105] Gager 1970, 328–9.

sense of the term (Wis 2:6; 5:17; 16:24; 19:6), it fits the linguistic context and it coheres with the traditions upon which, it is generally accepted, Paul is drawing in these verses, especially the cursing of the earth in Gen 3:17–19.

Having established the probable meaning of κτίσις in 8:19–22, we can now consider what Paul has to say about κτίσις (= non-human creation) in these verses. Paul characterizes the present state of the κτίσις as one of suffering and frustration, on the one hand, and of expectancy and hope, on the other. The organic relation between suffering and glory which holds for believers (vv. 17–18) thus also obtains for the non-human creation.

Paul states that the κτίσις has been made subject to futility: τῇ γὰρ ματαιότητι ἡ κτίσις ὑπετάγη (v. 20). The word ματαιότης, as Cranfield states, points to "the ineffectiveness of that which does not attain its goal".[106] The creation is unable to achieve its full potential, the end for which it was established. The κτίσις was subjected to futility, Paul insists, "not of its own will but by the will of the one who subjected it", οὐχ ἑκοῦσα ἀλλὰ διὰ τὸν ὑποτάξαντα (v. 20). With these words, Paul makes clear that ματαιότης was not inherent in or original to the creation. A previous state when the creation was not characterized by futility is presupposed.[107] The curse of Gen 3:17–19 is of course in view. Paul, in line with later Jewish reflection on that text, expands the scale of the judgement to cosmic dimensions. God is obviously the implied agent of the passive ὑπετάγη. A few scholars, though, opine that Adam is in view in the accusative construction διὰ τὸν ὑποτάξαντα.[108] That Adam is ὁ ὑποτάξαντα here, however, is unlikely for several reasons. Firstly, since God is both the agent of the previous ὑπετάγη and of the future passive ἐλευθερωθήσεται in v. 21, it would seem to follow that he is the implied subject of τὸν ὑποτάξαντα. Secondly, in Gen 3:17–19, it is God, not Adam, who pronounces the curse on the earth. Thirdly, only God could be said to have subjected creation "in hope", ἐφ' ἐλπίδι. Even so, the construction διά + accusative is probably intended to indicate Adam's sin as the occasion of the subjection. As Dunn puts it, "Paul was attempting to

---

[106] Cranfield 1975, 413. Sanday and Headlam (1902, 208) observe that the word is the opposite of τέλειος.
[107] So Meyer 1874, 76.
[108] G. W. H. Lampe 1964, 458; J. A. T. Robinson 1979, 102; Zeller 1985, 162.

convey too briefly a quite complicated point: that God subjected all things to Adam, and that included subjecting creation to fallen Adam, to share in his fallenness."[109]

The κτίσις, Paul further indicates, is presently held in "bondage to decay", τῆς δουλείας τῆς φθορᾶς. The created order has been made perishable, subject to the forces of dissolution and decay. Again the image of enslavement points to an imposed state rather than an inherent one. φθορά is not endemic to creation. This contrasts with 1 Cor 15:42–44, which, as we have observed, implies that φθορά is a natural (hence necessary and inescapable) characteristic of the present creation.

The "whole creation" (πᾶσα ἡ κτίσις),[110] Paul explains, is "groaning in labour pains" (συστενάζει καὶ συνωδίνει). The metaphor of childbirth appears both in Jewish and New Testament writings in eschatological contexts. Some scholars relate Paul's image here to the Jewish notion of the "messianic woes", the birth-pangs which would usher in the messianic age (cf. Mk 13:8 / Mt 24:8).[111] But the condition described in these verses has been going on ever since the fall of Adam and not just since the coming of Christ.[112] The image of childbirth may have suggested itself to Paul from the divine judgement placed on the woman in Gen 3:16 ("I will greatly increase your pangs in childbearing; in pain you shall bring forth children").[113]

The pain and frustration predicated of creation, however, is offset by the sense of hope and expectancy attributed to it. Paul describes the κτίσις in v. 19 in anthropomorphic terms as eagerly anticipating and yearning for the day when the sons of God will be revealed in glory

[109] Dunn 1988, 471. It is possible, as Zahn (1865, 536) suggests, that Paul's wording reflects Gen 8:21, where God declares that he will never again curse the ground because of humanity (διὰ τὰ ἔργα τῶν ἀνθρώπων). In a number of Old Testament texts, the earth is depicted as caught up in the sins of humanity: Isa 11:6–8; 24:5–6; Jer 4:28; 12:4; Ezek 34:25–31; Hos 2:18; Zech 8:12; cf. 4 Ezra 7:11ff; 9:17ff.

[110] The addition of πᾶς is to be understood as intensifying the earlier meaning of κτίσις, not as widening its earlier compass now to draw the rest of humanity into the picture: contra Shields 1980, 143; Vögtle 1970a, 199; Wilckens 1980, 153.

[111] Among those who think that Paul has in mind the Jewish doctrine of the "messianic woes": Black 1973, 116; Cranfield 1975: 416; Käsemann 1980, 232; Leenhardt 1961, 222; Michel 1966, 204.

[112] So Balz 1971, 108; Osten-Sacken 1975, 98ff; Siber 1971, 149ff. It seems unlikely that the phrase ἄχρι τοῦ νῦν has eschatological force: contra Käsemann 1980, 236. The words, as Cranfield recognizes (1975, 417), simply serve to emphasize the long continuance of the groaning and travailing; so also Moo 1991, 555.

[113] So Milne 1980, 17.

(ἡ γὰρ ἀποκαραδοκία τῆς κτίσεως τὴν ἀποκάλυψιν τῶν υἱῶν τοῦ θεοῦ ἀπεκδέχεται). The substantive ἀποκαραδοκία, which may well have been coined by Paul himself,[114] signifies confident expectation and hope.[115] Paul uses the word figuratively to suggest the picture of the creation stretching its neck and craning forward to catch a glimpse of its coming glory (κάρα, "head"; δέχομαι, "stretch"). The verb ἀπεκδέχομαι is consistently used by Paul of the eager waiting associated with the Christian hope (Rom 8:23, 25; 1 Cor 1:7; Gal 5:5; Phil 3:20). In view of the eschatological resonances of the word for Paul, he may be implying here that creation's state of anticipation has been heightened or awakened by the eschatological event of the death and resurrection of Christ and by the partial revelation of the sons of God in the present time (vv. 14–16). In v. 20, Paul stresses that the creation was subjected to futility in hope, ἐφ᾽ ἐλπίδι. It was with the hope and promise of a greater future that God placed the non-human creation under a temporary subjection.[116] The childbirth metaphor in v. 22 clearly also carries the note of hope and optimism. Creation's present suffering is not meaningless. It is part of a productive process which will result in a positive and joyous outcome.

There is thus both a negative and a positive aspect to what Paul says about the κτίσις in these verses. The greater weight, however, is on the positive side. Creation's current state of futility, frustration and bondage to decay is not a permanent one. The κτίσις is destined to be released from its present fetters and to share in a glorious future with the people of God. With confidence and assurance, but not without impatience, it eagerly awaits that momentous day.

There are several further observations about Paul's usage of κτίσις in this passage which may be made. Firstly, Paul uses κτίσις to make a set of "cosmological" statements. He talks in these verses about a fall and redemption which affects the wider cosmic order. This has been denied or resisted by a number of interpreters, reflecting a tendency among an earlier generation of scholars to minimize or relativize references to the wider universe in biblical texts. The insistence that κτίσις in Rom 8:19–21 designates non-Christian humanity is one of the ways in which the attempt to eliminate cosmology has been made. Another has been to

---

[114] Fitzmyer 1993, 507.
[115] The word occurs in Phil 1:20 where it is linked to ἐλπίς.
[116] Cranfield (1975, 414) suggests that Paul has in mind the promise of Gen 3:15 to which he alludes in Rom 16:20.

draw a firm line between the traditional elements in the text and Paul's own distinctive theological assertions. Following Bultmann's lead it has been argued that while cosmological motifs in this passage may have had a significant place in the traditions underlying Rom 8:19–22, they are of no real interest to Paul, whose concern is solely with human beings.[117] Cosmic elements have only been incorporated by Paul to make a statement about humanity and can easily be discarded without in any way interrupting or damaging the main flow of his thought. The weakness of this kind of reasoning has already been highlighted in the earlier discussion of Paul's adoption of the extended form of the Abrahamic promise in Rom 4:13. It is hardly conceivable that Paul could have taken up the motif of the fall and redemption of the wider creation in Rom 8:19–22 without wishing to align himself personally with it. As the introductory λογίζομαι of v. 18 clearly indicates, whatever sources on which he is dependent in these verses, he is expressing his *own* personal judgement and convictions. As noted above, Paul is not simply here passing on a received tradition, in an unthinking or mechanistic fashion, but is consciously reworking and reconfiguring established apocalyptic themes in a creative and distinctive way. There is no legitimate reason, therefore, for disputing or underplaying the cosmic dimension of Paul's talk of κτίσις in this textual unit.

Secondly, Paul draws a close linkage between the κτίσις and the children of God. The κτίσις awaits the revelation of God's children (v. 19). The κτίσις will be set free to enjoy the glory of God's children (v. 21). Not only does the κτίσις groan, but believers also groan inwardly (vv. 22–23). There is thus a bond of solidarity between believers and the κτίσις in the present, as they jointly experience suffering and expectation. And there is a solidarity between believers and creation in the future: the destiny of the κτίσις is bound up with, and is indeed contingent upon, that of the children of God (v. 21). The κτίσις is redeemed along with believers. The close association between Christians and the κτίσις set forth in this passage contrasts with the opposition of the church and the κόσμος which is emphasized in 1 Corinthians.

Thirdly, what Paul says about κτίσις here implies a high degree of continuity between the present creation and the new or renewed creation. The κτίσις is destined for deliverance (ἐλευθερωθήσεται). It is to be

---

[117] Baumgarten 1975, 170–8; G. W. H. Lampe 1964, 455; Schwantes 1962, 44ff, 92ff; Vögtle 1970b.

set free from its present slavery (ἀπὸ τῆς δουλείας) into a state of freedom (εἰς τὴν ἐλευθερίαν). Paul emphasizes that αὐτὴ ἡ κτίσις will be liberated. *This* creation will be redeemed. It will not "pass away", to be followed by another creation.[118] As indicated in the previous chapter the expected cosmic change of Jewish apocalyptic eschatology could be expressed either in terms of the destruction of this creation and the establishment of a completely new creation or in terms of a transformation or renewal of the existing creation. In 1 Cor 7:31a Paul's formulation points to the former. Here his words point un-ambiguously to the restoration of the present creation. This creation will be freed from its present, but temporary, subdued and enslaved condition so that it may at last fulfil the purpose for which it was made.

On the passage more generally, two additional observations may be drawn. As mentioned earlier, Paul takes up established apocalyptic motifs and creatively reworks them. It is interesting to note how Paul deviates from the world-view more typical of Jewish apocalypticism. He does not identify the present creation with this world/age in accordance with apocalyptic two world/age dualism.[119] He does not point up the evil and oppressive nature of the current order. He does not set in radical antithesis the present time of suffering and the future age of glory: the future glory is rather depicted as emerging from and growing out of the present period of suffering (8:18, 22). He does not highlight the disjunctive relation between the elect people of God and their wider environment.[120] And he completely avoids the sharp ethical and social dualisms characteristic of apocalyptic thought:[121] he draws no distinction, for example, between the "righteous" and the "unrighteous".

On the basis of this evidence, Bindemann concludes that Paul in this passage is correcting a Jewish apocalyptic vista of the world. This is probably going too far. But certainly, Paul is modifying the standard apocalyptic view of reality (if we may speak of such), softening and reducing the distinctive ethical, social, spatial and temporal dualities of the apocalyptic symbol system – the very dualisms he was keen to accentuate in 1 Corinthians!

---

[118] So Bruce 1985, 161; Gibbs 1971, 44; Lenski 1936, 542; Meyer 1874, 78; Moo 1991, 554; Murray 1959, 30; Philippi 1879, 15.

[119] Bindemann 1983, 75.

[120] Bindemann 1983, 30–1, 75.

[121] Bindemann 1983, 74–5.

Secondly, Paul's purpose in 8:18–39 is to legitimate the sufferings of his readers[122] (as Gager writes, the text furnishes "both justification of, and consolation for, present suffering ... to render tolerable a situation which would otherwise have been intolerable").[123] It is instructive to observe the way in which he does so, especially in vv. 18–22.

The kind of sufferings Paul has in mind in the transitional verse, v. 17, are specifically *Christian* sufferings, afflictions which are encountered and endured for the sake of Christ (συμπάσχομεν ἵνα καὶ συνδοξασθῶμεν), that is, persecution, in the broad sense of the word (cf. "distress, or persecution ... or sword", v. 35). These sufferings, which are by their very nature peculiar to believers, are located by Paul in vv. 18–22 within the wider frame of the general suffering which is part of the earthly lot, τὰ παθήματα τοῦ νῦν καιροῦ, the suffering which is "a *sine qua non* of a world which itself is groaning".[124] The result of this move is (as Gager states) that

> The suffering of the believer now appears not as an isolated instance, but as an integral and necessary stage in the cosmic birth process whose culmination will be the glorious liberty of the sons of God.[125]

Paul thus does not interpret his readers' sufferings as part of the "cosmic battle", between the forces of darkness and evil and the forces of light, though he could well have done so (cf. 1 Thess 2:18; 3:3–5).[126] Neither does he exhibit a concern to emphasize the damnation and punishment which persecutors may expect on the day of retribution (cf. 1 Thess 1:10; 5:3). He legitimates their afflictions in a manner which neither promotes any sense of alienation or marginalization nor sounds any note of hostility toward the perpetrators of their suffering. Rather, Paul links believers' specific afflictions with the general suffering that characterizes creation as a whole and emphasizes believers' solidarity with the world and its suffering.[127] He legitimates their experience of suffering and persecution in a way that is unlikely to encourage or reinforce a social dualism between insiders and outsiders.

[122] So Kuss 1963, 621; Nygren 1952, 335–6; Stuhlmacher 1989, 120; Ziesler 1989, 218–19.
[123] Gager 1970, 330.
[124] Pobee 1985, 112. So also Godet 1881/82, 87; Lenski 1936, 534; Moo 1991, 548.
[125] Gager 1970, 330.
[126] See Pobee 1985, 45–6; 110.
[127] So Beker 1985, 110.

The manner in which he handles the apocalyptic material on which he is drawing in this passage and the way in which he explains the sufferings of his readers suggest that it is not Paul's aim to generate among his readers a sectarian "response to the world".

To sum up, in 8:19–22 Paul uses κτίσις in connection with other terms to express the meaning that creation, though presently marked by suffering, is destined for a glorious future. Believers and creation groan together as they await the future hope. Creation will be redeemed alongside believers, set free to fulfil at last the goal for which it was made. The passage, though drawing on apocalyptic motifs and designed to comfort his readers in their present experience of persecution, is non-sectarian in tone. It neither stimulates nor sustains social alienation or exclusiveness.

6.3.7. Nor anything else in all creation (8:39)

In 8:31–39, Paul celebrates in hymnic style the ultimate triumph of believers over every threat, affliction and foe: nothing can wrest them from the love of God manifested in Christ. According to Leenhardt, three series of possible trials are delineated in this passage: firstly (vv. 32–34), the inner struggles of faith against the assaults of doubt; secondly (vv. 35–36), threats springing from the instrumentality of human beings; thirdly (vv. 38–39), "the mysterious forces of the universe which escape from all human control".[128]

The list of potential threats in vv. 38–39 contains ten items arranged in four pairs with two standing on their own. The first pair is "death" and "life" (θάνατος, ζωή). "Life" seems a strange opponent of Christians, but Paul probably means life insofar as it is marked by trials, hazards and woes. The next pair is "angels" (ἄγγελοι, most probably evil angels) and "principalities" (ἀρχαί), hostile powers. Next are "things present" and "things to come" (ἐνεστῶτα, μέλλοντα), that is current hardships and dangers yet to be experienced. "Powers" (δυνάμεις) stands alone and clearly denotes hostile spiritual forces. The final pair is "height" and "depth" (ὕψωμα, βάθος). The meaning of these terms is disputed. Some see a reference to heaven and Sheol (the "height" and "depth" of the three-storey universe). [129] Both ὕψωμα

---

[128] Leenhardt 1961, 240.
[129] So Cranfield 1975, 443; Wilckens 1980, 177; Ziesler 1989, 232. Cf. Wink 1984, 49–50.

and βάθος, however, were technical terms in astrology. Paul may thus have in view the celestial powers which were believed to control the destinies of human beings.[130] This would certainly fit with the earlier mention of ἄγγελοι, ἀρχαί and δυνάμεις.

Paul closes the list with the phrase τις κτίσις ἑτέρα. Here κτίσις means "creature", "created thing". The expression τις κτίσις ἑτέρα literally means "any other creature", though the NRSV translation "anything else in all creation" catches the significance of the words. The phrase is added, as Cranfield states, "in order to make the list completely comprehensive".[131]

As noted in chapter 1, Bultmann argues that the juxtaposition of κτίσις with such terms as θάνατος and ἀρχαί gives a negative shading to the word: it implies that creation has become "the field of activity for evil, demonic powers".[132] Certainly, this is a conclusion which can be drawn from the text. One may question, however, whether this is the inference intended by Paul. It is far more likely that the addition of τις κτίσις ἑτέρα is aimed at tempering the previous negative terms, by implicitly classifying them as κτίσεις, rather than at impugning κτίσις by the association. This reading undoubtedly chimes better with the stress in 8:31–39 on the invincibility of God's love toward believers and the comfort and assurance this affords.

The rhetorical effect of closing the catalogue with τις κτίσις ἑτέρα is to qualify the preceding items in such a way that these potential threats are now brought within the compass of God's creation and the sphere of his control. That the flow of linguistic influence between κτίσις and the other items on the list is bidirectional may be more obvious to us than it was to Paul. In any case, it seems clear enough where Paul's accent lies: for him, the collocation serves to neutralize the threats and powers and not to stigmatize κτίσις. Bultmann's interpretation of κτίσις in 8:39 seems to invert Paul's emphasis.

The phrase τις κτίσις ἑτέρα is added to make the point that all possible menaces to the believer are comprehended within God's creative and providential purposes: even the hostile spiritual powers are placed within the orb of the created order. There is nothing which can separate believers from the love of God in Christ precisely because there exists

---

[130] So Barrett 1957, 174; Black 1973, 127; Bruce 1985, 171; Caird 1956, 74.
[131] Cranfield 1975, 444.
[132] Bultmann 1952, 230.

no threat which is outside the bounds of God's creation, where he holds sovereign sway (cf. 8:19–22; 28–30).[133]

6.3.8. Riches and reconciliation for the world (11:12, 15)

In 11:11–27, Paul delineates a two-stage divine strategy with regard to Israel: Israel's hardening and opposition leads to the salvation of Gentiles, and the incorporation of the Gentiles will eventually lead to the redemption of Israel.

Paul affirms in v. 11 that, though Israel has stumbled, the slip is not a fatal one. μὴ γένοιτο is the resounding answer to the question of whether Israel has fallen to rise no more. Paul sees a divine game plan at work. Israel's trespass (τὸ παράπτωμα) has opened the way for salvation to come to the Gentiles, and this will in turn stir Jews to jealousy. Using a *qal-va-homer* formula (πόσῳ μᾶλλον), Paul argues in v. 12 that if their trespass means riches for the κόσμος, and their loss, riches for the Gentiles, how much will their full inclusion mean!

κόσμος in v. 12 denotes Gentile humanity in contrast to Jewish humanity. This is clear from the parallelism πλοῦτος κόσμου ... πλοῦτος ἐθνῶν.[134] The κόσμος, the non-Jewish world, has come into great wealth because of Israel's trespass. Paul here is picking up the familiar Jewish theme of the eschatological pilgrimage of Gentiles to Zion.[135] The use of πλοῦτος suggests an allusion to Isa 60:5 ("the wealth of the nations shall come to you"). Paul, however, deliberately inverts the traditional order: the Gentiles are coming in advance of Jews.

In vv. 13–14, Paul applies the principle of vv. 11–12 to his own ministry as apostle to the Gentiles. He magnifies his role in relation to the Gentiles in order to provoke his own people to jealousy with the result that he might bring some of them to salvation. In v. 15 he develops the contrast of v. 12 in a slightly different way, but the point is essentially the same. He speaks this time of the rejection and acceptance of Israel. The consequence of their rejection is the reconciliation (καταλλαγή) of the κόσμος, the Gentile world. The result of their acceptance is "life from the dead", that is, Israel's conversion will be the immediate precursor of the general resurrection at the end of time.[136]

---

[133] Cf. Wink 1984, 50.
[134] Cf. κόσμος in Luke 12:30. See further Str-B 2:191.
[135] Cf. Ps 22:27ff; Isa 2:2ff; 25:6ff; Jer 16:19; Mic 4:1ff; Zech 14:16.
[136] So Barrett 1957, 215; Black 1973, 144; Bruce 1985, 205; Cranfield 1979, 563.

In both v. 12 and v. 15, Paul uses κόσμος in a positive manner. In v. 12, the κόσμος, Gentile humankind, is the recipient of God's blessing, having come into a state of enrichment, and in v. 15, it is the object of God's reconciling activity. There are of course the presuppositions of the κόσμος once having been outside the range of such blessing and of the κόσμος as alienated from God (cf. 1:18–32). But Paul's emphasis is unambiguously on the new situation which has arisen for the κόσμος, the Gentile world, and the new relationship into which (potentially, at least) the κόσμος is brought.

These occurrences serve to further show how positively Paul can utilize κόσμος in Romans, throwing into bold relief the polemically and negatively charged usage of 1 Corinthians.

6.4. Related themes and emphases

Having examined Paul's usage of the key terms, it is now appropriate to highlight associated themes and theological emphases in chapters 1–11. This will enable us to establish whether tendencies evident in Paul's utilization of κόσμος and κτίσις are noticeable elsewhere in the theological section of the letter. We shall consider, very briefly, the lack of apocalyptic social dualities, the stress on the universal scope of salvation in Christ, the discussion of unrepentant Jews in chapters 9–11, the understanding of bodily resurrection that comes to expression in chapter 8 and the larger soteriological paradigm of Romans.

6.4.1. The lack of apocalyptic social dualisms

The antithesis between the church and "this world" or "this age", dominant in 1 Corinthians, is missing from Rom 1–11.[137] This is matched by the absence from Romans of the other social dualisms characteristic of 1 Corinthians: the contrasts between the "saved" and "perishing", "believers" and "unbelievers",[138] "saints" and "unrighteous"[139] and "those who are inside" and "those outside". This is not to deny that Paul paints a dismal picture of humanity under sin in 1:18 – 3:20. The soteriological contrast pattern of Rom 1–8, however, is one between the human plight and God's solution, not non-Christians and Christians

---

[137] Rom 12:2 is discussed in the next chapter. See pp. 201–2, 205.

[138] Strikingly, the term ἄπιστος, which features eleven times in 1 Corinthians, is completely absent from Romans. In Rom 15:31, Paul speaks of "disbelievers in Judea".

[139] ἄδικος is used only at 3:5 in the rhetorical question, "What should we say? That God is unjust to inflict wrath on us?"

as such. And Paul's proclamation of the wrath of God in the opening chapters serves as the dark foil to his overwhelmingly positive message of God's saving action in Christ.

6.4.2. The universal scope of salvation

In contrast somewhat with the strongly particularist understanding of salvation in 1 Corinthians, in Romans there is an emphasis on the universal scope of the gospel events (1:5, 16; 3:22, etc.). God's solution is as comprehensive and all-embracing as humanity's plight. This is made plain in 5:15–19 (cf. 11:30–32), especially v. 18: "just as one man's trespass led to condemnation for all, so one man's act of righteousness leads to justification and life for all" (οὕτως καὶ δι᾽ ἑνὸς δικαιώματος εἰς πάντας ἀνθρώπους εἰς δικαίωσιν ζωῆς). Whether Paul is here declaring that every single human being will be saved is much debated by scholars.[140] In my view, it seems wise to understand the implication of his words to be that God has objectively provided for the salvation of every human being and has made this salvation genuinely available to all.[141] What Paul is affirming here is that there is no one who is outside the scope of the salvific effects of Christ's death. Yet at the same time, as Cranfield observes, Paul's formulation does not actually foreclose the question as to whether all in the end will come to share the benefits of Christ's death.[142] The imprecision of his language may well be deliberate: he does not want his argument to end with a two-group antithesis of the saved and the perishing, but with the accent on God's purpose for the redemption of all.

6.4.3. Unbelieving Jews

In chapters 9–11, Paul discusses the question of Jews who resist the gospel. The case of unbelieving Jews is a matter which Paul treats with

---

[140] That Paul is affirming the final salvation of everyone is argued, for example, by Boring (1986) and de Boer (1988, 174–5). That Paul is contrasting two distinct groups of humanity, those "in Adam" and those "in Christ" (as in 1 Cor 15:22), is not a viable option for this passage: see Boring 1986, 286.

[141] It may well be, as Bultmann (1952, 302–3) has argued, that the participle, οἱ λαμβάνοντες in 5:17 implies a condition: the gift of grace must be received. Boring (1986, 286–7) contends that the participle here has a passive sense (those who have been made recipients), rather than an active sense (those who consciously take), but as Marshall (1989, 316–17) shows, the active meaning is more likely in view of Paul's use of the verb λαμβάνω elsewhere.

[142] Cranfield 1975, 290.

great sensitivity. The rejection of the gospel by the majority of his own kinspeople is something which causes him great sorrow, soul-searching and anguish (9:1–3). He does not write off unrepentant Jews in the style of Qumran sectarianism as "sons of darkness", doomed to perdition. On the contrary, he insists that God has not rejected his ancient people (11:1). In chapter 11, he outlines God's saving strategy in relation to Israel, a strategy presently at work. With astonishing boldness, Paul declares that in the end "all Israel" will be saved (11:26–27). Precisely how he conceives of this taking place is of course heavily debated, and need not detain us here. The point to stress is that Paul ends the whole discussion on an eminently positive note (11:25–32), with the proclamation of salvation rather than the pronouncement of judgement. He is at pains not to end up with an apocalyptic social dualism of elect Christians and reprobate Jews.

6.4.4. The resurrection body

In 8:19–22 Paul emphasizes the continuity between the present creation and the renewed creation: the κτίσις is not destined to pass away and to be replaced and by another κτίσις but to be rescued from its current bondage to decay. This emphasis corresponds to his stress in Rom 8 on the continuity between present bodily existence and resurrected bodily existence. The σῶμα, like the κτίσις, is subject to the forces of death and decay (cf. 6:12; 7:24; 8:10–11). As the κτίσις is destined to be released from its enslavement, so too the σῶμα. The σῶμα and the κτίσις together are to be redeemed (8:22–23).

In 1 Cor 15:42ff, Paul had explained resurrection as a replacement or exchange of one kind of body for another (the σῶμα πνευματικόν for the σῶμα ψυχικόν). But in Rom 8:11 and 23, resurrection is conceived as something that happens to *this* body. Believers' bodies will be made alive (ὁ ἐγείρας Χριστὸν ἐκ νεκρῶν ζῳοποιήσει καὶ τὰ θνητὰ σώματα ὑμῶν, 8:11) and redeemed (τὴν ἀπολύτρωσιν τοῦ σώματος ἡμῶν, 8:23). As Witherington states, "For the first time it is possible that Paul is suggesting that the resurrection body will be numerically and 'somatically' identical with the present body."[143] Witherington, in an attempt to relieve the tension between Rom 8 and 1 Cor 15:42ff on the matter, argues that "Paul likely is referring to the transformation of the living believers at the Parousia rather than to the

[143] Witherington 1992, 210.

resurrection of the dead."[144] This explanation, however, will hardly suffice: nowhere in Rom 8 nor elsewhere in the epistle does Paul make a distinction between believers alive at the parousia and those who have died. The reason for the difference is that in Romans Paul is operating with a stronger sense of continuity between this creation and the transformed creation and views bodily resurrection accordingly.

6.4.5. The soteriological paradigm of Romans

The redemptive scheme of 1 Corinthians is largely determined by the apocalyptic antithesis between this world/age and the next. The death of Christ signifies God's apocalyptic judgement on the present evil world. The apocalyptic event of the cross reveals that this world is a sinking ship. Salvation, therefore, consists in being rescued from this ship and being brought into the safe haven of the community of the new creation. Thus, humanity is divided between the "saved" and the "perishing", those who have been picked up from the submerging vessel, and those who remain upon it, going under with it, unaware or disbelieving of their perilous situation.

In Romans, a somewhat different emphasis emerges. Paul casts God's saving activity as that of the creator reclaiming his creation. The world has rebelled against its creator. But God has acted to restore the world to his sovereignty. On the sea-rescue analogy, salvation consists not so much in the rescue of human beings from a sinking ship, but in the recovery of the wayward vessel itself. The world itself is the object of God's redemption. The Christian community is not redeemed from this sinful and perishing world/age, but is a proleptic expression of the redemption of God's world.

6.5. Summary and conclusion

Paul uses κόσμος in this letter with the senses "inhabited world" (1:8), "world/universe" (1:20); "humanity" in general (3:6, 19; 5:12–13), "renewed world" (4:13) and "Gentile world" (11:12, 15). He employs κτίσις with the senses "act of creation" (1:20), "creature", "created thing" (1:25; 8:38) and "non-human creation" (8:19–22).

Paul's employment of κόσμος in Romans is non-pejorative. The slight exception is the use at 3:19, where it is stated that the κόσμος

---

[144] Witherington 1992, 210.

(= humanity) is "held accountable to God". But the degree of negativity present in this text is minimal in comparison with the negative statements on κόσμος in 1 Corinthians. In Romans, Paul can deploy the term in highly positive ways. In 1:20, the κόσμος is the vehicle of God's universal revelation. In 11:12 and 15, the κόσμος, the Gentile world, is the object of God's blessing and reconciling activity. Most striking of all, in 4:13 the word κόσμος is used to denote the future redeemed world, the inheritance of believers.

The pattern of usage of κόσμος in Romans contrasts markedly with that of 1 Corinthians. Nowhere in Romans does κόσμος bear the apocalyptic sense "this world", its characteristic meaning in 1 Corinthians. Nowhere in Romans does Paul use the term to build a contrast between the church and the wider world. Nowhere in this epistle does Paul use κόσμος to negate the "official" and "legitimated" meaning of κόσμος (= world/universe) in Greek usage and the world-view conventionally linked with the term. In fact, in 1:20, he uses the term with its legitimate meaning, presupposing the associated world-view and building his argument upon it.

κτίσις is also used in a favourable manner by Paul. Almost by definition, κτίσις is a term of positive evaluation for Paul: quite misguided is Bultmann's attempt to read negative associations into κτίσις at 1:25 and 8:38 and to play down the central role of the κτίσις in 8:19–22. In 8:19–22, Paul uses κτίσις to emphasize the continuity between the present world and its future transformation.

The linguistic role of κόσμος in 1 Corinthians as the main negative theological term of the epistle has been taken over in Romans by the triad ἁμαρτία, θάνατος and σάρξ. These three terms are used extensively in the discussion of chapters 5–8 to characterize humanity's state of estrangement from the creator.[145] ἁμαρτία occurs forty-eight times in Romans, by far the largest number of occurrences in a Pauline letter, or in any New Testament document. It appears forty-two times between 5:12 and 8:10. As Dunn states, "in Romans Paul sees sin . . . as the most negative and most dangerous force in human experience".[146] The role of ἁμαρτία as a "cosmological-apocalyptic" power-structure was highlighted in the discussion of 5:12ff above. The personification

---

[145] They appear as interrelated categories: sin and death are closely linked in 5:12, 21; 6:16, 23; 7:5, 10–11, 13; 8:2; sin and flesh in 7:5, 14, 25; 8:3; flesh and death in 7:5 and 8:6.
[146] Dunn 1988, 148.

of sin as an apocalyptic power extends into chapters 6–7 (6:6, 12, 16–17, 20, 23; 7:8, 11, 13, 14).[147] θάνατος occurs twenty-two times in Romans, again the largest number of instances in a single New Testament writing. Apart from the uses at 1:32 and 5:10, occurrences are concentrated between 5:12 and 8:38. Like ἁμαρτία it is cast in the role of an oppressive power (5:14, 17; 6:9; 8:38). σάρξ appears twenty-six times in Romans, again more often than in any other Pauline epistle. The majority of occurrences (sixteen of the twenty-six) are concentrated in the verses between 7:5 and 8:13. Paul uses the term in various ways: for physical flesh (2:28), for physical descent or kinship (1:3; 4:1; 9:3, 5, 8; 11:14), for humanity (3:20), for weak human nature (6:19). The main line of usage, though, is with reference to a sphere of opposition to God. It is this sense which dominates in chapters 7 and 8.

κόσμος, as observed above, is connected with ἁμαρτία and θάνατος in 5:12–13, but as their victim, not their villainous ally. κόσμος, as we have also noted, interchanges with πᾶσα σάρξ at 3:19–20.

In broad terms, Paul's s usage of κόσμος and κτίσις shows some similarities to the use of these terms in *Wisdom of Solomon*. The authors use the terms with similar senses: κόσμος as "world/universe" (Wis 9:9; 11:22; 13:2), "inhabited world" (9:3; 14:14; 17:18), "humanity" (2:24; 6:23; 10:1; 14:6); κτίσις as "non-human creation" (2:6; 5:17; 16:24; 19:6). Also, they make similar statements involving κόσμος and κτίσις. According to *Wisdom of Solomon*, God made/created the κόσμος (= world/universe) (9:9; 11:17); death entered the human κόσμος (2:24); there is salvation for the human κόσμος (6:23–24); the (personified) κτίσις is on the side of God's children (19:6); the κτίσις was fashioned anew (19:6).

The various theological emphases in Paul's usage statements on κόσμος and κτίσις cohere with the larger theological perspective of Romans: the universal sweep of the story of fall and redemption, embracing the *whole* of humankind; the setting of that story within the broad context of the understanding of God as creator and of the world as his creation; the juxtaposition serving to show that God's redeeming purposes derive from and express his faithfulness toward the world he has made.

---

[147] ἁμαρτία is also used to denote the act of sin or trespass (5:13, 20; 6:1; 7:5, 7; 11:27; 14:23).

All these observations could give rise to the following conclusion: this is how Paul talks about κόσμος – and κτίσις – when he is not writing with situational constraints imposed on him. In the absence of socio-rhetorical considerations forcing him into a narrow apocalyptic social and spatio-temporal dualism, Paul has the freedom to shed a more favourable light on the world as κόσμος and κτίσις and to reflect more deeply on how the world stands in a positive relation to its creator. Such a judgement would be in keeping with the opinion that Romans bears the character of a "theological treatise" in which Paul is more reflective than reactive, and more ruminative than responsive. Yet, both the shift in scholarly opinion as to the occasion of Romans and the methodological assumption of this study – that there is no socially-disinterested use of language – encourage us to look for signs that Paul's uses of κόσμος and κτίσις are not unaffected by social concerns. It is the pursuit of these indications that concerns the next chapter.

7

Social conflict with outsiders at Rome

7.1. Introduction

As noted at the beginning of the previous chapter, there is no scholarly consensus as to how far the theological argumentation of Rom 1–11 touches on the specific needs of the Romans readers. This renders unsound any attempt to look within these chapters for evidence of a socio-rhetorical dimension to Paul's usage of κόσμος and κτίσις. A more secure (but not risk-free) line of enquiry is to focus attention on the paraenetic material of Rom 12ff. A persuasive case can be made that the social and practical teaching in these chapters both develops out of the foregoing theological teaching and addresses the actual situation in Rome.

The basic approach in this chapter is to use Rom 12ff as a bridge to link Paul's talk of κόσμος and κτίσις in chapters 1–11 to the social situation of the community addressed. An examination of 12:14 – 13:10, where Paul instructs his readers on social relations with outsiders, will try to identify linguistic and conceptual links between what Paul says in this section and the κόσμος and κτίσις texts examined in the last chapter. Then an attempt will be made to show that the exhortations of 12:14 – 13:10 are context-specific to Rome, suggesting that Paul's admonitions reflect an awareness of recent developments in Rome and express his social concerns for his readers in the light of these circumstances.

The overall aim will be to show that Paul's usage of κόσμος and κτίσις in Rom 1–11 supports the line of advice he offers in Rom 12:14 – 13:10: that his readers should live, as fully as possible, in harmony with the surrounding society. This social objective for the community is to be understood against a background of political vulnerability and mounting conflict with outsiders at Rome. But before turning specifically to Rom 12–13, some general comments must be made on the context of utterance of this letter.

7.2. Context of utterance: general comments

We do not know how the Christian community in Rome came into being or who its founders were. The most probable explanation is that it emerged from the city's large Jewish community,[1] the somewhat loose structure of Roman Judaism providing an opening for the penetration of Christian preaching. The earliest members of the community would thus have been Christian Jews and former proselytes to Judaism.

Suetonius (*Claud.* 25) reports that Claudius expelled the Jews from the capital because of constant disturbances "at the instigation of *Chrestus*".[2] This probably happened in 49 CE.[3] It is generally accepted that *Chrestus* is a misspelt reference to Christ. A confusion between the names *Chrestus*, a common Roman slave name (but not a common Jewish name),[4] and *Christus* among Graeco-Romans – much to the annoyance of Christians – is well attested by the early Christian apologists.[5] The garbled reference to Christ suggests that Jews and Jewish Christians were banished from Rome for disturbances related to the preaching of the Christian message. It is unclear from Suetonius whether all the Jews in Rome were excluded or only those most directly involved. The latter seems more plausible.[6] Certainly Christian Jews were among those expelled (Acts 18:2).

[1] On the history of the Jewish colony in Rome, see Barclay 1996, 282–319; Clarke 1994, 466–71; Leon 1960; Penna 1982; Smallwood 1981, 201–19; Wiefel 1991. The number of Jews in Rome in the mid first century is estimated by Leon (135–6) at 50,000. The total population was around 1 million: Clarke 1994, 465.
[2] *Iudaeos impulsore Chresto assidue tumultuantis Roma expulit.*
[3] The evidence for the date of the edict is divided. Dio Cassius (*Hist.* 60.6.6) refers to an edict aimed at Jews in Rome in 41 CE. Orosius (7.6.15) dates the edict at 49 CE, a date supported by Acts 18:2. The conflict is best resolved by taking the decree mentioned by Dio as a limited ruling (Dio does not say that Claudius drove the Jews out but rather that he forbade them to hold meetings) and the decree related by Orosius and Acts 18:2 as a later and more drastic measure: so Barclay 1996, 305; Jewett 1979, 36–8; Momigliano 1981, 31–7; Smallwood 1981, 210–16; Watson 1986, 91–3.
[4] Leon (1960, 93–121) lists over 500 names taken by Jews in first-century Rome. *Chrestus* does not appear.
[5] Cf. Justin, *Apol.* 1.4; Tertullian, *Apol.* 3.5; Lactantius, D.I. 4.7. The confusion is even attested in the textual tradition of the New Testament. Codex Sinaiticus has χρηστιανος for χριστιανός at Acts 11:26; 26:28; 1 Pet 4:16.
[6] Leon (1960, 24) and Smallwood (1981, 216) argue that only the rioters were ejected. Acts 18:2 says πάντας τοὺς Ἰουδαίους.

As a result of the Claudian edict, the Roman churches would have lost much of their original Jewish membership. Gentile membership and leadership would have become the norm. When Christian Jews began to return to Rome after the edict had lapsed, they would have found a Christian community quite different in ethnic constituency and social ethos from the one they had left. They may have found it difficult to adjust, and this may have provoked Jewish–Gentile tensions in the churches.[7] This reconstruction is broadly corroborated by Paul's letter itself. When Paul writes in the late 50s,[8] he clearly assumes a predominantly Gentile community[9] and a degree of friction between Jewish and Gentile Christians within the congregations (14:1 – 15:13).[10]

Paul's letter presupposes a scattered community with different groups meeting at different locations. At least five such pockets can be identified from chapter 16. The scattered nature of the community accounts for Paul's failure to address the Roman believers as an ἐκκλησία.

The social level of the Roman believers is extremely difficult to assess. In his analysis of the names of Romans 16, Lampe comes to the conclusion that of the thirteen persons about whom a probability statement can be made, "more than two thirds ... have an affinity to slave origins".[11] But since, as Lampe admits, freedmen and women who engaged in commerce sometimes became wealthier than freeborn, servile status is not necessarily an indicator of socio-economic position. A number of the named individuals in Rom 16 seem to have been of some status, for example, Prisca and Aquila, Urbanus, Rufus and his mother. In general, however, the membership of the community in Rome was probably drawn from the lower strata of society. As Lampe demonstrates, the early Christian groups in Rome were mostly located in Trastevere and the district around the Via Appia near the Porta Capena: these were the poorest areas of the city.[12] Also, later evidence from the first and second

---

[7] See Wiefel 1991.

[8] The date 56–57 CE is argued for by Cranfield (1975, 16) and Dunn (1988, xliii). But a good case can be made for 57–58 CE: see Fitzmyer 1993, 85–7; cf. Black 1973, 20; Sanday and Headlam 1902, xiii.

[9] Cf. Rom 1:5–6, 13–15; 11:13–31; 15:7–12, 15–16. Only three of the names in chapter 16 occur also in the Jewish inscriptions of Rome: see P. Lampe 1991, 224–5. Brown and Meier (1983, 87ff) and J. T. Sanders (1993, 214ff), in arguing for a Jewish majority, insufficiently explain this evidence.

[10] That the division is on ethnic lines is indicated especially by 15:7–13. So Marcus 1989, 68.

[11] P. Lampe 1991, 228.

[12] P. Lampe 1987, 52.

centuries in Rome points to well-to-do members forming only a very small minority in the church.[13]

Paul played no part in the founding of the Roman churches. This clearly affects the way in which he writes to them. As Best points out, he avoids father/child language and methods of persuasion based on that model, he does not rebuke his readers, he does not call on them to obey him, and he does not directly argue with them.[14] His tone in Romans is much less authoritarian than in any other of his (undisputed) letters.

Paul wrote Romans from Corinth (Rom 16:1–2, 23). Why he wrote is a much debated issue. The old consensus was that Paul penned (or to be more precise, dictated; cf. 16:22) the letter essentially to meet his own needs, for example, to set out his theology as a "last will and testament",[15] or to rehearse the defence of his gospel which he would give at Jerusalem.[16] In recent discussion of the purpose of Romans, more attention has been given to the needs of the readers. Considerable weight has been placed on the section, 14:1 – 15:13. It is now generally accepted that the exhortations of this section have not simply been drawn form Paul's earlier experiences with the Corinthians (1 Cor 8–10)[17] but relate to a specific (and distinctly different) situation in Rome. On the basis of this section, it has been argued that Paul wrote Romans, at least partly, to resolve tensions between Jewish and Gentile Christians (or, between those who observe Jewish traditions and those who do not) in the Roman Christian community.[18] Certainly, a good of deal of the theological contents of the letter make sense in this light.

The current consensus is that Paul probably wrote Romans with several purposes in mind, relating both to his own interests and the perceived needs of the readers.[19] For the sake of this study, though, we shall emphasize the situational aspects of the letter, but focus on 12:14 – 13:10 rather than 14:1 – 15:13. This is the section of Paul's practical teaching which is most relevant to Paul's epistolary usage of κόσμος and κτίσις.

[13] P. Lampe 1991, 229.
[14] Best 1988, 150.
[15] So Bornkamm 1991.
[16] So Jervell 1991.
[17] *Contra* Karris 1991.
[18] Bruce 1991; Walters 1993; Watson 1986, 88–176.
[19] Donfried 1991b, lxx.

7.3. Romans 12–13: general paraenesis?

Rom 12–13 is sometimes labelled "general paraenesis".[20] The designation carries the following assumptions: that the section is only tangentially related to the theological exposition which has gone before; that it comprises loosely connected directives; that it does not address issues *specific* to the Roman congregations. If these suppositions are correct, this would obviously undermine any attempt to use these chapters as a bridge to link Paul's earlier talk of κόσμος and κτίσις with the Roman situation and Paul's efforts to affect it. But each of these assumptions must be challenged. We shall deal here with the alleged independence of Rom 12–13 from what precedes and the supposed lack of literary cohesion in the section. The question of its special relevance to Rome will be considered later.

Far from being detached from the foregoing theological arguments, there is good evidence to suggest that Paul's exhortations in chapters 12–13 find their foundation in and derive their shape from the theology which precedes. There are unmistakable linguistic and thematic ties between chapters 1–11 and 12–13. Rom 12:1–2 forms a summary statement or pivot for the exhortations which follow. The οὖν in 12:1 points to an argumentative link with the preceding material. A number of connections with earlier sections of the letter are clearly discernible in 12:1–2. The mention of "the mercies of God" links 12:1 to 11:30–32, verses which themselves constitute a climactic theological statement recalling and summing up key themes of the argument of chapters 1–11.[21] There are several striking verbal links between 12:1–2 and 1:18–32: ἀτιμάζεσθαι τὰ σώματα αὐτῶν (1:24), παραστῆσαι τὰ σώματα ὑμῶν (12:1); ἐλάτρευσαν τῇ κτίσει (1:25), τὴν λογικὴν λατρείαν ὑμῶν (12:1); εἰς ἀδόκιμον νοῦν (1:28), τῇ ἀνακαινώσει τοῦ νοός, εἰς τὸ δοκιμάζειν ὑμᾶς τί τὸ θέλημα τοῦ θεοῦ (12:2).[22] The echoes are so marked that it is difficult not to conclude with Thompson that the "action he [Paul] calls for in 12.1–2 ... represents a reversal of the downward spiral depicted in Romans 1".[23] The reference to discerning the will of God in 12:2 (εἰς τὸ δοκιμάζειν ὑμᾶς τί τὸ

---

[20] Käsemann 1980, x–xi; Michel 1966, 288–9; Schlier 1977, 349–50; Wilckens 1982, 1–2.

[21] Dunn 1988, 687–9.

[22] Cf. Dunn 1988, 708; Furnish 1968, 103–4; M. Thompson 1991, 81–3.

[23] M. Thompson 1991, 82.

CONSTRUCTING THE WORLD

θέλημα τοῦ θεοῦ) recalls 2:18 (καὶ γινώσκεις τὸ θέλημα καὶ δοκιμάζεις τὰ διαφέροντα). 12:1–2 also picks up key terms from chapters 6–8: παρίστημι (6:13, 16, 19), σῶμα (6:6, 12; 7:4, etc.), νοῦς (7:23, 25). Particularly strong are the links with 6:12–13[24] and 8:5–10.[25] There is also a connection between the call to be transformed (μεταμορφοῦσθε) in 12:2 and talk of conformity (συμμόρφους) to the image of Christ in 8:29.[26] These verbal and thematic ties lead to the conclusion that Paul is drawing together "previous threads of the discussion in a paraenesis which reflects the course of the complete discussion to this point".[27] A number of such links with Paul's teaching in chapters 1–11 can be detected throughout chapters 12–13.[28] These lines of continuity suggest that Paul in these chapters (and in chapters 14–15) is drawing out for his readers practical and social consequences of the theology expounded in Rom 1–11.[29] As Dunn points out, both in subject-matter and sequence, Rom 12–15 follows naturally from the overall argument of Rom 1–11.[30]

What, then, are we to make of the seemingly disconnected nature of the admonitions of 12:1–13:14? Again, when examined closely, these exhortations are by no means as piecemeal as they first appear. Link words which span the main paragraph divisions (παρακαλέω, 12:1, 8; ἀγαθός, 12:2, 9; διώκω, 12:13, 14; κακός/ἀγαθός, 12:21, 13:3–4; ὀφειλή/ὀφείλω, 13:7–8) tie the exhortations together. The arrangement of topics follows a logical progression of thought. Paul deals first, in 12:3–13, with relations inside the community, then, in 12:14 – 13:10, with life in the wider society,[31] covering relations with hostile outsiders (12:14–21), relations with the governing authorities (13:1–7) and duties toward neighbours (13:8–10). Key ethical themes structure the development: unity (12:3–8); love (12:9–13; 13:8–10); non-retaliation (12:14–21); submission (13:1–7).

[24] M. Thompson 1991, 79–80.
[25] M. Thompson 1991, 82.
[26] M. Thompson 1991, 84.
[27] Dunn 1988, 707.
[28] 12:12 recalls 5:3–5; 12:3, 16 echoes 11:20, 25; 12:14–21 echoes 2:1–11; 12:19 and 13:1–7 recall 1:18ff (see below pp. 206–7) and 2:7–15; the reference to σάρξ in 13:14 builds on 6:19; 7:5, 18, 25; and 8:1–13; the call to "put on" Christ in 13:14 recalls the Adamic soteriology of 6:6 and 8:29.
[29] W. T. Wilson 1991, 127–8.
[30] Dunn 1988, 705–6.
[31] There is some overlap. 12:12b and 12:13b have external relations in view, and 12:16a is aimed at internal relations.

The paraenesis of Rom 12–13, therefore, is not as "general" as sometimes thought. There are strong cohesive ties with what has gone before, indicating that these chapters (and Rom 12–15 as a whole) are rooted in the preceding theological exposition. Moreover, Rom 12–13 is marked by the cohesion, progression and thematization we would expect of integrated texts,[32] suggesting that, far from being a collection of loosely strung together precepts, this is a carefully and thoughtfully crafted unit of moral teaching.

7.4. Apocalyptic dualism in Romans 12:2 and 13:11–14

A possible sign of sharp discontinuity with what was gone before is the presence of the apocalyptic language of 12:2 and 13:11–14. In 12:2 Paul urges his readers not to conform to "this age", ὁ αἰὼν οὗτος. The two-age dualism of Jewish apocalyptic thought is clear. This is precisely the apocalyptic conception which was absent throughout 1:18 – 11:36. In 13:11–14, apocalyptic themes are particularly concentrated. In this subsection, we find for the first and only time in the epistle, an acknowledgement of the nearness of the parousia. Paul uses the motif of the imminence of the end to motivate believers to appropriate ethical conduct. We also have the typical apocalyptic contrasts between day and night, darkness and light, waking and sleeping. The configuration of apocalyptic symbols in Rom 13:11–14 is remarkably similar to that in 1 Thess 5:1–11. In that passage such imagery is used to construct a very sharp social contrast between insiders and outsiders.

Given their significant position, framing the series of admonitions in chapters 12–13,[33] 12:2 and 13:11–14 raise two key questions. Does the mention of ὁ αἰὼν οὗτος in 12:2 signal a change in outlook from 1:18–11:36, Paul's previous emphasis on the world as God's well-ordered creation giving way to a negative understanding of the world as "this world"? Secondly, does 13:11–14 now introduce into Paul's paraenesis a stark apocalyptic social duality, of the kind he has avoided so far? In sum, do the apocalyptic dualisms of these verses indicate a fundamental shift in theological and social perspective from Rom 1–11?

Notwithstanding the reference to ὁ αἰὼν οὗτος, the moral imperatives of 12:1–2 presuppose the strong affirmation of the created

---

[32] These are Fowler's (1996, 82–3) criteria of well-formed texts.
[33] So Furnish 1979, 123.

order which comes to expression in the previous chapters. The apocalyptic expectation of a cosmic change is implicit in 12:2 as the basic paradigm for Paul's directive. But it should be noted that the positive counterpart to conformity to "this age" is "transformation" and "renewal" (μεταμορφοῦσθε τῇ ἀνακαινώσει τοῦ νοός). This suggests that the underlying apocalyptic picture is that of cosmic transformation rather than that of cosmic destruction and re-creation. This is thoroughly consistent with 8:19–22 where Paul declares that creation is to be redeemed and transformed, not destroyed. The echoes of 1:18–32 in 12:1–2, noted above, indicate the ἀνακαίνωσις τοῦ νοός consists (at least partly) in a reorientation to God's original creative will.[34] The disobedient Gentiles deviated from the order given in creation and reaped the inevitable consequences. Believers, however, are being realigned to the order established in creation and are being enabled (presumably by the Spirit) to live in accordance with it. It is significant that Paul's exhortation focuses on the sacrificial presentation of the σῶμα. As Käsemann states, "When God claims our bodies, in and with them he reaches after his creation."[35] This is especially so in the light of Paul's statement in 8:23 that the σῶμα is to be redeemed along with the rest of creation. The moral actions called for in 12:1–2 are thus of a piece with the soteriological paradigm of chapters 1–11: redemption as the recovery of creation. Paul bases his moral appeal on the idea of a good and well-ordered creation and the belief that that order is (at least to some extent) re-affirmed in redemption.

Unlike 1 Thess 5:1–11, the dualistic language in Rom 13:11–14 is not used to stress the boundary between insiders and outsiders. There is no mention of outsiders in Rom 13:11–14. Rather, the imagery is employed to stimulate a concern for good social behaviour (μὴ κώμοις καὶ μέθαις, μὴ κοίταις καὶ ἀσελγείαις, μὴ ἔριδι καὶ ζήλῳ ... καὶ τῆς σαρκὸς πρόνοιαν μὴ ποιεῖσθε εἰς ἐπιθυμίας, vv. 13b–14). It is significant that Paul instructs his readers to conduct themselves εὐσχημόνως (v. 13a). The word εὐσχημόνως signifies, as Dunn states, "what would generally be regarded as decent, proper, presentable in responsible society".[36] What Paul is commending to his readers in these verse, therefore, is not a counter-cultural morality, but "conventional

---

[34] Stuhlmacher 1987, 10.
[35] Käsemann 1980, 330.
[36] Dunn 1988, 789.

respectability".[37] Paul is effectively "equating Christ and his movement with the accepted social values of his day".[38] This is hardly aimed at reinforcing a social dualism.

The understanding of the world as God's creation in chapters 1–11, therefore, is not undermined in Rom 12:1–2. Indeed it forms the theological basis for Paul's moral argumentation in these verses. As in chapters 1–11, the earlier emphasis on redemption as the restoration of creation tempers the apocalyptic dualism of this age and the next. Also, the apocalyptic contrast pattern set forth in 13:11–14 does not bring into Paul's paraenesis a social polarization of church and outside society. It is deployed to encourage exemplary social behaviour, conduct which would win the *approval* of outsiders. In sum, the dualistic language of 12:2 and 13:11–14 is no evidence of a difference in theological and social perspective between Rom 12–13 and chapters 1–11.

7.5. Paul's social teaching in Romans 12:14 – 13:10

In this section Paul counsels his readers on relations with the larger society. He calls for social harmony with outsiders, good citizenship and good neighbourliness.

7.5.1. Dealing with resentment from outsiders (12:14–21)

In this subsection, Paul instructs his readers on how to cope with hostility from outsiders. He warns them not to retaliate when provoked (vv. 14, 17, 19–21) but to respond with positive acts of love and kindness (vv. 14, 17, 20–21). The passage is marked by a complete absence of apocalyptic social dualism. Indeed, any apocalyptic traits in the subsection are difficult to find.[39] The "wrath" (of God) mentioned in v. 19 most probably refers to the present outworking of God's wrath in his ordered world (it is the present expression of God's wrath that Paul takes up a few verses later), not to the future eschatological judgement of God. The motivation for the loving treatment of hostile outsiders articulated in v. 20 – "for by doing this you will heap burning coals on their heads" (quoting Prov 25:21–22) – may seem to be the wish for their eschatological punishment. But it is generally recognized that the

---

[37] Dunn 1988, 789.
[38] Guerra 1995, 166.
[39] Zerbe's (1991, 225, 247–8) attempt to import apocalyptic dualism into this text on the basis of the word pair κακός / ἀγαθός is a clutching at straws.

phrase "burning coals" stands for the shame and repentance brought about in the perpetrators of evil when their actions are met with good.[40] The incentive for showing love in response to hatred is thus the hope that one might achieve reconciliation.

There is nothing in this passage that could be described as sectarian. The use of the basic moral categories κακός and ἀγαθός (vv. 17, 21) and the appeal to "take thought for what is noble in the sight of all" (προνοούμενοι καλὰ ἐνώπιον πάντων ἀνθρώπων, v. 17) indicate that Paul is recommending a "cross-boundary" standard of behaviour.[41] He urges his readers to adopt a style of conduct which pagans would recognize as good.

In this passage, Paul promotes peace, conciliation, and blessing toward non-Christians. The burden of Paul's advice is summed up in v. 18: μετὰ πάντων ἀνθρώπων εἰρηνεύοντες. The exhortations of 12:14–21 constitute a call for social harmony with the surrounding society, or as Bindemann puts it, in view of Paul's appeal to conventional social values, "Manhung zur Integration".[42]

7.5.2. Submission to the political authorities (13:1–7)

In this passage, Paul mounts a strong appeal for submission to the imperial authorities. The pericope represents an extension of the exhortation of 12:18 to "live peaceably with all".[43] Käsemann observes that the attitude of Paul here toward the government is based on a doctrine of creation.[44] Similarly Dunn writes of the theological perspective of this passage, "it is creation theology if it is anything".[45]

Some scholars have tried to inject an apocalyptic perspective into this passage by arguing that the terms ἐξουσίαι and ἄρχοντες refer to supernatural powers standing behind earthly rulers[46] and/or by claiming

---

[40] Cotterell and Turner 1989, 302–5; Cranfield 1979, 649; Dunn 1988, 750–1; Stuhlmacher 1989, 177; Travis 1986, 41; Wilckens 1982, 26; W. T. Wilson 1991, 195–6.
[41] So Bindemann 1983, 111–12
[42] Bindemann 1983, 111.
[43] So Fitzmyer 1993, 664. The thesis that this subsection is an interpolation – argued by Kallas (1964/65), Munro (1983, 57–8) and O'Neill (1975, 15) – has never won large support. There is no manuscript evidence for such a view. Moreover, it fails to account for the coherence of this section with the immediate and larger context.
[44] Käsemann 1969c, 205.
[45] Dunn 1986, 67.
[46] E.g. Cullmann 1963, 72–3.

that Rom 13:1–7 assumes the apocalyptic outlook of 12:2, the state being implicitly conceived of as belonging to ὁ αἰὼν οὗτος.[47] These attempts are wholly unconvincing. The suggestion that the terms ἐξουσίαι and ἄρχοντες point to spiritual powers may be quickly dismissed. As Carr has shown, the linguistic evidence is overwhelmingly against it.[48] Dunn remarks that the view "has now become something of a historical curiosity".[49] The suggestion that Paul views, or intends his readers to view, the state as part of ὁ αἰὼν οὗτος condemned in 12:2 is also implausible. Paul would be completely contradicting his earlier advice. Having told his readers that they *must not conform* to ὁ αἰὼν οὗτος because such conformity *is against* the will of God, he would now be telling them that they *must conform* to ὁ αἰὼν οὗτος because such conformity *is* the will of God! This is not to deny that 13:1–7 is meant to be read in the light of 12:1–2. However, Paul's advice in 13:1–7 is not to be linked with the negative command of 12:2, "Do not be conformed to this age", but with the positive appeal to discern the will of the God the creator and to live in the light of it.

Rom 13:1–7 resists all attempts to set it within an apocalyptic, dualistic framework. The political order is located incontrovertibly in the creative and providential purposes of God. Paul legitimates the imperial government by incorporating it within the reign of God. As Meeks states, "The apocalyptic element in Pauline thought ran counter to that kind of legitimation."[50]

The call for submission is framed largely in terms which are general and which would gain wide moral approbation.[51] Paul appeals to the basic moral categories of κακός and ἀγαθός (vv. 3–4). He invokes the ideal of ἔπαινος (v. 3), "a characteristic goal of Greek wisdom and philosophy".[52] He appeals to ἀνάγκη (v. 5) which, in a philosophical context and here (in view of the construction διὸ ἀνάγκη ὑποτάσσεσθαι … διὰ τὴν συνείδησιν), refers to "the way things

---

[47] E.g. Schrage 1988, 236.
[48] See Carr 1981, 115–18. The inference that ἄρχοντες in 1 Cor 2:6–8 refers to spiritual powers as well as human rulers is based on what Paul predicates of the term ἄρχοντες in these verses, not on the assumption that ἄρχοντες *per se* denotes jointly human and spiritual authorities.
[49] Dunn 1988, 760.
[50] Meeks 1983a, 170.
[51] Bammel (1984, 366) describes the terminology as "semi-philosophical".
[52] Dunn 1988, 763.

are ... and have to be" by nature and by destiny.[53] And he argues on the basis of συνείδησις (v. 5, cf. 2:14–16), a human being's natural awareness of right and wrong. Paul thus builds his appeal for submission upon general moral categories and not distinctively Christian ones. The opening words of the pericope, πᾶσα ψυχή, are significant in view of the wide terms of the admonitions. Paul addresses the Roman believers as *part of society as a whole*, not as demarcated from it or exempt from obligations toward it. It is their duty as *members of the wider society* to be subject.

As Käsemann points out, derivatives from the root ταγ- provide the leading idea in these verses:[54] ὑποτάσσω (v. 1, 5); τάσσω (v. 1); δαιταγή (v. 2); ἀντιτάσσομαι (v. 2). The basic notion is that of a well-ordered world. The governing authorities have been set up by God (αἱ δὲ οὖσαι ὑπὸ θεοῦ τεταγμέναι εἰσίν) as part of his ordering of human society. To oppose them, therefore, is to oppose what God has ordered (ὁ ἀντιτασσόμενος τῇ ἐξουσίᾳ τῇ τοῦ θεοῦ διαταγῇ ἀνθέστηκεν, v. 2). The call to submit (ὑποτασσέσθω) is essentially a call to recognize one's place in this order. It is not a call for unqualified obedience to rulers. Paul's appeal in 13:1–7 is more for "good citizenship",[55] on the assumption that the structures of society, especially the authority structures of society, reflect the will of God.

God's ordering of society is clearly viewed as good. There is no thought in this passage that the governing powers, appointed by God to administer (cf. διάκονος, λειτουργοὶ θεοῦ, vv. 4, 6) his human creation, are morally corrupt or unjust. On the contrary, the rulers are portrayed as upholders of the civic good (τὸ ἀγαθόν), conducting themselves properly and appropriately. The authorities hold no terror to those whose behaviour is good. They provoke fear only in those who do evil. The authorities reflect and preserve the good order of society.

The idea of a positively valued, ordered world was expressed in 1:18–32. Rom 13:1–7 shares this understanding. In both passages, it is assumed that there is a natural and moral order, reflecting the divine will, in accordance with which one is expected to live. Also, both passages articulate the idea that God's wrath in its present expression is a retributive process built into the fabric of the world. In 1:18–32, God's

[53] Dunn 1988, 765.
[54] Käsemann 1980, 351.
[55] J. I. H. MacDonald 1989, 543.

wrath operates in and through the natural, moral structures of human society. In 13:4–5, the divine wrath works through the political structures of society: the governing authorities are agents of God's wrath to wrongdoers (ἔκδικος εἰς ὀργὴν τῷ τὸ κακὸν πράσσοντι, v. 4). Paul's remark in 13:2b, those who resist the political authorities "receive judgment on themselves", ἑαυτοῖς κρίμα λήμψονται, recalls his comment in 1:27, that those who indulge in homosexual activity "receive in themselves the due penalty for their error", τὴν ἀντιμισθίαν ἣν ἔδει τῆς πλάνης αὐτῶν ἐν ἑαυτοῖς ἀπολαμβάνοντες.[56] Rom 13:1–7 thus presupposes the understanding of the world set forth in chapter 1, an understanding which has itself been significantly shaped by the view of the world linked with κόσμος (= world / universe). Paul in 13:1–7 builds on this world-view and draws out its social and ideological ramifications, giving a strong endorsement of the prevailing social and political order.

The climax of the pericope, v. 7, is an injunction to recognize the obligations which accrue to one's rank in society: to pay tax to whom tax is due, to give respect to whom respect is due, to give honour to whom honour is due. The thought is that one must act in accordance with one's social station and defer to those of a higher status, not upset the power relations of society, but respect and submit to the social arrangement. The burden of Paul's advice in 13:1–7 is that his readers recognize their place within society at large. They are not to be subversive; they are not to be a threat to the social status quo. In fact, they are to be model citizens.

Rom 13:1–7 reflects the strong emphasis on God as creator and the world as his well-ordered creation which emerges in the theological teaching of chapters 1–11, a perspective which his usage of κόσμος and κτίσις helps to construct. The social ethos of Paul's advice in 13:1–7, however out of line it may appear with the sectarian perspective of other epistles, is consistent with the view of the world that comes to the fore in Romans.

7.5.3. Love toward neighbours (13:8–10)

The call to love one another, following on from the advice in 12:14 – 13:7 about dealings with the wider society, should not be limited to relationships in the Christian community. It embraces even relations

[56] The translations here are my own.

with non-Christians.[57] "Neighbour" (πλησίον) is broad enough to take in all the people that the believers would come into contact with in the course of their everyday lives. Again the language of these verses is not the language of sectarianism or separatism. A basic duty toward one's neighbours is presupposed. In fact, in Christ, the debt of love toward society at large is increased.

7.5.4. Correlations

In the light of this brief analysis of 12:14 – 13:10, a number of correlations may be made with Paul's earlier talk of κόσμος and κτίσις.

1. Paul's refusal to use κόσμος (or the social antitheses of "saved" and "perishing", "those who are inside" and "those outside") to construct a social dualism of church and world matches the non-sectarian tone and outlook of his instructions in Rom 12:14 – 13:10. Paul stresses his readers' obligations toward the larger society. He encourages them to view themselves as integrated members of society, not as marginal to or subversive of it. Significantly, Paul couches his instructions in 12:17 – 13:7 in terms that would have "cross-boundary" appeal, recognizing, to some extent, the fundamental unity of humankind and a basic agreement between Christians and pagans on the norms and purposes and society.

2. The exhortation of 12:18 to live in a state of "peace" with outsiders, μετὰ πάντων ἀνθρώπων εἰρηνεύοντες, which encapsulates the burden of 12:14 – 13:10 as a whole, may be viewed as the social and ethical corollary of the belief that God has initiated the reconciliation of the κόσμος, the Gentile world (11:15; cf. the connection between peace and reconciliation in Rom 5:1, 10–11).

3. Paul's teaching in 13:1–7 reflects the understanding of the world set out in 1:18–32. The world is divinely arranged and exhibits a natural and moral order. Human beings have an intuited awareness of the divinely established order. One ought to live in accordance with that order. When God's order is contravened, the divine wrath comes into play. God's wrath operates in and through the world's structures. In 1:18–32 Paul incorporates aspects of the conventional world-view linked

---

[57] Paul's claim in 13:10 that "Love does no wrong to a neighbour" (κακὸν οὐκ ἐργάζεται) points back to 12:17, 21.

with κόσμος. In 13:1–7 he draws out some of the social and ideological implications of that world-view.

4. The emphasis on God's continued control over his creation, even though it has deviated from its intentions, is apparent in 1:18–32; 5:12–13; 8:19–22, 38–39. The emphasis is obviously present in 13:1–7.

5. The theme of creaturely submission (ὑποτάσσω) to the will of the creator in 13:1–7 echoes 8:19–22. The κτίσις submits to its creator (8:20). The submission of πᾶσα ψυχή to God's appointed rulers reflects the same cosmological, hierarchical pattern.

6. Rom 8:19–22 strongly indicates that God's redemptive work involves not the destruction of his creative work but its restoration and fulfilment. The understanding of redemption as the recovery of creation is the soteriological paradigm of Rom 1–11 as a whole. This perspective is presupposed in the ethical directives of 12:1–2 and 13:1–7. What it means to be a member of the redeemed community is not an abrogation or denial of what is means to be a citizen of God's well-ordered creation. Rather it involves a clearer perception of the created order and a renewed responsibility and enablement to live in accordance with it.

Paul's usage of κόσμος and κτίσις to build a fairly positive assessment of the world in chapters 1–11 thus correlates with and helps to promote the social values set forth in 12:14 – 13:10: social harmony with outsiders, integration into the larger society and good citizenship.

7.6. Romans 12:14 – 13:10 as context-specific to Rome

There is, then, a consistency between Paul's employment κόσμος and κτίσις in Rom 1–11 and his social exhortation of 12:14 – 13:10. To what extent do the admonitions of 12:14 – 13:10 and the social ideals which they express relate to circumstances in Rome? As noted above, the labelling of Rom 12–13 as "general paraenesis" entails the assumption that the section is unconnected to the situation in Rome. This assumption is partly based on the fact that these chapters, to some extent, draw on traditional Jewish ethical material. But this is no real argument against their special applicability to the Roman believers. As Wedderburn emphasizes,

Even if individual pieces amongst their contents were found to be in large measure traditional, that would still not account for Paul's use of precisely these pieces of tradition chosen out from amongst all the mass of traditional ethical material that lay to hand in early Christianity and Greek-speaking Judaism.[58]

Almost certainly Paul's instruction on paying taxes in 13:6–7 reflects an awareness on his part of particular circumstances in Rome.[59] The year 58 CE, we know from Tacitus (*Ann.* 13.50–1), was marked by complaint and unrest in the city of Rome over the collection of indirect taxes: the outcry was so great that Nero himself had to intervene in the matter. That Paul wrote this piece of advice to Christians in Rome at the very time when complaints would have been building up is almost beyond coincidence.

From what can be known and inferred about the history of the Roman Christian community, a strong case can be made for the situational nature of all the instructions of 12:14 – 13:10. Fortunately, we have two fairly solid pieces of historical information on which to build a reconstruction of the social context of the Roman churches: the Claudian edict of 49 CE and the Neronian persecution of 64 CE. From these fixed historical points, we can plot a course of events in Rome and within that development find a plausible socio-historical location for Rom 12:14 – 13:10.

7.6.1. Social consequences of the Claudian edict

The edict of Claudius in 49 CE, as Walters states, would have "accelerated the evolution of [Roman] Christianity's self-definition as a cult distinct from Judaism".[60] This in turn would have had the following consequences.

Firstly, it would have made the Roman churches more vulnerable to political interference. Although the political status of the Jews in Rome was never entirely secure (as the Claudian edict itself illustrates), the colony received a relatively favourable treatment from the Roman government. They were permitted to assemble for religious purposes and to live in accordance with their religious customs.[61] When the

---

[58] Wedderburn 1988, 78.
[59] See Friedrich, Pöhlmann and Stuhlmacher 1976. Cf. Dunn 1986, 60; Wedderburn 1988, 62–3.
[60] Walters 1993, 60.
[61] See Barclay 1996, 282–319.

Roman Christian community developed away from Judaism, it could not count on even these moderate privileges. Rather, it would have been liable to imperial policy toward *collegia illicita*.[62] Although technically illegal, such groups were generally tolerated by the authorities, because they were too numerous to regulate, on the one hand, and because they were too small and insignificant to attract official notice or cause concern, on the other.[63] However, when social disruptiveness or subversive activities drew attention to their presence, the government acted swiftly and firmly to stamp them out.[64] Spies were placed throughout the city to bring to light the activities of dangerous groups.

Secondly, the development away from Judaism would have made the Roman Christians more vulnerable to social opposition. The Jews constituted a well-established minority group in the capital with a sizeable presence and a recognized group identity. Though Roman Jews were subject to the scorn which was directed at Jews generally in Graeco-Roman society, as Barclay demonstrates, there did not develop in Rome the level of animosity towards the Jews that surfaced in some other parts of the empire.[65] As long as they were identified with the Jewish community, therefore, the Christians would have been socially tolerated. However, when the churches began to carve out an identity apart from the synagogues, the Roman believers would have become increasingly susceptible to the suspicion and intense hostility which often attended the emergence of Christianity – as a religious group distinct from Judaism – into public view.[66]

There were several features of the emerging Christian movement which provoked hostile reactions from Roman onlookers.[67] There was

---

[62] Julius Caesar in 64 BCE banned all *collegia* except those of ancient foundation (Suetonius, *Jul.* 42.3). Following the death of Caesar, the ban lapsed. Augustus reinstated it, requiring every new *collegium* to be licensed (Suetonius, *Aug.* 32). However, this regulation, it appears, was not strictly enforced. Inscriptional evidence indicates the existence of a vast number of associations during the early imperial period, only a very tiny minority of which would have been licensed: see Hardy 1906, 131. Thus, while the edict of Augustus expressed the general imperial policy toward *collegia*, as Hardy (134) states, it was not "a stringent rule literally observed, admitting of no exceptions and enforced with equal rigour in all parts of the empire".

[63] Hardy 1906, 135.

[64] Hardy 1906, 136.

[65] Barclay 1996, 310.

[66] The church at Corinth, as we have seen, was able to avoid this.

[67] See Benko 1980; 1984.

its *novelty*.[68] As a new religious grouping, it had no claim to legitimation on the basis of the axiomatic principle, *maior ex longinquo reverentia*. Tacitus, who was contemptuous of the Jews, had to concede that some aspects of the Jewish religion were vindicated by their antiquity (*Hist.* 5.5). The newness of Christianity marked out the movement as dangerous. As Benko points out, "The Romans had an exceptionally fine sense of time ... deeply rooted in their religion":[69] new and unproven religious practices, in the eyes of Romans, disturbed the harmony between the human and the divine spheres and thus endangered the security of the state.[70] Related to its newness, was its *strangeness*. It had none of the recognizable trappings of a religion. The Jews at least (up to 70 CE) had a temple and in each locality they had regular and identifiable places of worship – synagogues. The Christians had no temple, no altar and no shrine, that is, no designated places of worship. They had neither priests nor processions. There was no conspicuous ceremonial aspect to the faith. The Christian movement had none of the characteristic material features of Graeco-Roman religion. Then there was its *exclusivity*. The rejection and repudiation of Graeco-Roman religion by the Christians caused deep offence to Graeco-Romans. One of the most frequent charges made against Christians in the second century was that of "atheism", abandoning the gods.[71] This was no trivial matter: as MacMullen writes, "there was very little doubt in people's minds that the religious practices of one generation should be cherished without change by the next".[72] Abandonment of the ancient gods was not only a slight against ancestral tradition, it was also viewed as an extremely dangerous course of action by a society which lived in constant fear of the gods' anger.[73] Above all, there was its *antisocial* character. By withdrawing from the temples, festivals and other aspects of public worship, the Christians were seen to be withdrawing from the life of society itself.[74] Their shocking disregard for the duties and obligations

---

[68] Suetonius (*Nero*, 16.2) calls it "a new and wicked superstition" (*superstitionis novae ac maleficae*).

[69] Benko 1984, 21.

[70] Benko 1984, 22.

[71] Justin, *Apol.* 1.5–6; Tertullian, *Apol.* 10–11.

[72] MacMullen 1981, 2.

[73] See Fox 1986, 425–6.

[74] The antisocial nature of Christianity is reflected in Minucius Felix, *Oct.* 8, 10–12. Christians are secretive; they shun the light; they are silent in public but effusive in corners; they despise the temples and reject the gods, turning their backs on long

of family life made them appear especially misanthropic.[75] By abandoning family traditions and upsetting family relations, the Christians were looked upon as rocking the very foundations of society. Tacitus viewed Christianity as a dangerous cult, the very existence of which threatened the well-being and security of the Roman state. According to Tacitus (*Ann.* 15.44.5–6), Christians were guilty of *odium humani generis*, "hatred of the human race". As Wilken writes, by this Tacitus "did not simply mean that he did not like the Christians and found them a nuisance ... but that they were an affront to his social and religious world".[76]

As Christianity in Rome broke out of its Jewish matrix, it would have been subject to these reactions. As the social and religious offensiveness of emerging Christianity became more and more evident in Rome, the disapproval and hostility of outsiders would have increased. Harassment from outsiders would have been become a normative part of the social experience of the Romans Christians. The social conflict thereby generated would only have sharpened the profile of the Christian community as a disruptive social element.

7.6.2. Preconditions of the Neronian persecution

A development along these lines is largely confirmed by the events surrounding the Neronian persecution. The likely social consequences of the Claudian edict for the Roman Christians – social distinction from the Jews, political vulnerability, being subject to the contempt and suspicion of outsiders – are the social preconditions of Nero's persecution.

The persecution followed the fire of Rome of July 19, 64 CE.[77] The persecution was a localized event, confined to the capital. Having no precedent and being entirely limited to Rome, we must look to conditions and circumstances in the capital in order to account for its origin. The persecution is described by Tacitus (*Ann.* 15.44). According to Tacitus, it was widely believed that Nero himself was responsible for the fire. In

---

established religion; they fail to attend public entertainments, the processions and public banquets; they despise all honours and positions, showing themselves to be unpatriotic.

[75] Hardy 1902, 35–6.

[76] Wilken 1984, 66.

[77] The great fire is reported by Dio Cassius (*Hist.* 62.16), Pliny the Elder (*Nat. Hist.* 17:1–5), Suetonius (*Nero* 38) and Tacitus (*Ann.* 15:44).

order to offset this rumour, Nero fastened blame on the Christians and had them rounded up, tortured and executed. It is unclear from Tacitus' report whether the Christians were punished for the crime of arson or simply for being an offensive and intolerable element with society (the initial charge of incendiarism having been dropped). For him the important thing is the Christians' *odium humani generis*: this made them entirely deserving of the extreme punishments meted out on them, regardless of whether they actually were to blame for the disaster.

Accepting Tacitus' account of events,[78] several inferences can be drawn about Roman Christianity immediately prior to the fire of 64 CE. Firstly, the Roman Christians must have been a sufficiently *identifiable* social entity, quite distinct from the Jews, within the mass of the Roman population in order for Nero to target them.[79] This may have been due to their number. Tacitus states that an "immense multitude" was rounded up. But whatever the size of the community by this stage, it would still only have constituted an extremely tiny segment of the total population of the city. It seems likely that they had become a conspicuous group within their neighbourhoods of the city mainly because of the social offensiveness of their practices and beliefs. Tacitus reports that the populace knew them by the title "Christians". If the designation had begun to acquire its negative associations by this time (cf. 1 Pet 4:16),[80] the Roman Christians would have been known by the masses as social deviants.

Secondly, the Christians in Rome must have been sufficiently *unpopular* with the masses in order to make ideal scapegoats for Nero. Unless the Roman believers had achieved a large measure of notoriety, it is difficult to imagine how Nero could so swiftly and so successfully divert public attention away from himself and on to them. We know from sociology that when scapegoating occurs, it is directed toward a group in society against whom there is widespread prejudice and upon whom feelings of hostility can easily be vented.[81] Quite probably, the

---

[78] Keresztes (1980; 1989, 73ff) questions the accuracy of Tacitus' version of events. For a defence of Tacitus' account, see Sordi 1994, 29–31. Cf. Rudich 1993, 86; Warmington 1969, 126.

[79] This holds whatever the exact circumstances in which the Christians came to the notice of Nero.

[80] See Benko 1984, 1–24.

[81] Giddens 1993, 256–7. It was of course the complaint of Tertullian (*Apol.* 40.2) that when anything bad happened in the Empire, Christians got the blame. Cf. Fox 1986, 425–6.

Christians were widely regarded by the populace as an undesirable, intolerable and socially disruptive element within the city. It was probably the strength of public opposition to the Christians which enabled Nero to act against them as he did.[82]

Thirdly, the Christians must have been perceived as sufficiently *dangerous* and *subversive* as to make the charge of arson a plausible one. In the Graeco-Roman world, arson was viewed as a revolutionary act – the ancient equivalent of a terrorist bomb. That Christians could be suspected of arson strongly indicates that they were perceived as a threat to the established order.

A number of scholars have suggested that it was the Roman Christians' apocalyptic beliefs, specifically the belief in the destruction of the world by fire that made them credible targets of a charge of arson.[83] It is unclear, however, how widespread the idea of universal conflagration was in early Christianity.[84] We need not assume, though, that the Roman Christians specifically affirmed belief in cosmic conflagration in order to detect a connection between their eschatological views and the suspicion of arson in the minds of Roman onlookers. To Romans who had come into contact with the Christians, the action of setting fire to the city might well have seemed consonant with the Christian claim that Christ's return would usher in the end of history. The end of the world-cycle was readily enough linked with fire for pagans that the Christians need not have specifically spoken of a cosmic conflagration for such a connection to have been made.

To publicly proclaim the end of the present world would have been a highly risky thing to do in the capital of the Empire. The Roman order was legitimated by the belief that Augustus had inaugurated a golden age of peace.[85] Virgil declared that the Empire was eternal (*Aen.* 1.275ff); the city of Rome was the *urbs aeterna*.[86] To challenge these claims, even inadvertently, would have been politically highly dangerous.

---

[82] Sordi (1988, 31) deduces from Tacitus' account that even before the fire of 64 CE, the Christians were well known to the authorities and had already appeared before the tribunals on the charge of *superstitio illicita*.

[83] Edmundson 1913, 137; Ferguson 1987, 481; Grant 1970, 160; Smallwood 1981, 217–18; Stevenson 1957, 3

[84] Paul apparently knows nothing of it, unless 1 Cor 3:13–15 is an allusion to it. The earliest attested New Testament witness to the belief dates from a later period (2 Pet 3:10).

[85] Virgil, *Aen.* 6.791–5; Cf. *Ecl.* 4.4–10. On the *Pax Romana,* see Wengst 1987, 7–54.

[86] Eliade 1974, 135–6

Whether or not apocalyptic beliefs had anything to do with their being charged with arson, as we noted above, the Roman Christians' exclusive religious claims and anti-social behaviour would have been sufficient to mark them out as a menace to society and so make the stereotypical act of revolution seem conceivable.

By 64 CE, then, the Christians in Rome were an identifiable social group in the city, the objects of some measure of social hatred and were viewed as seditious and dangerous. The strong public feeling against the Roman believers which gave Nero the occasion to make them scapegoats for the fire clearly did not emerge overnight. We have to assume a gestation period of some years for Christians to acquire their subversive reputation and for the appropriate level of public aversion toward them to build up. That the seeds of public resentment and opposition were already developing at the time Paul wrote his epistle is highly likely.

7.6.3. The relevance to Rome

If the development suggested above carries any degree of plausibility, the context-specific nature of the admonitions of Rom 12:14 – 13:10 is plain to see. Instruction on duties toward the state, dealing with hostile outsiders and duties towards one's neighbours would have been of immediate and direct relevance to a community of Christians in a politically vulnerable situation, who were actually experiencing hostility from outsiders and who were commonly viewed as anti-social.

An actual situation of social conflict with outsiders is implicit in 12:14–21. No less than four times in these verses, Paul urges his readers to respond positively to ill-treatment at the hands of non-Christians and not to exact retribution (vv. 14, 17, 19–20, 21). Paul's concern that they must not retaliate, as Dunn points out,[87] is given the place of emphasis at both the beginning and end of the subsection (vv. 14 and 21). A warning against retaliation supposes prior provocation. A repeated warning not to strike back suggests a recurring pattern of provocative encounters. The style and tenor of these instructions implies that Paul is addressing a group facing harassment and abuse on a regular basis.[88]

---

[87] Dunn 1988, 755.

[88] It need not be supposed that the Roman Christians were encountering physical abuse at this stage (though this cannot be ruled out). Hostility, in the years preceding Nero's persecution, is likely to have taken the form of ostracism, verbal abuse (cf. 1 Peter 3:9,

7.6.4. Paul's social concerns for the community

The situation in Rome helps to explain the line of advice which Paul offers in 12:14 – 13:10. Paul promotes the ideals of social harmony, integration and orderly citizenship, it may be suggested, partly out of a concern for the well-being of the community in its highly and uniquely precarious socio-political situation.

Exposure to the hostility of the larger society and the intervention of the authorities was of course by no means confined to the Roman Christian community. Conflict with outsiders, to varying degrees, was the social experience of most early Christian communities. What made *this* situation unique, above all else, was its geographical location. To be viewed as a seditious group was one thing; to be viewed as a seditious group in *Rome*, the imperial capital, the seat of political power, was quite another. The believing community at Rome thus had to be particularly careful not to appear threatening to the socio-political order. The Roman Christians had already suffered under an imperial ruling. The next time the churches came to state notice on account of their disruptiveness, the punishment was bound to be harsher (as indeed it was).

Paul would have been aware of these socio-political realities (through some of his contacts mentioned in Rom 16). He would have been aware that, as Dunn puts it, "the little churches in Rome were an endangered species".[89] It may also have been in his mind that a government crackdown on the congregations at Rome, given their strategic location, could have serious repercussions for the status and treatment of Christian communities in other localities.

He therefore recommends concord with outsiders, integration into the life of the city and exemplary citizenship (partly) as a policy of social and political expediency. He advocates social behaviour which would be recognized as good and respectable by the surrounding society (partly) so that his readers might not be seen as radically undermining the values of society. He urges non-retaliation to provocation and a positive response to all acts of evil perpetrated against them (partly) so

---

16; 4:14), and the exacting of various degrees of social pressure. Social harassment would probably have grown in intensity as the social and religious offensiveness of Christianity became increasingly apparent.

[89] Dunn 1988, 755.

that they might not be seen as disruptive and disorderly. He commends good citizenship (partly) so that they might not be seen as a threat to the political order. He calls for good neighbourliness (partly) so that they might not be seen as antisocial and misanthropic. Paul's desire is that the Roman Christians show themselves to be *non-subversive* to the political order. As far as they can,[90] they are to give no cause for suspicion, no hint that they represent a danger to society and no reason to be marked out as seditious.

Paul's promotion of the ideals of harmonious relations with outsiders and integration into the larger society, which on the face of it stands in some tension with his social aim for the church at Corinth – distinction from the surrounding society – should, therefore, be seen in the light of the situation in Rome. Paul is not addressing a socially and ideologically compromised congregation, but a Christian community in a highly delicate, if not perilous, socio-political situation. His concern is that it avoids confrontation with the authorities since a further encounter with the state was sure to have disastrous consequences.

7.7. Conclusion

This chapter has argued that Paul's social teaching in Rom 12:14 – 13:10, correlates with his talk of κόσμος and κτίσις in chapters 1–11, reflects the social situation in Rome, and expresses his concerns and goals for the Roman churches in the light of their situation. Drawing these threads together, the following conclusions can be drawn with regard to the socio-rhetorical dimension of Paul's employment of κόσμος and κτίσις in Romans.

Paul's usage, from a socio-rhetorical perspective, is to be viewed in relation to the advice which he gives to his readers on dealings with the wider society in Rom 12:14 – 13:10. In this section, Paul advances the social ideals of social harmony with outsiders, (a degree of) integration with the larger society, good citizenship and good neighbourliness. These ideals relate, to a large extent, to the social situation in Rome, a situation of political vulnerability and mounting social tensions with outsiders, and Paul's concern for the well-being of the community in that social setting.

---

[90] Rom 12:18. Paul is of course aware of the *inherent* social and religious offensiveness of the gospel.

On the one hand, he avoids a line of linguistic employment which might *undermine* these social goals: the use of κόσμος (or κτίσις) to construct an apocalyptic and social dualism between the church and the wider society (as he avoids the social antitheses of "saved" and "perishing", "those who are inside" and "those outside", and so on). A stress on the opposition of church and world might have fostered or supported *introversionist* tendencies. Encountering acts of resentment from their non-Christian neighbours, the Roman Christians might have been tempted to reduce their social contacts with outsiders and withdraw from involvement in the larger community, as much as possible, so as to evade confrontation. Separatism of this kind would only have served to confirm accusations of misanthropy, led to rumours of furtive and clandestine activities and increased allegations of seditiousness. Alternatively, an emphasis on the antithetical relation of church and κόσμος might have stimulated confrontational and aggressive behaviour on the part of his readers.[91] Paul's repeated warning in 12:14–21 not to pay back in kind when provoked by opponents implies that his readers had been severely tempted to do so. Engaging in retaliatory measures would only have increased social conflict and added to their reputation as socially disruptive. A strongly apocalyptic perspective on "this world" might also have caused his readers to view the political rulers as agents of evil. Such an attitude, if publicly expressed, would obviously have led to conflict with the authorities.[92]

On the other hand, Paul adopts a line of usage which positively serves to *legitimate* his line of advice in 12:14 – 13:10. As was shown in the previous chapter, he uses the terms κόσμος and κτίσις to build a view of the world as God's good and well-ordered creation. This understanding of the world functions as the symbolic universe to sustain the social ideals he furthers in 12:14 – 13:10. It is precisely on the basis of this world-view that he is able to counsel conciliatory behaviour, social integration, good citizenship and neighbourliness, and to promote within the Roman congregations values which are held in common between Christians and outsiders. The social teaching of 12:14 – 13:10

---

[91] On the possibility of non-passive reaction to provocation, see Barclay 1993, 520–5.

[92] According to Bindemann (1983, 109–13), Roman Christianity was strongly marked by apocalyptic sectarianism, and Paul wrote to correct this social trend. This is going beyond the evidence. Whether Paul wrote to curb actual sectarian tendencies in Rome or to prohibit potential sectarianism is impossible to say.

is thus, to a large degree, drawn out of the earlier statements on κόσμος and κτίσις.

Paul uses κόσμος and κτίσις in Romans to construct a social world in (a measure of) *solidarity* with the wider society. His employment of the terms helps to generate a "response to the world" which corresponds, to a degree, to Troeltsch's church-type: a conservative social ethos, an endorsement of the existing socio-political order, an appropriation of the values of the larger society, a universal view of salvation.

In order to uncover the socio-rhetorical features of Paul's usage of κόσμος and κτίσις in Romans, the net has had to be cast wide. When compared to his use of κόσμος in 1 Corinthians, it is clear that Paul's employment of κόσμος and κτίσις in Romans has a less "strategic" place in the epistle's theological argument and social rhetoric: the deployment in Romans serves as a smaller ingredient in a somewhat less obvious theological, social and rhetorical mix. Yet, the correlations between Paul's usage of the terms in the theological argumentation of Rom 1–11, the ideals expressed in the social teaching of Rom 12–13 and the actual situation of Paul's Roman readers are sufficient to show that even in this letter there is a definite socio-rhetorical dimension to Paul's linguistic employment. In Romans, as in 1 Corinthians, Paul's usage serves to advance his particular social goals for the particular community addressed.

8

κόσμος and καινὴ κτίσις
in Galatians and 2 Corinthians

8.1. Introduction

We turn now to consider Paul's usage of κόσμος and καινὴ κτίσις in Galatians and 2 Corinthians. Each of these letters contains three occurrences of the term κόσμος and one instance of the phrase καινὴ κτίσις. This limited usage requires only a brief overview of the contexts of utterance and reference of these two letters. After examining the utterance and reference contexts of Galatians, we shall examine the key texts, Gal 6:14–15 and 4:3 (in that order), present some conclusions and then briefly repeat the procedure with 2 Corinthians.

8.2. Galatians: contexts of utterance and reference

Paul was the founder of the churches in Galatia (4:13–14, 19).[1] These Gentile congregations were the fruit of a successful, if perhaps un-planned (4:13–15), mission in the region. Fairly soon after the churches had been planted (1:6), a group of "troublemakers" (1:7; 5:10) or "agitators" (5:12), as Paul describes them, arrived in Galatia preaching "a different gospel" from Paul's (1:6–7). The troublemakers, who were almost certainly Jewish Christians, were insisting that Gentile believers had to be circumcised and had to observe the Jewish law if they were to be fully accepted by God. The intruders were clearly winning the Galatians over to their point of view, though Paul's converts had not as yet submitted to circumcision (5:2; 6:12). Paul writes to oppose the teaching of agitators and to convince the Galatians to remain loyal to the gospel as he had presented it to them and as they had originally accepted it.

---

[1] The vexed questions of the date and destination of Galatians may be left aside. They have no bearing on the argument presented here.

Paul addresses the Galatians as his "little children" (4:19), assuming a fatherly authority over them. His influence in the Galatian congregations, however, had been undermined (4:14–16) by the agitators. The intruders, it would appear, argued that Paul's apostleship was dependent on and secondary to that of the Jerusalem apostles (1:1 – 2:14). They also seem to have attacked Paul's character, casting doubts on his integrity (1:10; 5:11). Paul thus has to defend himself against their charges and justify to his readers the apostolic basis of his authority (1:11 – 2:10).

Paul vilifies his opponents, pronouncing them accursed (1:8–9) and impugning their motives and genuineness (6:12–13). He treats the Galatians in a different way. He rebukes them (1:6), calls them "foolish" (3:1) and declares his perplexity over their actions (4:20), but his tone with them is much less harsh than with the intruders (cf. 4:12). He endeavours to persuade them of the truth of his gospel through impassioned argumentation. He argues mainly on the basis of the Old Testament scriptures, interacting with and refuting the claims of the intruders (Gal 3–4).

The message of the intruders, as John Barclay has argued, probably met a felt need among the Galatians. Barclay points out that as a result of converting to Christianity, the Galatian Christians would have suffered a considerable loss of social identity.[2] On the one hand, the members of the Galatian churches would have had to dissociate themselves from their former paganism with all the social disruption that this would have entailed. And on the other hand, "neither were they members (or even attenders) of the Jewish synagogues although they had the same Scriptures and much the same theology as those synagogues".[3] The ambiguity of their social position would have made the message of the intruders seem highly attractive to Paul's converts. Submission to circumcision and law-observance would have meant their taking on a more recognizable and socially-acceptable set of religious characteristics.

Extending Barclay's observations, the effect of the agitators' message in the Galatian churches may be elucidated by insights from H. Tajfel's work on group identity and differentiation.[4] Tajfel points out that groups are usually socially and consensually defined as "superior" and "inferior"

---

[2] Barclay 1988, 58–9.
[3] Barclay 1988, 58–9.
[4] Tajfel 1978a, 1978b.

in relation to each other. What a society defines as inferior or superior characteristics differ according to culture and social context. When members of a socially inferior group become aware that their existing social reality "is not the only possible one and that alternatives to it are conceivable and perhaps attainable", the ensuing problem of identity can be resolved in one, or a combination, of three ways.

1. To become, through action and reinterpretation of group characteristics, more like the superior group.

2. To reinterpret the existing inferior characteristics of the group, so that they do not appear as inferior but acquire a positively valued distinctiveness from the superior group.

3. To create, through social action and/or diffusion of new "ideologies" new group characteristics which have a positively valued distinctiveness from the superior group.[5]

The first solution is that of assimilation to the superior group. Tajfel suggests that given the right conditions, this could be the solution to be tried first.[6] Solutions (2) and (3) usually appear in conjunction. For these solutions to be successful, two conditions must be met. First of all, group members must accept both the positive re-evaluation of the existing inferior characteristics of the group and the newly-created positive ones. Secondly, the validity of this "positively valued distinctiveness" must be recognized by the larger society.[7]

Tajfel's observations seem particularly applicable to events in Galatia since the Galatian situation has to do with the place of two minority groups – Judaism and (emerging) Christianity – within the larger society and that society's attitude toward them (going back to paganism, assimilating to the dominant culture, was not an option the Galatians were considering).

It may be posited, then, that when the agitators arrived in Galatia they not only addressed the Galatians' problem of social identity, but may well have made that problem more acute by showing that the Galatians' present social reality was not the only possible one. There was a valid (indeed, seemingly more valid) alternative: to assume the social and cultural identity of Jews, the social group with whom they

[5] Tajfel 1978b, 93–4.
[6] Tajfel 1978b, 94.
[7] Tajfel 1978b, 96.

had most in common. Though Jews were sometimes viewed with contempt, Judaism, as an ancient and national religion, would certainly have been judged by Galatian society at large as "superior" to the new, marginal and highly suspect, Christian movement. By becoming culturally Jewish, the Gentile Galatian believers could take on a more credible social identity among the social categorizations of the day and occupy a more secure place in Galatian society, one less exposed to social censure. Adopting the social and religious practices of the Jewish community would have seemed to the Gentile Galatians a more appealing option than the more painful route of carving out a distinctive group identity as Christians.

This is as much as need be said about the context of utterance. As to the context of reference, we note the apocalyptic strain of Paul's thought in the letter.[8] Paul declares that he received his gospel not from a human source but "through a revelation of Jesus Christ" (1:12, cf. 3:23). Paul's gospel centres on one who died "to set us free from the present evil age" (1:4). The death of Christ has activated the shift of ages. Consequently the universe is characterized by apocalyptic dualities. J. L. Martyn has shown how the theology of Galatians is structured by "apocalyptic antinomies".[9] The old distinctions between Jew and Gentile, slave and free and male and female are relegated to the old age (3:28). These former categorizations have now been replaced by new dualities activated by the apocalyptic event of the cross. Principal among these dualisms is the antimony of "flesh" and "Spirit" (5:16–24). Remarkably, the law is placed alongside the flesh against the Spirit on the wrong side of the apocalyptic partition (5:18). A series of antitheses is developed in 4:21–31 in the allegory of Hagar and Sarah, including the cosmic duality of "the present Jerusalem" and "the Jerusalem above" (4:25–26).

8.3. *Examination of texts*

There are only two texts to be considered: Gal 4:3 and 6:14–15. Both texts, however, are highly debated. An understanding of 6:14–15 will

---

[8] This is not to deny that there might also be elements of a salvation–historical point of view in the letter, but to concentrate on the theological perspective most relevant to the key texts. For the debate as to whether Galatians is apocalyptic or salvation–historical in theological outlook, see Dunn 1991, Gaventa 1991 and Martyn 1991. A mediating position is taken by Barclay (1988, 96–105).

[9] Martyn 1985. Gal 6:14–15 is the basis for Martyn's analysis.

provide something of a hermeneutical handle on the controversial phrase τὰ στοιχεῖα τοῦ κόσμου in 4:3. Hence, we shall treat 6:14–15 first.

8.3.1. The crucified world and the new creation (6:14–15)

The closing paragraph of the letter, Gal 6:11–18 (which, following Hellenistic epistolary convention,[10] Paul writes in his own hand), forms a summary capturing the essential concerns of the epistle. Betz has argued that 6:11–18 falls into the Graeco-Roman rhetorical category of *peroratio* and functions to sum up the case being argued and to elicit the appropriate response from the readers. He can thus insist on the importance of this passage for the interpretation of the whole of Galatians: he writes,

> It contains the interpretive clues to the understanding of Paul's major concerns in the letter as a whole and should be employed as the hermeneutical key to the intentions of the Apostle.[11]

Whatever the merits or demerits of Betz's rhetorical analysis, the summational force and broader hermeneutical significance of 6:11–18 is widely recognized. The denunciation of the agitators (vv. 12–13), the disavowal of circumcision (vv. 12–16), the emphasis on the cross of Christ (vv. 12, 14; cf. 2:18–20; 3:1–2, 10–14; 5:11), the mention of σάρξ (v. 12), the autobiographical, self-exemplary note (vv. 14, 17), all pick up key themes of the letter.

In vv. 12–13, Paul attacks the motives of the intruders. The reason they are compelling his readers to be circumcised is that they "want to make a good showing in the flesh", so "that they may not be persecuted for the cross of Christ"[12] and so that they may boast (καυχήσωνται) about their flesh (cf. 4:17).

The mention of "boasting" (καυχάομαι) in v. 13 provides the link with v. 14. Paul contrasts the misguided vaunting of his opponents with what he regards as the only rightful cause for boasting – the cross of Christ. By sharing in the crucifixion of Christ, Paul – speaking as the

---

[10] Betz 1979, 312.
[11] Betz 1979, 313.
[12] Paul does not specify the source of the persecution but most probably he means persecution from fellow Jews, of which he was once himself a perpetrator (1:13, 23; Phil 3:6). It is possible, as Jewett (1970/71) has argued, that the troublemakers' campaign arose as an attempt to evade Zealot-motivated reprisals against all Jews who compromised on Jewish purity, in the wake of a growing mood of Jewish nationalism.

CONSTRUCTING THE WORLD

archetypal Christian, describing a state of affairs not unique to himself but true for all believers – has died to the κόσμος and the κόσμος has died to him (δι' οὗ ἐμοὶ κόσμος ἐσταύρωται κἀγὼ κόσμῳ). Henceforth, he continues in v. 15, "neither circumcision nor uncircumcision is anything" but καινὴ κτίσις.

The debate continues as to the meaning of κόσμος and καινὴ κτίσις in these verses. The basic issue is whether the terms have an anthropological reference or a cosmological one. The question of the meaning of καινὴ κτίσις has received a vast amount of scholarly attention. Is Paul referring to the individual believer,[13] the believing community,[14] or a new cosmic order?[15] As mentioned at the beginning of this book, a consensus on the matter shows no sign of being reached.

In an exhaustive study of the term "new creation" and its background, Mell has shown that the expression "new creation" was an established, technical term in Jewish apocalypticism, referring to the new or transformed creation expected to follow the destruction or renewal of the world.[16] This is its sense in *Jub.* 4:26 (second century BCE) and *1 Enoch* 72:1. Mell demonstrates that the phrase "new creation" in apocalyptic texts equates with the terms "new heavens and new earth" (Isa 65:17; 66:22; *1 Enoch* 91:15; Rev 21:1; 2 Pet 3:13; *Bib. Ant.* 3:10), "renewed creation" (*4 Ezra* 7:75; *2 Apoc. Bar.* 32:6; 57:2; *Bib. Ant.* 32:17; 16:3), "renewal" (1QS 4:25) and "new world" (*2 Apoc. Bar.* 44:12).

In the light of Mell's study, we can now be reasonably confident of the *standard* sense of the term "new creation" in Paul's day. This in itself of course does not resolve the debate as to the meaning of καινὴ κτίσις in Gal 6:15, since Paul could be using the term in a *non-standard* way: he could be employing the apocalyptic image of a new or renewed cosmic order as a *metaphor* for the status of individuals following their conversion, or for the social identity of the new community, thus giving this cosmological term a new and unexpected anthropological

---

[13] W. D. Davies 1962, 119; Schwantes 1962, 26–31; Sjöberg 1950. These scholars draw attention to the use of the metaphor in rabbinic Judaism to describe a proselyte (*Gen. Rab.* 39.14; cf. *Jos. As.* 8:10–11; 15:5).

[14] Barclay 1988, 102; Baumgarten 1975, 163–70; Bruce 1982, 273; Reumann 1973, 97; Vögtle 1970a, 182.

[15] Aymer 1983, 116; Dunn 1993a, 343; Martyn 1985, 412; Mell 1989, 324; Tannehill 1967, 65.

[16] Mell 1989, 47–257.

spin. On principle, however, we should accept the cosmic meaning for the term unless there are fairly clear contextual markers to suggest otherwise.

Two such linguistic markers are often thought to be the use of the perfect tense of the verb ἐσταύρωται in v. 14 and the use of the present tense (ἐστιν) in v. 15. Paul views crucifixion to the κόσμος as a *past* event (with ongoing consequences) and sets forth καινὴ κτίσις as a *current* reality. Now for Paul, the cosmic change which results in a new or restored world-order is an object of *future* hope (1 Cor 7:31b; 15:27–28; Rom 8:19–22; Phil 3:20–21). This being so, it would seem to follow that he cannot be thinking here of the new created order itself but a personal or communal state of existence *analogous* to it. However, while the cosmic re-creation or renewal lies in the future for Paul, it is clearly his conviction that the change of the ages has somehow been triggered by the cross of Christ. The death and resurrection of Christ has in some sense set "this world" on its course toward final destruction (1 Cor 7:31b). The new age, in some undefined (and non-physical) way, has dawned (1 Cor 10:11). Hence Paul can declare that "this world" has already been judged and cast aside in the cross (1 Cor 1:20–21). The liberation of believers from this present evil age is presently underway (Gal 1:4). The tenses of Gal 6:14–15, therefore, reflect Paul's modification of the apocalyptic cosmic schema. For Paul, the cross has not brought about the expected cosmic transformation or re-creation, but it has in some way started the ball rolling toward that end. The tenses of vv. 14–15 do not, therefore, constitute sufficient contextual grounds for excluding the standard apocalyptic cosmological sense of καινὴ κτίσις (and κόσμος).

With the terms κόσμος and καινὴ κτίσις, Paul is invoking the apocalyptic spatio-temporal dualism of "this world" and "the world to come"/"the new creation". He is doing so without in any way reducing the cosmological overtones of this conception. His thought is this. In the event of the cross, God has declared that "this world" is on its way out and that a new cosmic order is on its way in. Believers, through participation in Christ's death and resurrection, have already been separated from the old world (cf. 1:4) and are in some proleptic sense already participating in the life of the new world.

While wanting to insist that καινὴ κτίσις refers to the new eschatological world, we can nevertheless agree with those who argue that Paul's focus in vv. 14–16 is on the believing community (καὶ ὅσοι τῷ κανόνι τούτῳ στοιχήσουσιν, v. 16). Paul is not saying that the community of Christ *is* the new creation. But he is suggesting that the church *belongs* to the new creation (they are *of* the new world, so to speak, though they are not yet *in* it).

The advance announcement of the death of the κόσμος and the birth of the καινὴ κτίσις is directly applied to the situation of the Galatians. In the light of the apocalyptic declaration, Paul states, οὔτε, ... περιτομή τί ἐστιν οὔτε ἀκροβυστία , "neither circumcision nor uncircumcision is anything".[17] Under the influence of the intruders, the Galatians believed that the distinction was indeed a crucial one. Paul claims that it belongs to the crucified κόσμος. It is a social and religious categorization with no place in the new reality which God is establishing and in which his readers participate.

The Gentile Galatians were in process of assimilating to Judaism (cf. 4:10). They were about to complete the process by undergoing circumcision. Paul indicates that by submitting to the rite, and thereby committing themselves to a Jewish lifestyle (cf. 5:3), his readers would be transferring back to the old κόσμος from which they had been separated.

The antithesis of κόσμος and καινὴ κτίσις in this passage thus has a very clear social function. It serves to underline the social and religious distinction between the Jewish community and the Galatian churches. Judaism (cf. 1:13–14), as a social, cultural and religious entity, belongs along with paganism to the dying κόσμος. To assimilate to Judaism, therefore, is to alienate oneself from the new creation.

8.3.2. The elements of the world (4:3)

In 4:3 (and 4:9), Paul mentions τὰ στοιχεῖα τοῦ κόσμου. The meaning of this phrase (both here and at Col 2:8, 20) is one of the most heavily debated issues in Pauline interpretation. Does the term mean "elementary religious teachings",[18] "the elements of religious distinction",[19] "the physical elements of the universe" (i.e. earth, water, fire and air),[20] "astral powers",[21] or "demonic powers"/

---

[17] The double οὔτε περιτομή . . . οὔτε ἀκροβυστία, also occurs in 5:6. There the contrast is "faith working through love".
[18] Belleville 1986, 68; Burton 1921, 510–18; Longenecker 1990, 166; Ridderbos 1956, 154.
[19] Martyn 1995.
[20] Schweizer 1988.
[21] Bruce 1982, 204.

"elemental spirits"?[22] A consensus on the matter seems as yet a long way off.

Conventional Greek usage, in this instance, does not greatly help in determining the meaning. The standard sense of τὰ στοιχεῖα τοῦ κόσμου in Paul's day would have been "the physical elements of the universe". But despite Schweizer's efforts to promote it, this sense does not fit the context in Gal 4:3 and 9. Thus, in defining the sense with which Paul is using the term, attention has to focus on Paul's text itself and the linguistic clues provided therein.

The widely recognized hermeneutical significance of 6:11–18 for Galatians as a whole was noted above. On this basis, 6:14–15 may be taken as a clue to the meaning of the utterances of 4:3 and 9. Four motifs are present or implicit when Paul speaks of κόσμος in 6:14–15 which are also present in his talk of τὰ στοιχεῖα τοῦ κόσμου in 4:3ff. In 6:14–15, Paul implies (1) that believers once belonged to the κόσμος. He contends (2) that they had been separated from the κόσμος through Christ. He implies (3) that the Jewish religion is part of the old κόσμος, and he insinuates (4) that by assimilating to Judaism his readers were going back to the κόσμος from which they had been redeemed.

In 4:3ff, Paul argues as follows, firstly, his readers were previously enslaved to τὰ στοιχεῖα τοῦ κόσμου (ὑπὸ τὰ στοιχεῖα τοῦ κόσμου ἤμεθα δεδουλωμένοι, v. 3). Secondly, they had been released from that enslavement (vv. 5, 7) and had come to know God and to be known by him (v. 9). Thirdly, being under τὰ στοιχεῖα τοῦ κόσμου is equivalent to being under the Jewish religion (ὑπὸ τὰ στοιχεῖα τοῦ κόσμου ... ὑπὸ νόμον, vv. 3–4).[23] Fourthly, in placing themselves under the law his readers were in process of returning to their former enslavement to the στοιχεῖα. Thus he asks them in v. 9, "How can you turn back again to the weak and beggarly στοιχεῖα? How can you want to be enslaved to them again?"

Given the correlation between the two texts, it seems likely that the word κόσμος has the same sense in both passages. The κόσμος of which Paul speaks in 4:3 is the crucified κόσμος of 6:14. It is "this

---

[22] Betz 1979, 204–5; Cousar 1982, 92–3; Reicke 1951, 261.
[23] Paul's characterizes the historical situation prior to the revelation of Christ as life "under" various entities: under a curse, 3:10; under sin, 3:22; under a disciplinarian, 3:25; under guardians and trustees, 4:2; under law, 3:23; 4:4, 5, 21; 5:18.

world", "the present evil age" (cf. 1:4). It is no neutral entity; it is the sphere of opposition and hostility to God.

What, then, is the meaning of στοιχεῖα? This, after all, is the crucial term. What, or who, they are may be inferred from what Paul says in 4:8–9. He calls the στοιχεῖα "weak and beggarly", ἀσθενῆ καὶ πτωχά. The adjectives are more likely to refer to personal beings than the physical elements or basic religious teachings, though of course a metaphorical application to inanimate objects or abstract principles cannot be ruled out. Paul describes his readers' pre-Christian enslavement to the στοιχεῖα as bondage to "beings that are by nature not gods", ἐδουλεύσατε τοῖς φύσει μὴ οὖσιν θεοῖς. The most obvious inference to be drawn is that Paul is referring to the deities whom his Gentile readers used to worship: the gods of pagan religion. Paul denies these entities the title θεοί, but he does not dispute their existence. The construction τοῖς φύσει μὴ οὖσιν θεοῖς immediately calls to mind the phrase λεγόμενοι θεοί in 1 Cor 8:5. There Paul agreed with the enlightened Corinthians that the gods of Graeco-Roman religion could not rightly be called θεοί. But he went on to argue in 10:20–21 – against the Corinthians – that standing behind the deities venerated by pagans are real spiritual powers. Gal 4:8 seems to reflect this reasoning.

Paul is using the term τὰ στοιχεῖα τοῦ κόσμου, in an irregular way (whether the phrase was one of his own coinage or one he picked up from others), for the malevolent spiritual forces, which from Paul's apocalyptic perspective, operate behind pagan religion. What is striking is that Paul envisages such forces operating in and through Jewish religion as well.

He describes the στοιχεῖα as "weak and beggarly" because the apocalyptic event of the cross has signalled their demise and because believers, insofar as they have been crucified to "this world", are no longer under their control.

Paul's point in 4:3 and 9 is that by submitting to the Jewish law, his readers were placing themselves again in slavery to the στοιχεῖα. And, "To return to the weak and beggarly στοιχεῖα was to cut themselves off from Christ, that is, from the new creation".[24] His talk of τὰ στοιχεῖα τοῦ κόσμου thus, like the contrast between κόσμος and καινὴ κτίσις, serves a boundary-stressing function. It underlines the social divide between Judaism and the Galatian churches.

[24] Cf. Minear 1979, 400.

8.4. Conclusions on Galatians

Paul employs κόσμος and καινὴ κτίσις in Galatians within an apocalyptic framework. The terms express the spatio-temporal dualism of "this world" and the "the new creation". The apocalyptic sense of κόσμος also obtains in the much debated reference at 4:3.

Paul's use of κόσμος in Galatians is comparable to that in 1 Corinthians. It has the negative, apocalyptic sense which dominates in 1 Corinthians, and it has a boundary-stressing function similar to that in the Corinthian letter. Yet, there are two obvious differences. Firstly, in Galatians, unlike 1 Corinthians, κόσμος is not the *dominant* negative term. That distinction goes to σάρξ. Of the negative quartet, ἁμαρτία, θάνατος, σάρξ and κόσμος, σάρξ is out on its own in Galatians. The term θάνατος is absent from the letter. ἁμαρτία only occurs three times, at 1:4, 2:17 and 3:22.[25] The word σάρξ, though, occurs eighteen times. Paul uses the term with a fairly neutral sense in several places (1:16; 2:16, 20; 4:13–14; 6:13). In the main, however, σάρξ is used with reference to a sphere of hostility toward God. It is set in sharp contrast to πνεῦμα (3:3; 4:29; 5:16–25; 6:8).[26] Secondly, in Galatians, the boundary which is stressed is not the boundary between the Christian community and the surrounding Graeco-Roman cultural and social environment (which is presupposed rather than argued for), but that between the Christians and the Jewish colony.

The crucial difference in situation addressed between 1 Corinthians and Galatians probably helps to explain why anti-κόσμος formulations are used so sparingly in this letter. The critical use of κόσμος is obviously an appropriate method of attack where the problem to be countered is assimilation to the larger society. It has less polemical value where the problem in view is assimilation to another minority group which is also at odds with the larger society. The polemical use of σάρξ, on the other hand, was appropriate to the Galatian dispute. The crisis in Galatia centred on the issue of circumcision. There is an obvious association between "flesh" and "the foreskin cut in circumcision". Paul exploits this linkage in Gal 6:12–13. It is not unreasonable to conclude that he

---

[25] The surprisingly limited use of ἁμαρτία in Galatians, as Barclay (1988, 211) suggests, may be put down to the fact that the term "was too closely connected to notions of law-breaking to be helpful in the context of the Galatian dispute".

[26] In the apocalyptic symbol system of Galatians, σάρξ aligns with κόσμος and ὁ αἰὼν οὗτος, and πνεῦμα with καινὴ κτίσις.

developed his anti-σάρξ polemic in Galatians partly on the basis of the connection.[27]

Paul may take up κόσμος sparingly in Galatians, but he deploys it to good socio-rhetorical effect. The terms κόσμος and καινὴ κτίσις serve as tools for constructing in Galatia a Christian social world *separate* from the Jewish community.

Paul's converts must not become Jewish proselytes in an attempt to resolve their crisis of social identity, for to do so would be return to the κόσμος from whence they came. Rather, in the knowledge that they belong to God's new creation, they are to construct for themselves a *new* social identity and develop a "positively valued distinctiveness"[28] from Judaism.

8.5. *2 Corinthians: contexts of utterance and reference*

Reconstruction of the situation underlying 2 Corinthians is greatly complicated by the likelihood that the canonical letter comprises at least two separate letters,[29] chapters 1–9 and chapters 10–13. These "letters" reflect different stages of the life of the church. Chapters 1–9 assume a state of partial reconciliation between Paul and the Corinthians after an earlier period of intense conflict (the reconciliation is only partial because tensions evidently remain). Chapters 10–13 reflect a church in outright rebellion against Paul under the influence of opponents of Paul from outside Corinth. Scholarly opinion has been divided on which is the earlier of the two letters. In recent discussion, the favoured view is that 2 Cor 1–9 is chronologically prior to chapters 10–13.[30]

For the purpose of this study, it is sufficient to make the general point that 2 Corinthians presupposes division between Paul and his readers over the issue of the legitimacy and extent of his authority as an apostle. The letter sequence and other matters, such as the identity of the opponents and whether their presence in the church can be detected in 2 Cor 1–9, are unimportant to the question on hand.

The central concern of 2 Corinthians is Paul's authority. But this does not necessarily mean that the problem of weak group boundaries

---

[27] Cf. Barclay 1988, 204.

[28] Tajfel 1978b, 94.

[29] As many as six fragments have been mooted: 1:1–2:13 and 7:5–16; 2:14 – 6:13; 6:14 – 7:1; 8; 9; 10–13.

[30] For a defence of the view that 2 Cor 10–13 precedes 2 Cor 1–9, see Horrell 1996, 296–312; Watson 1984.

addressed in 1 Corinthians had been resolved to Paul's satisfaction. If 2 Cor 6:14 – 7:1, with its clarion call for separation from unbelievers, belongs to 1 Cor 1–9 and comes from Paul's hand,[31] he obviously felt the church was still failing in this regard.

There is good evidence to suggest that the Corinthians' continued commitment to the ideals of the general culture lay, in some measure, behind their conflict with Paul. As Savage demonstrates,[32] in criticizing Paul for his refusal to boast (5:12; 11:18–21), his weak personal presence (10:1, 10), his unskilled speech (10:10; 11:16) and his refusal to accept financial support (2:17; 11:7–10; 12:14), the Corinthians were simply reflecting the cultural values of the larger society. Savage goes as far as to argue that the disagreement between Paul and his converts boiled down to "a conflict between two opposing perspectives: the worldly outlook of the Corinthians and Paul's own Christ-centred viewpoint".[33]

As to the theological context of reference of 2 Corinthians, we may note the presence of apocalyptic motifs in the letter. This is not to deny that other perspectives are also present, including Hellenistic thought-forms, but to focus on the one which is most relevant to the subject on hand. Paul is the recipient of "visions and revelations of the Lord" (12:1). He goes on to relate, in the third person, how he "was caught up into paradise and heard things that are not to be told, that no mortal is permitted to repeat". (12:4). The change effected by the apocalyptic event of the cross is cosmic in scope (5:19). Paul expects the "day of the Lord Jesus" (1:14), the judgement seat of Christ (5:10) and the resurrection of the dead (4:14, cf. 5:1–10). Reality is sundered by the cosmic duality of heaven and earth (5:1–5), the temporal duality of this age and (implicitly) the next age (4:4), and the social duality of "saved" and "perishing", "believers" and "unbelievers" (2:15; 4:3; 6:14, 15). The main elements of the apocalyptic viewpoint are thus evident in this letter.

8.6. Examination of texts

Having observed the key place of κόσμος in the rhetoric of 1 Corinthians, one is struck by the relative unimportance of the term in

---

[31] The integrity and authorship of this passage are heavily debated. There is no scholarly consensus on these matters. For discussion of the issues, see the commentaries.

[32] Savage 1996, 54–99.

[33] Savage 1996, 99.

2 Corinthians. The rate of usage drops significantly, from twenty-one occurrences in 1 Corinthians down to three instances in 2 Corinthians. Before trying to account for the diminution, we first look at the key texts: 1:12; 5:17, 19; 7:10.

8.6.1. Comportment in the world (1:12)

Paul was being accused of unreliability and dishonesty by some in the Corinthian church. In the face of such charges, he insists that he has behaved with frankness and godly sincerity. His conduct was not "in fleshly wisdom" (ἐν σοφίᾳ σαρκικῇ) but "by the grace of God" (ἐν χάριτι θεοῦ), "in the world" (ἐν τῷ κόσμῳ) and especially toward his readers (περισσοτέρως δὲ πρὸς ὑμᾶς).

κόσμος here has the sense "inhabited world". There is no obvious pejorative note to Paul's usage. As Furnish writes, "Nothing specifically negative is connoted."[34] A distinction is drawn between the "world" and the Corinthians (ἐν τῷ κόσμῳ ... δὲ πρὸς ὑμᾶς), but there is no emphasis on the social boundary between them. The thought is of witness in the world not separation from the world.

8.6.2. There is new creation (5:17)

In 5:15, Paul asserts that Christ died for all so that "those who live" (οἱ ζῶντες) might no longer live for themselves, but "for him who died and was raised for them". In v. 16, he contends that those who have died and risen with Christ have (or ought to have) a new way of perceiving and evaluating people. No longer do they perceive others κατὰ σάρκα, that is, from the old age point of view,[35] though once they regarded even Christ from this standpoint. They now operate with a completely new insight on reality.

If anyone is in Christ, Paul states in v. 17, "there is new creation",[36] εἴ τις ἐν χριστῷ, καινὴ κτίσις. As with Gal 6:15 there is great debate as to how the phrase καινὴ κτίσις in this verse is to be understood. Does it refer to the individual convert (as the microcosm of the "eschatological macrocosm of the new heaven and the new earth"),[37] the believing community or the new cosmic order? For the reasons outlined in discussing Gal 6:15, we may take the view that Paul uses

[34] Furnish 1984, 127.
[35] See Martyn 1967, 274.
[36] My translation.
[37] Stagg 1989, 173.

καινὴ κτίσις here with reference to the new or renewed created order. Nevertheless, the proposition expressed by the *sentence* as a whole embraces the individual and the community. Paul's meaning is that the individual believer (τις) as part of the believing community (ἐν χριστῷ), in advance of the coming physical destruction of the universe, already participates in the life of the new eschatological world. Though the final eschatological event lies in the future, for Christians, in some partial and non-material way, the old things have already passed away, and new things have already come (τὰ ἀρχαῖα παρῆλθεν, ἰδοὺ γέγονεν καινά). Again, the underlying thought is that Christ's death and resurrection has in some way set in motion the change of the ages.

Paul's assertion of καινὴ κτίσις in vv. 16–17 is partly polemical. It is aimed, to some extent, at his detractors in Corinth. Those who boast "in outward appearance"(τοὺς ἐν προσώπῳ καυχωμένους, v. 12) and measure Paul by this standard (criticizing his weak personal presence and lack of rhetorical skill), he is implying, are adopting a mode of perception which is κατὰ σάρκα. Paul's style of apostleship is not to be judged on the basis of the dominant cultural values which belong to this age but on the basis of the counter-cultural perspective of the καινὴ κτίσις. Paul thus invokes the apocalyptic motif of καινὴ κτίσις to underline the ideological (cf. οἴδαμεν ... ἐγνώκαμεν ... γινώσκομεν, v. 16) boundaries of the church and on that basis to vindicate his style of ministry.

8.6.3. The reconciliation of the world (5:19)

In v. 18–19, Paul focuses on God's purpose in reconciliation. In v. 19, he states that in Christ God was reconciling the world to himself, θεὸς ἦν ἐν Χριστῷ κόσμον καταλλάσσων ἑαυτῷ. The word κόσμος in this instance clearly bears the sense "humanity". This is apparent from the clause which follows, μὴ λογιζόμενος αὐτοῖς τὰ παραπτώματα αὐτῶν. Only of human beings could it be said that God was not counting their sins against them. As in Rom 11:15, talk of the reconciliation of the κόσμος presupposes its prior estrangement. But as with the Romans text, Paul's emphasis is on God's positive, saving action toward the κόσμος.

It is interesting to compare the relation of the terms καινὴ κτίσις and κόσμος in 2 Cor 5:17–19 with their linkage in Gal 6:14–15. In both passages, the terms occur in close proximity. While in Gal 6:14–15, κόσμος and καινὴ κτίσις stand in sharp antithesis, in

2 Cor 5:17–19, they do not. In Gal 6:14–15, the cross of Christ announces the birth of the new creation and the *death* of the κόσμος. In 2 Cor 5:17–19, the death of Christ announces the birth of the new creation and the *reconciliation* of the κόσμος.

8.6.4. The sorrow of the world (7:10)

At 7:8–12, Paul pauses to consider the effect of his "severe letter" on his readers (cf. 2:4, 9). The letter caused them sorrow, but the sorrow it provoked brought them to repentance (v. 9). This leads Paul, in v. 10, to draw a contrast between godly sorrow (ἡ κατὰ θεὸν λύπη) and the sorrow of the world (ἡ τοῦ κόσμος λύπη). The former produces repentance leading to salvation and brings no regret (μετάνοιαν εἰς σωτηρίαν ἀμεταμέλητον ἐργάζεται). The latter effects death (θάνατον κατεργάζεται). In this text, κόσμος is shaded negatively. It is associated with θάνατος and placed in opposition to θεός. It is difficult to be sure whether the word has the sense (sinful) humanity (hence ἡ τοῦ κόσμου λύπη would mean "human sorrow") or the apocalyptic sense "this world" (thus ἡ τοῦ κόσμου λύπη would mean "the sorrow which is a characteristic of this world/age"; cf. *4 Ezra* 7:12); probably the latter. Either way, it is interesting to note that Paul does not use κόσμος here to berate his readers. On the contrary, he commends for them precisely for *not* exhibiting the sorrow of the κόσμος.

8.7. Conclusions on 2 Corinthians

There is no consistent pattern to Paul's limited usage of κόσμος in 2 Corinthians. In each of its three occurrences, it has a different contextual sense. Only in 7:10 does it bear negative overtones. The use of the term is completely without a polemical edge. κόσμος makes no obvious contribution to the socio-rhetorical strategies of this letter. A polemical note can be detected, however, in the σάρξ/καινὴ κτίσις contrast in 5:16–17. The contrast serves to stress the ideological boundaries of the church and by extension to legitimate Paul's ministry and authority.

Of the negative terms ἁμαρτία, θάνατος and σάρξ, prominence is given in 2 Corinthians to θάνατος and σάρξ. ἁμαρτία only occurs at 5:21 (twice) and 11:7. θάνατος occurs nine times. It is set in opposition to ζωή at 2:16 and 4:10–12 and in contrast to πνεῦμα in

3:7–8. θάνατος, as we have seen, is negatively linked with κόσμος at 7:10. The word σάρξ occurs eleven times. The construction κατὰ σάρκα is used at 1:17; 5:16 (×2); 10:2, 3; 11:18. The expression designates the standpoint of the old age (cf. the synonymy of κατὰ σάρκα and τοῦ κόσμου in 1 Cor 1:26–28). In 2 Corinthians, Paul uses σαρξ where, on the basis of 1 Corinthians and Galatians, we might have expected him to use formulations involving κόσμος (5:16–17; 10:2–4).

The fact that Paul's apostolic authority is the central focus of this letter surely helps to account for the drop in rate of usage of κόσμος from 1 Corinthians. What is not so easy to explain is why he avoids the polemical use of κόσμος altogether. At points in the argument where he could have introduced the critical usage – when attacking "worldly" methods and attitudes – he has chosen not to do so. Several possibilities might be proposed as to why this is the case. From Paul's point of view, the polemical, boundary-emphasizing use of κόσμος may simply have served its purpose: having exploited the term to its fullest rhetorical potential, he may have considered there to have been little more polemical leverage to be gained from it. Or, κόσμος may by this time have become a less important term for the Corinthians. The terminological battle between Paul and the Corinthians seems at this point to have centred on σάρξ. His opponents in Corinth had been charging him with acting κατὰ σάρκα (1:12; 10:2–4). Instead of using κόσμος to vilify his detractors, therefore, he may have simply have opted to polemically redirect the charge of operating κατὰ σάρκα back at them. Or, the socio-rhetorical strategy involving κόσμος may not have worked as well as Paul had hoped. He had used the term in such a defamiliarized way that it had proved too confusing for his readers. All this is of course is highly speculative. The most that can be said is that for some reason Paul has given up the polemic use of κόσμος and has chosen to adopt other rhetorical and linguistic strategies to achieve his goals in writing.

The textual analysis of Paul's epistolary usages of κόσμος and κτίσις is now complete. It remains to draw together the threads of this investigation and to present our main conclusions.

9

Conclusions

9.1. Paul's epistolary uses of κόσμος and κτίσις

This study has attempted to analyze Paul's epistolary usages of the terms κόσμος and κτίσις in relation to the original social-historical situations within which they were employed. Implementing the interpretive framework set out in chapter 2, we have investigated the intended social functions of Paul's uses: the social goals they were designed to serve, the shape they were meant to give to the social and symbolic worlds of the readers addressed, and the "responses to the world" they were expected to generate.

In analyzing the context of utterance of 1 Corinthians, the problem of weak group boundaries in Corinth was highlighted: the Corinthians were insufficiently distinguishing themselves from outsiders in their beliefs, attitudes and conduct. Paul wrote 1 Corinthians to strengthen the social and ideological boundaries of the Corinthian community. The Corinthians would have used and understood the word κόσμος (= world/universe) in accordance with conventional Greek usage and would probably have accepted the world-view and ideology linked with the term. That ideology would probably have legitimated their social and cultural integration into their Graeco-Roman environment.

Paul's deployment of κόσμος in 1 Corinthians against this background indicates that he is using the term in a highly defamiliarizing way, uncoding some of the standard associations of the term and recoding quite different ones. He encodes a new social meaning, along apocalyptic lines, which radically subverts the world-view and ideology conventionally connected to the term. His negative and critical line of usage functions to stress the social and ideological distinction between the Christian community and the larger society and culture.

Paul's usage of κόσμος and κτίσις in Romans is largely positive. He employs the terms to develop an understanding of the world as God's good and well-ordered creation. In the process he draws on the world-view conventionally connoted by κόσμος (= world / universe).

The attempt to relate the usage of κόσμος and κτίσις in Romans to the situation in Rome had to proceed with caution in view of the lack of scholarly consensus on how far the letter is context-specific to Rome. The social teaching on relations with outsiders in Rom 12:14 – 13:10 was used as a bridge to try to link the usage to the community setting in Rome. This section reflects the Roman Christian community's increasingly vulnerable political status and its experience of mounting social conflict with outsiders in the years between the edict of Claudius and the persecution of Nero. The section expresses Paul's social aims for the community in the light of this situation: social harmony with the larger society and good citizenship. Paul's usage of κόσμος and κτίσις in the preceding part of the letter serves to support and legitimate these goals.

Paul wrote Galatians to stop his converts becoming proselytes to the Jewish religion. He uses the terms κόσμος and καινὴ κτίσις in this letter to stress the fundamental social and religious division between the Galatian Christian community and the Jewish colony, and to encourage his readers to develop a social identity distinct from Judaism.

In 2 Corinthians, there is no obvious pattern to Paul's limited employment of κόσμος. He does not use the term with any polemical intent or as part of any rhetorical strategy to advance his social goals for the Corinthian community. His use of the expression καινὴ κτίσις functions to stress the ideological boundaries of the church and to justify his ministry and leadership.

The ways in which Paul employs the terms in his letters are inextricably bound up with the situations he addresses (the use of κόσμος in 2 Corinthians is the exception). His usages not only *reflect* the situations which elicit his writing; they are intended to *affect* these situations. Paul writes with certain goals in view for the particular communities addressed and develops epistolary patterns of linguistic usage which serve those objectives.

9.2. κόσμος in Paul

In the light of this investigation, the following observations can be made about Paul's use of κόσμος. These comments are offered as a corrective to the overstated claims of Bultmann and Sasse in their theological analyses of κόσμος in Paul. Firstly, contrary to Bultmann's insistence that κόσμος is a "historical" term with Paul,[1] our analysis has shown that Paul predominantly uses κόσμος with a "cosmological" sense. κόσμος has a clear and exclusive reference to human beings on only ten or eleven occasions: it refers to humanity as a whole at Rom 3:6, 19; 5:12, 13; 2 Cor 5:19; 7:10 (possibly); it denotes Gentile humanity at Rom 11:12, 15; it specifies non-believers in contrast to believers at 1 Cor 6:2 (×2); 11:32. Unambiguously, the term refers to something more than or other than human beings in eleven instances. The term denotes the "inhabited world", the physical environment of human beings at Rom 1:8; 1 Cor 7:31a; 14:10; 2 Cor 1:12. It is applied to the whole universe at Rom 1:20; 1 Cor 4:9, 13; 5:10a; 8:4; Phil 2:15. And it designates the renewed creation at Rom 4:13. In every other instance the term has the sense "this world" in accordance with the spatio-temporal dualism of Jewish apocalypticism. In apocalyptic discourse, "this world" is a spatio-temporal reality. It embraces human beings but comprehends the non-human world as well. There are no linguistic grounds for deducing that Paul has taken over this standard conception in a demythologised and historicizing fashion, filtering out the cosmic aspect.

Secondly, Paul speaks of κόσμος with a spectrum of usage from strongly negative at the one end (for the world in its distance from and hostility to God), to highly positive at the other (for the world as God's good creation). According to Bultmann, κόσμος for Paul is a term which relates to a human being's "ruin", not "salvation".[2] In similar fashion, Sasse claims that κόσμος in Paul's writings is "reserved for the world which lies under sin and death". He remarks, "When the κόσμος is redeemed, it ceases to be κόσμος."[3] On the contrary, Paul can use the term on the positive "solution" side of his soteriology (Rom 11:12, 15; 2 Cor 5:19), and he can use the word with reference to the redeemed world, the object of eschatological hope (Rom 4:13). At the very least, this indicates that Bultmann's and Sasse's conclusions must not be taken – as they often are – as interpretive axioms.

Thirdly, Paul's predominant style of usage is negative. Pejorative references outnumber neutral and positive ones by two to one. However one ought not to draw the conclusion from this, as Bultmann and Sasse

---

[1] Bultmann 1952, 254.
[2] Bultmann 1955b, 78.
[3] Sasse 1965, 893.

do, that Paul's *typical* evaluation of κόσμος is negative and that the non-pejorative uses are completely unrepresentative of Paul's genuine theological thought. The most that can be claimed is that Paul's characteristic line of usage is negative in 1 Corinthians (where pejorative uses are overwhelmingly concentrated) and in Galatians. In Romans, the characteristic line of usage is neutral to positive. And even though the positive uses in Romans are less numerous than the negative ones in 1 Corinthians, they are not any less integrated into the theological thought of the letter.

Paul uses the term κόσμος in a remarkably complex, varied and subtle way, to an extent which has seldom been appreciated by scholars. The range of senses, nuances and associations with which Paul employs the word cannot be captured in a single, all-encompassing theological definition.

9.3. Paul's contrasting perspectives on the world

This study has highlighted the intriguing way in which Paul uses κόσμος in 1 Corinthians and κόσμος and κτίσις in Romans to build *contrasting* epistolary perspectives on the world. In 1 Corinthians, Paul uses κόσμος to construct a negative view of the social, cultural and physical world as "this world", alienated from God and doomed to perish. In Romans, Paul uses κόσμος and κτίσις to develop a positive understanding of the human and natural world as God's good and well-ordered creation, destined to be redeemed.[4] These perspectives have somewhat different soteriological and social ramifications.

An explanation for this contrast may be given on three levels. First of all, the contrasting views are related to the *dominant theological frameworks* of the letters. In 1 Corinthians, Paul's theological outlook is strongly apocalyptic. Consequently, he operates with a sharp antithesis between "the present world" and "the world to come". In Romans, on the other hand, the dualistic aspects of Paul's apocalyptic theology are tempered by a stress on God as creator and on his faithfulness and commitment to all that he has made. In this letter, there is a greater emphasis on the unity of God's creative and redeeming activity and on the continuity between the present world and its future transformation.

---

[4] The contrast is expressed over-sharply in order to make the point.

Secondly, the contrast may be explained in terms of the *different situational contexts* of the letters and Paul's different social goals for the two communities addressed. In 1 Corinthians, Paul responds to a problem of weak social and ideological boundaries. The Corinthians were adopting the practices, beliefs and attitudes of those outside the church and were failing to maintain or create a distinct social and moral identity. This induces Paul to stress the contrast between the church and its social and cultural environment. The Corinthians were involved in and committed to the larger society to a degree which, in Paul's view, compromised their participation in the life and values of the church. Paul thus counsels a dispassionate and detached approach to life in the wider world in the awareness that the "form of this world is passing away". The situation in Rome was vastly different. Paul writes to a group in an increasingly hostile social environment, living under the constant threat of interference from the authorities. The Roman situation, amongst other factors motivating the writing of this epistle, draws forth from Paul a more positive estimation of the world and its social ordering. On the basis of this assessment, Paul encourages his readers to see themselves as integrated into the wider society, and so offset accusations of subversiveness.

The third level of explanation has to do with Paul's fundamental theological convictions. The contrasting perspectives reflect a *theological tension* at the core of Paul's thinking. In an influential essay, N. A. Dahl pointed out that the New Testament belief in the church as the eschatological community of God has a double consequence. On the one hand, the belief entails "a contrast between the Church and 'the world'"; on the other hand, it engenders "a positive attitude to all things which God has created".[5] This tension is found to varying degrees throughout the New Testament. It is especially acute in Paul's theology. In 1 Corinthians, one side of the tension comes to prominence, in Romans, the other.

9.4. Response to the world

One of the aims of this study was to assess the extent to which Paul employs the terms κόσμος and κτίσις to generate a particular "response to the world". In 1 Corinthians, Paul utilizes κόσμος to promote a

---

[5] N. A. Dahl 1965, 423.

"response to the world" which may be described as "sectarian". One could further classify Paul's response in 1 Corinthians as a *revolutionist* response. In Romans Paul uses κόσμος and κτίσις to develop a "response to the world" which is, in some respects, characteristic of Troeltsch's "church-type". Paul promotes a conservative social ethos, endorses the existing socio-political order, appropriates the values of the larger society and stresses the universality of salvation.[6]

According to sociological theory, sect-type groups tend to develop into church-type groups through a process of institutionalization. Is the shift in orientation from 1 Corinthians to Romans to be explained in these terms? Did Paul start out with a radical vision of the church as an ethically pure community, with strong group boundaries, a counter-cultural value system and a totally committed membership? Did he gradually loose sight of his original ideals, come to soften his ethical position and his stance on boundaries, become willing to adopt the values of society, and so to demand much less of church members? The problem with this explanation is that the process of institutionalization usually occurs over at least a generation. The gap between 1 Corinthians and Romans is only a few years.

Is the shift rather to be explained in theological terms, as a reflection of Paul's diminishing expectation of the parousia? Did it gradually begin to dawn on Paul that the return of Christ was not imminent and that the world was not about to come to a catastrophic end? Did he then begin to develop a long-term social policy for his communities, abandoning his earlier interim ethic, encouraging his readers to accommodate themselves as much as possible to society, its norms and structures, in the realization that they were going to be around in the world for a while to come? The difficulty with this account is that Paul's sense of eschatological expectation is still strong in Romans (8:19–25; 13:11–12; 16:20).

Paul's different "responses to the world" in 1 Corinthians and Romans do not reflect either a sociological or theological development, but rather the different situations he is addressing. The situation of social and ideological compromise in Corinth causes him to adopt a radical, sectarian-like response. Circumstances in Rome induce him to counsel a more church-like approach as a policy of prudence and a strategy for survival for his readers.

---

[6] It is noteworthy that Troeltsch (1931, 342) traced the descent of the church-type to Paul.

The analysis confirms how unsatisfactory and misguided is the attempt to impose any one sect-type on the Pauline data in a model-like fashion. MacDonald's application of the *conversionist* sect to early Pauline Christianity obscures the key differences of world-view and social ethos highlighted in this study and puts one part of the evidence (the evidence for the church at Corinth) in a box where it does not belong. As indicated at the beginning of this study, such a use of sect-typology is in fact a *misapplication* of it. Wilson intended his typifications to be used as "hypothetical points of orientation",[7] not as all-encompassing explanatory schemes. That Paul's letters exhibit characteristics of more than one type is, on Wilson's own terms, precisely what we should expect of the emerging belief system of a new religious group.[8]

9.5. World-construction

We have attempted to interpret Paul's epistolary uses of κόσμος and κτίσις in terms of an "enterprise of world-building". A few observations may be added about the larger process of world-construction in Pauline Christianity and the role of Paul's letters in it.

Paul's missionary activity centred on the founding and nurturing of churches. It was his hope that these little communities would come to constitute for their members comprehensive "social worlds", all-embracing social orders providing structure and meaning for every aspect of their lives. In his church-planting endeavours, Paul laid the foundations of such worlds. He initiated the world-constructing process. But he did not, during this phase, bring that process to completion or even near to completion. The building work in any one of his congregations continued long after his initial founding of it.

World-construction, then, was an *ongoing* enterprise in Pauline Christianity. Paul's letter-writing ministry was part of this continuing process. He did not write to provide protective canopies for social worlds that had already been built. He did not write to maintain structures that were already in place. He wrote to communities in the course of construction, and he wrote to shape and direct the development. This

---

[7] B. R. Wilson 1973, 27.
[8] B. R. Wilson 1973, 26.

is also true of the letter to the Romans, a letter penned to a community which Paul had not actually founded (nor visited).

Paul wrote, of course, as one with enormous capacity and creative ability to influence the world-erecting process. Sometimes, however, his world-constructing efforts were hindered by the resistance of those whose worlds he was seeking to shape, and by the arrival on the scene of rival builders who sought to take over management of the construction project in Paul's absence.

In describing and explaining the world-building enterprise in Pauline Christianity, account must be taken of divergence and conflict between Paul and his addressees. In 1 Corinthians and Galatians, it is clear that the communities addressed had developed in ways unintended by Paul. Paul did not write to legitimate these developments but to repudiate them. He wrote to challenge and to change the audience situations. Paul's symbolic constructions in these letters were not used as instruments of legitimation but as tools of community critique. This means that we cannot take Paul's letters and simply read off from them the symbolic universe of Pauline Christianity as a whole. Paul's symbolizations served to *create* community, not primarily to *reflect* it.

Paul wrote to fashion the social and symbolic worlds of his readers in accordance with his general and unified vision for the churches. Yet at the same time, he also endeavoured to construct his readers' worlds in particular ways according to their distinctive needs and particular circumstances. Thus in 1 Corinthians, he wrote to forge a social world in tension with its social and cultural environment. In Romans, he wrote to construct a social world in solidarity with its environment. In Galatians, he wrote to build a social world distinct from the Jewish community. This indicates that there was a certain *ad hoc* nature about Paul's world-constructing efforts.

Paul constructed the worlds of his readers in relation to the social and symbolic order of Graeco-Roman culture. In pressing the distinction between the church and the larger society at Corinth, Paul subverted and challenged the dominant order. In encouraging harmonious relations between the church and outsiders at Rome, he (partially) legitimated it.

World-construction in Pauline Christianity was an immensely variegated and complex phenomenon involving a huge range of factors. The straightforward application of Berger's paradigm, in terms of a basic two-stage process of creation and maintenance, though heuristically helpful in the early days of sociological interpretation of Pauline Christianity, should now be seen as obscuring a more diverse and altogether much richer social reality.

Bibliography

ABBREVIATIONS USED IN BIBLIOGRAPHY

AB	Anchor Bible
AGJU	Arbeiten zur Geschichte des antiken Judentums und des Urchristentums
AJP	*American Journal of Philology*
AnBib	Analecta biblica
ANRW	*Aufstieg und Niedergang der römischen Welt*, ed. H. Temporini and W. Haase. Berlin, 1972–
ASNU	Acta seminarii neotestamentici upsaliensis
BEvT	Beiträge zur evangelischen Theologie
Bib	*Biblica*
BJRL	*Bulletin of the John Rylands Library*
BT	*The Bible Translator*
BTB	*Biblical Theology Bulletin*
BZNW	Beihefte zur *ZNW*
CBQ	*Catholic Biblical Quarterly*
ConB	*Coniectanea biblica*
CQ	*Classical Quarterly*
EDNT	*Exegetical Dictionary for the New Testament*. 3 vols, H. Balz and G. Schneider (eds). Eerdmans: Grand Rapids; T. & T. Clark: Edinburgh, 1990–3
EKKNT	Evangelisch-katholischer Kommentar zum Neuen Testament
FRLANT	Forschungen zur Religion und Literatur des Alten und Neuen Testaments
GCS	Griechische christliche Schriftsteller
HBT	*Horizons in Biblical Theology*

HTKNT	Herders theologischer Kommentar zum Neuen Testament
HTR	*Harvard Theological Review*
ICC	International Critical Commentary
Int	*Interpretation*
JBL	*Journal of Biblical Literature*
JDTh	Jahresbücher für deutsche Theologie
JLT	*Journal of Literature and Theology*
JPSTh	*Jahrbuch für Philosophie und spekulative Theologie*
JSNT	*Journal for the Study of the New Testament*
JSP	*Journal for the Study of the Pseudepigrapha*
JTS	*Journal of Theological Studies*
KBANT	Kommentare und Beiträge zum Alten und Neuen Testament
KD	*Kerygma und Dogma*
LTK	Lexikon für Theologie und Kirche
MS	Monograph Series
NCBC	New Century Bible Commentary
NIBC	New International Biblical Commentary
NICNT	New International Commentary on the New Testament
NIDNTT	*The New International Dictionary of New Testament Theology.* 4 vols. C. Brown (ed.). Paternoster Press: Exeter, 1975–8, 1986
NIGTC	New International Greek Testament Commentary
NovT	*Novum Testamentum*
NTS	*New Testament Studies*
OP	Occasional Papers
RB	*Revue biblique*
RelS	*Religious Studies*
RGG	*Religion in Geschichte und Gegenwart*
RTR	*Reformed Theological Review*
SBLDS	Society of Biblical Literature Dissertation Series
SE	*Studia evangelica*
SJLA	Studies in Judaism in Late Antiquity
SJT	*Scottish Journal of Theology*
SNTSMS	Society for New Testament Studies Monograph Series

SNTW	Studies of the New Testament and Its World
ST	*Studia theologica*
Sup	Supplement
TDNT	*Theological Dictionary of the New Testament*, G. Kittel and G. Friedrich (eds); Eng. trans. G. W. Bromiley, 10 vols. Eerdmans: Grand Rapids (1964–76)
TJ	*Trinity Journal*
TNTC	Tyndale New Testament Commentary
TPINTC	Trinity Press International New Testament Commentary
TynBul	*Tyndale Bulletin*
TZ	*Theologische Zeitschrift*
VC	*Vigiliae christianae*
WBC	Word Biblical Commentary
WMANT	Wissenschaftliche Monographien zum Alten und Neuen Testament
WUNT	Wissenschaftliche Untersuchungen zum Neuen Testament
ZAW	*Zeitschrift für die alttestamentliche Wissenschaft*
ZNW	*Zeitschrift für die neutestamentliche Wissenschaft*
ZTK	*Zeitschrift für Theologie und Kirche*

BIBLIOGRAPHY OF WORKS CITED IN THE TEXT

1. Primary Sources

All ancient sources and translations are from the *Loeb Classical Library*, with the following exceptions.

The Dead Sea Scrolls in English, translated by G. Vermes, 3rd edn. Penguin: London and Harmondsworth, 1987.

Eusebius, *Die Praeparation Evangelica, Eusebius Werke Band 8*, 2 vols, GCS. Akademie-Verlag: Berlin, 1954, 1956.

Die Fragmente der Vorsokratiker, 3 vols, H. Diels and W. Kranz (eds). Weidmannsche-Verlagsbuchhandlung: Berlin, 1951–2.

Fragments From Hellenistic Jewish Authors. Volume 2: Poets, C. R. Holladay. Scholars Press: Atlanta, 1989.

The Hellenistic Philosophers. Volume 1: Translations of the principal sources with philosophical commentary; Volume 2: Greek and Latin texts with notes and bibliography, A. A. Long and D. N. Sedley (eds). Cambridge University Press: Cambridge, 1987.

Justin Martyr and Athenagoras, translated by M. Dods, G. Reith and B. P. Pratten. The Ante-Nicene Christian Library, A. Robertson and A. Donaldson (eds). T. & T. Clark: Edinburgh, 1867.

Lactantius, *The Divine Institutions, Books I-VII,* translated by M. F. McDonald. The Fathers of the Church, Vol. 49. Catholic University of America Press: Washington, 1964.

The Letter of Aristeas: A linguistic study with special reference to the Greek Bible, H. G. Meecham. Manchester University Press: Manchester, 1935.

The Midrash Rabbah, 5 vols, H. Feldman and M. Simon (eds). Soncino Press: London, Jerusalem and New York, 1977.

Minucius Felix, *The Octavius of Minucius Felix.* Translations of Christian Literature: Series II, Latin Texts, translated by J. H. Freeze. SPCK: London; Macmillan: New York, 1918.

The Mishna: translated from the Hebrew with introduction and brief explanatory notes, H. Danby. Clarendon Press: Oxford, 1933.

Novum Testamentum Graece, E. Nestle, K. Aland *et al.* (eds), 27th edn. Deutsche Bibelgesellschaft: Stuttgart, 1993.

"Ocellus Lucanus": Text und Kommentar, R. Harder (ed.), Neue Philologische Untersuchungen 1. Weidmannsche Buchhandlung: Berlin, 1926.

Orosius, *The Seven Books of History Against the Pagans,* translated by R. J. Defarrari. The Fathers of the Church: a new translation. Catholic University of America Press: Washington, 1964.

The Old Testament Pseudepigrapha, 2 vols; J. H. Charlesworth (ed.). Darton, Longman & Todd: London, 1983, 1985.

The Presocratic Philosophers: a critical history with a selection of texts, ed. G. S. Kirk and J. E. Raven. Cambridge University Press: Cambridge, 1957.

Septuaginta, A. Rahlfs (ed.). Deutsche Bibelgesellschaft: Stuttgart, 1993.

The Testaments of the Twelve Patriarchs: a critical edition of the Greek text, M. de Jonge, in co-operation with H. W. Hollander, H. J. De Jonge and T. Korteweg. E. J. Brill: Leiden, 1978.

The Writings of Tertullian, Vol. 1, translated by S. Thelwall and P. Holmes. The Ante-Nicene Christian Library, A. Robertson and A. Donaldson (eds). T. & T. Clark: Edinburgh, 1869.

2. Secondary Literature

ACHTEMEIER, P. J. 1985. *Romans*, Interpretation. John Knox Press: Atlanta.

ADAMS, E. 1997a. "Abraham's Faith and Gentile Disobedience: textual links between Romans 1 and 4", *JSNT* 65, 47–66.

—— 1997b. "Historical Crisis and Cosmic Crisis in Mark 13 and Lucan's *Civil War*", *TynBul* 48.2, 329–44.

ALETTI, J.-N. 1988. "Rm 1,18 – 3,20: Incohérence ou cohérence de l'argumentation paulinienne?", *Bib* 69, 47–62.

ALLISON, D. C. 1988. *The End of the Ages Has Come: an early Christian interpretation of the passion and resurrection of Jesus*, SNTW. T. &. T. Clark: Edinburgh.

AUER, A. 1970. "World", in J. B. Bauer (ed.), *Encyclopedia of Biblical Theology*, 3 vols. Sheed & Ward: London and Sydney, 3:1001–6.

AUNE, D. 1994. "Human Nature and Ethics in Hellenistic Philosophical Traditions and Paul: some issues and problems", in Engberg-Pedersen (ed.), 256–312.

AYMER, A. J. D. 1983. *Paul's Understanding of "Kaine Ktisis": continuity and discontinuity in Pauline eschatology*, PhD Dissertation. Graduate School of Drew University: Madison, New Jersey.

BALCH, D. L. 1983. "1 Cor 7:32–35 and the Stoic Debates about Marriage, Anxiety, and Distraction", *JBL* 102, 429–39.

BALZ, H. R. 1971. *Heilsvertrauen und Welterfahrung: Strukturen der paulinischen Eschatologie nach Römer 8, 18–39*, BEvT 59. Kaiser: Munich.

—— 1991. "κόσμος", *EDNT* 2:309–12.

BAMMEL, E. 1984. "Romans 13", in E. Bammel and C. F. D. Moule (eds) *Jesus and the Politics of His Day*. Cambridge University Press: Cambridge, 365–83.

BANDSTRA, A. J. 1964. *The Law and the Elements of the World: an exegetical study in aspects of Paul's teaching*. J. H. Kok: Kampen.

BARCLAY, J. M. G. 1987. "Mirror-Reading a Polemical Letter: Galatians as a test case", *JSNT* 31, 73–93.

—— 1988. *Obeying the Truth: a study of Paul's ethics in Galatians*, SNTW. T. & T. Clark: Edinburgh.

—— 1992. "Thessalonica and Corinth: social contrasts in Pauline Christianity", *JSNT* 47, 49–74.

—— 1993. "Conflict in Thessalonica", *CBQ* 55, 512–30.

—— 1996. *Jews in the Mediterranean Diaspora: From Alexander to Trajan (323 BCE – 117 CE)*. T. & T. Clark: Edinburgh.

BARR, J. 1961. *The Semantics of Biblical Language*. Oxford University Press: Oxford.

BARRETT, C. K. 1957. *A Commentary on the Epistle to the Romans*. A. & C. Black: London.

—— 1962. *From First Adam to Last: a study in Pauline theology*. A. & C. Black: London.

—— 1964. "Christianity in Corinth", *BJRL* 46, 264–97.

—— 1968. *A Commentary on the First Epistle to the Corinthians*. A. & C. Black: London.

BARTH, K. 1952. *The Epistle to the Romans*, translated by E. C. Hoskyns, 6th edn. Oxford University Press: London.

BASSLER, J. M. 1982. *Divine Impartiality: Paul and a theological axiom*, SBLDS 59. Scholars Press: Chico, California.

—— 1984. "Divine Impartiality in Paul's Letter to the Romans", *NovT* 26, 43–58.

—— (ed.) 1991. *Pauline Theology, volume 1: Thessalonians, Philippians, Galatians, Philemon*. Augsburg Publishing House; Fortress Press: Minneapolis.

BAUMBACH, G. 1979. "Die Schöpfung in der Theologie des Paulus", *Kairos* 21, 196-205.

BAUMGARTERN, J. 1975. *Paulus und die Apokalyptik*, WMANT 44. Neukirchener Verlag: Neukirchen-Vluyn.

BECKER, J. 1989. *Paulus. Der Apostel der Völker*. J. C. B. Mohr (Paul Siebeck): Tübingen.

BEKER, J. C. 1980. *Paul the Apostle: the triumph of God in life and thought*. Fortress Press: Philadelphia; T. & T. Clark: Edinburgh.

BEKER, J. C. 1985. "Suffering and Triumph in Paul's Letter to the Romans", *HBT* 7, 105–19.

BELLEVILLE, L. 1986. "'Under Law' in Galatians 3.21 – 4.11", *JSNT* 26, 53–78.

BENKO, S. 1980. "Pagan Criticism of Christianity during the First Two Centuries A.D.", *ANRW* 23.2, 1055–118.

—— 1984. *Pagan Rome and the Early Christians.* Indianapolis University Press: Bloomington and Indianapolis.

BERGER, P. L. 1969. *The Social Reality of Religion.* Faber & Faber: London.

—— and LUCKMANN, T. 1967. *The Social Construction of Reality: a treatise in the sociology of knowledge.* Penguin: London.

BEST, E. 1988. *Paul and his Converts.* T. & T. Clark: Edinburgh.

BETZ, H. D. 1979. *Galatians: a commentary on Paul's letter to the churches in Galatia,* Hermenia. Fortress Press: Philadelphia.

BIERINGER, R. (ed.) 1996. *The Corinthian Correspondence.* Leuven University Press: Leuven.

BINDEMANN, W. 1983. *Die Hoffnung der Schöpfung: Römer 8, 18–27 und die Frage einer Theologie der Befreiung von Mensch und Natur,* Neukirchener Studienbücher 14. Neukirchener Verlag: Neukirchen-Vluyn.

BLACK, M. 1973. *Romans,* NCBC. Marshall, Morgan & Scott: London.

BOCKMUEHL, M. N. A. 1990. *Revelation and Mystery in Ancient Judaism and Pauline Christianity,* WUNT 2. 36. J. C. B. Mohr (Paul Siebeck): Tübingen.

BORGEN, P. 1984. "Philo. Survey of research since World War II", *ANRW* 21.1, 98–154.

BORING, E. M. 1986. "The Language of Universal Salvation in Paul", *JBL* 105, 269–92.

BORNKAMM, G. 1969. "The Revelation of God's Wrath", in G. Bornkamm, *Early Christian Experience*, translated by P. L. Hammer. SCM Press: London, 47–70.

——1991. "The Letter to the Romans as Paul's Last Will and Testament", in Donfried (ed.), 16–28.

BRATCHER, R. G. 1980. "The Meaning of *kosmos*, 'World', in the New Testament", *BT* 31, 430–4.

BRAUCH, M. T. 1977. "Perspectives on 'God's Righteousness', in Recent German Discussion", in E. P. Sanders, *Paul and Palestinian Judaism. A comparison of patterns of religion.* Fortress Press: Philadelphia, 523–42.

BRAUN, H. 1962. "Die Indifferenz gegenüber der Welt bei Paulus und die Epiktet", in H. Braun, *Gesammelte Studien zum Neuen Testament und seiner Umwelt.* J. C. B. Mohr (Paul Siebeck): Tübingen, 159–67.

BROWN, R. E., and MEIER, J. P. 1983. *Antioch and Rome: New Testament cradles of Catholic Christianity.* Geoffrey Chapman: London.

BRUCE, F. F. 1971. *1 and 2 Corinthians*, NCBC. Oliphants; Marshall, Morgan and Scott: London.

—— 1982. *The Epistle of Paul to the Galatians: a commentary on the Greek text*, NIGTC. Paternoster Press: Exeter.

—— 1985. *The Letter of Paul to the Romans*, TNTC. Inter-Varsity Press: Leicester; Eerdmans: Grand Rapids.

—— 1991. "The Romans Debate – Continued", in Donfried (ed.), 175–94.

BULTMANN, R. 1952. *Theology of the New Testament*, Vol. 1; translated by K. Grobel. SCM Press: London.

—— 1955. "The Understanding of Man and the World in the NewTestament and in the Greek World", in R. Bultmann, *Essays Philosophical and Theological,* translated by J. C. G. Greig. SCM Press: London, 67–89.

BURNET, J. 1930. *Early Greek Philosophy*, 4th edn.; A. & C. Black: London.

BURTON, E. de W. 1921. *A Critical and Exegetical Commentary on the Epistle to the Galatians,* ICC. T. & T. Clark: Edinburgh.

BUSSMANN, C. 1975. *Themen der paulinischen Missionspredigt auf dem Hintergrund der spätjüdisch-hellenistischen Missionsliteratur,* Europäische Hochschulschriften Reihe 23; Theologie Serie Vol. 3. Herbet Lang: Bern; Peter Lang: Frankfurt.

BYRNE, B. 1979. *"Sons of God - Seed of Abraham": a study of the idea of the sonship of God of all Christians in Paul against the Jewish background,* AnBib 83. Biblical Institute Press: Rome.

—— 1990. *Inheriting the Earth: the Pauline basis of a spirituality for our time.* St. Paul Publications: Homebush, New South Wales.

BYTOMSKI, F. 1911. "Die genetische Entwicklung des Begriffes κόσμος in der Heiligen Schrift", *JPSTh* 25, 180–201; 389–413.

CAIRD, G. B. 1956. *Principalities and Powers. A study in Pauline theology.* Clarendon Press: Oxford.

CALVIN, J. 1894. *Commentaries on the Epistle of Paul the Apostle to the Romans*, translated and edited by J. Owen. The Calvin Translation Society: Edinburgh.

CAMPBELL, W. S. 1991. "Romans III as a Key to the Structure and Thought of Romans", in Donfried (ed.), 251–64.

CARR, W. 1981. *Angels and Principalities. The background, meaning and development of the Pauline phrase "hai archai kai hai exousiai",* SNTSMS 42. Cambridge University Press: Cambridge.

CARTER, T. L. 1997. "'Big Men' in Corinth: Using 'Grid and Group' to look at 1 Cor. 1–4", *JSNT* 66, 45–71.

CHADWICK, H. 1954/55. "'All Things to All Men' (1 Cor. ix. 22)", *NTS* 1, 261–75.

CHOW, J. K. 1992. *Patronage and Power: a study of social networks in Corinth,* JSNTSup 75. Sheffield Academic Press: Sheffield.

CHRISTOFFERSON, O. 1990. *The Earnest Expectation of the Creature: the flood-tradition as matrix of Romans 8:18–27*, ConB New Testament Series 23. Almqvist and Wiksell: Stockholm.

CLARKE, A. D. 1993. *Secular and Christian Leadership in Corinth: a socio-historical and exegetical study of 1 Corinthians 1–6*, AGJU 18. E. J. Brill: Leiden, New York, Köln.

—— 1994. "Rome and Italy", in D. W. J. Gill and C. Gempf (eds), *The Book of Acts in its First Century Setting: Volume 2: The Book of Acts in its Graeco-Roman Setting.* Eerdmans: Grand Rapids; Paternoster Press: Carlisle, 455–81.

CLAVIER, H. 1964. "Breves Remarques sur la Notion de ΣΩΜΑ ΠΝΕΥΜΑΤΙΚΟΝ", in Davies and Daube (eds), 342–62.

CONZELMANN, H. 1975. *1 Corinthians*, translated by J. W. Leitch. Hermeneia. Fortress Press: Philadelphia.

COOPER, J. G. 1989. *Body, Soul and Life Everlasting: biblical anthropology and the Monism–Dualism debate.* Eerdmans: Grand Rapids.

CORNFORD, F. M. 1934. "Innumerable Worlds in Presocratic Philosophy", *CQ* 28:1–16.

—— 1937. *Plato's Cosmology. The Timaeus of Plato translated with a running commentary,* International Library of Psychology, Philosophy and Scientific Method, 1977 reprint. Routledge & Kegan Paul: London and Henley.

COTTERELL, P., and TURNER, M. 1989. *Linguistics and Biblical Interpretation.* SPCK: London.

COUSAR, C. B. 1982. *Galatians,* Interpretation. John Knox: Louisville, Kentucky.

CRANFIELD, C. E. B. 1975. *The Epistle to the Romans,* Vol. 1, ICC. T. & T. Clark: Edinburgh.

—— 1979. *The Epistle to the Romans,* Vol. 2, ICC. T. & T. Clark: Edinburgh.

CROMBIE, I. M. 1963. *An Examination of Plato's Doctrines.* Routledge & Kegan Paul: London; The Humanities Press: New York.

CULLMANN, O. 1963. *The State in the New Testament,* revised edn. SCM Press: London.

—— 1967. *Salvation in History,* translated by S. G. Sowers. SCM Press: London.

DAHL, M. E. 1962. *The Resurrection of the Body. A study of 1 Corinthians 15.* Studies in Biblical Theology. SCM Press: London.

DAHL, N. A. 1965. "Christ, Creation and the Church", in Davies and Daube (eds), 422–43.

—— 1977. "Paul and the Church at Corinth according to 1 Corinthians 1:10 – 4:21", in N. A. Dahl, *Studies in Paul: Theology for the early Christian mission.* Augsburg Publishing House: Minneapolis, 40–61.

DAVIES, G. N. 1990. *Faith and Obedience in Romans: a study in Romans 1–4,* JSNTSup 39. Sheffield Academic Press: Sheffield.

DAVIES, W. D. 1962. *Paul and Rabbinic Judaism: some rabbinic elements in Pauline theology.* SPCK: London.

—— 1974. *The Gospel and the Land: early Christianity and Jewish territorial doctrine.* University of California Press: Berkeley, London.

DAVIES, W. D. and DAUBE, D. (eds) 1956. *The Background of the New Testament and its Eschatology*. Cambridge University Press: Cambridge.

DAVIS, J. A. 1984. *Wisdom and Spirit: an investigation of 1 Corinthians 1:18 – 3:20 against the background of Jewish Sapiential Traditions in the Graeco-Roman Period*. University Press of America: Lanham, New York, London.

DE BOER, M. C. 1988. *The Defeat of Death: apocalyptic eschatology in 1 Corinthians 15 and Romans 5*, JSNTSup 22. Sheffield Academic Press: Sheffield.

DEMAREST, B. A. 1991. "General and Special Revelation: epistemological foundations of religious pluralism", in A. D. Clarke and B. W. Winter (eds), *One God, One Lord in a World of Religious Pluralism*. Tyndale House: Cambridge, 135–52.

DEMING, W. 1995. *Paul on Marriage and Celibacy: The Hellenistic background of 1 Corinthians*, SNTSMS 83. Cambridge University Press: Cambridge.

DINKLER, E. 1962. "Weltbild III. Im NT", *RGG* 6:1618–22.

DODD, C. H. 1932. *The Epistle of Paul to the Romans*. Hodder & Stoughton: London.

DONFRIED, K. P. (ed.) 1991a. *The Romans Debate: revised and expanded edition*. T. & T. Clark: Edinburgh.

—— 1991b. "Introduction 1991: the Romans debate since 1977", in Donfried (ed.), xlix-lxxii.

DÖRRIE, H. 1973. "Die Erneueruhng des Platonismus im ersten Jahrhundert vor Christus", in H. Dörrie, *Platonica Minora*. Wilhelm Fink: München, 154–65.

DOUGHTY, D. J. 1975. "The Presence and Future of Salvation in Corinth", *ZNW* 66, 61–90.

DOUGLAS, M. 1973. *Natural Symbols: explorations in cosmology*. Penguin: Harmondsworth.

DRAGONA-MONACHOU, M. 1976. *The Stoic Arguments for the Existence and the Providence of the Gods*, S. Saripolis' Library 32; National and Capodistrian. University of Athens Faculty of Arts: Athens.

DUNN, J. D. G. 1975. "Rom. 7,14–25 in the Theology of Paul", *TZ* 31, 257–73.

DUNN, J. D. G. 1977. *Unity and Diversity in the New Testament: an inquiry into the character of earliest Christianity.* SCM Press: London.

—— 1980. *Christology in the Making: an inquiry into the origins of the doctrine of the incarnation.* SCM Press: London.

—— 1986. "Romans 13:1–7 – A Charter for Political Quietism", *Ex Auditu* 2, 55–68.

DUNN, J. D. G. 1988. *Romans*, 2 vols, WBC 38A & 38B. Word Books: Dallas.

—— 1991. "The Theology of Galatians: the issue of covenantal nomism", in J. M. Bassler (ed.), 125–46.

—— 1993. *The Epistle to the Galatians*, Black's New Testament Commentaries. A. & C. Black: London.

EDMUNDSON, G. 1913. *The Church in Rome in the First Century: an examination of various controverted questions relating to its history, chronology, literature and traditions,* The Bampton Lectures for 1913. Longmans: London, New York, Bombay, Calcutta.

EHRHARDT, A. 1964. "Creatio Ex Nihilo", in A. Ehrhardt, *The Framework of New Testament Stories.* Manchester University Press: Manchester, 200–33.

ELDERS, L. 1965. *Aristotle's Cosmology: a commentary on the De Caelo,* Philosophical Texts and Studies 13. Van Gorcum & Comp. N.V.: Assen.

ELIADE, M. 1974. *The Myth of The Eternal Return, or, Cosmos and History,* translated by W. R. Trask, Bollington Series XLVI. Princeton University Press: Princeton, New York.

ELLIOT, J. H. 1981. *A Home for the Homeless: a sociological exegesis of 1 Peter, its situation and strategy.* Fortress Press: Philadelphia.

ELLIS, E. E. 1978. *Prophecy and Hermeneutic in Early Christianity: New Testament essays,* WUNT 18. J. C. B. Mohr (Paul Siebeck): Tübingen.

—— 1990. "*Soma* in First Corinthians", *Int* 44, 132–44.

ENGBERG-PEDERSEN, T. (ed.) 1994. *Paul in his Hellenistic Context,* SNTW. T. & T. Clark: Edinburgh.

ESLER, P. F. 1987. *Community and Gospel in Luke–Acts: the social and political motivations of Lucan theology*, SNTSMS 57. Cambridge University Press: Cambridge.

—— 1994. *The First Christians in their Social Worlds: social-scientific approaches to New Testament interpretation*. Routledge: London and New York.

ESSER, H. H. 1975. "κτίσις", *NIDNTT* 1:378–87.

FEE, G. D. 1987. *The First Epistle to the Corinthians*, NICNT. Eerdmans: Grand Rapids.

FERGUSON, E. 1987. *Backgrounds of Early Christianity*. Eerdmans: Grand Rapids.

FIORE, B. 1985. "'Covert Allusion' in 1 Corinthians 1–4", *CBQ* 47, 85–102.

FITZGERALD, J. T. 1988. *Cracks in an Earthen Vessel: an examination of the catalogues of hardships in the Corinthian correspondence*, SBLDS 97. Scholars Press: Atlanta, Georgia.

FITZMYER, J. A. 1993. *Romans*, AB 33. Geoffrey Chapman, Doubleday: London.

FLENDER, H. 1968. "Das Verständnis der Welt bei Paulus, Markus und Lukas", *KD* 14, 1–27.

FOERSTER, W. 1964. "δαίμων, διαμόνιον", *TDNT* 2:1–20.

—— 1965. "κτίζω, etc.", *TDNT* 3:1000–32.

FOWLER, R. 1991. "Critical Linguistics", in K. Malmkjaer and J. M. Anderson (eds), *The Linguistics Encyclopedia*. Routledge: London and New York, 89–93.

—— 1996. *Linguistic Criticism*, 2nd edn. Opus. Oxford University Press: Oxford and New York.

—— and KRESS, G. 1979. "Critical Linguistics", in R. Fowler, R. Hodge, G. Kress and A. Trew (eds), *Language and Control*. Routledge & Kegan Paul: London, 185–213.

FOX, R. L. 1986. *Pagans and Christians in the Mediterranean World from the Second Century AD to the Conversion of Constantine*. Penguin: London.

Friedrich, J., Pohlmann, W., and Stuhlmacher, P. 1976. "Zur historischen Situation und Intention von Röm 13, 1–7", *ZTK* 73, 131–66.

Furnish, V. P. 1968. *Theology and Ethics in Paul*. Abingdon Press: Nashville.

—— 1979. *The Moral Teaching of Paul: selected issues*. Abingdon Press: Nashville.

—— 1984. *II Corinthians*, AB 32A. Doubleday: Garden City, New York.

Gager, J. G. 1970. "Functional Diversity in Paul's Use of End-Time Language", *JBL* 89, 325–37.

—— 1975. *Kingdom and Community: the social world of early Christianity*. Prentice-Hall: Englewood Cliffs, New Jersey.

Gamble, H. Y. 1977. *The Textual History of the Letter to the Romans: a study in textual and literary criticism*, Studies and Documents 42. Eerdmans: Grand Rapids.

Garlington, D. B. 1990. "Romans 7:14–25 and the Creation Theology of Paul", *TJ* 11, 197–235.

Gärtner, B. 1955. *The Areopagus Speech and Natural Revelation*, translated by C. H. King, ASNU 21. Almqvist & Wiksells: Uppsala.

Gaventa, B. R. 1991. "The Singularity of the Gospel. A reading of Galatians", in J. M. Bassler (ed.), 147–59.

Geertz, C. 1975. "Ethos, World View, and the Analysis of Sacred Symbols", in C. Geertz, *The Interpretation of Cultures: selected essays by Clifford Geertz*. Hutchinson: London, 126–41.

Gerber, U. 1966. "Röm viii 18ff als exegetisches Problem der Dogmatik", *NovT* 8, 58–81.

Gibbs, J. G. 1971. *Creation and Redemption: a study in Pauline theology*, NovTSup 26. E. J. Brill: Leiden.

Giddens, A. 1993. *Sociology: second edition fully revised and updated*. Polity Press: Cambridge.

Gieraths, H. 1950. *Knechtschaft und Freiheit der Schöpfung: Eine historisch-exegetische Untersuchung zu Röm 8, 19–22*. PhD Dissertation, Rheinischen Friedrich-Wilhelms-Universität: Bonn.

Gill, D. W. 1989. "Erastus the Aedile", *TynBul* 40, 293–301.

GILLMAN, J. 1988. "A Thematic Comparison: 1 Cor 15:50–57 and 2 Cor 5:1–5", *JBL* 107, 439–54.

GODET, F. 1880/81. *Commentary on St. Paul's Epistle to the Romans*, Vol. 1, translated by A. Cusin, Clark's Foreign Theological Library New Series Vol. 2. T. & T. Clark: Edinburgh.

GODET, F. 1886. *Commentary on St. Paul's First Epistle to the Corinthians*, Vol. 1, translated by A. Cusin, Clark's Foreign Theological Library New Series Vol. 27. T. & T. Clark: Edinburgh.

GOOCH, P. W. 1993. *Dangerous Food: 1 Corinthians 8–10 in its context.* Wilfrid Laurier University Press: Waterloo, Ont.

GOULD, J. B. 1970. *The Philosophy of Chrysippus,* Philosophia Antiqua 17. E. J. Brill: Leiden.

GOULDER, M. D. 1991. "ΣΟΦΙΑ in 1 Corinthians", *NTS* 37, 516–34.

GRACE, G. W. 1987. *The Linguistic Construction of Reality.* Croom Helm: London.

GRANT, M. 1970. *Nero.* Weidenfeld & Nicolson: London.

GROSHEIDE, F. W. 1953. *Commentary on the First Epistle to the Corinthians*, NICNT. Eerdmans: Grand Rapids.

GUERRA, A. J. 1995. *Romans and the Apologetic Tradition: Purpose, genre and audience of Paul's letter*, SNTSMS 81. Cambridge University Press: Cambridge.

GUHRT, J. 1975. "κόσμος", *NIDNTT* 1:517–26.

—— 1978. "αἰών", *NIDNTT* 3:826–33.

GUNDRY-VOLF, J. M. 1996. "Controlling the Bodies: A theological profile of the Corinthian sexual ascetics (1 Cor 7)", in R. Bieringer (ed.), 1996, 519–41.

GUTHRIE, W. K. C. 1962. *A History of Greek Philosophy. Volume 1. The early Presocratics and the Pythagoreans.* Cambridge University Press: Cambridge.

—— 1965. *A History of Greek Philosophy. Volume 2. The Presocratic tradition from Parmenides to Democritus.* Cambridge University Press: Cambridge.

HAEBLER, C. 1967. "Kosmos. Eine etymologisch-wortgeschichtliche Untersuchung", *Archiv für Begriffsgeschichte* 11, 101–18.

HALL, D. R. 1983. "Romans 3.1–8 Reconsidered", *NTS* 29, 183–97.

HALLIDAY, M. A. K. 1978. *Language as Social Semiotic: the social interpretation of language and meaning.* Edward Arnold: London.

HARDY, E. G. 1906. *Studies in Roman History.* S. Sonnenschein: London.

HARRIS, M. J. 1983. *Raised Immortal: Resurrection and immortality in the New Testament.* Marshalls Theological Library. Marshall, Morgan & Scott: London.

HARRIS, O. G. 1984. "The Social World of Early Christianity", *Lexington Theological Quarterly* 19, 102–14.

HARRISVILLE, R. A. 1980. *1 Corinthians*, Augsburg Commentary on the New Testament. Augsburg Publishing House: Minneapolis.

HAUCK, F. 1965. "περικάθαρμα", *TDNT* 3:430–1.

HAWTHORNE, G. F., MARTIN, R. P., and REID, D. G. (eds) 1993. *Dictionary of Paul and his Letters.* Inter-Varsity Press: Downers Grove and Leicester.

HAYS, R. 1996. *The Moral Vision of the New Testament: a contemporary introduction to New Testament ethics.* HarperCollins: New York (1996); T. & T. Clark: Edinburgh (1997).

HÉRING, J. 1962. *The First Epistle of Saint Paul to the Corinthians*, translated by A. W. Heathcote and P. J. Allcock. Epworth Press: London.

HESTER, J. D. 1968. *Paul's Concept of Inheritance*, SJTOP 14. Oliver & Boyd: Edinburgh.

HIERZENBERGER, G. 1967. *Weltbewertung bei Paulus nach 1 Kor 7, 19–31: Eine exegetisch-kerygmatische Studie.* Patmos-Verlag: Düsseldorf.

HOFIUS, O. 1971/72. "Eine altjüdische Parallele zu Röm. iv. 17b", *NTS* 18, 93–4.

HOLLANDER, H. W., and DE JONGE, M. 1985. *The Testaments of the Twelve Patriarchs: a commentary*, Studia in Veteris Testamenti Pseudepigrapha. A.-M. Denis, E. De Jonge (eds); E. J. Brill: Leiden.

HOLMBERG, B. 1990. *Sociology and the New Testament: an appraisal.* Fortress Press: Minneapolis.

HOLTZ, T. 1990. "αἰών", *EDNT* 1:44–6.

HOOKER, M. D. 1959/60. "Adam in Romans 1", *NTS* 6, 297–306.

—— 1966/67. "A Further Note on Romans 1", *NTS* 13, 181–3.

HOOKER, M. D. 1973. "Were There False Teachers in Colossae?", in B. Lindars and S. S. Smalley (eds), *Christ and the Spirit in the New Testament*. Cambridge University Press: Cambridge.

HORRELL, D. 1996. *The Social Ethos of the Corinthian Correspondence: interests and ideology from 1Corinthians to 1 Clement*, SNTW. T. & T. Clark: Edinburgh.

HORSLEY, R. A. 1976. "Pneumatikos vs. Psychikos: distinctions of spiritual status among the Corinthians", *HTR* 69, 269–88.

—— 1977. "Wisdom of Word and Words of Wisdom in Corinth", *CBQ* 40, 574–89.

—— 1980. "Gnosis in Corinth: 1 Corinthians 8.1–6", *NTS* 27, 32–51.

HURD, J. C. 1965. *The Origins of 1 Corinthians*. SCM Press: London.

HYLDAHL, N. 1955/56. "A Reminiscence of the Old Testament at Romans i. 23", *NTS* 2, 285–8.

JACKSON, H. 1988. *Words and their Meaning*. Longman: London and New York.

JAEGER, W. 1965. *Paideia: the ideals of Greek culture:Volume 1: archaic Greece, the mind of Athens*, translated by G. Highet. Basil Blackwell: Oxford.

JENNI, E. 1952. "Das Wort '*olam* im Alten Testament", *ZAW* 64, 197–248.

—— 1953. "Das Wort '*olam* im Alten Testament", *ZAW* 65, 1–35.

JEREMIAS, J. 1954. "Zu Röm 1 22–32", *ZNW* 45, 119–21.

—— 1955/56. "Flesh and Blood Cannot Inherit the Kingdom of God (1 Cor. xv. 50)", *NTS* 2, 151–9.

JERVELL, J. 1960. *Imago Dei: Gen 1:26f im Spätjudentum, in der Gnosis und in den paulinischen Briefen*. FRLANT (Neue Folge) 58. Vandenhoeck and Ruprecht: Göttingen.

—— 1991. "The Letter to Jerusalem", in Donfried (ed.), 53–64.

JEWETT, R. 1970/71. "The Agitators and the Galatian Congregation", *NTS* 17, 98–212.

—— 1971. *Paul's Anthropological Terms: a study of their use in conflict settings*, AGJU 10. E. J. Brill: Leiden.

JEWETT, R. 1979. *Dating Paul's Life*. SCM Press: London.

JOHNSTON, G. 1963/64. "ΟΙΚΟΥΜΕΝΗ and ΚΟΣΜΟΣ in the New Testament", *NTS* 10, 352–60.

JONAS, H. 1963. *The Gnostic Religion. The message of the alien God and the beginnings of Christianity*. Beacon Press: Boston.

KAHN, C. H. 1960. *Anaximander and the Origins of Greek Cosmology*. Columbia University Press: New York; Oxford University Press: London, Bombay, Karachi.

—— 1973 *The Verb "Be" and its Synonyms: philosophical and grammatical studies*. Reidel: Dordrecht.

KALLAS, J. 1964/65. "Romans xiii. 1–7: an interpolation", *NTS* 11, 365–74.

KARRIS, R. J. 1991. "Romans 14:1 – 15:13 and the Occasion of Romans", in Donfried (ed.), 65–84.

KÄSEMANN, E. 1969a. "On the Subject of Primitive Christian Apocalyptic", in E. Käsemann, *New Testament Questions of Today*. SCM Press: London, 108–37.

—— 1969b. "'The Righteousness of God' in Paul", in E. Käsemann, *New Testament Questions of Today*. SCM Press: London, 168–82.

—— 1969c. "Principles of the Interpretation of Romans 13", in E. Käsemann, *New Testament Questions of Today*. SCM Press: London, 188–95.

—— 1971a. "On Paul's Anthropology", in E. Käsemann, *Perspectives on Paul*. SCM Press: London, 1–31.

—— 1971b. "The Faith of Abraham in Romans 4", in E. Käsemann, *Perspectives on Paul*. SCM Press: London, 79–101.

—— 1980. *Commentary on Romans*, translated by G. W. Bromiley, Eerdmans: Grand Rapids; SCM Press: London.

KECK, L. A. 1977. "The Function of Rom 3:10–18: observations and suggestions", in J. Jervell and W. A. Meeks (eds), *God's Christ and His People: studies in honour of Nils Astrup Dahl*. Universitatforlaget: Oslo, Bergen, Tromsø, 141–57.

KEE, H. C. 1980. *Christian Origins in Sociological Perspective: methods and resources*. Westminster Press: Philadelphia.

KERESZTES, P. 1980. "The Imperial Roman Government and the Christian Church 1. From Nero to the Severi", *ANRW* 23.1, 247–315.

—— 1989. *Imperial Rome and the Christians from Herod the Great to about 200 A.D.,* Vol. 1. University Press of America: Lanham, New York, London.

KERSCHENSTEINER, J. 1962. *Kosmos: Quellenschichtliche Untersuchungen zu den Vorsokratikern,* Zetemata 30. C. H. Beck'sche Verlagsbuchhandlung: München.

KIM, S. 1984. *The Origin of Paul's Gospel,* 2nd edn. WUNT 2.4. J. C. B. Mohr (Paul Siebeck): Tübingen.

KIRK, G. S. 1954. *Heraclitus, The Cosmic Fragments. Edited with an introduction and commentary.* Cambridge University Press: Cambridge.

KLEINKNECHT, H. 1965. "θειότης", *TDNT* 3:123.

KLOSTERMANN, E. 1953. "Die adäquate Vergeltung in Röm 1 22–31", *ZNW* 32, 1–6.

KÖSTER, H. 1973. "φύσις, etc.", *TDNT* 9: 251–77.

KOVACKS, J. L. 1989. "The Archons, the Spirit and the Death of Christ: Do we need the hypothesis of Gnostic opponents to explain 1 Cor 2.6–16?", in M. L. Soards and J. Marcus (eds), *Apocalyptic and the New Testament,* Festschrift for J. L. Martyn. Sheffield Academic Press: Sheffield, 217–36.

KRAFTCHICK, S. 1987. "Paul's Use of Creation Themes: a test of Romans 1–8", *Ex Auditu* 3, 72–87.

KRANZ, W. 1938. "Kosmos als philosophischer Begriff frühgriechischer Zeit", *Philologus* 93, 430–48.

KUCK, D. W. 1992. *Judgment and Community Conflict: Paul's use of apocalyptic judgment language in 1 Corinthians 3:5 – 4:5,* NovTSup 66. E. J. Brill: Leiden.

KÜMMEL, W. G. 1974. *Römer 7 and das Bild des Menschen im Neuen Testament. Zwei Studien.* Theologische Bücherei Neues Testament 53. Chr. Kaiser Verlag: München.

—— 1982. *Introduction to the New Testament.* Revised edn. SCM Press: London.

KUSS, O. 1963. *Der Römerbrief,* 3 vols. Verlag Friedrich Pustat: Regensburg.

LADD, G. E. 1975. *A Theology of the New Testament*. Lutterworth Press: Guildford and London.

LAMPE, G. W. H. 1964. "The New Testament Doctrine of Ktisis", *SJT* 17, 449–62.

LAMPE, P. 1987. *Die stadtrömischen Christen in den ersten beiden Jahrhunderten*, WUNT 2.18. J. C. B. Mohr (Paul Siebeck): Tübingen.

—— 1991. "The Roman Christians of Romans 16", in Donfried (ed.), 216–30.

LAPIDGE, M. 1978. "Stoic Cosmology", in Rist (ed.), 161–85.

—— 1989. "Stoic Cosmology and Roman Literature, First to Third Centuries A.D.", *ANRW* 36.3, 1379–1429.

LEENHARDT, F. J. 1961. *The Epistle to the Romans*, translated by H. Knight. Lutterworth: London.

LEMON, L. T., and REIS, M. J. (eds) 1965. *Russian Formalist Criticism: four essays*. University of Nebraska Press: Lincoln, New England.

LENSKI, R. C. H. 1936. *The Interpretation of St. Paul's Epistle to the Romans*. Lutheran Book Concern: Columbus, Ohio.

LEON, H. J. 1960. *The Jews of Ancient Rome*. The Jewish Publication Society of America: Philadelphia.

LEVISON, J. R. 1988. *Portraits of Adam in Early Judaism: from Sirach to 2 Baruch*, JSPSup 1. Sheffield Academic Press: Sheffield.

LINCOLN, A. T. 1981. *Paradise Now and Not Yet: studies in the role of the heavenly dimension in Paul's thought with special reference to his eschatology*. Cambridge University Press: Cambridge.

LINDEMANN, A. 1996. "Die paulinische Ekklesiologie angesichts der Lebenswirklichkeit der christlichen Gemeinde in Korinth", in Bieringer (ed.), 63–86.

LITFIN, D. 1994. *St. Paul's Theology of Proclamation: 1 Corinthians 1–4 and Greco-Roman rhetoric*, SNTSMS 79. Cambridge University Press: Cambridge.

LIVINGSTONE, E. A. (ed.) 1980. *Studia Biblica III. Papers on Paul and other New Testament authors*. Sixth International Congress on Biblical Studies, Oxford, 3–7 April 1978. JSNTSup 3. Sheffield Academic Press: Sheffield.

LONG, A. A. 1974. *Hellenistic Philosophy: Stoics, Epicureans, Sceptics.* 2nd edn. Duckworth: London.

LONGENECKER, R. N. 1964. *Paul, Apostle of Liberty.* Harper & Row: New York and London.

—— 1990. *Galatians,* WBC 41. Word Books: Dallas.

LÖWE, R. 1935. *Kosmos und Aion. Ein Beitrag zur heilsgeschichtlichen Dialektik des urchristlichen Weltverständnises.* Bertelsmann: Gütersloh.

LUCE, J. V. 1992. *An Introduction to Greek Philosophy.* Thames & Hudson: London.

LUZ, U. 1968. *Das Geschichtsverständnis des Paulus,* BEvT 49. Chr. Kaiser Verlag: München.

MACDONALD, J. I. H. 1989. "Romans 13.1–7: a test case for New Testament interpretation", *NTS* 35, 540–9.

MACDONALD, M. Y. 1988. *The Pauline Churches: a socio-historical study of institutionalization in the Pauline and Deutero-Pauline writings,* SNTSMS 60. Cambridge University Press: Cambridge.

MACMULLEN, R. 1981. *Paganism in the Roman Empire.* Yale University Press: New Haven and London.

MALHERBE, A. 1994. "Determinism and Free Will in Paul: the argument of 1 Corinthians 8 and 9", in T. Engberg-Pedersen (ed.), *Paul in his Hellenistic Context,* SNTW. T. & T. Clark: Edinburgh, 231–55.

MALINA, B. J. 1986. *Christian Origins and Cultural Anthropology: practical models for biblical interpretation.* John Knox: Atlanta.

MANSFIELD, J. 1979. "Providence and the Destruction of the Universe in Early Stoic Thought. With some remarks on the 'mysteries of philosophy'", in M. J. Vermaseren (ed.), *Studies in Hellenistic Religions.* E. J. Brill: Leiden, 129–88.

—— 1981. "Bad World and Demiurge: a Gnostic motif from Parmenides and Empedocles to Lucretius and Philo", in R. Van Den Broek and M. J. Vermaseren (eds), *Studies in Gnosticism and Hellenistic Religions: presented to Gilles Quispel on the occasion of his 65th birthday.* E. J. Brill: Leiden, 261–314.

MARCOVICH, M. 1967. *Heraclitus. Greek text with a short commentary.* Los Andes University Press: Merida, Venezuela.

MARCUS, J. 1989. "The Circumcision and the Uncircumcision in Rome", *NTS* 35, 67–81.

MARSHALL, I. H. 1989. "Does the New Testament Teach Universal Salvation?", in T. A. Hart and D. P. Thimell (eds), *Christ in Our Place: the humanity of God in Christ for the reconciliation of the world: essays presented to Professor James Torrance.* Pickwick: Allison Park, 313–28.

MARSHALL, P. 1987. *Enmity in Corinth: social conventions in Paul's relations with the Corinthians,* WUNT 2.23. J. C. B. Mohr (Paul Siebeck): Tübingen.

MARTIN, D. B. 1995. *The Corinthian Body.* Yale University Press: New Haven and London,

MARTIN, T. W. 1996. *By Philosophy and Empty Deceit: Colossians as Response to a Cynic Critique,* JSNTSup 118. Sheffield Academic Press: Sheffield.

MARTYN, J. L. 1967. "Epistemology at the Turn of the Ages: 2 Corinthians 5:16", in C. F. D. Moule and R. R. Niebuhr (eds), *Christian History and Interpretation: Studies Presented to John Knox.* Cambridge University Press: Cambridge, 269–87.

—— 1985. "Apocalyptic Antinomies in Paul's Letter to the Galatians", *NTS* 31, 410–24.

—— 1991. "Events in Galatia: modified covenantal nomism versus God's invasion of the cosmos in the singular gospel: a response to J. D. G. Dunn and B. R. Gaventa", in J. M. Bassler (ed.), 160–79.

—— 1995. "Christ, the Elements of the Cosmos, and the Law in Galatians", in White and Yarbrough (eds), 16–39.

MATLOCK, R. B. 1996. *Unveiling the Apocalyptic Paul: Paul's Interpreters and the Rhetoric of Criticism,* JSNTSup 127. Sheffield Academic Press: Sheffield.

MEEKS, W. A. 1972. "The Man from Heaven in Johannine Sectarianism", *JBL* 91, 44–72.

—— 1983a. *The First Urban Christians: the social world of the apostle Paul.* Yale University Press: New Haven, London.

MEEKS, W. A. 1983b. "Social Functions of Apocalyptic Language in Pauline Christianity", in D. Hellhom (ed.), *Apocalypticism in the Mediterranean World and the Near East: proceedings of the International Colloquium on Apocalypticism, Uppsala, August 12– 17, 1979*. J. C. B. Mohr (Paul Siebeck): Tübingen, 687–705.

—— 1993. *The Origins of Christian Morality: the first two centuries*. Yale University Press: New Haven, London.

MELL, U. 1989. *Neue Schöpfung: Eine traditionsgeschichtliche Studie zu einem soteriologischen Grundsatz paulinischer Theologie*, BZNW 56. De Gruyter, Berlin, NewYork.

MEYER, H. A. W. 1874. *The Epistle to the Romans*, Vol. 2. T. & T. Clark: Edinburgh.

MICHEL, O. 1966. *Der Brief an die Römer*, MeyerK 4. Vandenhoeck & Ruprecht: Göttingen.

MILLAR, A., and RICHES, J. K. 1981. "Interpretation: a theoretical perspective and some applications", *Numen* 28/1, 29–53.

MILNE, D. W. 1980. "Genesis 3 in the Letter to the Romans", *RTR* 39, 10–18.

MINEAR, P. 1979. "The Crucified World: the enigma of Galatians 6,14", in C. Andresen and G. Klein, *Theologia Crucis – Signum Crucis*, Festschrift für E. Dinkler zum 70. Geburtstag. J. C. B. Mohr (Paul Siebeck): Tübingen, 395–407.

MITCHELL, M. M. 1991. *Paul and the Rhetoric of Reconciliation. An exegetical investigation of the language and composition of 1 Corinthians*. Westminster/John Knox Press: Louisville, Kentucky.

MOLES, J. L. 1996. "Cynic Cosmopolitanism", in R. B. Branham and M.-O. Goulet-Cazé (eds), *The Cynics: the Cynic movement in antiquity and its legacy*, Hellenistic Culture and Society, Vol. 23. University of California Press: Berkeley, Los Angeles, London.

MOMIGLIANO, A. 1981. *Claudius: the emperor and his achievement*. Reprint. Greenwood Press: Connecticut.

MOO, D. J. 1991. *Romans 1–8*, The Wycliffe Exegetical Commentary. Moody Press: Chicago.

MORRIS, L. 1958. *The First Epistle of Paul to the Corinthians: an introduction and commentary*, TNTC. Inter-Varsity Press: Leicester.

MOULE, C. F. D. 1962. *The Birth of the New Testament*. A. & C. Black: London.

MOXNES, H. 1980. *Theology in Conflict: studies in Paul's understanding of God in Romans*, NovTSup 53. E. J. Brill: Leiden.

MUNCK, J. 1959. *Paul and the Salvation of Mankind*, translated by F. Clarke. SCM Press: London.

MUNRO, W. 1983. *Authority in Paul and Peter. The identification of a pastoral stratum in the Pauline corpus and 1 Peter*. Cambridge University Press: Cambridge.

MURRAY, J. 1959. *The Epistle to the Romans. The English text with introduction, exposition and notes*, Vol. 1. Eerdmans: Grand Rapids.

MUSSNER, F. 1961. "Kosmos", *LTK* 6:575–7.

NEYREY, J. H. 1991. "The Symbolic Universe of Luke–Acts: 'They turn the world upside down'", in J. H. Neyrey (ed.), *The Social World of Luke–Acts: models for interpretation*. Hendrickson: Peabody, Massachusetts, 271–304.

NORTH, C. R. 1962. "World, The", in *The Interpreter's Dictionary of the Bible: an illustrated encyclopedia*, Vol. 4. Abingdon Press: New York and Nashville, 873–8.

NYGREN, A. 1952. *Commentary on Romans*, translated by C. C. Rasmussen. SCM Press: London.

O'NEILL, J. C. 1975. *Paul's Letter to the Romans*, Pelican New Testament Commentary. Penguin: Harmondsworth.

ONSETI, K. L., and BRAUCH, M. T. 1993. "Righteousness, Righteousness of God", in Hawthorne, Martin and Reid (eds), 827–37.

ORR, W. F., and WALTHER, J. A. 1976. *1 Corinthians. A new translation, introduction with a study of the life of Paul, notes and commentary*, AB 32. Doubleday: Garden City, New York.

OSTEN-SACKEN, P. V. D. 1975. *Römer 8 als Beispiel paulinischer Soteriologie*, FRLANT 122. Vandenhoeck & Ruprecht: Göttingen.

OVERMAN, J. A. 1990. *Matthew's Gospel and Formative Judaism: the social world of the Matthean community*. Fortress Press: Minneapolis.

PAIGE, T. 1992. "Stoicism, ἐλευθερία and Community in Corinth", in M. J. Wilkins and T. Paige (eds), *Worship, Theology and Ministry in the Early Church*, JSNTSup 87. Sheffield Academic Press: Sheffield, 180–93.

PAINTER, J. 1993. "World, Cosmology", in Hawthorne, Martin and Reid (eds), 979–82.

PALLIS, A. 1920. *To The Romans: a commentary*. The Liverpool Booksellers Co.; Oxford University Press: Liverpool.

PARRY, R. St J. 1937. *The First Epistle of Paul the Apostle to the Corinthians*. Cambridge University Press: Cambridge.

PAULSEN, H. 1974. *Überlieferung und Auslegung in Römer 8*, WMANT 43. Neukirchener Verlag: Neukirchen-Vluyn.

PEARSON, B. A. 1973. *The Pneumatikos-Psychikos Terminology in 1 Corinthians. A study in the theology of the Corinthian opponents of Paul and its relation to Gnosticism*, SBLDS 12. Scholars Press: Missoula, Montana.

PENNA, R. 1982. "Les Juifs à Rome au temps de l'apôtre Paul", *NTS* 28, 321–47.

PETZKE, G. 1992. "κτίζω, etc.", *EDNT* 2:325–6.

PHILIPPI, F. A. 1879. *Commentary on St. Paul's Epistle to the Romans*, Vol. 2, translated by J. S. Banks. T. & T. Clark: Edinburgh.

PILCH, J. 1992. "Understanding Healing in the Social World of Early Christianity", *BTB* 22, 26–33.

PLUMMER, A. 1915. *A Critical and Exegetical Commentary on the Second Epistle of St Paul to the Corinthians*, ICC. T. & T. Clark: Edinburgh.

POBEE, J. S. 1985. *Persecution and Martyrdom in the Theology of Paul*, JSNTSup 6. Sheffield Academic Press: Sheffield.

POGOLOFF, S. M. 1992. *Logos and Sophia. The rhetorical situation of 1 Corinthians*, SBLDS 134. Scholars Press: Atlanta.

POPKES, W. 1982. "Zum Aufbau und Charakter von Römer 1:18–32", *NTS* 28, 490–501.

PUHVEL, J. 1976. "The Origins of Greek *Kosmos* and Latin *Mundus*", *AJP* 97, 154–67.

RÄISÄINEN, H. 1990. *Beyond New Testament Theology. A story and a programme*. SCM Press: London; Trinity Press International: Philadelphia.

REICKE, B. 1951. "The Law and This World according to Paul. Some thoughts concerning Gal 4 1–11", *JBL* 70, 259–76.

REID, D. G. 1993. "Elements / Elemental Spirits of the World", in Hawthorne, Martin and Reid (eds), 229–33.

RENSBERGER, D. 1989. *Overcoming the World: politics and community in the Gospel of John*. SPCK: London.

REUMANN, J. 1973. *Creation and New Creation: the past, present, and future of God's creative activity*. Augsburg Publishing House: Minneapolis.

RICHES, J. 1995. "Defamiliarisation and conceptual change", unpublished paper.

RIDDERBOS, H. N. 1956. *The Epistle of Paul to the Church of Galatia*, translated by H. Zylstra, NICNT. Eerdmans: Grand Rapids.

—— 1975. *Paul: an outline of his theology*, translated by J. R. DeWitt. Eerdmans: Grand Rapids.

RIST, J. M. (ed.) 1978. *The Stoics*. University of California Press: Berkeley, Los Angeles, London.

ROBBINS, V. K. 1984. *A Socio-Rhetorical Interpretation of Mark*. Fortress Press: Philadelphia.

ROBERTSON, A., and PLUMMER, A. 1914. *A Critical and Exegetical Commentary on the Epistle of St. Paul to the Corinthians*, ICC. T. & T. Clark: Edinburgh.

ROBINSON, J. A. T. 1979. *Wrestling With Romans*. SCM Press: London.

ROMANUICK, K. 1967/68. "Le Livre de la Sagesse dans la Nouveau Testament", *NTS* 14, 498–514.

RUDICH, R. 1993. *Political Dissidence under Nero: the price of dissimulation*. Routledge: London and New York.

RUEF, J. S. 1971. *Paul's First Letter to Corinth*, The Pelican New Testament Commentary. Penguin: Harmondsworth.

RUNIA, D. T. 1981. "Philo's De Aeternitate Mundi: the problem of its interpretation", *VC* 35, 105–51.

—— 1986. *Philo of Alexandria and the Timaeus of Plato*, Philosophia Antiqua 44. E. J. Brill: Leiden.

SAMPLEY, J. P. 1991. *Walking Between the Times – Paul's Moral Reasoning.* Fortress Press: Minneapolis.

SAND, A. 1967. *Der Begriff "Fleisch", in den paulinischen Hauptbriefen.* Biblische Untersuchungen. Verlag Friedrich: Regensburg.

SANDAY, W., and HEADLAM, A. C. 1902. *The Epistle to the Romans,* ICC. T. & T. Clark: Edinburgh.

SANDBACH, F. H. 1975. *The Stoics.* Ancient Culture and Philosophy. Chatto & Windus: London.

SANDERS, E. P. 1991. *Paul.* Past Masters Series. Oxford University Press: Oxford.

SANDERS, J. T. 1993. *Schismatics, Sectarians, Dissidents, Deviants. The first one hundred years of Jewish–Christian relations.* SCM Press: London.

SASSE, H. 1964a. "ἀΐδιος", *TDNT* 1:168.

—— 1964b. "αἰών, etc.", *TDNT* 1:197–209.

—— 1965. "κοσμέω, etc.", *TDNT* 3:867–98.

SAVAGE, T. 1996. *Power through Weakness. Paul's understanding of the Christian ministry in 2 Corinthians,* SNTSMS 86. Cambridge University Press: Cambridge.

SCHLATTER, A. 1935. *Gottes Gerechtigkeit.* Calwer Verlag: Stuttgart.

SCHLIER, H. 1965. "καθήκω", *TDNT* 3:437–40.

—— 1977. *Der Römerbrief,* HTKNT. Herder: Freiburg, Basel & Wien.

SCHLOVSKY, V. 1965. "Art as Technique", in Lemon and Reis (eds), 3–24.

SCHMIDT, K. L. 1964. "παράγω", *TDNT* 1:129–30.

SCHMITHALS, W. 1971. *Gnosticism in Corinth: an investigation of the letters to the Corinthians,* translated by J. E. Steely. Abingdon Press: Nashville and New York.

SCHMITZ, E. D. 1976. "γινώσκω", *NIDNTT* 2:392–406.

SCHNACKENBURG, R. 1967. "Das Verständnis der Welt nach dem Neuen Testament", in R. Schnackenburg, *Christliche Existenz nach dem Neuen Testament: Abhandlungen und Vorträge: Band I.* Kosel-Verlag: München, 157–85.

—— 1968. "Zwischen den Zeiten. Christliche Existenz in dieser Welt nach Paulus", in R. Schnackenburg, *Christliche Existenz nach dem Neuen Testament: Abhandlungen und Vorträge: Band II.* Kosel-Verlag: München, 9–32.

SCHNEIDER, J. 1971. "σχῆμα, etc.", *TDNT* 7:954–8.

SCHOFIELD, M. 1991. *The Stoic Idea of the City*. Cambridge University Press: Cambridge.

SCHRAGE, W. 1964. "Die Stellung zur Welt bei Paulus, Epiktet und in der Apokalyptik: Ein Beitrag zu 1 Kor 7, 29–31", *ZTK* 61, 125–54.

SCHRAGE, W. 1988. *The Ethics of the New Testament*, translated by D. E. Green. T. & T. Clark: Edinburgh

—— 1991. *Der Erste Brief an die Korinther, 1 Teilband, 1 Kor 1,1 – 6,11*, EKKNT. Benziger Verlag: Zürich. Neukirchener Verlag: Neukirchener-Vluyn.

—— 1995. *Der Erste Brief an die Korinther, 2 Teilband, 1 Kor 6,12 – 11,16*, EKKNT. Benziger Verlag: Zürich; Neukirchener Verlag: Neukirchener-Vluyn.

SCHULZ, S. 1973. "Evangelium und Welt. Hauptprobleme einer Ethik des Neuen Testaments", in H. D. Betz and L. Schottroff (eds), *Neue Testament und christliche Existenz*. J. C. B. Mohr: Tübingen, 483–502.

SCHWANTES, H. 1962. *Schöpfung der Endzeit: Ein Beitrag zum Verständnis der Auferweckung bei Paulus*. Calwer Verlag: Stuttgart.

SCHWEIZER, E. 1988. "Slaves of the Elements and Worshippers of Angels: Gal 4:3, 9 and Col 2:8, 18, 20", *JBL* 107, 455–68.

SCROGGS, R. 1966. *The Last Adam: a study in Pauline anthropology*. Fortress Press; Blackwell: Philadelphia.

—— 1975. "The Earliest Christian Communities as Sectarian Movement", in *Christianity, Judaism and Other Graeco-Roman Cults: studies for Morton Smith at sixty*, SJLA 12, Vol 2. Leiden, 1–23.

SHIELDS, B. E. 1980. *Creation in Romans*, PhD Dissertation. Evangelisch-theologisch Facultät an der Eberhard-Karls-Universität, Tübingen.

SIBER, P. 1971. *Mit Christus leben. Eine Studie zur paulinischen Auferstehungshoffnung*. Theologischer Verlag: Zürich.

SIDER, R. J. 1975. "The Pauline Conception of the Resurrection Body in 1 Corinthians xv. 35–54", *NTS* 21, 428–39.

SJÖBERG, E. 1950. "Wiedergeburt und Neuschöpfung im palästinischen Judentum", *ST* 4, 44–85.

SMALLWOOD, E. M. 1981. *The Jews under Roman Rule. From Pompey to Diocletian. A study in political relations*. E. J. Brill: Leiden.

SOLMSEN, F. 1960. *Aristotle's System of the Physical World. A comparison with his predecessors*. Cornell University Press: Ithaca, New York.

SORDI, M. 1994. *The Christians and the Roman Empire*, translated by A. Bedini. Routledge: London and New York.

STAGG, F. 1989. "Exegesis of 2 Corinthians 5:14–21", in J. P. Lewis (ed.), *Interpreting 2 Corinthians 5:14–21: an exercise in hermeneutics*, Studies in the Bible and Early Christianity, Vol. 17. The Edwin Mellen Press: Lewiston, Lampeter, 163–78.

STÄHLIN, G. 1968. "περίψημα", *TDNT* 6:84–93.

STAMBAUGH, J., and BALCH, D. 1986. *The Social World of the First Christians*. SPCK: London.

STARK, W. 1967. *The Sociology of Religion: a study of Christendom. Vol. 2, Sectarian Religion*. Routledge & Kegan Paul: London.

STEVENSON, J. (ed.) 1957. *A New Eusebius. Documents illustrative of the history of the church to A.D. 337*. SPCK: London.

STONE, M. E. 1989. *Features of the Eschatology of IV Ezra*. Harvard Semitic Studies 35. Scholars Press: Atlanta, Georgia.

—— 1990. *Fourth Ezra: a commentary on the Book of Fourth Ezra*, Hermenia. Fortress Press, Minneapolis.

STOUGH, C. 1978. "Stoic Determinism and Moral Responsibility", in Rist (ed.), 203–31.

STOWERS, S. K. 1984. "Paul's Dialogue with a Fellow Jew in Romans 3:1–9", *CBQ* 46, 707–22.

STUHLMACHER, P. 1987. "The Ecological Crisis as a Challenge for Biblical Theology", *Ex Auditu* 3, 1–15.

—— 1989. *Der Brief an die Römer*, Das Neue Testament Deutsch 6. Vandenhoeck & Ruprecht: Göttingen and Zürich.

—— 1991. "The Theme of Romans", in Donfried (ed.), 333–45.

—— 1992. *Biblische Theologie des Neuen Testaments: Band I: Grundlegung von Jesus zu Paulus*. Vandenhoeck & Ruprecht: Göttingen.

SUTER, D. W. 1979. *Tradition and Composition in the Parables of Enoch*, SBLDS 47. Scholars Press: Missoula.

SWEET, J. P. M. 1965. "The Theory of Miracles in the Wisdom of Solomon", in C. F. D. Moule (ed.) *Miracles: Cambridge Studies in their Philosophy and History*. Mowbray: London, 115–26.

SYREENI, K. 1994. "The Symbolic World of Matt 6:1–18", *NTS* 40, 22–41.

TAJFEL, H. 1978a. "Social Categorization, Social Identity and Social Comparison", in H. Tajfel (ed.), *Differentiation between Social Groups. Studies in the social psychology of intergroup relations.* Academic Press (in association with European Association of Experimental Social Psychology): London, New York, San Francisco, 61–76.

—— 1978b. "The Achievement of Group Differentiation", in H. Tajfel (ed.), *Differentiation between Social Groups. Studies in the social psychology of intergroup relations.* Academic Press (in association with European Association of Experimental Social Psychology): London, New York, San Francisco, 77–98.

TANNEHILL, R. C. 1967. *Dying and Rising with Christ: a study in Pauline theology*, BZNW 32. Verlag Alfred Töpelmann: Berlin.

TENNANT, F. R. 1903. *The Sources of the Doctrines of the Fall and Original Sin*. Cambridge University Press: Cambridge.

THEISSEN, G. 1982. *The Social Setting of Pauline Christianity: essays on Corinth*, translated by J. H. Schütz. T. & T. Clark: Edinburgh.

—— 1987. *Psychological Aspects of Pauline Theology*, translated by J. P. Galvin. Fortress Press: Philadelphia; T. & T. Clark: Edinburgh.

THISELTON, A. C. 1977/78. "Realized Eschatology at Corinth", *NTS* 24, 510–26.

THOMPSON, A. L. 1977. *Responsibility for Evil in the Theodicy of IV Ezra: a study illustrating the significance of form and structure for the meaning of the book*, SBLDS 29. Scholars Press: Missoula, Montana.

THOMPSON, M. 1991. *Clothed With Christ: the example and teaching of Jesus in Romans 12:1–15:13*, JSNTSup 59. Sheffield Academic Press: Sheffield.

TIDBALL, D. 1997. *The Social Context of the New Testament*, Paternoster: Carlisle. First published under the title *An Introduction to the Sociology of the New Testament*. Paternoster: Exeter (1983).

TODD, R. B. 1978. "Monism and Immanence: the foundations of Stoic physics", in Rist (ed.), 137–60.

TOMASHEVSKY, B. 1965. "Thematics", in Lemon and Reis (eds), 61–95.

TRAVIS, S. H. 1986. *Christ and the Judgment of God. Divine retribution in the New Testament*, Foundations for Faith. Marshall, Morgan & Scott: Basingstoke.

TROELTSCH, E. 1931. *The Social Teachings of the Christian Churches*, Vol. 1, translated by O. Wyon. Allen & Unwin: London; Macmillan: New York.

VIARD, A. 1952. "Expectatio creaturae (Rom. viii, 19–22)", *RB* 59, 337–52.

VLASTOS, G. 1955. "On Heraclitus", *AJP* 76, 337–68.

—— 1975. *Plato's Universe*. Clarendon Press: Oxford.

VÖGTLE, A. 1970a. *Das Neue Testament und die Zukunft des Kosmos*, KBANT. Patmos-Verlag: Düsseldorf.

—— 1970b. "Röm 8, 19–22: eine schöpfungstheologische oder anthropologisch-soteriologische Aussage?", in A. Deschamps and A. Halleux (eds), *Mélanges bibliques en homage au R. P. Bé de Rigaux*. Ducolot: Gemblaux, 351–66.

VÖLKL, R. 1961. *Christ und Welt nach dem Neuen Testament*. Echter-Verlag: Würzburg.

VOLZ, P. 1966. *Die Eschatologie der Jüdischen Gemeinde im neutestamentlichen Zeitalter nach den Quellen der rabbinischen, apokalyptischen und apokryphen Literatur*. Georg Olms: Hildesheim.

VON RAD, G. 1972. *Wisdom in Israel*, translated by J. D. Martin, SCM Press: London.

VOS, G. 1986. *The Pauline Eschatology*. Presbyterian and Reformed Publishing Co. Phillipsburg, New Jersey.

WALTER, N. 1989. "Gottes Zorn und das 'Harren der Kreatur', Zur Korrespondenz zwischen Römer 1,18–32 und 8, 19–22", in *Christus Bezeugen*, Festschrift für Wolfgang Trilling zum 65. Geburtstag. St. Benno-Verlag: Leipzig, 218–26.

WALTERS, J. C. 1993. *Ethnic Issues in Paul's Letter to the Romans: changing self-definitions in earliest Roman Christianity.* Trinity Press: Valley Forge.

WARMINGTON, B. H. 1969. *Nero Reality and Legend.* Chatto & Windus: London.

WATSON, F. 1984. "2 Cor. x-xiii and Paul's Painful Letter to the Corinthians", *JTS* 35, 324–46.

—— 1986. *Paul, Judaism and the Gentiles: a sociological approach*, SNTSMS 56. Cambridge University Press: Cambridge.

WEDDERBURN, A. J. M. 1980. "Adam in Paul's Letter to the Romans", in Livingstone (ed.), 413–30.

—— 1987. *Baptism and Resurrection: studies in Pauline theology against its Graeco-Roman background*, WUNT 1.44. J. C. B. Mohr: Tübingen.

—— 1988. *The Reason for Romans*, SNTW. T. & T. Clark: Edinburgh.

WELBORN, L. L. 1987. "On the Discord in Corinth: 1 Corinthians 1–4 and Ancient Politics", *JBL* 106, 85–111.

WENGST, K. 1987. *Pax Romana and the Peace of Jesus Christ*, translated by J. Bowden. SCM Press: London.

WHITE, L. M., and YARBOROUGH, O. L. 1995. *The Social World of the First Christians: essays in honor of Wayne A. Meeks.* Augsburg Fortress, Minneapolis.

WIEFEL, W. 1991. "The Jewish Community in Rome and the Origins of Roman Christianity", in Donfried (ed.), 85–101.

WILCKENS, U. 1971. "σοφία, etc.", *TDNT* 7:465–528.

—— 1978. *Der Brief an die Römer,* Vol. 1, EKKNT. Benziger Verlag: Zürich; Neukirchener Verlag: Neukirchen-Vluyn.

—— 1980. *Der Brief an die Römer,* Vol. 2, EKKNT. Benziger Verlag: Zürich; Neukirchener Verlag: Neukirchen-Vluyn.

—— 1982. *Der Brief an die Römer,* Vol. 3, EKKNT. Benziger Verlag: Zürich; Neukirchener Verlag: Neukirchen-Vluyn.

WILDE, J. A. 1978. "The Social World of Mark's Gospel: a word about method", in P. J. Achtemeier (ed.), *Society of Biblical Literature 1978 Seminar Papers*, Vol. 2. Scholars Press: Missoula, Mont, 47–70.

WILKEN, R. L. 1984. *The Christians as the Romans Saw them.* Yale University Press: New Haven and London.

WILLIAMS, C. J. F. 1966. "Aristotle and Corruptibility", *RelS* 1, 95–107, 203–15.

WILLIS, W. 1985. *Idol Meat in Corinth: the Pauline argument in 1 Corinthians 8 and 10.* Scholars Press: Chico, California.

WILSON, B. R. 1973. *Magic and the Millennium: a sociological study of religious movements of protest among tribal and Third-World peoples.* Heinemann: London.

WILSON, R. McL. 1982. "Gnosis at Corinth", in M. D. Hooker and S. G. Wilson (eds), *Paul and Paulinism: essays in honour of C. K. Barrett.* SPCK: London, 102–14.

WILSON, W. T. 1991. *Love Without Pretense: Romans 12:9–12 and Hellenistic-Jewish wisdom literature,* WUNT 46. J. C. B. Mohr (Paul Siebeck): Tübingen.

WIMBUSH, V. L. 1987. *Paul the Worldly Ascetic: response to the world and self-understanding according to 1 Corinthians 7.* Mercer University Press: Macon, GA.

WINK, W. 1984. *Naming the Powers: the language of power in the New Testament.* Fortress Press: Philadelphia.

WINTER, B. W. 1990. "Theological and Ethical Responses to Religious Pluralism – 1 Corinthians 8–10", *TynBul* 41, 209–26

—— 1991. "Civil Litigation in Secular Corinth and the Church. The forensic background to 1 Corinthians 6:1–8", *NTS* 37, 559–72.

WITHERINGTON III, B. 1992. *Jesus, Paul and the End of the World: a comparative study in New Testament eschatology.* Paternoster: Exeter.

—— 1994. *Paul's Narrative Thought World: the tapestry of tragedy and triumph.* Westminster Press/John Knox: Louisville, Kentucky.

—— 1995. *Conflict and Community in Corinth: a socio-rhetorical commentary on 1 and 2 Corinthians.* Eerdmans: Grand Rapids.

WÜLLNER, W. 1973. "The Sociological Implications of 1 Corinthians 1.26–28 Reconsidered", *SE* 6:666–72.

—— 1982. "Tradition and Interpretation of the 'Wise-Powerful-Noble' Triad in 1 Cor 1,26", *SE* 7:557–62.

Wuthnow, R., Hunter, J. D., Bergesen, A., and Kurzweil, E. 1984. *Cultural Analysis. The work of Peter L. Berger, Mary Douglas, Michael Foucault and Jurgen Habermas.* Routledge & Kegan Paul: London and New York.

Zahn, T. 1865. "Die seufzende Creatur, Röm. 8, 18–23, mit Rücksicht auf neuere Auffassungen", *JDTh* 10, 511–42.

Zeller, D. 1985. *Der Brief an die Römer.* Regensburger Neues Testament. Verlag Friedrich Pustet: Regensburg.

Zerbe, G. M. 1991. *Non-Retaliation in Early Jewish and New Testament Texts: ethical themes in social contexts,* JSPSup 13. Sheffield Academic Press: Sheffield.

Ziesler, J. 1989. *Paul's Letter to the Romans,* TPINTC. Trinity Press: Philadelphia; SCM Press: London.

—— 1990. *Pauline Christianity.* Revised edn. Oxford University Press: Oxford.

Zimmerman, H. 1968. "Welt", in H. Haag (ed.) *Bibel Lexikon.* Benziger Verlag, Tübingen, 1883–6.

Index of references

Index of names

Index of subjects

Adam 15, 63n, 76, 144–6, 153n, 154–5,
  170–5, 178–9, 188n, 200n
Abraham 154, 160, 167–71
alienation, social 97, 124, 183–4
apocalyptic 17, 31, 96, 106–16, 119, 125,
  130–5, 138, 142, 146n, 147–8, 153,
  155, 166, 168, 172–5, 181–2, 184,
  187, 189–93, 201–5, 215–16, 219,
  224, 226–8, 230–1, 233, 235–6, 239,
  241–2

body 48, 55, 66, 92–4, 96, 99n, 123, 143,
  145–6, 189–90, 200, 202
boundaries, group xiv, 37, 85–103, 105,
  125–6, 129–30, 139, 143–4, 149, 202,
  204, 208, 230–2, 234–7,
  239–40, 243–4

church-type: see sect, sectarian
circumcision 221–2, 225–6, 228, 231
collegia 93, 102, 211
conflagration, cosmic 53–5, 57, 67–8,
  215
critical linguistics 23, 25–8
cross (of Jesus) 108, 112–14, 135, 139,
  148, 190, 224–5, 227, 230, 233, 236
Cynic, Cynics 74, 162, 164n

death, power of 13, 15–16, 18, 76,
  119–20, 148, 153–4, 169, 172–4, 184,
  189, 191–2, 231, 236–7, 241
defamiliarize, defamiliarization 27–30, 33,
  113, 115, 121, 125, 129, 139, 147, 237,
  239

edict of Claudius 196–7, 210, 213, 240

flesh 13, 18, 93, 114–15, 146, 148, 166,
  191–2, 200n, 225, 231–2, 234,
  236–7
functionalism 31

Gnosticism 69, 94
group/grid 99

habitualization 26–7, 29, 74, 113
Hellenistic dualism 102

identity, social 24–5, 98–9, 103, 211,
  222–4, 226, 232, 240, 243
ideology 30, 36n, 69–75, 80, 102–3, 113,
  139, 147–8, 239
indestructibility of the cosmos 48, 50–2,
  55, 60–1, 67–8, 136
integration, social 88, 100, 102–3, 113,
  117, 124, 136, 142, 147, 204, 208–9,
  217–19, 239, 243
Israel 152, 156n, 164, 186, 189

kingdom (of God) 30, 95, 107, 129,
  146–8, 170

legitimation 5–6, 23, 25–26, 28–29, 36,
  70–1, 74–5, 80, 102, 113, 139, 147,
  183, 191, 205, 212, 215, 219, 236,
  239–40, 246
linguistic change 28–30

marriage 72, 91, 96–7, 107, 130–1,
  136–39
microcosmic–macrocosmic link 46–7,
  53, 56, 62, 66–7, 69–72, 80, 102,
  116–17, 148, 234

natural theology 53, 62, 158
new creation 19, 109, 115, 133, 148, 170,
  182, 190, 225–8, 230–2, 234–6,
  240

outsiders 10, 37–8, 85, 88n, 97–8,
  126, 129, 183, 187, 195, 200–4, 208–9,
  213, 216–19, 239–40, 243, 246
over-realized eschatology 95–6